Religious Minorities at Risk

Religious Minorities at Risk

MATTHIAS BASEDAU, JONATHAN FOX, AND
ARIEL ZELLMAN

OXFORD
UNIVERSITY PRESS

Oxford University Press is a department of the University of Oxford. It furthers
the University's objective of excellence in research, scholarship, and education
by publishing worldwide. Oxford is a registered trade mark of Oxford University
Press in the UK and certain other countries.

Published in the United States of America by Oxford University Press
198 Madison Avenue, New York, NY 10016, United States of America.

© Oxford University Press 2023

All rights reserved. No part of this publication may be reproduced, stored in
a retrieval system, or transmitted, in any form or by any means, without the
prior permission in writing of Oxford University Press, or as expressly permitted
by law, by license, or under terms agreed with the appropriate reproduction
rights organization. Inquiries concerning reproduction outside the scope of the
above should be sent to the Rights Department, Oxford University Press, at the
address above.

You must not circulate this work in any other form
and you must impose this same condition on any acquirer.

CIP data is on file at the Library of Congress

ISBN 978–0–19–769394–0

DOI: 10.1093/oso/9780197693940.001.0001

Printed by Integrated Books International, United States of America

Contents

Foreword	vii
Acknowledgments	ix
1. Introduction	1
2. What are Deprivation, Discrimination, Inequality, and Grievances?	25
3. From Deprivation, Discrimination, and Inequality to Grievances	71
4. Religious Minorities, Mobilization, Protest, Conflict, and Violence in Theory	117
5. An Empirical Examination of the Grievances to Mobilization Model	161
6. Conclusions	221
Appendix: Supplementary Analyses and Robustness Checks	245
References	303
Index	323

Foreword

In what turned out be the last time I spoke with Ted R. Gurr at the February 2017 International Studies Association annual conference held in Baltimore, Maryland, I told him about the project that eventually resulted in this book. I asked for and received his blessing to call the project the Religious Minorities at Risk (RMAR) project after his groundbreaking Minorities at Risk (MAR) project. To my lasting regret, Professor Gurr passed away later that year.

This project, or at least my part in it, is deeply connected to the work of Ted R. Gurr and in many ways has taken me full circle to the beginnings of my academic career. In 1992, my second year as an unfunded graduate student at the University of Maryland, I took a course on ethnic conflict with Ted R. Gurr. One of the central texts for the course was his 1993 *Minorities at Risk* book, which had not yet been published. I and the other students received copies from Professor Gurr in the form of bound photocopies of a printout, I assume from Word, of the book. This was the beginning for me of my knowledge of grievance theory.

After completing the class, Professor Gurr brought me into the next phase (phase 3) of the MAR project as a research assistant. It was on that job where I truly learned how to construct, develop and collect a cross-national events-based dataset. He was fully involved in all stages of the project and provided an excellent example of how to both supervise and educate at the same time. Shortly thereafter he agreed to be my dissertation supervisor and allowed me to use the MAR project resources to develop religion variables for use with the MAR dataset. This became my dissertation, *Religion, Ethnicity, and the State: A General Theory on Religion and Conflict as Applied to Ethnic Conflict With the State* which, in turn, became the basis for a series of publications which launched my career.

Several years later, I launched the Religion and State (RAS) project, which diverged from Ted. R. Gurr's work theoretically and focused on government religion policy. However, the methodology for data collection and analysis remained at its core the skills I learned from my time with the MAR project.

viii FOREWORD

I also found myself following his model for supervising my own students and research assistants

During this period, I watched with dismay as after Professor Gurr's retirement, his critics began to systematically dismantle his work, undermine its credibility, and in some cases steal his ideas and insights to claim as their own. Always a class act, he brushed this off as inevitable academic behavior. Until the end he remained convinced that grievances matter, as do I along with this book's other two authors.

In this book, we provide the fruit of joining my RAS project's Religion and State-Minorities (RASM) module to the work on the conflict behavior of religious minorities by my colleague Matthias Basedau as well as the indispensable theoretical and empirical talents of my colleague at Bar Ilan University, Ariel Zellman. This book would not have happened without all three of its authors. Together we built and analyzed the RMAR dataset. Together with them, I have returned full circle to research and illuminate the original insights that began when I first met Ted R. Gurr and restore one of the first basic insights he bestowed upon me to its proper place in academic discourse, grievances matter.

Jonathan Fox

Acknowledgments

Like most research projects this one would not have been possible without a village of colleagues who helped along the way. We would like to thank Peter Henne, Daniel Philpott, Jocelyne Cesari, Lene Kuhle, Yasemin Akbaba, Chris Bader, Patrick James, Shmuel Sandler, Jeff Haynes, Torkel Brekke, Nilay Saiya, and Dane Mataic, all of whom commented on aspects of this project. We would like to thank the research assistants who helped collect the data including Mora Deitch, Tanya Haykin, Vita Roy, Tom Konzack, Chris Huber, Sherrie Feigleson, and Eytan Meir as well as Arne Pieters for his help with the earlier stages of the analysis. As we note at length in the foreword, we also thank Ted R. Gurr for his early support for this project as well as his foundational work which inspired this project.

We thank the Israel Science Foundation (Grant 23/14), the German-Israel Foundation (Grant 1291-119.4/2015), the John Templeton Foundation, and the German Ministry of Development Cooperation (Bundesministerium für Wirtschaftliche Zusammenarbeit und Entwicklung) for funding this project. We also thank the Association of Religion Data Archives for their help with the data. The opinions expressed in this study are solely those of the authors and do not necessarily reflect those of any of the funders.

1

Introduction

The post–Cold War era has been one of contradictory expectations regarding the role of religion in world politics. Proponents of the secular modernist worldview have long projected their aspirations for a postreligious world. In its most extreme iteration, one may have believed that the growth of cultural liberalism, economic prosperity, procedural democracy, and scientific achievement must be met with the decline of atavistic and divisive social and political ideologies (Fox, 2015; Gorski & Altinordu, 2008). As such, the fall of the Iron Curtain and the collapse of the Soviet Union should have heralded a new era of peace and secular enlightenment.

Quite to the contrary, the competition between religious and secular political actors to influence government policy has become an increasingly more prominent feature of politics in both the West and non-West (Fox, 2015, 2019, 2020). More concerning has been the global resurgence of bloody, ostensibly identity-based civil wars and separatist insurgencies, from the Balkans to the Middle East and North Africa to the Caucasus and East Asia that seemingly characterized the 1990s and 2000s. As secular ideological and otherwise superpower-supported proxy warfare fell to the wayside, religious and ethnic ideological conflict have displaced them in terms of both their duration and lethality (Walter, 2017; Toft, 2021; Basedau et al., 2022). Arguably among the most globally destabilizing conflicts of this period have been those involving and in response to nonstate violent fundamentalist religious actors, whether al-Qaeda, Boko Haram, the Islamic State (Da'esh), or the Lord's Resistance Army (Dunn, 2010; Hoffman, 2004; Raineri & Martini, 2017; Tamm, 2016; Zenn, 2020), to say nothing of religiously inspired foreign fighters who have flooded into far-flung conflict zones, from Afghanistan to Syria to Ukraine (Hegghammer, 2010; MacKenzie & Kaunert, 2021; Mishali-Ram & Fox, 2022; Pokalova, 2019).

Among the most fascinating observations regarding religious conflict in the past thirty years has been its great heterogeneity. Despite average levels of religious discrimination and outright oppression increasing worldwide, in democratic and nondemocratic contexts alike, the extent to which

Religious Minorities at Risk. Matthias Basedau, Jonathan Fox, and Ariel Zellman, Oxford University Press.
© Oxford University Press 2023. DOI: 10.1093/oso/9780197693940.003.0001

2 RELIGIOUS MINORITIES AT RISK

aggrieved groups actually mobilize to demand redress vary widely. For instance, Muslims and Jews across the West express grievances over perceived Islamophobia (Obaidi et al., 2018) and anti-Semitism (Fox & Topor, 2021), respectively. Christians, in turn, are among the most restricted religious minorities in the world (Fox, 2020) and often express grievances. Yet whereas some deeply oppressed religious minorities have engaged in sustained insurgencies, prompting even more massive repression by their host states (e.g., Muslims in Chechnya or Rakhine, Myanmar), others have suffered similar levels of state repression despite engaging in much less violent resistance (e.g., Uyghurs in China) or none altogether (e.g., Christians in Pakistan).

Addressing this puzzle, this book raises key questions about why and under what conditions religious minorities express grievances regarding their treatment by the state and society at large and what they choose to do about it. Whether religious minorities are even capable of or motivated to engage in collective organization is one matter. How they choose to engage when mobilized—whether through peaceful protest, resort to spontaneous violence such as rioting, organized violence including terrorism, or outright rebellion—is another.

These questions are far from simple, and we do not pretend to have uncovered all the answers. We, however, propose that the most systematic manner to understand observed patterns requires a multistep approach, first identifying under what conditions religious minorities express different kinds of collective grievances, and second understanding how different grievances and associated structural conditions translate to different mobilizational strategies. So parsed, we can better understand why some groups mobilize when others do not; why some resort to violent methods while for others peaceful protest is sufficient; and hopefully in the process gain greater understanding on how to avoid such violent situations altogether.

Accordingly, in this study we examine the conflict and mobilization behavior of religious minorities between 2000 and 2014. Drawing on classic grievance theory (Gurr, 1993a, 1993b, 2000) which was originally developed to explain ethnic conflict, we argue that deprivation, discrimination, and inequality (DDI) lead to the formation of grievances over these issues which, in turn, leads to conflict behavior including protests, riots, and violence. Of course, other factors including a groups capacity, opportunity structure, and regime, among many others, also play important roles.

In this chapter, we outline why we feel using the lens of grievance theory is important and how our arguments fit into the larger literature focusing primarily on the domestic conflict and civil war literature as well as the religion and conflict literature. More specifically, this chapter proceeds as follows. First, we discuss why grievance theory is important. Second, we examine the intellectual history of our study. Third, we discuss our original data collection. Fourth, we summarize our findings and their limitations. Finally, we outline the structure of our study.

In the rest of this book, we further develop these themes as well as present evidence showing that grievance theory's explanation for political mobilization, protest, and conflict by minorities provides a good explanation for the behavior of religious minorities.

Grievances and Common Sense, or Why Grievances Are Important

That grievances are a central cause of violence and conflict is common wisdom. It is not difficult to find examples of this common wisdom across politics, the media, and culture. For example, journalist Richard Engel argues that "only a few ingredients need to combine to create an insurgency . . . The recipe is, simply, a legitimate grievance against a state, a state that refuses to compromise, a quorum of angry people, and access to weapons."[1] Poet Robert Frost states that "poetry is about grief. Politics is about grievance."[2] In his Letter From a Birmingham Jail, Martin Luther King Jr. stated,

> In spite of my shattered dreams, I came to Birmingham with the hope that the white religious leadership of this community would see the justice of our cause and, with deep moral concern, would serve as the channel through which our just grievances could reach the power structure.[3]

However, we cannot always rely on common wisdom. Karl Deutsch (1963) argues in his article "the limits of common sense" that common sense is not always reliable and often contradictory. For example, common sense has it that birds of a feather flock together but also that opposites attract. Our common sense can show us relationships and patterns that are real but "it

---

[1] https://www.thepostemail.com/2018/06/10/dont-you-feel-it-anger-and-frustration-are-everywhere/.
[2] https://allupdatehere.com/robert-frost-quotes/.
[3] https://www.africa.upenn.edu/Articles_Gen/Letter_Birmingham.html.

4 RELIGIOUS MINORITIES AT RISK

is also true that we can understand in our fertile imagination very many relations that do not exist at all" (Deutsch, 1963, p. 53). For this reason, if we want to take our insights seriously "we must test them. We can do this by selecting . . . data, verifying them [and] forming explicit hypotheses as to what we expect to find. And we then finally test these explicit hypotheses by confrontation with the data. In the light of these tests we revise our criteria of relevance" (Deutsch, 1963, p. 53).

The role of grievances in conflict is a good example of this phenomenon. There exists a debate in the literature where some argue that grievances are central to understanding the causes of violence conflict, and civil war, particularly when it involves minorities. Others argue that grievances are irrelevant and other factors such as greed, resources, opportunity, and mobilization drive conflict.

This study delves into this issue by taking Deutsch's advice and engages in a data driven test of the hypothesis that grievances are a central cause of conflict among religious minorities. More specifically, we examine the conflict behavior of religious minorities using a new and innovative data collection, the Religious Minorities at Risk (RMAR) dataset. Our findings show that grievances do matter and are an integral part of the conflict process for religious minorities. Our tests that demonstrate this, we argue, are as rigorous and comprehensive as Karl Deutsch would have demanded. This is in part because RMAR contains more detailed cross-country data on more minorities than has existed before. This is true not only for religious minorities, but for any type of minority.

Our central argument is that this conflict behavior is driven by a two-stage process where DDI causes the minority to form grievances and these grievances, in turn, influence conflict behavior. This model follows the work of Ted. R. Gurr's (1993a, 1993b, 2000a) development of a similar model for ethnic conflict based on his Minorities at Risk (MAR) project which inspired RMAR's project name. However, RMAR applies this model to religious minorities and, we argue, provides some important methodological improvements over that foundational work.

While the empirical study of domestic unrest and civil war dates back six decades and the empirical study of religion and conflict dates back to the 1990s, these issues and their intermingling with religion are far older than that. For example, chapter 2, verse 3 of the Jewish religious text *The Ethics of the Fathers*[4] states, "Be careful of the government, for it will befriend a man

---

[4] The Ethics of the Fathers is a Jewish religious text with sayings attributed to prominent Rabbis who lived between 200 BCE and 200 CE.

only for its own needs. It appears to be his friend when it needs him but will not stand with him in the time of his distress."[5] This ancient piece of wisdom contains two observations directly relevant to our study. First, people seek redress from governments but often receive no such redress. Second, governments are independent actors that follow their own interests. This verse also implies that governments are often the source of people's distress.

The empirical study of domestic conflict and civil war has long recognized and addressed these principles. More specifically, it has long recognized that governments discriminate against minorities and these minorities often seek redress for their grievances over this discrimination as well as DDI from other sources. When these minorities do not receive this redress, they often engage in conflict.

However, there is little agreement over the details of this process. In fact, there are fundamental debates over basic issues. We situate this study at the center of these debates and aim to examine them from a new perspective, both theoretical and empirical, using the RMAR data, which is the first conflict dataset to focus on religious minorities while others either focus on ethnic groups or use the country, rather than groups, as the unit of analysis. For this reason, particularly in Chapters 3 and 4, we discuss this debate with two goals in mind. First, to situate our arguments and findings within this debate. Second, to integrate the empirical literature on religion and conflict into this debate.

For example, as we discuss in more detail in Chapter 4, among the prominent debates in the field is one where one side holds that grievances motivate conflict. The other side argues that grievances are ubiquitous across minorities and, therefore, do not differentiate between groups that engage in conflict behavior and these who do not. Rather, what matters is a group's capacity to engage in political mobilization. A third perspective argues that grievances are relevant, but they are synonymous with DDI and, therefore, only DDI need be measured. While it is unlikely that any single study can settle this debate, we provide important new evidence that grievances matter. DDI and grievances may be ubiquitous, but they are not uniform across religious minorities. They vary and this variation predicts both nonviolent and violent conflict behavior by religious minorities and, we argue, by implication other types of minorities. Also, we find that DDI heavily influences grievances, but this relationship is far from automatic.

---

[5] Translation by the authors.

6 RELIGIOUS MINORITIES AT RISK

That being said, capacity also matters. Group capacity influences both the grievance formation process and conflict behavior by religious minorities. However, this is not a process that, as some argue (e.g., Fearon & Laitin, 2003; McCarthy & Zald, 1977; Tilly, 1978), does not involve grievances in any meaningful way. Rather the capacity, resources, and opportunity factor is tied up intimately with both how grievances are formed and how grievances influence conflict behavior. Thus, we diverge from a trend in the conflict literature which has it that only one explanation must be correct. Rather, we argue it is both grievances *and* capacity that matter.

A Brief Intellectual History of Our Study

This study straddles two academic literatures. The first focuses on domestic conflict and civil war with an emphasis on conflict behavior by minorities. The second is the religion and politics literature that studies conflict and violence. While both literatures involve studies which use both empirical-quantitative methodology and classical comparative politics approaches, this study is situated firmly in the empirical-quantitative element of these disciplines. While we discuss the relevant previous studies in later chapters, particularly Chapters 3 and 4, it is important to take a step back from the particulars of the findings of these literatures and examine how our study fits into the larger picture.

The Domestic Conflict and Civil War Literature

While the history of the empirical study of domestic conflict and civil war is likely familiar to many readers, we posit that a discussion of this history in this chapter and our reexamination of the debates within that literature in Chapters 3 and 4 are important for several reasons. First, our study makes fundamental claims regarding these debates, which makes a review of the debates and their origin story essential for both situating our study, its arguments, and its findings in this literature as well as explaining why all of this is important. We believe this review must include a discussion of how these arguments developed over time to properly accomplish this goal.

Second, our arguments and findings are deeply embedded within this body of theory to the extent that they can only be fully appreciated within their context. Third, as we very much take sides in this debate, we feel that a fair presentation of all aspects of the debate is an essential element in explaining why we argue that grievances matter. For example, when we argue grievances matter, this invokes a large body of theory and argument that debates this very issue, including quite a few which posit that the entire grievances argument is invalid and offer alternative theories. Accordingly, any study claiming that grievances would be remiss if it did not address and counter these arguments and theories head on, as we do in Chapters 3 and 4.

Fourth, within this literature there are many different conceptions and definitions of DDI and grievances. In order to understand our arguments and findings it is important to understand how our uses of these concepts are similar and different from previous uses. In particular, the distinction between individual-level grievances and group-level grievances is key to our arguments and, we argue, key to understanding previous studies of civil war and conflict.

Fifth, we argue that there are many common misconceptions about this literature. Understanding this is essential to appreciating the import of our study. For example, as we discuss in more detail in Chapters 3 and 4, much of the evidence presented in this debate is not as it appears. This is because many studies that purport to measure DDI and grievances actually use other measures which, we argue, are questionable surrogates for these phenomena. Sixth, this literature contains important and influential critiques of previous studies based on the theoretical tradition we follow in this study. Our discussion of these critiques and why we feel they do not apply to our study is critical to justifying its validity. Seventh, we posit that this discussion is essential for readers who are less familiar with this literature.

Consequently, our critical review of this literature is aimed at influencing how the reader sees and interprets this literature in light of the arguments and findings we present in this study. That is, we see this review as a conversation with the relevant previous studies and arguments intended to form a new synthesis, which views the findings and arguments from these studies from a new perspective drawn from the theoretical context and empirical findings of our study.

Empirical studies of the causes of domestic conflict and civil war date back to the 1960s. This is around the time of political science's behavioral revolution when a new generation of researchers began to apply the scientific method of

8 RELIGIOUS MINORITIES AT RISK

formulating falsifiable hypotheses and testing them with empirical data. One of the earliest theories in this literature was relative deprivation (RD) theory, which posited that when a group compared itself to some point of comparison and found its situation lacking, this could lead to violence, conflict, rebellion and revolution. The most influential formulation of this argument was Gurr's (1970) argument that DDI can cause frustration, which leads to anger, which leads to violence. For Gurr (1970) this DDI was mainly caused by a gap between "value expectations" and "value capabilities." He wrote, "value expectations are the goods and conditions of life to which people believe they are rightfully entitled. Value capabilities are the goods and conditions they think they are capable of attaining or maintaining, given the social means available to them" (Gurr, 1970, p. 13). The larger this gap, the more likely it will cause frustration and anger, which leads to aggression and violence.

While there are many intellectual strands and theories within the larger domestic conflict and civil war literature, RD theory and the work of Ted R. Gurr is the strand that most influences our study from among this larger body of theory. During the 1970s and 1980s, RD was a popular theory due to its face validity. That is, the intuition that DDI inspires civil war, rebellion, and revolution "ought" to be correct. This is because it was based on common wisdom. It was the basis for hundreds, perhaps thousands, of published studies in peer review forums during this period (Brush, 1996; Lichbach, 1989; Rule, 1988).

As is the case with many popular theories in academia, it has its critics. While there were numerous theoretical critiques, which we discuss in more detail in Chapter 3, the most important critique was empirical. Specifically, the empirical literature, the vast majority of which focused on economic DDI, simply did not support the theory (Brush, 1996; Fox, et. al., 2017; Lichbach, 1989; Osborne & Sibley, 2013; Rule, 1988; Smith et. al., 2012).

Gurr (1993a, 1993b, 2000a) accepted these findings but did not give up on the proposition that DDI can lead to conflict, violence, rebellion, and revolution. He took these findings as a flaw not in this central concept but in how it was originally theorized and tested. He created the MAR project which transformed and updated his approach to the relationship between DDI and conflict in at least four ways, all of which fundamentally influence the present study.

First, he chose to focus on ethnic minorities. This focus was exceptional at the time because for much of the post–World War II era modernization theory which was influential in political science predicted, among other

INTRODUCTION   9

things, that tribalism in the form of ethnicity and religion was becoming a thing of the past. It was seen as disappearing due to process inherent in modernity (Fox, 2002a, 2004). More specifically during this period,

> many social scientists, especially political scientists, argued that modernization would reduce the political significance of ethnicity. They argued that factors inherent in modernization, including economic development, urbanization, growing rates of literacy and education, as well as advancements in science and technology, would inevitably lead to the demise of the role of primordial factors like ethnicity in politics. While the modernization literature usually dealt with ethnicity in general, its predictions were also intended to apply specifically to religion. In fact, modernization theory predicted that the same factors which were believed to be causing the demise of ethnicity would lead to the process of the secularization of society. (Fox, 2002a, p. 33)

Second, this focus on ethnic minorities was also methodologically revolutionary. Previously nearly all cross-country empirical studies used the country as the unit of analysis. MAR used the ethnic minority as the unit of analysis. Thus, each country had multiple ethnic minorities which were studied individually. This recognized that the status of a specific minority and its behavior could be different than that of other minorities in the same country. While this insight may seem obvious, no previous cross-country events data conflict study had been constructed at the group level.

Third, Gurr (1993a, 1993b, 2000a) reformulated his theory. He argued that DDI causes a group to form grievances. As we discuss in more detail in Chapters 3 and 4, these grievances are qualitatively different from the frustration and anger individuals feel as theorized by RD theory. Rather these are grievances expressed at the group-level by leaders, organizations, and representatives in a format intended to seek redress for these grievances. This makes them more politically relevant. It is these grievances, according to Gurr, that begin the process that leads to conflict. Thus, conflict is a two-stage process, the first is DDI leading to grievances and the second is the grievances launching the conflict process.

The theory was also more sophisticated in that it took into account other factors. Perhaps most importantly, it incorporated other theory strands, such as mobilization literature, which argues that conflict is driven by opportunity, resources, and capacity. It recognized the role of regime and a wide variety of traits of ethnic minorities. It also created multiple dependent

10   RELIGIOUS MINORITIES AT RISK

variables for violence and peaceful protest in order to examine the causes of different types of mobilization and conflict behavior.

Fourth, Gurr (1993a, 1993b, 2000a) explicitly expanded his measurement of forms of DDI and grievances beyond those addressing economic issues. He looked at economic, political, and cultural DDI, as well as grievances. His model also looked at beliefs in past autonomy (both mythical and real) among an ethnic minority and how it spurred demands for autonomy. He also looked at the stress on minorities caused by demographic, ecological, and migration factors.

The diverse analyses of the MAR dataset largely support this model (e.g., Gurr, 1993a, 1993b, 2000; Sorens, 2009).[6] However, this theory also attracted theoretical, methodological, and empirical critiques, which we describe in more detail in Chapter 4. As a result the MAR project has experienced a slow demise.

In this book we follow all of these innovations as we focus on grievances expressed by minorities, albeit religious ones, and test multiple types of DDI, grievances, and conflict behavior. In doing so we revive Gurr's original concepts that minorities are a useful unit of analysis and, using our RMAR data, that a two-stage approach—from DDI to grievances and grievances to conflict behavior—provides a better theoretical framework to understand why and how minorities mobilize than those that neglect this intermediate step of grievance formation and expression. The main difference between MAR and RMAR is that RMAR focuses on religious minorities, and unlike MAR, which included only some ethnic minorities, RMAR includes all religious minorities that meet a minimum population threshold. Other than the MAR and RMAR datasets, no major cross-country data collection has been based around this theoretical foundation or measured group-level grievances. Thus, we argue that this study of RMAR constitutes the most methodologically sound test of the grievance argument to date.

The Religion, Violence, and Conflict Literature

The empirical religion and conflict literature began more recently but heavily influences this study. The same theories that predicted the demise of

---

[6] See also Ayres & Saideman (2000); Akbaba & Tysas (2011); Birnir & Satana (2013); Birnir et. al. (2017); Fox (2002a, 2004); Ishiyama (2000); Jenne et al. (2007); Saideman & Ayres (2000); Saideman et al. (2002); Tsutsui (2004).

INTRODUCTION   11

ethnicity also predicted the demise of religion. This likely deterred the empirical study of religion and conflict for several decades (Fox, 2015, 2018). As a result, the first empirical studies of violence and conflict that took the religion factor into account were published in 1997 (Fox, 1997; Rummel, 1997; Walter, 1997).

During this early period, Fox (1997, 1999a, 1999b, 1999c, 2000a, 2000b, 2000c, 2000d, 2001a, 2001b, 2001c, 2002a, 2002b, 2002c, 2003a, 2003b, 2004) published a series of studies based on the MAR dataset with additional variables measuring the impact of religious DDI, grievances, legitimacy, and institutions on the conflict behavior of 105 ethnoreligious minorities. This research program used Gurr's model. It confirmed the model in that religious forms of DDI cause religious grievances. However religious grievances only increased the extent of rebellion where autonomy issues were also present in a conflict. Subsequent to these studies, it was over a decade before the empirical literature produced a study which included a variable explicitly measuring religious grievances.

In contrast, most other early studies used only religious demography variables. One focused specifically on religion and conflict (Ellingsen, 2005). The rest were written in the context of Samuel Huntington's Clash of Civilizations theory (Henderson & Singer, 2000; Roeder, 2003; Tusicisny, 2004) or focused on another cause of conflict but included a religious demography variable as a control or a measure of diversity (Collier & Hoeffler, 2002; Ellingsen, 2000; Reynal-Querol, 2002; Rummel, 1997; Walter, 1997).

Beginning in 2005, studies began to appear that included variables measuring religion's relevance to conflict (Pearce, 2005), whether groups involved in the conflict made religious demands of some kind (Bercovitch & Darouen, 2005; Svensson, 2007), and whether a conflict involved religious outbidding (Toft, 2007). After this, studies on religion and conflict using a wide variety of variables became more common. These studies measured religious DDI, ideology, beliefs, incompatibilities, demands, and outbidding as well as demography variables. Much of it theorized that grievances are important to the conflict process, but none explicitly measured grievances.

This changed with the development of the Religion and Conflict in Developing Countries (RCDC) dataset, which examines the role of religion in conflict in 130 developing countries in Asia, Latin America, the Middle East, and sub-Saharan Africa between 1990 and 2010. RCDC uses the country year as its unit of analysis rather than a minority but is the first cross-country study since the MAR project to explicitly include a grievance

12 RELIGIOUS MINORITIES AT RISK

variable. This variable is a general grievances variable which measures "whether or not a religious community feels discriminated against" (Basedau et al., 2016, p. 239). The study found these grievances to influence the onset of interreligious and theological conflicts. As we discuss in the next section, the RCDC dataset is a precursor to the data used in the present study.

Thus, this study diverges somewhat from the bulk of previous religion and conflict studies. Unlike the demographic-based studies we do not assume that religious identity or diversity alone causes conflict. Also, we do not focus on religious ideology. Rather we argue that conflict behavior by religious minorities is caused at least in part by DDI and grievances.

This lack of empirical focus on ideology is not because we feel it has no influence. Rather, it is because we argue its influence is at the subgroup level. There is diversity within most religious populations on a wide range of factors, including, but not limited to, intensity of belief, how they interpret their religion, and their willingness to apply their religious beliefs and ideology in the political domain. Thus, it is difficult to identify any consistent stand on these three issues among any religious population as a whole, including religious minorities, precisely because there is little agreement on them. Surveys and experiments may identify their effect, but they are typically confined to very small and probably not universally representative samples (e.g., Hoffmann et al., 2020; Basedau et al., 2022). Higher levels of agreement on these issues can be found at the organizational level. That is, like-minded members of a group form an organization that represents their beliefs, but these organizations tend, in practice, to represent only some members of the group which places them at the subgroup level of analysis. As we discuss in Chapter 4, this is implicit in the religion and conflict's empirical literature as most studies which focus on ideology use organizations as their unit of analysis.

DDI and grievances are factors more appropriate to the study of religious minorities. DDI is often directed at the minority in general. However, as we discuss in more detail in Chapter 2, DDI is related to religious ideology because religious ideology is one of the prominent motivations for religious DDI. Grievances, as we conceive and operationalize them, are demands for redress expressed by group representatives, which makes them politically relevant. This has significant continuity with the empirical religious and conflict literature since other common variables in that literature include the presence of religious issues and demands which include demands for redress of grievances. Thus, these variables are related to grievances but do not explicitly measure them.

The Religious Minorities at Risk (RMAR) Dataset

This study uses the RMAR dataset to examine the dynamics and causes of conflict behavior by religious minorities. RMAR constitutes the combined efforts of two projects, the RCDC project and the Religion and State-Minorities (RASM) project. In this section, we provide an overview of the genesis and the content of the RMAR dataset.

The Genesis of RMAR

RMAR is the result of a confluence of serendipity between two projects which initially developed separately. The Religion and State (RAS) project was designed to study government religion policy. From its beginning, it included a wide variety of variables looking at how governments support religion, restrict and regulate the majority religion, and engage in DDI against minority religions (Fox, 2008, 2015). Over time it developed a module known as the RASM dataset which, unlike RAS's focus on the state as the unit of analysis, focuses on DDI against religious minorities using the minority as the level of analysis. The project developed complex detailed variables measuring DDI both by governments and society which we describe in more detail in Chapter 2 (Fox, 2016, 2020; Fox & Topor, 2021).

As noted, the RCDC project focuses on religious conflict behavior. Its original version did not include DDI variables except for differences in economic status of religious groups but does include grievance variables. The major initial publications based on both datasets appeared around the same time (Fox, 2016; Fox & Akbaba, 2015a; Fox & Akbaba, 2015b; Basedau et al., 2016). The projects joined forces to produce a study that recoded RCDC to the minority-level in the 130 countries covered in the project. Basedau, Fox et al. (2019) used this data in what became the pilot study for RMAR. It showed that the RASM DDI variables did predict grievances generally, but grievances themselves (again measured generally) did not predict violence (in the form of organized state based or nonstate conflict). Based on this pilot, the projects jointly collected the RMAR dataset.

RMAR is in some respects also a direct descendant of MAR. The government based DDI variable in RASM—governmental religious discrimination (GRD)—began as a variable developed by Fox (2002a) to measure discrimination in his MAR-based studies of ethnoreligious conflict. The variable

14 RELIGIOUS MINORITIES AT RISK

structure which identifies and codes multiple types of DDI separately then combines them into a larger DDI index is the same structure used by Gurr's MAR project for many of its DDI variables. This is not a coincidence since Fox's data was developed originally as part of a dissertation supervised by Gurr and Fox was one of the research assistants for the MAR project. This variable structure transferred to RAS and eventually RASM adding multiple components to the GRD variable and developing a similar societal religious discrimination (SRD) variable, both of which are included in RMAR as its primary DDI variables.

The RMAR Dataset

The RMAR dataset includes data on 771 religious minorities in 183 countries and covers 2000 to 2014.[7] This includes all countries with a population of at least 250,000 and a sampling of smaller countries. It uses the minority as the unit of analysis and includes all minorities that meet a population threshold of at least 0.2 percent of the country as well as smaller Christian minorities in Muslim-majority countries, Muslim minorities in Christian-majority countries and Jewish minorities in both Muslim-majority and Christian-majority countries.[8] RMAR defines a religious minority as a religious group which is a different religion or a different denomination of the same religion as the majority religion. Examples of the latter include Orthodox Christians in a Catholic-majority country and Shi'a Muslims in a Sunni Muslim-majority country.

Thus, RMAR is the first cross-national, events-data, minority-conflict behavior dataset that uses religious minorities as the level of analysis. It is different from MAR as well as other ethnic group-based data collections such as the Ethnic Power Relations (EPR) dataset in several important respects. First, it focuses on religious rather than ethnic minorities. Second, it includes all minorities within its universe of analysis which meet a minimum population cutoff. MAR originally included ethnic minorities which were either politically active or subject to DDI. Later versions of MAR included a sampling

---

[7] The RAS dataset component of RMAR covers 1990 to 2014, but the RCDC component covers only 2000 to 2014.

[8] Robustness checks for all models examined in this book confirm that excluding groups below this threshold has no significant impact upon neither our variables of interest nor our analyses. These models are provided in the Appendix.

of other ethnic minorities but no version included all ethnic minorities. This resulted in some methodological critiques we describe in more detail in Chapter 4. However, as RMAR is fully inclusive, these critiques do not apply. Third, the time-period included in MAR and RMAR differ.

RMAR uses coding procedures developed originally by Gurr (1993a, 1993b, 2000a). Each country in the dataset was assigned to a coder who produced a report on the larger religion–state and government religion policy in the country, which included treatment of religious minorities. The reports are based on a wide range of sources including (1) government reports such as the US State Department International Religious Freedom reports, (2) reports on religious freedom and related issues by intergovernmental organizations such as the United Nations and the European Union, (3) country reports on political developments such as quarterly reports by the Economist Intelligence Unit (EIU) and yearbooks such as the Africa Yearbook, (4) reports by advocacy groups such as Human Rights Without Frontiers and Forum 18, (5) a search for media sources both on the internet and in the Lexis-Nexis database, and (6) government documents such as constitutions and laws. If available (7), we also referred to secondary data in the form of scholarly articles and books. Information on conflict behavior is based on these sources. This report was the basis for the DDI codings. A separate coder used this report and other sources such as well-recognized conflict databases such as the UCDP dataset, and the Global Terrorism Database (GTD) to code the grievance, capacity, and conflict behavior variables. Thus, the data is based on a wide variety of sources. All codings were supervised and verified by the project's primary investigators (PIs) Jonathan Fox and Matthias Basedau.[9]

We discuss the structure of the variables we use in the study in Chapters 2, 3, and 5 where they are initially used. This discussion also includes descriptive information of the variables' distributions.

Looking at the bigger picture, RMAR includes the following characteristics which are in combination unique. First, it uses the religious minority as its unit of analysis. Second, it includes all relevant minorities, not just a sample. Third, it includes multiple DDI and grievance measures, and it measures different types and intensities thereof. Fourth, it includes measures for other factors such as group capacity. Finally, it includes multiple variables

---

[9] For a more detailed discussion of data collection and reliability for RMAR see, Fox (2020) and Fox et al. (2018) as well Basedau, Fox, et al. (2021).

16 RELIGIOUS MINORITIES AT RISK

for conflict behavior including both violent and nonviolent mobilization. We argue this provides an unprecedented opportunity to examine the conflict behavior of religious minorities.

Theory and Findings

Our core theoretical argument and empirical finding is that grievances matter. It is a simple argument. We argue, following Gurr (1993a, 1993b, 2000a), that DDI causes groups to form group-level grievances which are expressed by group leaders, representatives, and organizations in a manner seeking to redress these grievances. These grievances, in turn, motivate mobilization for conflict and conflict behavior.

While this theory has been present and debated in the literature for decades, we posit it is one that has not been satisfactorily tested, or at least not tested to everyone's satisfaction. As noted, the only previous direct tests of this theory were performed using the MAR data looking at the conflict behavior of ethnic minorities. This data has been heavily criticized for methodological flaws. While, as we discuss in Chapters 3 and 4, we disagree with much of this criticism, the criticism has been accepted by much of the relevant academic community, many of whom support competing theories. Thus, correct or not, this criticism of MAR has undermined the face validity of its claims.

The RMAR dataset provides a new view of grievance theory as well as a fresh start for it for three reasons. First, it does not have the methodological flaws attributed to MAR by its critics. Second, it focuses on religious rather than ethnic minorities. Thus, not only does RMAR provide a new and better test of grievance theory, it also constitutes the most comprehensive and systematic test to date of the conflict behavior of religious minorities. Third, the empirical results presented in this study provide essential new understandings in the precise paths by which DDI can lead to grievances and grievances can lead to conflict behavior.

The latter is particularly important because, while grievance theory is at its core simple, its application in practice is complex for two reasons. First, there are multiple types of both DDI and grievances, each having their own influences on the process. That is, each type of DDI influences the multiple types of grievances differently, and each type of grievance influences the multiple types of conflict behavior we examine differently. We summarize our key empirical findings in Figure 1.1.

INTRODUCTION 17

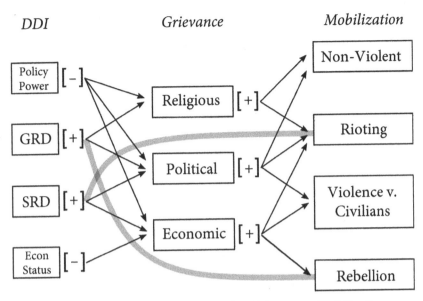

Figure 1.1 Predicted Causal Pathways: DDI to Grievance to Mobilization

We find that GRD (governmental religious discrimination) predicts levels of political and religious grievances but not economic grievances. However, SRD (societal religious discrimination) predicts levels of political and economic grievances but not religious grievances. Finally, whereas inclusion of minorities in policy-making processes (the inverse of political deprivation) tends to decrease all grievance types, improved economic status (the inverse of economic inequality) seems to primarily diminish economic grievances. Thus, while we confirm that DDI leads to grievances, specifics matter. This is particularly interesting because, as we discuss in Chapters 3 and 4, many consider the link between DDI and grievances automatic. If one is present so must be the other. On a superficial level, our findings show this to be true in that each type of DDI causes some type of grievance, and all types of grievance we examine are predicted by some type of DDI. However, when breaking both DDI and grievances into types, we find that distinct pathways between the specific types of DDI and grievances emerge. In addition, while a relationship exists it is by no means automatic as there are numerous cases where DDI and grievance levels do not match. Thus, the general principle holds but the devil is in the details and these details are critically important for understanding the grievance formation process. This, we argue, is an insight absent in many parts of the literature, particularly among critics of grievance theory.

18 RELIGIOUS MINORITIES AT RISK

The link between grievances and conflict behavior is, if anything, more complex. We examine the impact of religious, political, and economic grievances on nonviolent political mobilization and three types of violence—rioting, violence against civilians (most of which would be considered by most analysts to be terrorism), and organized rebellion (frequently labeled "intrastate armed conflict"). Nonviolent mobilization is defined as events where minority members organize peacefully in order to voice grievances. These can include demonstrations, rallies, strikes, press conferences, campaigns, boycotts, or dialogues. They are predicted by political and economic grievances but not religious grievances.

Rioting—which includes riots and other unorganized violence by group members—is the only type of violence predicted by all three types of grievances measured by RMAR. Organized violence is predicted by political and economic grievances. Religious grievances actually predict a reduced intensity in organized violence. Finally, economic grievances weakly predict rebellion. However, more intense political and religious grievances predict lower likelihoods of rebellion. It is important to note that unlike rioting and organized violence, the incidence of rebellion among religious minorities is so rare that this may be a statistical artifact.

We argue that these findings for conflict behavior are explained by a government's desire and ability to address grievances. We posit that as a minority's conflict behavior becomes more intense, a government has greater incentives to address these grievances to avoid domestic instability. However, some grievances are simpler to address than others. Religious grievances, as coded by RMAR, are essentially complaints over religious DDI such as restrictions on religious practices and institutions, which is exactly what is measured by GRD. Addressing them requires little more than repealing the offending policy. This has some cost as these types of restrictions are rarely present without significant political constituency supporting them, but changing such policies usually requires no more than passing a law or changing bureaucratic regulations. Political grievances involve issues of political exclusion and marginalization. These issues can be addressed, but they are procedurally more difficult to address than the issues raised by religious grievances. Redress often includes provision of political representation, recognition of religious authority in civil matters, or forms of group self-determination—from communal self-governance to territorial autonomy. It also involves politicians from the religious majority ceding a portion of their power and influence. This accommodation of grievances most commonly occurs before conflict. However, if and when violence does occur, this usually results in the hardening of states' restrictive policies and actions.

Finally, economic grievances are often based on long-term economic marginalization. While some economic DDI may be due to government policies, much of it is due to societal attitudes and prejudice which are more difficult to address. That is, a country can pass a law banning discrimination in the workplace and education, for example, but this rarely results in true equality and certainly is even less likely to achieve this goal in the short term. Even assuming good intentions and societal cooperation—an uncertain assumption at best—redressing long-term economic DDI takes considerable political will and time.

This link between grievances and conflict behavior is made even more complicated because some forms of DDI appear to directly influence conflict behavior even beyond grievance formation, albeit to a more subtle degree. SRD makes rioting more likely. We argue this is because SRD constitutes discreet incidents of harassment, violence, and goading of minorities. Such incidents can cause collective anger, which can result in spontaneous forms of violent protest, that is, rioting. It has less influence on organized and purposeful violence. GRD makes rebellion more likely. We believe that in this case GRD is acting as a proxy for repressive governments, which successfully repress nonviolent mobilization and violence not reaching the level of rebellion, making rebellion the only possible outlet.

In sum, the DDI to grievances to conflict process is theoretically simple but in practice complex. Specific types of DDI and grievances have different influences on different types of conflict behavior. Nevertheless, we find the basic model to be valid.

The second element of the complexity of this model is that it is not only DDI and grievances that matter. Much of the civil war and domestic conflict literature tends to take an exclusivist approach wherein if one theory is correct, the other must be wrong. We take a different approach that allows for and recognizes multiple influences on conflict behavior.

As we discuss in more detail in Chapter 4, a broad literature posits that group opportunity, resources and capacity are what determines levels of conflict. That is, conflict is not determined by DDI and grievances but, rather, those who are most able to mobilize are the ones who are most likely to engage in conflict. Yet a significant challenge faced by much of recent scholarship in this regard is an empirical inability to differentiate between group-level discrimination and group-level mobilizational capacity, As we explain at various points in Chapters 2, 3, and 4. projects like the EPR dataset operationalize discrimination against ethnic minorities in terms of relative exclusion from, access to, and control over state executive power apparatuses, "disregarding access to legislative and judicial institutions" (Vogt et al., 2021, p. 5) for "politically relevant ethnic groups." This approach, in essence, limits analysis only to those groups likely to have relatively high mobilizational capacities.

By contrast, our study investigates all religious minorities that meet a low demographic threshold (0.2 percent of the total population as well as a sampling of smaller minorities of general scholarly interest). We then directly measure both explicit governmental and societal discrimination against specific religious minorities, as well as collective expression of grievance by these specific minorities, measurements previously collected (to a less complex degree) only by the Minorities at Risk project. Finally, we separately measure whether these minority groups are (1) politically organized outside of government, (2) politically represented in a country's legislature, and (3) exercise influence over executive policymaking. We argue that by disaggregating group-level discrimination and grievance from measurements of political power, we can better understand the above detailed measures not merely as proxies for political deprivation but as directly indicative of group organizational capacity.

Having done so, we confirm that group capacity indeed significantly influences grievance formation and conflict behavior, however these effects augment rather than exclude the influence of DDI and grievances. In the grievance formation process, we find two capacity variables to be particularly influential. The presence of minority organizations increases the levels of all three types of grievances. Thus, groups which have the capacity to organize political parties and organizations to represent their interests are more likely to seek redress. This finding is unsurprising. However, groups which are included in the government and, thus, have the power to influence policy express lower levels of all three types of grievances. We believe that this is because when a group can influence policy from within a government, there is less of a need to publicly seek redress of grievances. As Grzymala-Busse (2015) argues, when religious organizations are able to influence policy behind closed doors, this is more effective than open politics such as the public expression of grievances.

In contrast to policy power's deep influence on the grievance formation process, it has little direct influence on the conflict process except that it may reduce the likelihood of rebellion. Though this finding, while logical for the same reasons as described above, has marginal significance. The presence of group organizations predicts nonviolent mobilization, rioting, and organized violence but not rebellion. Group representation in government—which measures only the presence of elected representative, not influence on policy—influences all forms of violent behavior measured by RMAR. Finally, groups which are a larger proportion of the population are more likely to engage in nonviolent mobilization as well as all three forms of violent behavior.

Thus, capacity matters. Yet the capacity argument has been tested multiple times, so this finding in isolation is not new. Our findings, including this one, are new, however, in at least six ways when examined in the larger context of this study. First, DDI and grievances matter in addition to capacity, and as it seems grievances matter more for protest and conflict than the underlying DDI variables. Second, the influence of DDI and grievances is primarily through a two-stage model with grievances mediating most, but not all, of the influence of DDI on conflict behavior. Third, our multitheory approach yields better results than arguments that one theory precludes the validity of others. Fourth, our findings are not subject to the methodological critiques that have been applied to previous grievance-based studies. Fifth, the capacity factor is intimately tied up in the DDI to grievances to conflict model, especially at the grievance formation level. Thus, including DDI and grievances in capacity arguments has, we argue, more than additive value.

Finally, our findings all apply to religious minorities. This study constitutes the most comprehensive examination of conflict behavior by religious minorities to date. Neither the general literature on domestic conflict and civil war nor the religious conflict literature contains many studies that focus on religious minorities. In fact, most of the previous cross-country empirical studies of religious minorities, and all of them that include grievance variables, include among their authors at least one of this study's authors. As we discuss in more detail in Chapters 3 and 4, these previous studies are based on data that is more limited and less comprehensive than the RMAR dataset.

All of this raises an interesting issue. Despite many claims that religion has a unique influence on conflict, we find that the behavior of religious minorities is largely consistent with behavior typically theorized to match the interests and behaviors of other, primarily ethnic, minority types. The DDI to grievance to conflict model in which group capacity plays a critical role is certainly not unique to religious minorities. What is unique is the

22   RELIGIOUS MINORITIES AT RISK

role of religious DDI and grievances. That is, even though religious DDI and grievances play a role that is analogous to other types of DDI and grievances, religious grievances and DDI include unique elements. These can be found both in their content and their idiosyncratic influence on the path to conflict. We demonstrate that each type of DDI and grievances is unique. Thus, religion adds a unique element, just as the autonomy issue does for ethnic minorities (Gurr, 1993a, 1993b, 2000a).

Put differently, each type of minority has its own traits, which makes it unique and will influence the process by which they mobilize for conflict. This is true of religious and ethnic minorities as well as others based on sexuality, gender identity, and other bases for identity. Each will have its unique issues and grievances and will experience different constellations of DDI. This makes each identity type unique. In addition, each type of DDI and grievance will forge unique paths to conflict. However, we posit that all of these paths will follow the general pattern of DDI to grievances to conflict.

Research Strategy and Structure

In Chapter 2, we begin with a discussion of DDI and grievances. These are the central causal variables in our model. We discuss how RMAR defines and measures these concepts. We provide descriptive statistics for these variables as well as illustrative examples of the many components of these measures. We also discuss the theoretical background of these concepts.

Chapter 3 examines the first stage of our two-stage model, the influence of DDI on grievances. It begins with a discussion of the evolution of theories which posit a link between DDI and grievances. We find that while this is a much discussed and debated topic, tests of this relationship are rare. In fact, much of the literature simply assumes this relationship exists to the extent that DDI variables are sometimes considered nearly synonymous with grievances. We also discuss the many different conceptions of grievances and how variables based on these different conceptions can have different influences on conflict dynamics. As noted, we find that while DDI does cause grievances the paths between DDI and grievances depend much upon the specific types of DDI and grievances in question.

Chapter 4 is devoted to the theoretical debate over the link between grievances and conflict behavior. In particular, we dive deeply into the empirical branches of grievance theory, its critics, and proposed alternative theories as well as the religion and conflict literature. We demonstrate that there is considerable disagreement over the grievance theory literature, and this disagreement includes both theoretical and empirical elements. We also demonstrate that while our study is well situated within these literatures, it offers a unique analysis of the conflict behavior of religious minorities, including the religious influences on this behavior. Chapter 5 provides the empirical testing of the RMAR data on the link between grievances and conflict behavior, which we describe in the previous section.

Chapter 6 summarizes and discusses the theoretical, empirical, and political implications of our findings. Again, we find that grievances matter in a manner consistent with our two-stage model, but that capacity also plays an important, interrelated role. The results are complex, and likely in some specifics unique to religious minorities, but we argue our two-stage model should be generalizable in many respects to the conflict behavior of other types of minorities. Religion, in the form of religious DDI and grievances, also matters. We do not claim that this study is the final word on the topic. However, we do claim it provides sufficient evidence to require that grievances be taken seriously in models seeking to explain domestic conflict and civil war, especially when involving minorities.

2

What are Deprivation, Discrimination, Inequality, and Grievances?

In this book, we posit that the core process that causes religious minorities to engage in conflict is a simple one. When religious minorities experience deprivation, discrimination, and inequality (DDI) this can cause them to form grievances. In turn, these grievances motivate various forms of mobilization, protest, and conflict. Of course, this general statement, while accurate, camouflages a conflict process that is far more complex, especially in how grievances translate into mobilization and conflict, and in that it is influenced by a myriad of other factors. However, it clearly begins with DDI, among other factors, causing grievances.

While the origins and causes of DDI are an important topic of study, it is not the focus of this book. Previous studies, many using the same DDI variables as are used in this study, have identified a wide variety of causes of and motivations for DDI against religious minorities. These include religious ideologies, secularism, state support for religion, belief in conspiracy theories concerning the religious minority, whether the minority is seen as a political or existential threat, protection of national culture, and anticult policies, among others (Fox, 2016, 2020; Fox & Topor, 2021; Peretz & Fox, 2021). This study, in contrast, focuses on DDI as a primary independent variable, rather than as a dependent variable.

We discuss why and how DDI causes grievances in Chapter 3. In this chapter we set the foundation for this discussion by describing what we mean by DDI and grievances. This includes both a theoretical perspective and how we measure these phenomena in practice. That is, in this chapter we define and discuss in detail the primary independent variables in this study. In doing so we provide illustrative examples of various religious minorities, which are intended to provide insight on the connection between the real-world DDI that occurs against them and how those translate into the measures we use in this study.

Religious Minorities at Risk. Matthias Basedau, Jonathan Fox, and Ariel Zellman, Oxford University Press.
© Oxford University Press 2023. DOI: 10.1093/oso/9780197693940.003.0002

Deprivation, discrimination, inequality, and grievances are terms that most people understand intuitively. However, in this chapter we use more precise definitions necessary for a methodical analytical process. We begin with a discussion of how social science theory conceives of DDI, a body of theory that provides the intellectual roots for our measures of discrimination. We then discuss our practical definitions of DDI based on the variables include in the Religious Minorities at Risk (RMAR) dataset which is a combination of variables originally collected in Religion and State-Minorities (RASM) and Religion and Conflict in Developing Countries (RCDC) datasets with additional variables unique to RMAR. Our variables for religious and societal DDI are taken from the RASM dataset. RMAR includes a number of additional variables measuring DDI against religious groups regarding economic status and political representation or inclusion in government. In addition, RMAR provides rather fine-grained and innovative data on grievances, distinguishing their type—religious, political, economic—as well as their level of intensity.

What Are Deprivation, Discrimination, and Inequality in Theory?

To discriminate means to treat differently. It can also mean to distinguish or differentiate. Thus, the word does not necessarily have a negative connotation if one recognizes that in a world with abundant variety, there will be many differences. However, in our case, we focus on the type of discrimination where one group is treated poorly in comparison to another. When applied to a majority-minority context, this means that there is some form of restriction or other form of harm placed on a minority that is not placed on the majority. This involves two distinct components. First, the restriction or other form of harm itself and second, differential treatment.

Deprivation and inequality are also relative terms in our context. It is not possible for something to be unequal in a vacuum. It must be unequal compared to some other point of comparison. While it is possible for deprivation to exist without a reference for comparison, in the context of this study we use the term to describe how minorities are deprived of a right, privilege, or access in some manner in comparison to the country's majority. However, unlike discrimination, which requires a positive act by the party engaging in the discrimination, deprivation and inequality are not necessarily

DEPRIVATION, DISCRIMINATION, INEQUALITY, AND GRIEVANCES? 27

intentional. They focus more on outcomes. Given these distinctions we use the acronym DDI (deprivation, discrimination, and inequality) when referring to the larger phenomena, which encompasses all three of them, and use the individual terms when we wish to specify that specific term.

Thus, if some form of restriction is placed on everyone in a state, including the majority, there is no differentiation in the treatment, and this would not be considered DDI. Put differently, DDI as we use the term involves differential treatment, status, or outcomes where a minority is singled out for a form of restriction that is not placed on the majority, is denied basic privileges and rights that are granted to the majority, or is in practice otherwise deprived or unequal as compared to a country's majority.

Take for example two extreme cases: North Korea and Saudi Arabia. While the Democratic People's Republic of Korea's (DPRK) constitution promises that "citizens have freedom of religious beliefs,"[1] in practice there is no such freedom, and religious freedom is severely restricted within its borders. The government promotes Marxism and a pseudo-religious ultranationalist ideology known as *Juche* (often defined as "self-reliance") of which leader-worship is a central element. While the government created religious federations for several religions including Buddhists, Chondokyists,[2] Protestants, and Catholics, these are controlled by political operatives and very few North Koreans participate in these organizations. They also seem intended more to focus international attention away from the DPRK's repression of all religions than provide venues for religious activity. Despite this high level of repression of all religions, there is still some religious discrimination in the DPRK because the government singles out some religions for an even greater dose of repression. For example, "the government considers the spread of Christianity to be a direct threat" (Fox, 2020, p. 182) and therefore represses Christians even more than other religions. However, most of the restrictions in the DPRK are not classified as DDI because they are lacking the second component of our conception of the term: differential treatment. That is, since most restrictions are applied to all religions, they are repression not discrimination. In contrast, Saudi Arabia promotes a specific version of Sunni Islam called Wahhabism. All other religions are officially

---

[1] Constitution, *Korea (Democratic People's Republic of)'s Constitution of 1972 with Amendments through 1998*, https://www.constituteproject.org/constitution/Peoples_Republic_of_Korea_1998.pdf?lang=en.

[2] This is a syncretic belief system largely based on Confucianism, but which also incorporates elements of Taoism, Shamanism, Buddhism, and Catholicism.

banned. Of the 35 types of governmental religious discrimination (GRD) discussed below, 30 are present against minorities in Saudi Arabia but not Wahhabi Islam. Thus, unlike the DPRK, there is a stark difference between the religious freedom of the majority and minorities in Saudi Arabia.

These two cases demonstrate the difference between a focus on religious discrimination as restrictions targeted against religious minorities as opposed to more general repression or restrictions on religious freedom. This distinction is what differentiates between the concept of discrimination and other theoretical lenses to examine restrictions that apply more generally.

Other concepts such as religious repression, religious persecution, and religious freedom paint with a broader brush. While there is no doubt that they include restrictions placed on religious minorities that are not placed on the majority, they also include restrictions on the religious freedoms of the majority. For example, Farr (2008) argues that "religious persecution is generally associated with egregious abuse—torture, rape, unjust imprisonment—on the basis of religion. A political order centered on religious liberty is not free of such abuses, to be sure, but it also protects the rights of individuals and groups to act publicly in ways consistent with their beliefs." There is no distinction between majorities and minorities in this definition. Farr would almost certainly include religious DDI as a form of religious persecution, but he also includes many forms of persecution that are not DDI as we define it.

Inboden (2013, p. 171–173) is more explicit, using a more expansive definition. His discussion of "religious persecution" in pre-9/11 Afghanistan includes the imposition of the Taliban's version of Islam on all residents of the country as well as persecuting religious minorities. For him the Taliban's religious intolerance included "the destruction of the sixth-century Buddhas of Bamiyan statues in March 2001, or the imprisonment of two American women missionaries that same year. And those who consistently suffered the most under Taliban rule were Afghan Muslims who did not share the Taliban's Islamist predilections."

Many other definitions of religious freedom share this inclusive trait. For example, Gill (2013, p. 7) states that "anything that increases the cost to an individual or group with respect to their ability to believe, practice, and proselytize their religious faith would be considered an infringement upon religious freedom. Conversely, any reduction in such costs enhances religious freedom." Saiya (2017b, p. 43) similarly defines religious freedom as "the right of individuals or communities to manifest religion or belief in teaching, practice, worship, and observance and to bring their faith into the public square." This is also true of definitions of religious persecution. For example, Jenkins (2007, p. 3) defines religious persecution as "an effort by a government to repress major activities by a given religious group, commonly with the goal of eliminating that group in the long or short term."

This broader definition is also present in prominent data collections. For example, Grim and Finke's (2006, 2007, 2011) cross-country measures of government restrictions on religion measure such restrictions regardless of to whom they are applied. This is unsurprising given that they base their conception of religious freedom on Article 18 of the UN's 1948 Universal Declaration of Human Rights, which states that "everyone has the right to freedom of thought, conscience and religion; this right includes freedom to change his religion or belief, and freedom, either alone or in community with others and in public or private, to manifest his religion or belief in teaching, practice, worship and observance." They also define religious persecution as "physical abuse or physical displacement due to one's religious practices, profession, or affiliation" (Grim & Finke, 2007, p. 643).

Many also address the concept of religious freedom through the lens of human rights. Human rights, like religious freedom, does include the idea that DDI in general and discrimination in particular violate human rights but is nevertheless broader and includes violations of the rights of people in general including members of the majority. It is common for those discussions of religious freedom to explicitly define it as a subset of human rights.[3] Others like Carnevale (2019, p. 2) consider religious freedom to be "at the historical origin of the human rights discourse." Nevertheless, he still considers religious freedom to be "a growing subfield of the emerging sociology of human rights" (Carnevale, 2019, p. 4). Martin (2005, p. 828) similarly argues that "the modern formulation of human rights grew up under the influence of Western Christianity and Judaism." Also, as noted earlier in this chapter, many international agreements protecting human rights include religious freedom among those human rights (Dinstein, 1991). Even those who argue that religious freedom is somehow unique often place it within the context of human rights. For example, Finke and Martin (2014, p. 689) argue that "religion holds a distinctive relationship with the state and larger culture. While all human rights depend on political support and state protections, the

---

[3] See, for example, Bettiza (2019, p. 60), Breskaya et al. (2018), Durham (1996), Glendon (2019, p. 1), Henne (2018), Little (1996), Marshall (2008, p. 12), Philpott (2019), Rieffer-Flanagan (2014), and Tiedmann (2015).

30   RELIGIOUS MINORITIES AT RISK

nature of religion-state relationships poses unique challenges for protecting religious freedoms and carries increased risks if these freedoms are not protected."

The concept of religious freedom has additional complexities in that many argue it is a normative agenda that can cause harm. One central contention is that "religious freedom is really a project of Judeo-Christian proselytization in disguise" (Joustra, 2018) and is, therefore, really an imposition of Western Christian values on others. That the United States' policy for promotion of religious freedom originated in the lobbying efforts of Evangelical Christians, among others, lends some credence to this contention. Another is that by prioritizing religious freedom we may be relegating the secular to second-class status (Joustra, 2018; Philpott, 2019).

In contrast, our conception of DDI is far narrower. It focuses on the treatment and status of minorities and requires that religious minorities be treated differently from the religious majority or in some manner be deprived or unequal compared to the majority. As we discuss in more detail in Chapter 3, this distinction is important because it is precisely in instances where minorities are singled out for treatment different from the majority that grievances are most likely to form.

The rest of this chapter discusses how we apply this concept of religious DDI and other forms of DDI in practice as well as our conception of grievances expressed by religious minorities over these forms of DDI.

Governmental Religious Discrimination

As noted in Chapter 1, the RMAR dataset combines the RASM and RCDC datasets and a number of newly created variables. GRD is taken from the RASM dataset. Its strategy for measuring GRD is based on the methodology developed by Gurr (1993a, 1993b, 2000a) in his Minorities at Risk (MAR) dataset to measure discrimination against ethnic minorities. Within each broader category of discrimination, MAR developed a list of potential specific types of discrimination that might occur, measured each of them separately on a scale, and combined these component scales to form a composite variable.

The GRD variable used here is defined as "restrictions placed by governments or their agents on the religious practices or institutions of religious minorities that are not placed on the majority religion. This measure

DEPRIVATION, DISCRIMINATION, INEQUALITY, AND GRIEVANCES? 31

is intentionally narrow and specific in order to isolate a specific type of government discriminatory behavior that is unambiguously related to religion" (Fox, 2020, p. 20).

This distinguishes it from the other DDI measures used in this study. The others measure forms of DDI which are directed at religious minorities. However, other than that the object of the DDI is a religious minority, these aspects of DDI have no characteristics that are unique to religion. All of them could be applied, and often have been applied, to other types of minorities such as those based on ethnicity, race, sexual preference, or gender identity.

The GRD measure includes 35 specific types of GRD, each measured on the following scale:

0. Not significantly restricted or the government does not engage in this practice.
1. The activity is slightly restricted or the government engages in a mild form of this practice.
2. The activity is significantly restricted or the government engages in a severe form of this practice.

Thus, the resulting measure in theory runs from 0 to 70. However, in practice, the highest coding in our observed data from 2000 to 2014 is 52, which identifies Iran as engaging in superlatively high levels of discrimination against the Baha'i across our entire temporal range. The next highest case is Christians in Laos with a score of 47 between 2011 and 2014.

These 35 types of GRD are divided by Fox (2016, 2019, 2020) into four categories: restrictions on religious practices, restrictions on religious institutions and clergy, restrictions on proselytizing and conversion, and other restrictions.

Overall, 74.45 percent of minorities in the study experienced at least one of these types of GRD at some point between 2000 and 2014. We provide detailed information on each of these 35 types of GRD in the following sections of this chapter. It is important to note that all of these forms of GRD are actions and policies set by governments or their representatives, including regional and local governments. They are not based upon general attitudes, opinions, or public statements of leaders, political representatives, or civil society groups. We organize our discussion along the four categories of GRD and provide illustrative examples. These examples tend to be among the more extreme cases. Thus, they are not intended to represent the median case

32 RELIGIOUS MINORITIES AT RISK

but rather to give the reader a better idea of the actions and events that are behind the data.

Restrictions on Religious Practices

Restrictions on religious practices are common. As shown in Table 2.1, at least one of these 12 types of restriction was placed on 41.52 percent of minorities at some point between 2000 and 2014. These restrictions are important because "even the smallest and seemingly inconsequential restriction on the right to free exercise is unlikely to be seen as trivial by the religious community that is restricted" (Fox, 2020, p. 31).

The most common types of restrictions on religious practices are restrictions on the public observance of religion, when minorities are forced

Table 2.1 GRD Restrictions on Religious Practices, 2000–2014

	% Groups Experiencing Discrimination			
			2000 to 2014	
	2000	2014	All Years	At Least Once
Public observance of religion	17.31	18.64	18.09	21.11
Private observance of religion	6.13	8.74	7.82	8.95
Forced observance: religious laws of another group	11.98	14.34	12.49	15.23
Make/obtain materials necessary for religious rites/customs/ceremonies	3.20	2.87	3.04	3.31
Circumcisions or other rite of passage ceremonies	0.00	0.26	0.25	0.26
Religious dietary laws	1.60	1.83	1.59	1.84
Write/publish/disseminate religious publications	16.78	17.47	17.05	17.87
Import religious publications	13.98	13.95	13.46	14.98
Religious publications for personal use	4.26	6.13	5.05	6.59
Religious laws concerning marriage and divorce	6.79	7.17	7.19	7.57
Religious laws concerning burial	7.86	9.00	8.51	9.62
Religious symbols or clothing	3.06	4.56	3.95	5.86
Number of cases	751	767	11425	11425
At least one of the above	*33.82*	*38.98*	*36.37*	*41.52*

DEPRIVATION, DISCRIMINATION, INEQUALITY, AND GRIEVANCES? 33

to observe the religious practices of the majority, and the various types of restrictions on religious publications. All three of these types are enforced against religious minorities in Iran. Among these, the Baha'i are the most heavily restricted. They are seen by the state as heretics and apostates, referred to as a "deviant sect," and are systematically harassed, arrested, persecuted, discriminated against, and killed. The government prohibits the Baha'i from teaching and practicing their faith, and they are discriminated against in almost every facet of life. This results in significant limitations on religious practices. As their faith is illegal, so are Baha'i religious practices and ceremonies both in public and private. Baha'i marriages and divorces are not officially recognized. While the government allows a civil attestation of marriage to serve as a marriage certificate, there have been cases of Baha'i being charged criminally with having sex outside of marriage because their marriages were not recognized by the state. The government prohibits the Baha'i community from official assembly and from maintaining administrative institutions. The government regularly confiscates Baha'i property including religious materials. They are generally prevented from burying and honoring their dead in accordance with their religious tradition, and their cemeteries are occasionally destroyed by the state. In January 2009, for instance, the Baha'i cemetery in Ghaemshahr was attacked for the fourth time in eight months and almost completely destroyed. According to witnesses, municipality officials razed the cemetery with a bulldozer at night. Similarly, in January 2009, government workers entered a Tehran cemetery and demolished an entire section known as the burial ground of "infidels."[4]

Christians in Iran also experience significant restrictions on their religious practices despite Iran's constitution recognizing Christianity as a legal religion. This discrimination is targeted primarily at "unrecognized" churches, which are mostly evangelical churches that are seen, often accurately, as seeking converts. Unsanctioned Christian house churches are illegal, and routinely raided by police. Christians are often arrested on various charges including of apostasy, illegal activities of evangelism,

---

[4] United Kingdom, Home Office (2013). Country of Origin Information Report—Iran, September 26, http://www.refworld.org/docid/5385a43d4.html; Erdbrink, T. (2016). An Ayatollah's daughter prompts a debate on religious persecution in Iran, *The New York Times*, May 18, http://www.nyti mes.com/2016/05/19/world/middleeast/iran-bahais-kamalabadi-hashemi-meeting.html; MacEoin, D. (2014). The Baha'is in Iran, *Gatestone Institute*, June 10, http://www.gatestoneinstitute.org/4347/bahais-iran.

34   RELIGIOUS MINORITIES AT RISK

anti-government propaganda, espionage, and activities against Islam. With few exceptions, even "recognized" churches are no longer allowed to hold services in Farsi (the first language of most Iranian Christians) and are not allowed to hold services on Fridays. All of this effectively restricts religious practices and ceremonies in these forums. Government officials frequently confiscate Christian Bibles and pressure publishing houses printing Bibles or nonsanctioned, non-Muslim materials to cease operations.[5] Iran's Islamic dress code is enforced on all people in the country regardless of religion. GRD in Iran is not limited to restrictions on religious practices. Many of the other categories of restriction described in the following sections are also present.

Restrictions on Religious Institutions and Clergy

Restrictions on religious institutions and clergy are even more common than restrictions on religious practices. As shown in Table 2.2, they were present against 57.11 percent of religious minorities in this study at some point between 2000 and 2014. These restrictions have serious consequences. Clergy and institutions are essential to organized religion. They are crucial for preserving theology and doctrine as well as the continuity of their religious practices across generations: "They are central to most religious ceremonies and rites of passage. Without them, practicing a religion and even maintaining its presence in a location becomes more difficult" (Fox, 2020, p. 35).

All seven of these types of restrictions are present against at least some of the eight minorities in Russia included in this study (Animists, Buddhists, Hindus, Jews, Muslims, Catholics, Protestants, and other non–Russian Orthodox Christians). This discrimination comes from both the federal and local governments. While Russia officially recognizes Judaism, Islam, and Buddhism as "traditional" religions this does not completely exempt them from restrictions on their religious institutions and clergy. Registration has become particularly difficult since the passage of the 1997 *Law On Freedom of Conscience and Religious Associations*. Unregistered religions are illegal

---

[5] United Kingdom: Home Office, Country of Origin Information Report—Iran; US State Department Report on International Religious Freedom, 2001–2014, https://2009-2017.state.gov/j/drl/rls/irf//index.htm.

DEPRIVATION, DISCRIMINATION, INEQUALITY, AND GRIEVANCES? 35

Table 2.2 GRD Restrictions on Religious Institutions and Clergy, 2000–2014

| | % Groups Experiencing Discrimination | | | |
| | | | 2000 to 2014 | |
	2000	2014	All Years	At Least Once
Building/leasing/repairing/maintaining places of worship	26.63	30.38	28.39	31.63
Access to existing places of worship	10.12	14.32	11.79	14.89
Formal religious organizations	9.59	12.89	11.11	13.15
Ordination of and/or access to clergy	8.52	8.74	8.55	10.29
Minority religions (as opposed to all religions) must register	31.16	32.94	32.8	34.64
Minority clergy access to jails.	14.91	14.34	14.56	15.23
Minority clergy access to military bases	20.24	19.69	19.77	20.35
Minority clergy access to hospitals and other public facilities	11.58	11.6	11.41	11.95
# cases	751	767	11425	11425
At least one of the above	*51.4*	*55.15*	*53.11*	*57.11*

and their institutions can be restricted or banned. This often includes denial of access to existing places of worship. The Russian Orthodox Church (ROC) has considerable influence over which religions are allowed to register.[6] The 2002 *Law on Extremism* criminalizes a broad spectrum of speech and activities. Among the forms of "extremist activity," it has been used to restrict a broad range of religious activity. In particular numerous Muslim and Jehovah's Witness organizations and individuals have been targeted under this law.[7] Local governments often deny land or permits to build minority places of worship, particularly to Jews, Muslims, and non–Orthodox Christian denominations. For example, there is a general dearth of mosques and restricted access to those that exist. There are only four mosques in Moscow and Muslims continue to have difficulty obtaining approval for a fifth. Sochi, a city in which 20,000 Muslims reside, has no mosque. The deputy mayor of Sochi denied a 2010 request to construct a mosque, stating that a mosque 20 kilometers away was sufficient for the

---

[6] Religion in Russia: A question of faith (2013). *The Economist*, February 2, http://www.economist.com/news/books-and-arts/21571111-new-look-religion-post-1991-russia-question-faith.

[7] Arnold, V. (2015). Russia: 65 known 'extremist' religious literature cases in 2014, *Forum 18 News Service*, March 31, http://www.forum18.org/archive.php?country=10; Clark, E. A. (2013, p. 297).

36 RELIGIOUS MINORITIES AT RISK

needs of the city's Muslims.[8] In June 2014 a regional court in Kaliningrad deemed a nearly completed mosque illegal. The community had to organize "round-the-clock protection" of the mosque to prevent attempts to destroy the building.[9] Local governments also often take active measures to prevent these groups from renting facilities to hold religious activities. For example, in May 2013 Jehovah's Witnesses submitted a request to the Gorodetskiy District to rent a stadium for a convention. The request was denied after the administration consulted an Orthodox priest. Russian courts apply a strict interpretation of the law on public demonstrations to keep evangelical Protestants and Jehovah's Witnesses from gathering for worship. While this is technically a limitation on religious practices, it also applies to religious institutions because the banned activities, such as prayer and Bible study, are activities that often take place under the auspices of religious institutions. Protestant churches find it hard or impossible to get visas for visiting pastors.[10]

The ROC and its clergy have preferred and often exclusive access to public institutions such as schools, hospitals, prisons, police, and the military forces. Nearly all religious facilities in prisons are Russian Orthodox.

Restrictions on Conversion and Proselytizing

Restrictions on conversion and proselytizing directed against religious minorities who live in the country are less common than the other types of GRD thus far discussed. As shown in Table 2.3, they were present against 27.45 percent of religious minorities at some point between 2000 and 2014. Restrictions against foreign proselytizers and missionaries are far more common and were present in 48.1 percent of countries in 2014 (Fox, 2019, p. 21).

This type of GRD represents an interesting struggle between religions as well as between religion and nationalism. On one hand, many religions

---

[8] US State Department Report on International Religious Freedom, 2001–2014; Arnold, V. (2014). Russia: Still no mosque for Sochi, protestants struggle to keep church, *Forum 18 News Service*, March 4, http://www.forum18.org/archive.php?country=10&page=3.

[9] Arnold, V. (2014). Russia: Obstructions to building places of worship, *Forum 18 News Service*, June 5, http://www.forum18.org/archive.php?country=10&page=2.

[10] Russia: Religious Freedom Survey, 2012, *Forum 18 News Service*, http://www.forum18.org/arch ive.php?article_id=1722; US Department of State International Religious Freedom Report, 2013, http://www.state.gov/j/drl/rls/irf/religiousfreedom/index.htm#wrapper.

DEPRIVATION, DISCRIMINATION, INEQUALITY, AND GRIEVANCES? 37

Table 2.3 GRD Restrictions on Conversion and Proselytizing, 2000–2014

	% Groups Experiencing Discrimination			
			2000 to 2014	
	2000	2014	All Years	At Least Once
Conversion to minority religions	9.99	9.52	9.85	10.17
Forced renunciation of faith by recent converts to minority religions	3.99	4.43	4.33	4.62
Forced conversions	1.60	3.26	2.72	3.13
Efforts/campaigns to convert members of minority religion (no force)	7.86	9.52	8.93	10.39
Proselytizing by permanent residents to members of the majority religion	18.91	21.12	20.12	21.62
Proselytizing by permanent residents to members of minority religions	11.45	13.3	12.34	13.65
# cases	751	767	11425	11425
At least one of the above	*23.7*	*26.21*	*25.41*	*27.45*

consider seeking converts a central religious obligation. In addition, when one believes there is one Truth that is essential to our existence, one is highly motivated to share that truth and possibly intolerant of others who do not share it. For the same reasons, many religious people consider members of other religions seeking to poach from their own religious community as an existential threat. Even secular governments can see proselytizing as a threat for at least three reasons. First, if the proselytizing religion is considered foreign this can be seen as undermining national culture. Second, in cases where religious demography has political significance, this can be seen as an effort to change the political status quo (Fox, 2020). Third, many autocratic governments see religious institutions as potential bases for mobilization against the government (Koesel, 2014; Sarkissian, 2015).

Sudan provides a good example of a religiously motivated government. Article 26 of Sudan's 1991 Criminal Code criminalizes apostasy for Muslims. Converts away from Islam who do not recant may be sentenced to death (Article 126).[11] Until 2011, this law was rarely enforced, but since then and through the end of the study period it was enforced vigorously. For example,

---

[11] Criminal Act 1991 Sudan; *In search of confluence: Addressing discrimination and inequality in Sudan*, Equal Rights Trust.

38 RELIGIOUS MINORITIES AT RISK

in July 2011 alone, over 170 Sudanese were arrested for apostasy.[12] In April 2014, a woman whose parents had converted to Christianity before her birth and raised her as a Christian was arrested and sentenced to death. She was freed and allowed to leave the country after massive international pressure.[13] In May 2014, a woman with a Muslim father who had been raised as a Christian by her Christian mother was convicted of apostasy for marrying a Christian man and refusing to embrace Islam. She was sentenced to death, but after international protest was allowed to leave the country.[14]

While proselytizing is not prohibited by law, it is restricted in practice. Foreign religious organizations are allowed into the country for humanitarian purposes but are closely monitored. Those suspected of proselytizing are deported. For example, in October 2012, two English teachers were deported on charges of proselytizing.[15] Similarly, in February 2009 the government expelled a US humanitarian aid organization due to the presence of Arabic-language Bibles in their offices.[16] In December 2012, police arrested two Coptic priests and briefly detained a Coptic bishop for reportedly converting a Muslim woman to Christianity. In July 2014, a Korean Christian suspected of proselytizing was deported, and his music store was confiscated. In November 2014, another Korean Christian suspected of conducting religious activities was deported.[17] In an effort to prevent Muslim children from being adopted and raised by non-Muslims, Christian orphanages are under surveillance and pressure, particularly not to accept male orphans.[18]

The government also engages in policies seeking to convert people to Islam. The *1992 Prisons and Treatment of Prisoners Law* states that the minister of justice can release any prisoner who memorizes the Quran during

---

[12] *Human rights and freedom of religion or belief in Sudan* (2012). UN Human Rights Council.

[13] Second Sudanese woman jailed for her faith, *Baptist News*, http://www.bpnews.net/42656/2nd-sudanese-woman-jailed-for-her-faith; US Department of State, *Religious freedom report Sudan 2014*; Green, C. (2014). Pregnant Christian to hang in Sudan for abandoning Islam, *The UK Independent*, May 16; Death row mother rearrested as she tries to flee Sudan (2014), *Irish Examiner*, June 25; Sudan "apostasy" woman Meriam Ibrahim arrives in US (2014), *BBC News*, August 1, http://www.bbc.com/news/world-us-canada-28596412.

[14] Sudan profile timeline, *BBC News*; US Department of State, *Religious freedom report sudan 2014*; Sudan "Apostasy" woman Meriam Ibrahim arrives in US, *BBC News*.

[15] US State Department Report on International Religious Freedom, 2001–2014; *Human rights and freedom of religion or belief in Sudan* (2012), UN Human Rights Council.

[16] US State Department Report on International Religious Freedom, 2001–2014; Heavens, A. (2009). Sudan expels US aid group over bibles, *Reuters*, January 31, http://uk.reuters.com/article/idUKLV258132; Darfur, Sudan, thirst no more, http://www.thirstnomore.org/#/where-weve-been/darfur-sudan.

[17] US State Department Report on International Religious Freedom, 2001–2014.

[18] US State Department Report on International Religious Freedom, 2001–2014.

DEPRIVATION, DISCRIMINATION, INEQUALITY, AND GRIEVANCES? 39

his prison term, encouraging non-Muslims to convert to Islam to take advantage of the parole option. Non-Muslims cannot get government jobs and non–Muslim owned businesses do not get government contracts. This has resulted in many conversions to Islam for economic purposes. Residents of government-run camps for displaced persons reported multiple types of pressure to convert to Islam. Children in camps for vagrant minors were required to study the Quran and pressured to convert. Islamic humanitarian aid organizations in Sudan's war zones withheld services unless people converted to Islam. Christian leaders also report that prisoners' sentences are reduced if they convert to Islam. They also report that government forces were giving rewards to persons who converted to Islam. Some women have converted to Islam in an attempt to qualify for land and government benefits as well as charity assistance given to widows of war casualties.[19]

Laos provides an example of secular and nationalist motivations for these types of restrictions. Proselytizing by foreigners is prohibited by law. Other religious groups require government permission to preach or disseminate religious materials outside their house of worship. In practice many local governments enforce this against the country's Christian minority and harass converts to Christianity. For example, in August 2012, a preacher's residency status was revoked after he converted hundreds of people in the region to Christianity. In 2013, several pastors were arrested for copying and distributing Christian videos. They were reportedly beaten in prison.[20] Efforts by local authorities to pressure Christians to recant their faith are common. In most cases, these families have been Christian for several generations, but the government sees them as converts. In July 2009, local officials confiscated livestock from Christians in their village. In January 2010, local

---

[19] US State Department Report on International Religious Freedom, 2001–2014; Colvin, A. (n.d.). Sudan, *International Coalition for Religious Freedom*, http://www.religiousfreedom.com/index.php?option=com_content&view=article&id=105&Itemid=29; *United States Commission on International Religious Freedom Annual Report 2010*. (2010). US Commission on International Religious Freedom, http://www.uscirf.gov/index.php?option=com_content&view=article&id=3310.

[20] Pastors released after arrest for "spreading Christian religion" (2013). *Christian Today*, April 8, http://www.christiantoday.com/article/pastors.released.after.arrest.for.spreading.christian.religion/32072.htm; US State Department Report on International Religious Freedom, 2001–2014; Lao police arrested and detained Christian pastors for spreading Christian religion through movie CDs (2013). *Human Rights Watch for Lao Religious Freedom*, February 7; US Department of State, *Religious Freedom Report Laos 2012, 2014*; Laos: Christians arrested on charges of proselytizing, *Official Vatican Network*, http://www.news.va/en/news/asialaos-christians-arrested-on-charges-of-prosely; Crackdown on churches spreading in southern Laos (2012). *Worthy News*, May 15, http://www.worthynews.com/11484-crackdown-on-churches-spreading-in-southern-laos.

officials in the same village forced Christians out of their village when they would not renounce their faith. The provincial governor interceded on their behalf, citing their Constitutional right to belief, but the Christians did not return to their former homes and, rather, established a new village nearby. In 2010, the local government in a southern district forced 65 Christian farmers from their homes and land, destroyed their crops, held them in a camp without food, and prevented others from bringing them food in order to force them to recant their Christian faith. In 2012, two members of the military were discharged after they converted to Christianity. In 2014, local authorities in Natahal, a village in the south of the country, banned Christianity and expelled those who refused to officially recant their beliefs. In 2014, a man who converted to Christianity was arrested and held for 10 days, during which time he was pressured to recant his conversion.[21]

Laos is officially a communist country, which is generally hostile to religion. Yet it is also overtly hostile to Buddhists, the country's majority religion, who convert to Christianity. Fox (2020, p. 180) argues,

> There are two likely explanations for this incongruity. First, officials of at least some local governments are paying lip service to Communism yet still adhere at least to some extent to Buddhism. Second, Buddhism is seen as part of the national culture, and Christianity is seen as foreign. In fact, government policy is to see that all religious activities serve the national interest. Thus, nationalism is likely a significant influence on this behavior. Likely, the explanation is a combination of nationalism and ideology.

Other Forms of GRD

This category includes nine types of GRD that do not fit into the above three categories. As shown in Table 2.4, overall 49.44 percent of religious minorities experienced at least one of these types of GRD at some point between 2000 and 2014.

---

[21] US Department of State, *Religious Freedom Report Laos 2014*; Laos fires Christian converts from security forces (2012). *NewsLife Asia*, June 22, http://www.bosnewslife.com/22169-laos-dismisses-christian-converts-from-security-forces; Food denied to 65 Laotian farmers to force them to renounce Christianity (2011). *AsiaNews*, February 25, http://www.asianews.it/news-en/Food-denied-to-65-Laotian-farmers-to-force-them-to-renounce-Christianity-20878.html.

DEPRIVATION, DISCRIMINATION, INEQUALITY, AND GRIEVANCES? 41

Table 2.4 Other Forms of GRD, 2000–2014

| | % Groups Experiencing Discrimination | | | |
| | | | 2000 to 2014 | |
	2000	2014	All Years	At Least Once
Religious schools/education	14.91	16.82	15.93	17.23
Mandatory education in the majority religion	18.51	18.38	19.37	21.68
Arrest/detention/harassment other than for proselytizing	9.32	12.78	11.23	14.74
Failure to protect rel. minorities against violence or punish perpetrators	5.99	7.56	6.56	7.83
State surveillance of religious activities	8.66	11.21	9.80	12.38
Child custody granted on basis of religion	8.52	9.78	8.87	10.51
Declaration of some minority religions dangerous or extremist sects	3.46	4.17	3.94	4.33
Anti-religious propaganda in official/ semi-official government publications	8.39	8.60	8.43	9.61
Other forms of governmental religious discrimination	12.12	14.08	12.36	16.06
# cases	751	767	11425	11425
At least one of the above	*40.88*	*45.76*	*43.32*	*49.44*

Seven of these types of restrictions are present in Belarus, a Christian Orthodox–majority country, particularly against non-Orthodox, non-Catholic Christians. Much of these restrictions are placed on minorities, which are unable to register. The government may, and often does, arbitrarily deny or revoke a group's registration. This is especially common for religious minorities perceived as nonindigenous. All religious activity by unregistered groups is prohibited and violators are subject to heavy fines or jail terms. This includes religious education and setting up religious schools.

Police surveil and regularly raid private residences where unauthorized religious services are held. Clergy and participants may be arrested, fined, or charged with criminal offenses for participating in or organizing services for unregistered religious groups. Police surveil and even film services by registered Protestant groups and often charge them with engaging in illegal activities. There have been multiple cases of criminal charges being brought against individuals for holding unauthorized religious services. Criminal charges were brought against a Catholic layman running a charity organization and

42 RELIGIOUS MINORITIES AT RISK

a Christian group running a drug and alcohol rehabilitation program. Hare Krishna and Jehovah's Witness members were detained after preaching or distributing religious literature in public places.[22] Antiminority propaganda is common in the state-run media. For example, in 2009, a state-owned national television station broadcast several programs about the Unification Church, calling it a sect and alleging that the church employs destructive methods and activities. Members of minority religions are reluctant to report abuses, fearing retribution. Authorities only sporadically or ineffectively investigated anti-Semitic acts.[23]

Governmental Religious Discrimination from 2000 to 2014

As shown in Figure 2.1, there has been a considerable percentage increase in the average GRD experienced by religious minorities globally since 2000, approaching 12 percent by 2014. In 2000, 65.51 percent of the minorities in this study experienced at least one form of GRD. By 2014 this increased to 68.52 percent. Overall, 74.45 percent of religious minorities experienced some form of GRD at some point between 2000 and 2014. This is important because it establishes that GRD is common, but there is variance over location, specific minorities within a location, and time. This means that comparisons across minorities as well as comparisons of the same minority over time are valid comparisons.

Societal Religious Discrimination

Our variable for societal religious discrimination (SRD) is also taken from the RASM dataset. SRD is defined as "societal actions taken against religious minorities by members of a country's religious majority who do not represent the government" (Fox, 2020, p. 56). Unlike most previous measures of SRD,

---

[22] US State Department Report on International Religious Freedom, 2001–2014; Glace, O. (2014). Belarus: Religious freedom survey, September 2014, *Forum 18 News Service*, September 16; Glace, O. (2014). Belarus: Homeless shelter officially closed, March 6; Baptists fined, *Forum 18 News Service*; Glace, O. (2013). Belarus: Praying in homeless shelter a crime, *Forum 18 News Service*, July 2; Fagan, G. (2009). Ideology official targets rehabilitation program, *Forum 18 News Service*, March 30.

[23] US Department of State, *Religious Freedom Report Belarus 2010*; US Department of State, *Religious Freedom Report Belarus 2010, 2011, 2012, 2013*.

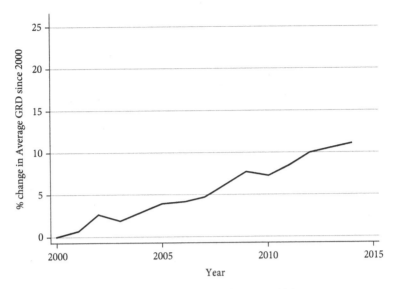

Figure 2.1 Percentage Change in Average GRD since 2000

which measure attitudes or include attitudes as a component of discrimination (e.g., Grim & Finke, 2011; Zick et al., 2011), this SRD variable focuses exclusively on *actions taken against religious minorities* in the real world. It includes 27 distinct types of actions in the following categories: economic discrimination, speech acts, attacks on property, nonviolent harassment, violence, and other types of SRD (Fox, 2020). As with GRD, general attitudes, opinions, or public statements of leaders, political representatives, or civil society groups are insufficient to establish SRD according to our data. The presence of each of these acts in a given year against a given minority is measured on the following scale:

0. There are no reported incidents of this type of action against the specified minority.
1. This action occurs on a minor level.
2. This action occurs on a substantial level.

The resulting variable ranges from 0 to 54. However, in practice the highest score is 47, which refers to Egyptian societal discrimination against Copts from 2012 to 2014. The next highest levels of societal discrimination outside of Egypt, with a SRD score of 36, are observed in Myanmar against Muslims in 2012 and in Pakistan against Christians in 2006 and 2011–2012.

44 RELIGIOUS MINORITIES AT RISK

It is important to emphasize that this variable focuses on actions taken against religious minorities by members of the majority group. We focus on this because this study examines the conflict between religious minorities and the state, and it is precisely action taken by members of the majority that are most likely to cause grievances against the state and the religious majority that, in most countries, is at least a part of the governing coalition or selectorate.[24]

Overall, 54.22 percent of minorities in the study experienced at least one of these types of SRD at some point between 2000 and 2014. We provide detailed information on each of these 27 types of SRD in the next sections of this chapter. We organize our discussion along the six aforementioned categories of SRD and provide illustrative examples intended to give the reader a better idea of the actions and events that are behind the data.

Economic Discrimination

The three types of economic discrimination measured here are listed in Table 2.5. These are all acts taken by societal actors rather than the government. So, for example, laws barring a minority from a specific profession or economic activity are not included in these measures.

15.96 percent of minorities experiences some form of economic SRD between 2000 and 2014. The Muslim minority in Denmark experienced all three types. One study from 2009 showed that chances of an applicant being called for a job interview varied by a ratio of 1:32 depending on whether the applicant used a typically Danish name or a typically Muslim one. The report concluded that Muslims "typically have significantly higher unemployment rates, lower labor income, and they are less likely to find and keep their jobs than the majority population."[25] In another survey, 27 percent of minority respondents said that they had experienced discrimination in housing. These complaints centered on being overlooked in housing allocations, especially in private housing corporation waiting lists. There were also some isolated reports of denial of service at some businesses.[26]

---

[24] The RAS dataset includes variables for minority on minority violence and harassment but they are not included as independent variables in this study.

[25] Euro-Islam.Info, *Islam in Denmark*, http://www.euro-islam.info/country-profiles/denmark/.

[26] Euro-Islam.Info, *Islam in Denmark*, http://www.euro-islam.info/country-profiles/denmark/; US State Department Report on International Religious Freedom, 2001–2014.

DEPRIVATION, DISCRIMINATION, INEQUALITY, AND GRIEVANCES? 45

Table 2.5 SRD Economic Discrimination, 2000–2014

	% Groups Experiencing Discrimination			
			2000 to 2014	
	2000	2014	All Years	At Least Once
In the workplace	10.25	11.08	10.52	13.42
Boycott of business/denial of access to businesses, stores, etc.	1.07	1.56	0.93	2.31
Other economic discrimination	1.46	2.22	1.87	2.85
# cases	751	767	11425	11425
At least one of the above	*11.05*	*12.78*	*11.74*	*15.96*

Speech Acts

Speech acts are public antiminority speech, propaganda, or rhetoric by non-governmental actors such as the media, clergy, or political parties as well as the dissemination of antiminority publications. They do not represent private acts of speech by individuals in forums such as social media, which are unfortunately quite common. Rather, they are made by public figures and leaders or in media outlets or other public forums.

As shown in Table 2.6, 27.74 percent of minorities have experienced this type of speech act at least once between 2000 and 2014. The Jews in Greece experienced particularly high levels, receiving the highest score in each of the four categories. Members and supporters of the Golden Dawn party, including its leader Nikos Michaloliakos, often make anti-Semitic statements including Holocaust denial, espousing conspiracy theories that a Jewish lobby is conspiring against Greece, and criticizing Greek citizens of Jewish heritage. The July 2012 issue of the newspaper *Eleftheri Ora*, associated with the Golden Dawn party, included excerpts from the *Protocols of the Elders of Zion* (a classic anti-Semitic document) with an introduction by Father Eustathios Kollas, honorary president of the Greek Orthodox Priests Association. During an October 2012 plenary session of parliament, a member of Golden Dawn read passages from the *Protocols of the Elders of Zion*. In January 2009, the official LAOS (another right-wing Greek political party) newspaper announced that "it is now widely known throughout the world that the Jew stinks of blood." Giorgos Karatzaferis, leader of LAOS, is a notorious Holocaust denier and regularly accuses the Jews of conspiracy against Greece. He has used

46   RELIGIOUS MINORITIES AT RISK

Table 2.6 SRD Speech Acts, 2000–2014

| | % Groups Experiencing Discrimination | | | |
| | | | 2000 to 2014 | |
	2000	2014	All Years	At Least Once
Antiminority propaganda/statements/ articles in the media	11.45	14.99	13.00	18.19
Antiminority rhetoric by majority religion's clerics	6.66	8.08	7.45	10.98
Antiminority rhetoric in political campaigns or by political parties	6.39	8.21	6.95	10.2
Dissemination of antiminority publications	4.26	4.82	4.81	9.19
# cases	751	767	11425	11425
include all of above	*16.25*	*21.51*	*18.81*	*27.74*

party-owned media channels to denounce Greek Jewish politicians and to claim that Jews were responsible for the World Trade Center attacks on 9/11.[27]

This behavior is not limited to Greece's far right. Senior clergy of the Greek Orthodox Church expressed anti-Semitic attitudes such as that Jews control the banks. In 2010, the Greek Orthodox Church's Bishop of Piraeus made anti-Semitic statements on national television. The Greek Orthodox Church's Holy Week liturgy includes anti-Semitic passages. Public school textbooks contain negative references to Jews, and some bookstores sell anti-Semitic books such as the *Protocols of the Elders of Zion*.[28]

Anti-Semitic articles and cartoons are commonplace in the Greek media. In March 2008, three journalists from *Eleftheros Kosmos* were handed a seven-month suspension for insulting Jews. In December 2008, the newspaper *Eleftherotypia* printed anti-Semitic cartoons, and the website of the Communist Party of Greece has animation of a Star of David turning into a swastika. In November 2008, a headline in a mainstream Greek newspaper announced Barack Obama's election as "The end of Jewish Domination."[29]

---

[27] Margaronis, M. (2012). In austerity-ravaged Greece neo-Nazi party Golden Dawn is on the rise, *The London Guardian*, October 27, 48; US State Department Report on International Religious Freedom, 2001–2014.

[28] US State Department Report on International Religious Freedom, 2001–2014.

[29] Anti-Defamation League Press Release, Headline in Greek newspaper puts anti-Semitism on full display, http://www.adl.org/PresRele/ASInt_13/5386_13.htm; US State Department Report on International Religious Freedom, 2001–2014.

DEPRIVATION, DISCRIMINATION, INEQUALITY, AND GRIEVANCES? 47

Table 2.7 SRD Attacks on Property, 2000–2014

| | % Groups Experiencing Discrimination | | | |
| | | 2000 to 2014 | | |
	2000	2014	All Years	At Least Once
Vandalism of religious property (places of worship, community centers, schools, cemeteries, etc.)	11.05	15.38	13.90	23.54
Vandalism of other minority property	4.66	4.82	4.66	9.54
Antireligious graffiti	6.13	8.74	7.81	11.9
# cases	751	767	11425	11425
At least one of the above	*12.78*	*16.69*	*15.37*	*26.37*

Attacks on Property

Attacks on property include vandalism and graffiti. RASM includes arson in the violence category rather than this one because arson has the potential to harm and kill (Fox, 2020). As shown in Table 2.7, this form of SRD is nearly as common as speech acts because 26.37 percent of minorities experienced attacks on their property at some point between 2000 and 2014.

The Jewish minority in the United States experiences all of these types of discrimination. Anti-Jewish graffiti is quite common in the United States. There are numerous incidents every year of vandalism and anti-Semitic graffiti on Jewish schools, Synagogues, cemeteries, other Jewish institutions, Jewish homes, and other locations. The vandalism incidents are mostly broken windows and turned-over gravestones. Graffiti incidents where anti-Jewish graffiti is found at non-Jewish schools and universities are also common. Swastikas are the most common form of anti-Jewish graffiti. Other examples include Nazi phrases such as "Sieg Heil" or "Heil Hitler." Documented graffiti incidents also include phrases like "fuck Jews," "Jew rats," "no Jews allowed," "I hate Jews," "kill the Jews," "white power," and "you will not replace us," among others.[30] This is not unique to the United States. According to police statistics in Canada, among the hundreds of yearly hate crimes against Jews in Canada, about 85 percent include graffiti and

---

[30] For a detailed listing of similar incidents in the US see the Anti-Defamation League's listing of anti-Semitic incidents in 2017 at https://www.adl.org/media/10943/download.

48 RELIGIOUS MINORITIES AT RISK

vandalism.[31] Similar incidents are regular occurrences in Western countries with large Jewish communities including Australia, France, Germany, and the United Kingdom.

Nonviolent Harassment

Nonviolent harassment includes "acts of harassment and persecution against individuals and groups that fall short of violence and do not constitute an over threat of violence" (Fox, 2020, p. 70). As shown in Table 2.8, 28.35 percent of religious minorities in the study experienced nonviolent harassment at some point between 2000 and 2014. There are few minorities that experience significant levels nonviolent harassment which do not also experience violence, but this discussion focuses on nonviolent harassment, and in the two illustrative examples we discuss in this chapter, the nonviolent harassment is more prominent.

Timor-Leste became independent from Indonesia in 2002, and its population is approximately 98 percent Catholic. There are significant levels of harassment of its Protestant minority. Attitudes toward Protestants are generally friendly in Dili, Timor's capital. However, outside of the capital, Protestants are viewed with suspicion. There are multiple incidents of harassment of religious services. For example, in 2009, Catholic youth disrupted church activities of a Protestant church and harassed participants. Out of ongoing fears for the safety of his congregation, the pastor elected to hold services privately. Similarly, in March and April 2013, a local Catholic youth group harassed members of a Protestant missionary church and prevented them from holding religious services. In August 2014, members of a local Catholic youth group harassed a foreign missionary at her home and insisted that she seek approval from the Catholic Church to carry out religious work. Much of this harassment is motivated by conversion from Catholicism to Protestant denominations. Some Protestant leaders reported harassment of converts by family, members of their community, and local leaders.[32]

---

[31] Statistics Canada (2012). Police-reported hate crime in Canada 2012, http://www.statcan.gc.ca/pub/85-002-x/2014001/article/14028-eng.pdf; Statistics Canada (2011). Police-reported hate crime in Canada 2011, http://www.statcan.gc.ca/pub/85-002-x/2013001/article/11822-eng.pdf.

[32] *Religious identity and conflict in Timor-Leste: An ewer program policy brief*, September 2009, http://www.cicr-columbia.org/wp-content/uploads/2011/06/Policy-Brief-2-Religion.pdf; US State Department Report on International Religious Freedom, 2009–2014, https://2009-2017.state.gov/j/drl/rls/irf//index.htm.

DEPRIVATION, DISCRIMINATION, INEQUALITY, AND GRIEVANCES? 49

Table 2.8 SRD Nonviolent Harassment, 2000–2014

	% Groups Experiencing Discrimination			
			2000 to 2014	
	2000	2014	All Years	At Least Once
Nonviolent harassment of clergy	2.26	2.74	2.42	3.87
Nonviolent harassment of proselytizers or missionaries	3.2	3.39	3.29	3.66
Nonviolent harassment of converts away from the majority religion	7.86	8.08	8.02	8.38
Nonviolent harassment of other members of religious minorities	13.72	16.95	16.04	20.13
Expulsion or harassment so severe that it leads to a significant number of minority members leaving a town or region	2.93	3.91	3.30	5.23
Organized demonstrations and public protests against religious minorities	1.33	2.35	1.77	7.15
# cases	751	767	11425	11425
At least one of the above	*21.04*	*24.12*	*23.04*	*28.35*

Harassment of the Christian minority in Israel is also motivated to a great extent, though not exclusively, by missionary efforts. Israel's Christians fall into several categories. They include indigenous Christians, such as members of the Armenian Church; foreign clergy who are mostly present at holy sites and Church-owned property in the holy land; missionaries; and messianic Jews (also known as Jews for Jesus), who are seen by many in Israel as similar to the missionaries. Most Jews in Israel are opposed to missionary activity, and some are hostile to Jewish converts to Christianity. Missionaries face harassment, discrimination, and, occasionally, physical assault by organizations such as *Yad L'Achim* and *Lev L'Achim*. There have been multiple protests outside of the meeting places and businesses of messianic Jews. For example, In August 2011, in Holon, approximately 15 Ultra-Orthodox men disrupted a Jehovah's Witness religious meeting held at a sports hall. Many of these incidents also include low level violence such as breaking of windows and stone throwing. Most of the protesters are Ultra-Orthodox men. There were also numerous incidents of Ultra-Orthodox Jews insulting and spitting at priests and nuns.[33]

---

[33] US State Department Report on International Religious Freedom, 2001–2014, https://2009-2017.state.gov/j/drl/rls/irf//index.htm; Posner, S. (2012). Kosher Jesus: Messianic Jews in the Holy

50 RELIGIOUS MINORITIES AT RISK

Table 2.9 SRD Violence, 2000–2014

| | % Groups Experiencing Discrimination | | | |
| | | 2000 to 2014 | | |
	2000	2014	All Years	At Least Once
Overt threats of violence	8.12	10.82	9.39	16.67
Violence targeted against clergy	2.13	3.52	2.95	9.76
Violence targeted against proselytizers or converts	2.4	2.87	2.79	4.58
Other violence against minority due to their religious affiliation	9.72	12.13	11.34	17.72
Large-scale violence against minority due to their religious affiliation	2.53	3.00	2.72	8.29
Lethal violence against minority due to their religious affiliation	4.53	6.39	5.01	13.66
Arson, bombing, or concerted attacks against religious property	6.26	7.43	7.09	18.9
Arson, bombing, or concerted attacks against other property	3.6	4.3	4.01	9.2
# cases	751	767	11425	11425
At least one of the above	*15.58*	*19.95*	*18.00*	*33.13*

Violence

Violence is the most extreme form of SRD. As shown in Table 2.9 it is also the most common. 33.13 percent of religious minorities experienced violence directed against them at some point between 2000 and 2014.

Between 2000 and 2014, societal violence against religious minorities in Pakistan, including Christians, Hindus, Sikhs, and Ahmadis, was among the highest in the world. There are multiple violent attacks yearly, killing hundreds every year. Many of them are by organized groups often classified as terrorists. This includes mass attacks involving as many as 40 perpetrators as well as smaller-scale attacks and shootings. Additional common forms of violence include gang rape, arson, bombings, suicide bombings, and mob violence. Also, organized groups often target minority places of worship using threats, intimidation, and other unlawful means to force the religious

Land, *The Atlantic*, November 29, http://www.theatlantic.com/international/archive/2012/11/kos her-jesus-messianic-jews-in-the-holy-land/265670/.

DEPRIVATION, DISCRIMINATION, INEQUALITY, AND GRIEVANCES? 51

communities to abandon their properties or force a sale by the government.[34] These groups often have political ties that give them both power and protection. Thus, they are rarely arrested and often acquitted for "lack of evidence" (Ispahani, 2013). In some cases, when minorities complain to the authorities about the violence, charges are filed against the victims on some pretext, often blasphemy. In fact, many argue that government discrimination against minority religions and support for Islam in Pakistan encourages these societal groups to engage in violence against religious minorities (Henne et al., 2020; Saiya, 2017a).

Some typical incidents include one reported in Kasur: in response to a grievance over property damage, a group of 12 armed men beat three Christian women, then paraded them naked through the streets. According to media reports, the police were slow to respond to the attack, and no charges were filed against the assailants. In fact, a police official summarily dismissed the victims' claims, saying "the Christians are accusing innocent people." Also in 2011, unidentified shooters shot and killed four Hindu doctors in a town in Shikarpur District, Sindh. It is believed the attack was a response to an alleged relationship between a Muslim woman and a Hindu man.[35] In 2014 in Gujranwala, Punjab, a mob attacked an Ahmadi man's house in response to allegations that he had committed blasphemy. They set the house on fire, killing a woman and two children as well as injuring nine others.[36]

There also are coerced conversions of religious minorities to Islam. According to the Movement for Solidarity and Peace in Pakistan, an estimated 1,000 Christian and Hindu women are kidnapped or otherwise forced to convert and marry Muslim men every year (Rahman, 2012).[37]

While Pakistan is effectively a worst-case scenario for antiminority violence, the Muslims in the United Kingdom experience lower, but still significant, levels of violence. In 2013, for example, 193 anti-Muslim incidents were reported. While the majority of them were nonviolent incidents, such as online harassment, they included 17 physical attacks on people and attacks on 10 Mosques. In one such attack, the Al-Rahma Islamic Centre Mosque in London was burned down in a suspected arson attack. Police sought to

---

[34] US State Department Report on International Religious Freedom, 2001–2014.

[35] US State Department Report on International Religious Freedom, 2011, https://2009-2017.state.gov/j/drl/rls/irf//index.htm.

[36] Kharal, A., & Tanveer, R. (2014). Three Ahmadis, including two minors, killed in Gujranwala, *The Express Tribune*, July 28.

[37] Kassar, G. A. (2014). Pakistan: SAP-PK for law against forced conversion, marriages, *Indian Muslim Observer*, October 26.

52 RELIGIOUS MINORITIES AT RISK

find and arrest perpetrators. For example, in June 2013, police arrested four youths on suspicion of arson for a fire at the Darul Uloom Islamic School in Chislehurst. In October 2013, a Ukrainian student received a life sentence for the murder of Mohammed Saleem, a Birmingham grandfather walking home from prayers at his mosque in May.[38]

Other Types of SRD

The three types of SRD shown in Table 2.10 are those that do not fit into the other categories. Overall, 19.89 percent of religious minorities experienced at least one of these types of SRD at some point between 2000 and 2014.

In Georgia, efforts to both deny access to existing religious sites and prevent the construction of new ones are often led by the country's Orthodox clergy or the Georgian Orthodox Church (GOC) itself. For example, in 2009, GOC groups prevented repairs to a local mosque and threatened village members if the construction continued. In 2012 GOC leaders participated in protests against the restoration of a historic mosque in Batumi. Also in 2012, GOC priests and congregants in the village of Nigvziani blocked individuals from entering a private home used as a Muslim prayer house. They demanded the closure of the prayer house and the eviction of all worshippers. Police did not intervene. In a similar 2012 incident in the village of Tsinksaro, GOC congregants threatened local Muslims and their imam, and prevented them from gathering to worship in a private home. In 2013, GOC congregants protested the building of a Mosque in Samtatskaro and prevented Muslims from holding prayer services once it was built. This escalated when a mob surrounded the imam's house and intimidated him and his family, assaulted his wife, and threatened to burn down the house and drive them from the village. There was an investigation, but no one was charged with a crime.[39]

---

[38] US State Department Report on International Religious Freedom, 2013, https://2009-2017. state.gov/j/drl/rls/irf//index.htm; Erlanger, S. (2014). As hate crimes rise, British Muslims say they're more insular, *The New York Times*, February 13, http://www.nytimes.com/2014/02/14/world/eur ope/as-hate-crimes-rise-british-muslims-say-theyre-becoming-more-insular.html?module=Sea rch&mabReward=relbias%3As%2C%7B%221%22%3A%22RI%3A6%22%7D.

[39] Tolerance and Diversity Institute (2014). *Assessment of the Needs of Religious Organizations in Georgia*; US State Department Report on International Religious Freedom, 2001–2014; Corley, F. (2013). Georgia: Will police protect Muslim prayers from mobs? *Forum 18 News Service*, July 4; United Nations Association of Georgia, *Joint Submission on Minority Rights in Georgia for the United Nations Universal Periodic Review* (November 2015).

DEPRIVATION, DISCRIMINATION, INEQUALITY, AND GRIEVANCES? 53

Table 2.10 Other Types of SRD, 2000–2014

| | % Groups Experiencing Discrimination | | | |
| | | | 2000 to 2014 | |
	2000	2014	All Years	At Least Once
Efforts to deny access to or close existing religious sites	1.73	2.22	2.1	4.85
Efforts to prevent religious sites from being built/opened/rented	2.53	5.74	4.43	9.33
Other acts against minority	6.26	7.82	7.05	11.4
# cases	751	767	11425	11425
At least one of the above	*9.05*	*13.17*	*11.29*	*19.89*

Similar incidents occurred against other religious minorities. For example, in 2009, a mob of 150 people threatened and insulted Jehovah's Witnesses at their worship hall. Police arrived at the scene but did not intervene, and later that night four Jehovah's Witness members were physically assaulted. Similarly in 2012, Jehovah's Witnesses were physically assaulted when leaving a prayer ceremony. Authorities did not investigate or prosecute, despite there being sufficient evidence to identify the perpetrators. In several municipalities there have been petition campaigns and public protests allowing buildings to be used or built for Jehovah's Witness meetings. For example, Jehovah's Witnesses have not been able to rent facilities for large meetings in Tblisi since 2004.[40]

SRD in 2000 to 2014

As shown in Figure 2.2, the percentage increase in average SRD experienced by religious minorities since 2000 has been quite dramatic, reaching over 25 percent by 2014. In 2000, 37.55 percent of the minorities in this study experienced at least one form of SRD. By 2014, this increased to 42.76 percent. Overall, 54.22 percent of religious minorities experienced some form of SRD at some point between 2000 and 2014. This is important because it establishes

[40] Tolerance and Diversity Institute, *Assessment of the Needs of Religious Organizations in Georgia*; US State Department Report on International Religious Freedom, 2001–2014.

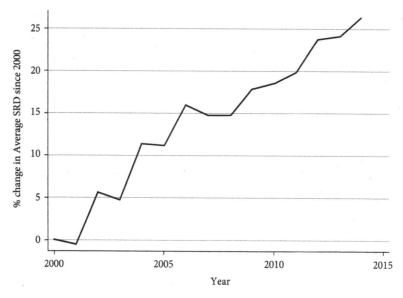

Figure 2.2 Percentage Change in Average GRD since 2000

that SRD is common but there is variance over location, specific minorities within a location, and time. This means that comparisons across minorities as well as comparisons of the same minority over time are valid comparisons.

Political Deprivation and Organizational Capacity

One of the interesting conundrums of measuring political deprivation is that political deprivation often includes restrictions on a group's organizations. Thus, political deprivation measures also in effect measure organizational capacity. Accordingly in this section we describe our political deprivation variables and how they can also be measures of organizational capacity.

DDI can come in different shapes and affect minorities in different areas. While GRD and—arguably to a lesser extent, SRD—primarily refer to religious practices in the broader sense, they do not capture the extent to which the minority and their members enjoy representation in legislative and other political bodies or can directly influence policy making. The distinction is important, because a religious community can fully enjoy religious freedoms but at the same time may be excluded from politics—and vice versa. More importantly, exclusion from political representation and policy making has

DEPRIVATION, DISCRIMINATION, INEQUALITY, AND GRIEVANCES? 55

been argued to be an important form of deprivation that may spark extra-systemic articulation of interest, including violent and nonviolent protest (e.g., Gurr, 1970, 2000; Tilly, 1978; see Chapters 3 and 4). For ethnic minorities and groups, there exist datasets such as the MAR dataset[41] or the Ethnic Power Relations (EPR) dataset (e.g., Cederman et al., 2010; Wimmer et al., 2009).[42] For religious minorities, however, almost no data is available worldwide regarding the political inclusion or the lack thereof. Data previous to RMAR is confined to samples of ethno-religious minorities that are ethnic minorities that at the same time differ in terms of faith from other ethnic groups (e.g., Akbaba & Tydas, 2011).

In order to account for political deprivation, the RMAR dataset includes a special effort to collect data for two distinct variables. The first one refers the exclusion from political representation. These variables are conceptually modeled roughly similarly to the EPR dataset[43] and, as we discuss below, include elements of both political deprivation and capacity. The variable *political representation* distinguishes between three levels:

−1: There is explicit evidence that the minority—through individual members or its organizations—is politically *not represented* (i.e., excluded).

0: There are no reports that the minority is excluded or included.

1: There are explicit reports that the minority *is politically represented* or included.

Representation refers usually to parliaments at the national level. However, we also count inclusion or exclusion at the regional level in federal states or local bodies of representation below the national level in unitary states. This distinction can be important when religious minorities are regionally concentrated in one area of the country and therefore might only be represented at the regional but not the national level. Parliament or legislative bodies usually refers to democratic institutions, but we also look at functionally equivalent institutions in authoritarian regimes such as councils or legislative

---

[41] Minorities at Risk Project (2009). Minorities at risk dataset; Center for International Development and Conflict Management, December 23, 2020, http://www.mar.umd.edu/.

[42] We discuss the EPR dataset in more detail in Chapter 4.

[43] The EPR dataset provides data on ethnic groups' access to state power, links to rebel organizations, their settlement patterns, transborder ethnic kin relations, and intraethnic cleavages. For more details, see https://icr.ethz.ch/data/epr/. We discuss studies using this dataset in more detail in Chapter 4.

56 RELIGIOUS MINORITIES AT RISK

bodies not based on free and fair elections. However, representation does not equal actual impact on decision-making, for instance, when the groups does not participate in government. Hence, a second variable asks for exclusion from government. The variable minority *policy power* specifies on four levels per minority and year whether:

-1: There are explicit reports that the minority through individual members or its organizations is *not represented*, i.e., excluded in political decision making at the local or national level, i.e., government.

0: There are *no reports* that the minority is excluded or included.

1: There are explicit reports that the minority *is included*, e.g., through members of cabinet or as part of coalitions at the national or local level (e.g., in federal states); majors of big cities are also counted.

2: Explicit reports that the minority *dominates* government.

We follow the same principles as for political representation and include the national and local level. Both for the lack of representation and nonparticipation in policy making we do not assume that exclusion or participation is necessarily a result of intentional discrimination, we just record the fact as such. Several reasons come to mind for such nondiscriminatory exclusion: A religious minority might, following quietist principles, voluntarily opt for staying out of politics; it might be too small to attain effective inclusion, or, with regards to decision making, simply consistently fail to be part of government.

While potentially measuring political deprivation, these variables also measure mobilizational capacity—which, as noted, reminds us of the difficulty of measuring one in isolation of the other. Capacity includes the ability to organize, and we indeed separately measure whether groups are politically organized outside of their representation and/or participation in government. Political representation of religious minorities in legislative bodies therefore represents an additional type (and likely greater level) of capacity, as does inclusion in executive policymaking roles, only the latter of which is measured by the EPR project.

Here it is critical to note that political representation does not necessarily imply policy power. For instance, although Arab parties have until recently never joined Israeli governing coalitions, they have consistently been represented in the Israeli parliament since 1949. Conversely, inclusion in governmental decision-making is measured as the provision that minorities, as individuals or as a collective, have an explicit influence on policy outcomes at the local or national level, as was the case with the Ra'am Islamist party's participation in Israel's governing coalition that took power in 2021. Altogether, then, these variables measure various aspects of inclusion and exclusion from the political system along an ordinal spectrum. However, as our empirical approach explicitly disaggregates measures of group-level discrimination and grievance from measurements of political power, this allows us to treat the variables detailed above not merely as proxies for political deprivation but also as directly indicative of group organizational capacity.

Table 2.11 provides an overview on what we found regarding the exclusion from political representation and decision making (see Basedau et al.,

Table 2.11 "Objective" Status of Religious Minority

	% Groups			
			2000 to 2014	
	2000	2014	All Years	At Least Once
Minority Representation				
Excluded from political representation	5.27	4.28	4.85	5.88
Not excluded from political representation	81.69	79.38	78.58	85.00
Explicitly politically represented	13.04	16.34	16.57	22.18
Minority Policy Power				
Excluded from political decision-making	16.86	15.43	15.90	18.86
Not excluded from political decision-making	70.49	68.09	68.09	74.26
Explicitly included in political decision-making	9.22	12.58	12.14	19.21
Dominates political decision-making	3.43	3.89	3.87	6.87
Minority Economic Status				
Poorer on average compared to rest of population	16.60	16.34	16.91	16.58
Economic parity on average with rest of population	5.27	5.84	5.62	5.67
Wealthier on average than rest of population	8.30	8.04	8.12	8.23
Missing data	69.83	69.78	69.91	69.91
# cases	759	771	11487	11487

58 RELIGIOUS MINORITIES AT RISK

2019). At first glance, it is remarkable that we found no explicit mentioning of inclusion or exclusion for the large majority of minorities. This unsurprisingly especially holds true for the smaller groups in dataset of 771 minorities. However, in the year 2000, around 5 percent of all groups were explicitly excluded from representation at any level. This is a strong form of exclusion and holds true for around 5 percent of all groups in at least one year between 2000 and 2014. One prominent example is Christians in the Turkish controlled part of Cyprus. In China, religious groups seem to be completely unrepresented and left out of government, mirroring the atheist ideology of the Communist party. China excludes no less than five minorities such as Muslims, including the mostly ethnic Turkish Uyghurs, and the traditional Chinese religion Falun Gong. In several sub-Saharan countries adherents of African Traditional Religion (ATR)—sometimes also referred to as Animists—suffer from nonrepresentation.

The picture substantially changes when we look at the actual policy power of minorities. Almost one-fifth of all groups were excluded from policy making in at least one year during the period of investigation. On average almost 16 percent are excluded in any given year. Exclusion from government is still comparatively rare, but up to 19 percent in at least one year during this period show this characteristic. Logically, examples comprise the nonrepresented minorities such as the ATR adherents in several aforementioned African countries. Likewise, China does not allow five minorities in government. In many Gulf states like Bahrain, Qatar, or Saudi Arabia, Hindu or Buddhist believers do not enjoy participation in government nor other bodies. Hinduism and Buddhism are faiths often adhered to by labor migrants from South Asia mostly and these groups suffer from other forms of discrimination too.

Remarkably, exclusion from government does not seem to occur in Latin America. In Western Europe, Spain, Ireland, and Sweden apparently do not include Muslims in government. Generally, Latin America is a region with little deprivation or discrimination of religious minorities (see, e.g., Basedau et al., 2019), politically or otherwise (e.g., Fox, 2016, 2020). Overall, there are no strong trends over time, but the number has slightly decreased from 2000 to 2014.

Regarding inclusion, another almost 20 percent have participated in decision making at some point in time, with an average of around 12 percent yearly from 2000 to 2014; again, many groups are not specifically mentioned and we can assume that they are either too small to make a difference or that at least their exclusion or inclusion is not part of the political discourse. We also find evidence that a larger number of groups of 113 religious minorities explicitly participate in government and this number has somewhat increased during this period as well. Examples of groups included in government often compromise minorities that hold grievances (before). Not rarely, the inclusion of minorities mirrors attempts to overcome intergroup tensions and accommodate grievances. In Egypt, for instance, Christian Copts are part of the government. There is an inclusive power-sharing agreement called "confessionalism" in Lebanon. The Indian government includes Muslims, and the Indonesian government includes Christians. In the Fiji islands, Hindus and Muslims have participated in government. Hindus have been involved in a power struggle with the Christian majority, leading to several military coups. Many Western countries like France, Germany, the Netherlands, Norway, or the United Kingdom have seen increasing participation in government of members of the Muslim minority in their countries.

Between 3 and 4 percent even dominate policy making. It is interesting how often such "minority rule" is connected to violence, especially in Africa and the Middle East. In Cote d'Ivoire, the civil war from 2002 to 2011 resulted in a shift of power from the Christian to the Muslim minority.[44] Christian President Laurent Gbagbo was eventually removed in a contested election in 2011 that, after heavy fighting, brought Muslim Alassane Ouattara into office. Other examples include Sunni Muslims in Iraq under Saddam Hussein before the Iraq war in 2003, which then led to the Shi'a majority, previously discriminated, to dominate politics. In Syria, Alawites, a Muslim minority close to Shi'a Islam, dominate at the highest ranks of the state and the military. Syria's civil war since 2011 has also been a struggle between religious minorities and the Sunni majority. Lebanon constitutes a special case, where "confessionalism" has cemented a power-sharing agreement between Christians (mainly Maronites, belonging to the Roman Catholic Church), Sunni, and Shi'a Muslims.

Economic Deprivation

A final form of deprivation analyzed in this study refers to the economic status of religious minorities. It has been convincingly argued that

---

[44] These two groups are minorities in the sense that they both do not form majorities (around 40% of the population respectively).

60 RELIGIOUS MINORITIES AT RISK

economic deprivation and discrimination can be a strong motivation for dissatisfaction, grievances, political protest, and outright armed rebellion (e.g., Cederman et al., 2011; Gurr, 1970; Stewart, 2008). Empirical evidence, however, is limited, because comprehensive, valid, and reliable data on the group level is hard to come by, and this holds true even more for religious groups. As we discuss in more detail in Chapter 3, empirical evidence on so-called horizontal inequalities—as opposed to vertical inequality—typically is available for ethnic groups at best and often uses geographical disparities rather than hard data on group members. If so (e.g., Østby, 2013), data is limited to certain regions such as (parts of) sub-Saharan Africa.

RMAR takes a different approach and identifies whether our several sources explicitly mentioned that religious minorities were, on average, poorer, equally wealthy, or wealthier than the rest of the population. While this will arguably only insufficiently capture reality, it will accurately capture clear-cut cases of economic inequality and in addition mirror the discourse over relative inequality—and this discourse and the related perceptions might directly inform the reactions by the group members. Besides missing information, the variable "economic status" can take three values:

0. Minority members are on average poorer
1. Are equally wealthy
2. Are richer compared to the country's average

As is the case with political deprivation, we stress that this variable does not capture whether economic status results from any kind of deliberate act of the state or nonstate societal actors—such information is partially captured by some of the SRD variables (described earlier in this chapter). We should also caution that in case members of different minorities on average occupy different professions (e.g., herding versus sedentary farming) but are not necessarily richer or poorer, we do not assume economic differences in status per se.

The lower part of Table 2.11 shows an overview of the economic status of religious minorities vis-à-vis the economic average and wealth of the country. Like for political representation and unsurprisingly, we do not find any kind of information for the vast majority of groups, which had to be expected given the small size of many groups and also the difficulty to obtain data. However, for at least a slightly less than one-fifth of all groups (16.58 percent

DEPRIVATION, DISCRIMINATION, INEQUALITY, AND GRIEVANCES?   61

for the whole period) we could identify a relatively poorer status, while only around 8 percent are apparently more well-to-do compared to the average citizen of a given country. Frequently, lower economic status is tied to migration. Religious minorities such as Muslims in Western Europe are often at the same time largely migrants and thus almost inevitably less wealthy compared to the indigenous population. The same holds true for labor migrants with Hindu or Buddhist beliefs in Gulf states. Interestingly, many Muslim minorities in sub-Saharan Africa, in cases such as Burundi, Eritrea, Ghana, Kenya, and Tanzania, are economically less strong than their compatriots of other faiths.

Being richer on average could be supported by evidence in 63 cases. It is also frequently connected to small minorities that engage in the education and trade sectors such as Jewish communities worldwide and Hindus in Africa, the Caribbean, and Europe. In rare examples Muslims are better off in terms of wealth. Angola constitutes such a case, where Muslims are a small minority of immigrants from other African countries who are usually traders and thus tend to be more well-to-do (Tiesler, 2007).[45] In the United States, Muslims seem also economically favored along with three other religious minorities, Hindus, Jews, and Mormons, as well as Orthodox Christians. Almost 6 percent of all religious minorities seem to be on par with the rest of their country. It is likely, however, that in many other cases this fact—no significant differences—just remains unreported. Regarding larger trends, our data shows very little variation over time. As it seems, economic status overall is not subject to rapid and substantial change.

What Are Grievances in Theory?

While grievances are often discussed in the conflict literature, they are rarely defined. Most of the literature focuses on how grievances influence conflict, a topic we discuss in more detail in Chapters 4 and 5, or what causes grievances, a topic we discuss in more detail in Chapter 3. However, most of these discussions never explicitly define what is meant by grievances, except perhaps to discuss how grievance variables are coded.

---

[45] Terdiman, M. (2013). Islam, state and Christianity in Angola: Research on Islam and Muslims in Africa, February 14, https://muslimsinafrica.wordpress.com/2013/02/14/islam-state-and-christianity-in-angola/.

Cao et al. (2018, p. 765) provide a typical example of this phenomenon when they argue that "grievances caused by between-group inequalities provide motivations for members of the disadvantaged group to revolt. However, whether such motivations translate into violence depends on the ways that relevant local institutions operate as bridges between the local population and the government." Thus, in this case grievances are defined by what causes them and what effect they have.

However, explicit definitions are not completely absent in the literature. Collier and Hoeffler (2002, p. 14) briefly define grievances as "the opposition to perceived or actual injustice." Cederman et. al (2010, p. 114) allude that grievances are "matters of motivation and legitimacy." However, these cannot really be considered comprehensive definitions. Basedau et al. (2017, pp. 222–223) argue that "grievances . . . are the subjective and explicit perception of being discriminated against (or being subjectively marginalized or otherwise deprived)."

The conflict literature does indirectly provide a definition of grievances. It links them to events and actions over which a group might be upset, express complaint, or seek redress. In an early example, Gurr (1970, p. 245) argues that "to understand grievances, we must first examine where people stand in society and what goods and bads they experience from society and government." Collectively the literature follows this approach. While it is rarely stated explicitly, this literature implicitly defines grievances as public expressions of upset or complaint and/or expressions of a desire to seek redress over some "bad" that has occurred to the groups, usually—but not necessarily—an intentional "bad" perpetrated by others such as the government or the majority group (e.g., Akbaba & Tydas, 2011; Fox, 2002; Gurr, 1993a, 1993b, 2000). The grievance variables we use in this study follow this model.

Definition and Measurement of Grievances

Generally, we define grievances—in contrast to DDI—as the explicit expression of the feeling of being treated unfairly. We define grievances more specifically in the RMAR codebook as follows:

A grievance is the explicitly verbalized subjective feeling of being marginalized. Grievances can refer to several forms of deprivation or marginalization.

Grievances are different from objective deprivation (though often closely related). In this project, we look at grievances regarding religious, political and economic reasons.

There are several distinct aspects in this definition as we explicitly distinguish grievances from any objective state of DDI and marginalization, thus clearly marking the distinction between objective state and the subjective expression of a perception. This makes a lot of sense from a conceptual point of view but also provides several empirical advantages. It enables us to distinguish between two different phenomena and explore and investigate their relation. In addition, also following the suggestions from the aforementioned pilot study (Basedau et al., 2017), we do not treat all grievances as equal but acknowledge different types of grievances, namely grievances related to religious practice (religious), to political inclusion (political), or regarding economic status (economic). Moreover, we assess the levels of intensity which may wildly differ but are commonly treated as being more or less the same in the literature. The levels of *grievance intensity* can generally take three levels beyond their absence:

0. No grievances exist or are reported.
1. Mild, when statements point to unfortunate situations only.
2. Moderate, when minorities or their members demand change.
3. Intense, when minority members urge change and consider action when they express their grievances.

One may argue that it is challenging to clearly distinguish between the different levels. Therefore, we tried to explicitly and clearly define "breaking points." When group members refer to dissatisfaction only, we consider them mild; when they explicitly demand change, grievances are at least moderate and not just mild. Intense grievances, finally, are coded when the minority or their members not only demand changes but also urges them and explicitly considers taking action—or actually takes limited action in the form of lawsuits.[46] Both type and intensity are likely to be either affected by specific forms of DDI—and may well affect the form and intensity of mobilization,

---

[46] Please note that we limit such actions to lawsuits. Any "mobilized" form of action such as any demonstration, press conferences, and so forth are coded as protest events. However, we rarely detected lawsuits.

64 RELIGIOUS MINORITIES AT RISK

protest activities, and the likelihood of violent reactions by minorities (see Chapters 3, 4, and 5).

Findings on Types and Intensity of Grievances

What do we find regarding the types and intensities of grievances? As a starting point, we can examine general trends (see also Basedau et al., 2019). In Table 2.12 we see that, during the entire period under investigation, a majority of minorities expressed grievances at least once (55.75 percent). In each year, on average, between one in five to one in four minorities complained about being treated unfairly in one way or another (22.86 percent). The average intensity of grievances stands at 0.56, slightly more than the average between no grievances and mild grievances; we should consider, however, that around half of all groups covered in our sample do not express any grievances in any of the years in the period under investigation (339 minorities).

At the same time, intermediate and intense grievances are not uncommon among those who feel marginalized, counting more than 200 cases for each level and more than 400 altogether. Regarding intense grievances, several groups almost instantly come to mind, scattered around all world regions and faiths. For example, in India and Indonesia no less than five minorities each have voiced strong dissatisfaction. Christians in the MENA region such as the Copts in Egypt or Shi'a Muslims in mostly Sunni majority countries also frequently hold strong grievances. No world region is free from strong grievances, including Western democracies in West Europe and North America. Here, Muslim minorities in particular are apparently very dissatisfied, often in relation to growing Islamophobia. Many Jewish communities—not only in Europe—voice grievances in relation to persisting and growing anti-Semitism. Smaller religious communities, such as Jehovah's Witness or Scientology in Germany[47] and other Western democracies, also heavily complain about being mistreated.

There are significant trends over the years from 2000 to 2014. Table 2.12 and Figures 2.3 and 2.4 show that both frequency and intensity of grievances have considerably increased over this period. Numbers have more than

---

[47] In 2001, the German government via its embassy in Washington complained about a "campaign" by Scientology, denying Scientology's accusations; see https://web.archive.org/web/20060813194 020/http://www.germany.info/relaunch/info/archives/background/scientology.html.

Table 2.12 Expressed Grievances by Religious Minority

	2000	2014	2000 to 2014 All Years	2000 to 2014 At Least Once
Grievances of Any Kind				
% groups expressing grievance	13.03	27.89	22.86	55.75
Average intensity of grievance expressed (0-9)	0.329	0.725	0.56	
Political Grievances				
% groups expressing grievance	9.22	20.23	15.36	47.24
Average intensity of grievance expressed (0-3)	0.17	0.39	0.27	
Religious Grievances				
% groups expressing grievance	6.85	16.34	13.15	41.87
Average intensity of grievance expressed (0-3)	0.07	0.16	0.13	
Economic Grievances				
% groups expressing grievance	2.37	4.80	4.05	15.70
Average intensity of grievance expressed (0-3)	0.02	0.05	0.04	
# cases	759	771	11487	11487

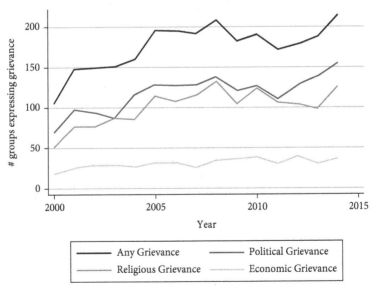

Figure 2.3 Number of Groups Expressing Grievances by Type, 2000–2014

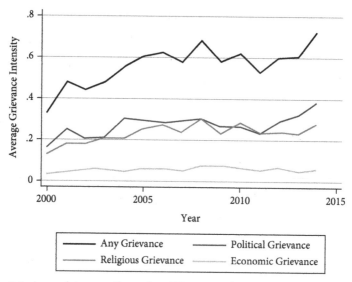

Figure 2.4 Annual Average Intensity of Grievance by Type, 2000–2014

doubled. In 2000, only around 13 percent of all minorities expressed any kind of grievances, in 2014 we count almost 28 percent. Similarly, the average intensity has more than doubled, increasing from 0.329 to 0.725. Apparently, the increases in several forms of DDI, especially GRD and SRD, are mirrored by increasing grievances by religious minorities.

We next take a closer look at the types of grievances as well as their intensities.

Religious grievances refer first and foremost to GRD and partly to SRD. We measure religious grievances by the question, "Does this minority feel discriminated against or marginalized regarding religious practice?" We subsume as religious practice, for instance, worshipping, construction of places of worship, pilgrimage, religious dress code and diet, religious education, and respect of religious holidays. Well-known examples are grievances by Muslim minorities in Western countries about dress code restrictions in head scarf or burka and burkini bans. Christian minorities in Muslim countries often complain about systematic constraints on religious practice. Jewish and Muslim minorities alike have objected to laws banning the ritual slaughter of animals. Less well-known examples include Rastafaris in Jamaica or other Caribbean countries about not being allowed to use Cannabis—as "smoking weed" is part of their religious practice (Basedau et al., 2017, fn. 10; see also Edmonds, 2012).

DEPRIVATION, DISCRIMINATION, INEQUALITY, AND GRIEVANCES? 67

Figures 2.3 and 2.4 as well as numbers in Table 2.12 show that more than 40 percent of all religious minorities have expressed such religious grievances at one point. On average, more than 13 percent expressed a religious grievance in one year. The average religious grievance level stands at 0.27. However, an alarming finding is that religious grievances have strongly increased. Less than 7 percent of all minorities felt discriminated in 2000, but in 2014 the number has more than doubled and stands at more than 16 percent. Likewise, intensity is more than twice as high in 2014 compared to 2000. Summing up, religious grievances follow the general trend both in grievances and in religious discrimination.

Political grievances, first and foremost, capture expressions of marginalization regarding political inclusion and rights, not directly related to freely expressing and practicing religious belief. In this sense, political grievances, for instance, refer to the dissatisfaction over the lack of political representation or participation in policy making—and thus directly correspond to the two variables of political deprivation. However, we also include dissatisfaction over denied rights of association and expression, missing autonomy rights, or societal discrimination. Such dissatisfaction often also refers to a lack of protection by the state from societal hostilities that sometimes become lethal. Muslim minorities in Western and other countries with Muslim minorities such as India or Sri Lanka often refer to this type of DDI as "Islamophobia," and in doing so, are effectively expressing their grievances over this DDI. It is no exclusive feature of Muslim minorities of course. In Egypt for instance, the Copts, a Christian minority, have urged the government to better protect them from attacks from extremist Muslims.

Looking at the numbers (Table 2.12 and Figures 2.3 and 2.4) reveals a similar situation as is present for religious grievances albeit on an even stronger level. Nearly half of religious minorities expressed dissatisfaction over their political status at least once between 2000 and 2014. More than 15 percent of all groups express political grievances per year on average. The number of groups with political grievances has more than doubled from 2000 to 2014. The same holds true for the average intensity level. Interestingly, the political grievances do not exactly mirror the trends regarding our numbers on political representation and inclusion where we could not identify a clear-cut increase, but in fact a slight decrease in exclusion (see Table 2.11).

Findings and related trends differ with regards to *economic grievances*. Our guiding question here reads: "Does this minority feel discriminated against regarding economic opportunities?" Such economic aspects include job

68   RELIGIOUS MINORITIES AT RISK

opportunities in private enterprises and with the state, revenue distribution, development programs, (unfair) taxes, and the right to do business and trade goods. Economic grievances obviously correspond to economic status but also to some of the SRD variables, for example, being denied jobs in private enterprises. When we look at the numbers and figures it first becomes obvious that the overall level of economic grievances is much lower than that of religious and political grievances. Less than 16 percent of all groups expressed economic grievances at least once during the period of investigation—which is considerably less than the more than 40 percent regarding religious freedoms, but similar to political grievances. Although we find a slight uptick regarding both the numbers of groups with economic grievances and the average intensity, basically they remain at a low level—and more starkly compared to the other forms of grievances. However, a few examples for strong grievances in economic terms exist. For example, Muslims in Western democracies express strong economic dissatisfaction. Only in the Middle East do we find similarly frequent strong economic grievances, expressed, for instance, by Christian minorities in Bahrain, Egypt, Iraq, Israel, and Turkey.

Deprivation, Discrimination, Inequality, and Grievances

This chapter has taken a closer look at objective levels of DDI experienced by religious minorities on the one hand and grievances on the other. We have demonstrated the need to define them carefully and distinguish between the two—in particular because objective conditions such as DDI and subjective perceptions and discourses such as grievances are not the same. Our fine-grained innovative data has allowed us to paint a nuanced picture with regard to these differences showing trends for a number of important variables.

Several key trends emerge. Both grievances and DDI vary both across groups and across time. This is of key importance because, as we discuss in more detail in Chapter 4, one of the key critiques of grievance theory is that DDI and grievances are ubiquitous. Because of this alleged uniform ubiquity, especially with regard to grievances, these critics argue that they are a poor explanation for conflict behavior. This demonstration that, at least for religious minorities, they vary across groups and time is a critical counter to that critique.

There are strong increases for both discrimination by governments (GRD) as well as the societal discrimination of minorities (SRD). Trends for economic status and political inclusion are less clear-cut as no strong increase can be observed. However, we identify a substantial number of minorities that do suffer from DDI in economic and political terms. Regarding subjective discrimination—what members of minorities actually voice—we find evidence that grievances by minorities on religious disadvantages and also political exclusion are substantial and have also increased. In contrast, economic grievances are neither strong nor show an upward trend. At first glance, there is apparently a correlation between rising GRD and SRD on the one hand and increasing subjective religious and political grievances on the other. The next chapter explores this relationship more closely.

3

From Deprivation, Discrimination, and Inequality to Grievances

The first step in our basic conflict model is that when a minority experiences deprivation, discrimination, and inequality (DDI), this can cause grievances. While it seems obvious that DDI ought to cause grievances, in fact, many dispute this connection, or at least that this relationship is important in explaining conflict behavior. There are few empirical studies which directly test this relationship, and the evidence derived from these studies is mixed. This mixed evidence and theoretical dispute is, we argue, associated at least in part to three interrelated elements of the literature. First, there is no agreement on definitions. DDI and grievances are defined differently across the theoretical literature and measured differently across the empirical literature. In some cases these definitions are unclear or not fully specified.

Accordingly, it is important to define our terms, which we do in detail in Chapter 2. In the empirical portion of this study, we refer to grievances expressed collectively by a minority group, usually through its leaders, organizations, or representatives, which are often associated with demands for redress of these grievances. That being said, in our discussion of the theory we make an effort to not only distinguish between differing definitions of these terms but also discuss how these differing definitions influence conclusions.

Second, there is a "disconnect" between many of the theories and the empirical tests of these theories. That is, while there are crucial exceptions, much of the empirical literature which posits that some form of DDI leads to grievances does not actually test this proposition. Some studies that claim to measure DDI do not actually measure DDI. Also, among nonsurvey-based studies involving cross-country data, with some important exceptions, variables labeled as measuring grievances do not measure grievances.

Third, as we discuss in more detail in this chapter, one of the most important distinctions is between individual-level and group-level grievances. While this relates to the first two points, this distinction is sufficiently crucial that it deserves separate attention. This is because the empirical literature

Religious Minorities at Risk. Matthias Basedau, Jonathan Fox, and Ariel Zellman, Oxford University Press.
© Oxford University Press 2023. DOI: 10.1093/oso/9780197693940.003.0003

looking at the individual-level tends to find much less of a link between DDI and grievances than does the empirical literature, which looks at group-level grievances. As noted, the empirical portion of our study focuses on group-level rather than individual-level grievances.

Overall, we argue that while the issue is addressed to some extent in the literature, DDI as a cause of grievances by minorities is undertheorized and undertested. In this chapter we critically assess the relevant literatures with three goals in mind. First, we seek to situate our study in the existing theoretical debates. Second, we establish that, despite arguments to the contrary, the relationship between DDI and grievances has rarely been tested in the cross-national empirical literature. Thus, our study's analysis of this relationship is an important contribution. Third, we build on these literatures to develop a more mature theory as well as provide an improved and more thorough empirical test of this relationship. Our results show that objective DDI predicts grievances expressed at the group-level by religious minorities.

Within these general observations, however, there is considerable nuance. We find that although governmental religious discrimination (GRD) informs the intensity of political grievances and both the expression and intensity of religious grievances, it does not influence economic grievances. Societal religious discrimination (SRD) predicts the intensity of political and economic grievances but not religious grievances. We also find that better politically represented minority groups tend to express more grievances in general with greater intensity, however having influence over governmental policy substantially reduces the expression of these grievances. These patterns are substantially replicated for political grievances and somewhat less consistently for religious and economic grievances. Thus, while we find a connection between DDI and grievances, the details matter.

This chapter proceeds as follows. First, we examine the theoretical literature on the link between DDI and grievances. Second, we similarly examine other influences on grievances. This includes the mobilization of grievances by group leaders and the influence of group power. Third, we present our empirical evidence.

Deprivation, Discrimination, Inequality, and Grievance

Among the most intriguing and important characteristics of the theoretical literature is that the vast majority of theory that addresses the topic does not actually focus on the relationship between DDI and grievances. Although grievances are commonly theorized to be an intermediate step between DDI and political mobilization and conflict, few scholars directly measure their expression or test its relationship to DDI.

Furthermore, the discussions of the DDI-grievances link tend to be given far less attention than to the direct causes of violence, conflict, and political mobilization. DDI is far more often addressed as the cause of mobilization and conflict than as the cause of grievances. In some cases, this occurs to the extent that the link between DDI and grievances is ignored or DDI is conflated with grievances. Most of those who do address the causes of grievances do so in passing or as a secondary issue while focusing on the causes of mobilization or conflict. In some studies, these causes of mobilization and conflict include DDI. Others do not directly address DDI and focus on grievances or some factor analogous to grievances as the cause of mobilization and conflict.

Also, most of this literature focuses on ethnolinguistic or racial groups rather than religious minorities. There are notable exceptions to these trends in the literature and we discuss these exceptions below.

Relative Deprivation Theory

The earliest conflict-based body of theory which posits a link between DDI and grievances does not focus specifically on grievances. Relative deprivation (RD) theory was first applied as an explanation for collective conflict and violence in the 1960s and 1970s. It posits that conflict occurs when individual group members compare their condition to some point of comparison and find their situation lacking. This comparison is what makes them feel relatively deprived. The critical point of comparison can, in theory, be almost anything. Popular comparisons include what members of a group believe they deserve (expectations), the status of other groups in the same country, especially the majority group, and the situation in other countries. It is clear that deprivation, inequality, and discrimination can all trigger such comparisons and cause "frustration" and "anger" which, in turn, lead to conflict and violence. While this body of theory predates most of the theories which focus on grievances, "frustration" and "anger" effectively play the role of grievances in this body of theory. In practice, most studies of RD, particularly those that empirically test the theory, focus on

74 RELIGIOUS MINORITIES AT RISK

economic inequalities or poor objective economic conditions (e.g., Dahl, 1971, p. 95; Davies, 1962; Feierabend & Feierabend, 1973; Gurr, 1970; Olson, 1963).

For our purposes we will focus on those formulations of the theory that focus on DDI. According to RD theory, the presence of this DDI causes frustration and anger which, in turn, may lead to various forms of political organizing, violence, and conflict. Implied in the theory is that DDI must be recognized as such by individuals for them to form frustrations. These frustrations are analogous to grievances, but the theories that focus on grievances rather than frustrations postdate the use of RD theory in the conflict literature by around two decades. Also, as we discuss below, RD focuses on the individual-level while most conflict theories that focus on grievances focus on collective grievances at the group-level, as does the theory and model we present in this study.

There is considerable evidence that many writers in this literature acknowledged this interpretation. For example, Gurr (1970) in his book *Why Men Rebel*, perhaps the most important single work on RD in this era, refers to frustration and anger far more often than grievances, but it is clear from the context that Gurr (1970) considered grievances an essential part of the process. This can be seen from the following examples from this text. When discussing the dynamics of anger, Gurr (1970, p. 59) argues that "the greater its intensity, the longer it persists; many men carry the burden of profound grievances throughout their lives and pass them on to their children." When discussing the sources of previous frustrations, Gurr (1970, p. 78) argues that "the announcement of a reform program to deal with popular grievances tends to reduce the immediate potential for violence." In some instances, he also posits a direct link between inequality and grievances. For example, he argues that "if opportunities are differentially low for these groups, their perceived capabilities are likely to be especially low and their sense of grievance intense" (Gurr, 1970, p. 128). He also clearly argues that grievances can lead to political mobilization and conflict: "many groups . . . regard the institutionalized procedures for participation and for expressing grievances as ineffective. Their initial grievances or deprivations are consequently intensified by a perceived decline in their participatory value capabilities, leading to increasingly aggressive protest" (Gurr, 1970, p. 145).

It is important to emphasize that while the concept of grievances is inherent in RD theory, it was not theorized as central to RD theory. Perhaps the most obvious demonstration of this is that, as we discuss in more detail

DEPRIVATION, DISCRIMINATION, INEQUALITY TO GRIEVANCES   75

below, Gurr (1993a, 1993b, 2000a) later reformulated his theories of conflict to better and more directly address grievances.

Over the next two decades, RD theory was tested in hundreds of empirical studies, which found little support for the theory. This literature focused primarily on economic DDI as the cause of conflict. Intensive reviews of this literature show that it produced no consistent findings. While a minority of studies did support RD theory's predictions, the overwhelming majority did not. Lichbach (1989) attributes these divergent results to measurement issues,[1] and the use of different controls and problem sets. Brush (1996) similarly tracks 649 studies that cite Gurr (1970) and finds that most empirical studies did not support RD, and those studies which are favorable to RD tend to provide no empirical evidence. Osborne and Sibley (2013, p. 992) and Smith et al. (2012) similarly find inconsistent results in studies on individual-level RD in the psychology and social psychology literatures. From our perspective, the most important aspect of these studies is that few of them actually test RD theory as it is formulated. Specifically, few of these studies tested the link between objective DDI and grievances (Fox et al., 2017). We can divide these studies into two categories, the cross-national studies and the survey-based studies.

Cross-national studies have mostly tested the link between objective DDI and collective action (violent or otherwise) without addressing the "frustration" or grievances portion of the model. That is, they skipped over frustration, anger, and grievances in their empirical tests. They measured objective conditions such as economic inequality and directly tested its influence on some form of conflict or collective action (Sayles, 1984, p. 456). Thus, these studies "black boxed" the multistep RD model by looking only at its initial input and final output. Some of these studies did not even directly measure DDI and, rather, measure ethnic diversity or polarization variables, which are based entirely on demographics. They based this on the assumption that demographic diversity or polarization can sufficiently approximate DDI, a problematic supposition at best (Cederman et al., 2013, pp. 20–21).

Many survey-based studies do use grievances as a dependent variable, but they do not focus on objective DDI. Rather the most common independent variable is perceived DDI. That is, they link an individual's perception of DDI to that individual's upset over similar issues. However, many of them do not even measure grievances. Like the cross-national studies they

---

[1] See also Muller (1980).

76 RELIGIOUS MINORITIES AT RISK

directly correlate perceived DDI with variables such as willingness to support for some form of political action or whether the respondent has engaged in some form of political action. In addition, most of these studies survey respondents in a specific location where civil violence occurred. In practice this means that these respondents represent a narrow population where there is little or no variance in objective DDI (Muller, 1980).

Thus, all individuals in a given survey are reacting to the same level of objective DDI, and the independent variable measures the differences in how they perceived their objective situation. Yet, perceiving DDI is arguably an integral step in grievance formation, and it is clear that perceptions do not always match reality. Thus, these perceived DDI variables arguably include an element of grievances within them and are, at the very least, an intermediate step in the theorized process that begins with objective DDI and ends with political mobilization, violence, or conflict. That is, if perceived DDI does not constitute a form of proto-grievances in and of itself, it is certainly grievance-adjacent and qualitatively different from objective DDI.

In sum, while the RD literature is the theoretical origin of the concept that DDI causes grievances, this aspect of the theory is underdeveloped, and the conflict-based empirical portion of this literature largely did not properly test this proposition. This is important for our purposes because it establishes that our arguments and findings are consistent with the theory in this literature, and that previous empirical tests do not undercut our findings.

Does Discrimination Really Lead to Grievances among Individuals?

While, as we discuss later in this chapter, the cross-national conflict literature essentially moved away from RD to new paradigms beginning in the 1990s, the survey-based literature has delved deeper into the question of whether DDI causes grievances among individuals. This body of theory, located largely within the discipline of social psychology, argues that objective DDI is often unrelated to grievances among individuals. This literature is important because by contrasting it to the group-level literature, it provides evidence that the dynamics of grievance formation are different between the individual and group-levels. Nevertheless, it provides insights that are relevant to group-level grievance theories including the one presented on this study.

This literature attributes this absence of a DDI-Grievance relationship at the individual-level of analysis to several factors. First, grievances are more likely to form when objective conditions influence individuals personally. In fact, surveys whose respondents include a wide range of groups including those based on ethnicity, race, gender, immigrants, and sexual orientation, find that many individuals feel that discrimination affects "them" but not "me" (Foster & Matheson, 1999). Second, grievances may only form under certain social conditions, such as when it is considered socially appropriate (Gill & Matheson, 2006, pp. 150–151). Third, the nature of an individual's link to the group can also be important. Individuals whose identification with the group is relatively weak may be less likely to form grievances. Accordingly, individuals with a dual identity, such as both to a minority and to a state, may be less likely to form grievances (van Stekelenberg & Klandermans, 2013, pp. 890–895). Fourth, "the distress associated with discrimination experiences may sometimes motivate denial of its occurrence" (Gill & Matheson, 2006, p. 150). Finally, the literature contains an understanding that people's perceptions often do not exactly match reality (Kunst & Obaidi, 2020, p. 56).

Like the earlier survey-based conflict literature, this social psychology literature finds that perceived discrimination can influence grievances and conflict behavior. However, it finds that objective DDI generally influences grievances only to the extent that it influences perceptions of DDI. It also recognizes that group-level dynamics and mobilization are likely a key factor in how individuals form both grievances and the perception of DDI (Kunst & Obaidi, 2020, p. 56). While Gurr's (1970) treatment of RD theory acknowledged RD was based on perceptions and expectations, it contained an assumption that perceptions of DDI closely matched reality. A half century of research has shown that this assumption has limited utility at the individual-level.

The conflict literature includes criticisms that parallel these findings. Cederman et al. (2013, pp. 21–22) argue that RD is based on assumptions of group unity which are not always accurate. Rule (1988, p. 202) argues that this is particularly problematic because it views all aspects of the conflict process, including grievances as "the sum across a large population of individuals" rather than any collectively organized action. This also assumes that these disparate individuals both have similar standards of justice and perceive injustice in a similar manner. Cramer and Kaufman (2011) argue that perceptions of inequality are often more important than objective reality.

78 RELIGIOUS MINORITIES AT RISK

It is worth noting that many of the social psychology studies which produce this finding of a "disconnect" between objective DDI and grievances introduce problematic assumptions. Like their predecessors in the RD-conflict literature, they mostly survey small homogeneous groups, usually within a single country or smaller geographic location, where all respondents experience similar levels of discrimination. For example, Foster and Matheson (1999) survey female psychology student's feelings about women's status compared to men. Thus, they assume women are unequal to men and measure perceptions of inequality among these students. Whatever objective DDI exists based on their status as women who are sufficiently privileged to attend Carleton University, it should be similar for all respondents.

However, there are some studies that do have variation on the independent variable, DDI, which confirm these findings. Fox et al. (2017) examine 19,480 respondents to the World Values Survey in 82 countries who they identified as religious minorities and matched them to levels of GRD as measured by the RASM data set. They found that objective DDI, as measured by GRD, did not significantly influence grievances as measured by "the extent to which respondents have confidence in their parliament, the civil services in their country, their government and the police" (Fox et al., 2019, p. 504).

This lack of correlation between individual-level DDI and grievances combined with the findings of this study lends credence to the argument that if one wants to look at the influence of DDI on grievances, one must look at the group-level.

Discrimination, Inequality, and Group-Level Grievances

Given the empirical failures of RD theory, Gurr (1993a, 1993b, 2000a), reformulated his arguments to focus on group-level grievances. While, as noted, an early version of this concept was present in his earlier work (Gurr, 1970), it was not part of the theoretical or empirical focus. Nor was it well developed. This reformulation addresses this issue and strongly influences the conception of grievances used in the current study.

Gurr's (1993a, 1993b, 2000a) Minorities at Risk (MAR) project focuses on ethnic minorities and looks at political, cultural, economic, and autonomy grievances. It posits that all but autonomy grievances are caused by DDI. The project uses the ethnic minority as the unit of analysis rather than the state as a whole or individuals, the most common units of analysis for previous

DEPRIVATION, DISCRIMINATION, INEQUALITY TO GRIEVANCES 79

studies, as well as most subsequent studies that do not use the MAR data. This allowed tests that were specific to ethnic minorities, and most states included in the analysis had multiple minorities. The study demonstrated that DDI, grievances, and conflict behavior were usually group-specific which indicates that the group-level of analysis is the most appropriate level of analysis for this type of study.

However, the DDI-grievances link was not the focus of this study. Rather, it focused more on the causes of ethnic conflict. Nevertheless, the project did address this relationship as part of the larger whole, and this discussion focuses on that aspect of the project.

Gurr's concept of grievances combines RD theory's focus on "discontent" and "unjust deprivation" with a group mobilization perspective (Gurr, 1993b, p. 167). Unlike his previous work on RD theory (Gurr, 1970), Gurr's MAR-based concept of grievances is explicitly group-level. He argues that the concept of grievances has little political relevance unless they are held collectively and advanced in "pursuit of group interests by group leaders and political entrepreneurs" (Gurr, 1993b, p. 167). Thus, this view of grievances specifically looks at group-level grievances rather than a group of individuals who each feel their own individual-level grievances but there is no group representative or organization actively expressing these grievances and seeking redress for them. This is qualitatively different from RD theory which is based more on individual-level dynamics. These insights were influenced by earlier work focusing on the collective nature of political grievances by Horowitz (1985) and Tilly (1978).

Gurr (1993b, p. 68) realizes that this conception has its complexities but firmly based his theoretical and empirical analysis on this collective conception of grievances:

> The authenticity of representatives' claims is difficult to judge, because contending organizations often claim to represent the groups, because observers seldom have direct access to a cross-section if group members, and because governments that are challenged by minority-based movements usually try to discredit or minimize the claims. The grievances of most communal groups come from their political movements. Their statements and strategies provide the basis for our coding of group grievances.

Gurr (1993a, pp. 68–69) acknowledges that collective interests are not always unitary and that some expressions of grievances are likely more "authentic" than others. In addition, not all group members will hold the same intensity of grievance as other members and some may not hold any grievances at all. However, "what counts politically is the organized expression of subjective interests" (Gurr, 1993a, p. 69). That is, what counts at the group-level is the organized expression of grievances perhaps combined with efforts to seek redress for those grievances.

Gurr's (1993a, 1993b, 2000a) grievance variables measure grievances publicly expressed by group representatives over political issues, economic issues, cultural issues, and autonomy issues. Other than autonomy issues—which are not posited to be caused by DDI but rather by the perception that the group was autonomous in the past—the variables for each of these types of grievances are composite variables made up of scaled variables measuring the presence of grievances expressed by group leaders over more specific types of DDI or specific demands made by these group leaders against the state. For example, economic grievances are based on six ordinal scales such as demands for greater public funds, greater economic opportunities, improved working conditions, and protection of land, jobs, and resources (Gurr, 1993b, p. 170).

Gurr argues that these grievances are caused by a combination of collective disadvantages, which include discrimination and repression by governments and other inequalities such as economic inequalities. The causal factors also include group identity and cohesion as well as "ecological conditions," many of which can be classified as forms of deprivation such as "high birth rates, poor public health conditions, migration, and land scarcity" (Gurr, 1993b, pp. 167, 173, 178).

Unlike most studies, Gurr (1993a, pp. 75–86, 1993b, 178–179) explicitly tests the causes of these grievances and finds that DDI significantly increases levels of political, cultural, and economic grievances. Economic discrimination, but not economic "differentials" (Gurr's measure for economic inequality), significantly increases all three types of grievances. Thus, in this case, it is active government efforts to discriminate rather than simple inequality which are important. Political discrimination and inequality both influence political grievances.

Gurr's MAR project is one of the few which collected both DDI and grievance variables. Consequently, nearly all other studies which directly test the DDI-grievances relationship are also based on MAR. For example, Fox (2002a) added religious discrimination and religious grievance variables to the MAR data set for those ethnic minorities in MAR which are also

DEPRIVATION, DISCRIMINATION, INEQUALITY TO GRIEVANCES   81

religious minorities. Fox's discrimination and grievance variables are modeled after the MAR variables, and the religious discrimination variable is a direct precursor to the GRD variable used in this study. While Fox finds a strong correlation between religious discrimination and grievances, there is little discussion of why there would be a relationship between discrimination and grievances other than to base it on the logic of Gurr's (1993a, 1993b, 2000a) MAR-based arguments. However, he does argue that restrictions on religious minorities can result in a desire to defend the religion and that desire to defend "can be described as the formation of grievances" (Fox, 2002a, p. 151).

Akbaba & Tydas (2011) make use of this Fox-MAR data to discuss the discrimination-grievance relationship more explicitly. They argue that "severe inequalities in access to political, economic and social resources between culturally defined groups serve as the basis for inter-group hostility" (Akbaba & Tydas, 2011, p. 273). They also argue that "restrictions on religion create an antagonistic and divisive atmosphere in which there is lack of trust and tolerance between both sides and a great deal of religious cleavage" (Akbaba & Tydas, 2011, p. 274). However, their empirical tests focus on how discrimination directly influences conflict.

This body of empirical work has been criticized for selection bias. MAR includes ethnic minorities which are politically active or experience discrimination. Thus, it includes no "null cases" and may not be a representative sample of all ethnic groups (Fearon, 2003; Fearon & Laitin, 1996, 2003; Hug, 2003; 2013). More specifically they argue that

> this data set breaks new ground as regards political relevance, but unfortunately at the price of introducing potential selection bias. While the sample includes some "advantaged" minorities, it remains incomplete since Gurr and his colleagues do not include many powerful groups, some of which may decide to challenge the incumbent government. (Cederman et al., 2013, p. 27)

Interestingly, this argument has only partial applicability because, if accurate, it would cause a bias toward results being less significant without the null cases. Thus, findings that a factor is insignificant would be suspect but significant findings should be more reliable, all else being equal. It also applies specifically to tests including DDI and grievances but not necessarily to other factors such as "ethnic group characteristics that are unrelated to grievances,

82 RELIGIOUS MINORITIES AT RISK

such as whether they are religiously or linguistically defined" (Cederman et al., 2013, p. 28). Also, Sorens (2009) added "null" cases to MAR to counter the selection bias critique and reported similar results. Later versions of MAR also included null cases and largely support the results of the original studies (Birnir et al., 2015).[2] In addition, studies that converted MAR to country-level data, which eliminates the selection-bias issue according to some who raise this critique (e.g., Cederman et al., 2013), found a link between discrimination and conflict (Piazza, 2011). Thus, Gurr's findings are confirmed using versions of MAR that are not subject to this critique.

Given this, we contend that the correlations found by Gurr (1993a, 1993b, 2000a) between discrimination and grievances are likely valid. Yet, it is clear that there is some disagreement in the literature on the validity of the MAR data. However, as the RMAR data used in our study includes all cases which meet a minimum population cutoff there is no selection bias in RMAR and these critiques should not apply.

Hug (2013) argues that MAR in later versions added cases which should have been included in earlier versions or corrected codings based on new and better information, which calls into question the entire coding process. This did occur, but if this disqualifies MAR, we posit it would disqualify any event-based data set, since information is always imperfect and no events-based data set of which we are aware, including the RMAR data set used in this study, would be immune to this critique. This critique also seems to penalize the MAR project for seeking to improve the data's accuracy when new information becomes available. We posit that it is sufficient that a data set be sufficiently close to representing real-world events, that is, providing a reasonable representation of those events.

The concept of grievances used in the present study are modeled after this conception of grievances developed by Gurr (1993a, 1993b, 2000a). Thus, this view of grievances a group-level demands for redress including all the nuances of Gurr's theorization are also applicable to our conception of grievances. In addition, the consistent empirical results supporting the DDI-grievances link both provides a foundation for applying similar tests to religious minorities and implies that the findings of this study may be part of a larger phenomenon that is applicable to a variety of minority types.

---

[2] For a discussion of these issues see Birnir et al. (2015), Cederman et al. (2013), and Fearon and Laitin (1997, 2003).

Horizontal Inequality and Grievances

In a series of studies with several collaborators Lars E. Cederman (Cederman & Girardin, 2007; Cederman et al., 2010; Cederman et al., 2011; Cederman et al., 2013; Cederman et al., 2015; Cederman et al., 2017; Wimmer et al., 2009), using data from his Ethnic Power Relations (EPR) data set, presents what, in their later work they call the horizontal inequality argument: "The horizontal inequality argument states that inequalities coinciding with cultural cleavages may enhance group grievances, which in turn may facilitate mobilization for conflict" (Østby, 2013, p. 207). That is "if vertical inequality compares individuals and households without sorting them into categories, horizontal inequality compares entire group identities to each other without paying any attention to the internal diversity of each category" (Cederman et al., 2013, pp. 31–32).

As we note in Chapter 4, they heavily criticize Gurr's (1993a, 1993b, 2000a) conflict models. This criticism focuses on either whether grievances cause some form of conflict or DDI directly causes some form of conflict but does not address the grievance formation process. They also present their horizontal inequality argument as an alternative to grievance theory. Thus, we consider it important to address these arguments and discuss why we posit the grievances argument provides a superior theoretical and empirical foundation for explaining conflict behavior by religious minorities.

We find that one of the most interesting aspects of their argument is that despite their critique of Gurr's arguments and that most of their discussion focuses a direct link between inequality and conflict, their arguments inherently accept the proposition that DDI should lead to some form of grievance. Thus, they do not directly contradict this central element of Gurr's model which is also a central element of this study. In fact, their arguments largely parallel those of Gurr (1970, 1993a, 1993b, 2000a) in some, but not all, respects making the same arguments using a different terminology.

They, relying on Stewart (2008), focus on political and economic inequalities. Nevertheless, if one looks closely, their language could have been taken directly out of the RD and grievances literatures and uses terms such as "anger," "resentment," "frustration," and "grievance." For example, their strategy to deal with "the operationalization and measurement of grievances" is "to take one step back in order to detect structural situations that can be safely assumed to cause frustrations in the first place" (Cederman et al., 2013, p. 3). They specifically argue that "violations of norms of justice and equality will typically arouse feelings of anger and resentment among members of the disadvantaged group" (Cederman et al., 2011, p. 481). They also explicitly state that "objectively measurable differences in group status or economic development will make grievances more likely" (Cederman et al., 2013, p. 39). Furthermore they "postulate that, on average, grievances will be experienced roughly in proportion to the degree of violation" (Cederman et al., 2013, p. 41).

Also following (Stewart, 2008) and Gurr (1993a, 1993b, 2000a), they define grievances at the group-level. They argue that this is because "for inequalities to be transformed into grievances, they have to be politicized" (Cederman et al., 2013, p. 37). This requires a collective element. In fact, they argue that horizontal inequalities cannot exist outside of the context of a well-defined group because the concept of horizontal inequality applies only to cases which involve identity groups. Interestingly they also argue that articulating grievances can itself help to strengthen group identity. Like Gurr (1993a, 1993b, 2000a), they argue that "in concrete terms . . . someone has to identify what is unfair about the status quo. In most cases, this task falls on the group's leadership" (Cederman et al., 2013, p. 40).

Despite this centrality of DDI causing grievances to their theory, this is not a proposition they test empirically. Their data contains no measure for grievances and their tests examine the direct influence of DDI on conflict. Thus, just as is the case for most earlier tests of RD theory, their empirical tests "black box" the DDI to grievances process. Unlike many of these previous studies they explicitly acknowledge this:

> Our strategy is to explore the role of grievances indirectly by investigating the empirical link between inequalities and civil war outbreak at the level of groups. Of course, it is in principle possible to measure grievances directly and to trace mobilization processes explicitly but such detailed analysis is beyond the scope of the current study. (Cederman et al., 2013, p. 35)

They argue that this is appropriate because "political and economic inequalities afflicting entire ethnic groups, rather than merely individuals, are especially likely to fuel resentment and justify attempts to fight perceived injustice" (Cederman et al., 2013, p. 3).

Thus, while on one hand arguing that the DDI to grievances to conflict relationship matters, on the other hand, they argue, it is not necessary to test this relationship because grievances and DDI are sufficiently closely related that a measure of one is effectively a measure of the other. Accordingly, they feel that there is no point in testing the DDI-grievances relationship or measuring grievances at all. This diversion from Gurr's model, we argue, is a fundamental limitation in both their theory and empirics for two reasons that we demonstrate in the empirical portion of this. First, while DDI and grievances are correlated, they diverge from each other sufficiently that one cannot assume the presence of grievances just because DDI is present. Also, one certainly cannot assume that levels of grievances will always be directly proportional to levels of DDI. Second, not all types of DDI lead to all types of grievances. That is, specifics matter, and the relationship between DDI and grievances is not automatic.

While they include a larger number of ethnic minorities than MAR, their EPR data set, like MAR, includes minorities they consider "politically relevant." In comparison to MAR, their discrimination variable is simplistic, as it places all groups into nine categories based on the extent to which they are included or excluded from central power. Also, unlike MAR, which is based on evaluations of primary and secondary sources, EPR is based entirely on expert evaluation (Cederman et al., 2013, pp. 65–69). Given this methodology, the use of a more basic coding scheme is likely appropriate.

Finally, as discussed in Chapters 1 and 2, their DDI measurements essentially conflate not only DDI and grievances, but also DDI and capacity. Like the political representation and policy-power variables used in this study, which are described in more detail in Chapter 2, their variable measures exclusion from political power as a central element of DDI. However, as we have also previously discussed, both representation and exercise of policy power are important indicators of collective political capacity. Lacking independent measures of collective grievance, and by limiting case selection to "politically relevant ethnic groups," the relative influence of DDI and organizational capacity, not to mention collective grievance, is nearly impossible to determine.

Deprivation, Discrimination Inequality, and Grievances in the Religious Conflict Literature

The argument that DDI can cause grievances is also noted in the religion and conflict literature. This helps to both bridge the gap between the religion and conflict literature and the grievance argument and provide a strong

86 RELIGIOUS MINORITIES AT RISK

theoretical basis for applying this argument to religious minorities. The discussion in this literature also helps to flesh out how the DDI-grievances relationship manifests among religious minorities as opposed to ethnic minorities.

As noted above Fox's (2002a, 2004) and Akbaba and Tydas's (2011) studies of ethnoreligious minorities argue for a DDI-grievances link. However, most of these studies mention the issue in passing while focusing on other issues and few test this proposition. For example, Ben-Nun Bloom (2015, p. 836) argues that "religious regulation promotes intrastate conflict because it leads to increasing grievance on the part of religious organizations and groups that are restricted from freely practicing their beliefs." Grim and Finke (2007, p. 636) argue that grievances over religious issues are reduced when all religions are treated equally by the state. Saiya (2017, p. 49) similarly argues that religious freedom "has the effect of reducing conflict by removing one of the chief grievances people of faith have against the state." Gurses (2015, p. 143) argues that minorities seek to redress grievances caused by "discriminatory and often repressive state polices." Others link grievances to income disparities (Fox, 2002a), religious favoritism (Henne et al., 2020, p. 1949), restrictions on religion (Lu & Yang, 2018, p. 199), or "social class, political marginality, and cultural defensiveness" (Demerath, 2001, p. 176).[3]

Nevertheless, a few studies examine the issue in greater depth. Perhaps the most detailed discussion can be found in David Muchlinski's (2019) article "The Politics and Effects of Religious Grievances," which devotes considerable attention to the causes of religious grievances. His arguments largely echo those in the RD and ethnic conflict literature. "Differences in religious groups' access to political, economic, or social power are directly responsible for contributing to the formation of religious grievances" (Muchlinski, 2019, p. 2). He also argues that objective discrimination is not sufficient for grievance formation but rather that religious groups must also "understand that their disadvantaged social position is directly attributable to policies that deprive them of political and economic equality" (Muchlinski, 2019, p. 2). Thus, he echoes the social psychology literatures' argument that the impact of objective DDI is mediated through perceived DDI.

Muchlinski (2019, pp. 2–4) also discusses, in particular, how restrictions on religion can lead to grievances. These restrictions can have a variety of

---

[3] See also Henne (2019, p. 71); Hoffman & Jamal (2014, p. 595); Kim & Choi (2017, p. 315); and Saiya (2019b, p. 5).

DEPRIVATION, DISCRIMINATION, INEQUALITY TO GRIEVANCES   87

manifestations which he argues can be placed on a continuum of non-violent to violent restrictions. Like Fox (2020), he argues variations in regulation of religion can be traced to levels of democracy and state support for religion. Muchlinski (2019, p. 4) also indicates that the form of grievances which are most relevant are group-level grievances when he argues that "religious minority groups that preach messages critical of the ruling regime are especially likely to be singled out for religious repression."

We are aware of only one study that has systematically tested the relationship between discrimination and grievances for religious minorities, explicitly distinguishing between the objective form of discrimination and grievances. Using an earlier version of the data used here, Basedau et al. (2017) combined RAS data on GRD with grievances of religious minorities (and involvement in violent conflict). While they find that neither grievances nor discrimination influences violent conflict, they do a find a systematic, significant link between being subject to GRD and voicing grievances. The relationship is far from deterministic, however. In sum, the authors caution against the results, citing the limited scope of the study. Geographically, the study looks at some 400 minorities in developing countries only in the period between 1990 and 2008. Topically, it does not include forms of DDI other than GRD and the grievance variable measures nonspecific grievances. The authors explicitly conclude that the further study of the effects of discrimination and inequality on grievances and conflict requires more exact information on the nature and intensity of discrimination, deprivation, and grievances, as well as more fine-grained data on relevant characteristics of religious minorities including their organizational resources and other relevant features.[4]

In sum, while there is some discussion of the link between DDI and grievances in the religion and conflict literature, this discussion has been limited and, other than Fox's (2002a) religious version of the MAR analysis, which was limited to 105 ethnoreligious minorities, and Basedau et al. (2017), which uses a precursor to the RMAR data set, it has not been tested systematically. Both of these studies are direct precursors to the present study and use data far more limited than the data used in this study and found

---

[4] This study uses only a subset of the minorities included in RMAR and includes only the religious discrimination variable. It basically joined earlier versions of RASM and RCDC which had been collected separately. In fact, this study provided the basis for a coordinated joint data collection effort which resulted in RMAR.

88 RELIGIOUS MINORITIES AT RISK

a correlation between DDI and grievances. This indicates a more advanced and complete test of the DDI-grievances link is warranted.

Linking Specific Types of DDI and Grievances

As we discuss in detail in Chapter 2, SRD and GRD are distinct phenomena. While related, they both show different dynamics and are not always correlated (Fox, 2020; Grim & Finke, 2011). They represent different types of actions taken by different parts of the sociopolitical spectrum. Yet both represent a form of objective DDI that is posited in the body of literature described in this chapter to cause grievance formation by minorities. In this section we discuss the reasons we hypothesize specific types of DDI may be causes of religious, political, and economic grievances.

GRD measures restrictions placed on religious practices, institutions and clergy that are not placed on the majority religion. Such restrictions would likely cause a religious minority to "feel discriminated against/marginalized regarding religious practice (e.g. worshiping, construction of places of worship, pilgrimage, religious dress code and diet, religious education, respect of religious holidays)" (RMAR Codebook). As these restrictions come from the government, they could also result in grievances against the government including issues of "political and inclusion and rights" (RMAR Codebook). However, GRD is not consistently linked to economic issues. We therefore do not expect it to predict economic grievances. We formalize these predictions in the below hypotheses:

> H3.1: GRD directed against a religious minority will cause that minority to form political grievances.

> H3.2: GRD directed against a religious minority will cause that minority to form religious grievances.

> H3.3: GRD directed against a religious minority will not influence levels of economic grievances.

SRD measures actions taken by societal actors against minority religions including economic discrimination, speech acts, harassment, property crimes, and violence. In addition to the economic discrimination, many of these categories influence economic issues. For example, property crimes can cause damage, which can be expensive. Violence can also have economic consequences. Accordingly, we expect SRD to predict economic grievances.

The presence of these actions often becomes a political issue. To the extent SRD occurs politicians can be held responsible for not taking sufficient actions to deal with SRD. Given this we expect SRD to predict political grievances. SRD also targets religious minorities because of their religion. It often singles out visible members of the minority who are identified by their religious dress or presence at religious centers such as places of worship. It also includes attacks directed at religious institutions. For these reasons we argue that SRD can cause the formation of religious grievances. We formalize these predictions in the following hypotheses:

H3.4: SRD directed against a religious minority will cause that minority to form political grievances.

H3.5: SRD directed against a religious minority will cause that minority to form religious grievances.

H3.6: SRD directed against a religious minority will cause that minority to form economic grievances.

The argument that economic inequality is a basic cause of grievance has been present in the literature for over fifty years because it is a central element of RD theory. We formalize this prediction in the following hypothesis:

H3.7: A minority economic status that is lower than that of the majority will cause that minority to form grievances.

Other Determinants of Grievance: Political Opportunities versus Political Deprivation

While we theorize that DDI is an important cause of grievances, it is clear that the process which leads to grievances is complex and involves other factors. In fact, one of the most common theoretical criticisms of RD theory is that DDI is sufficiently common that wherever conflict or violence breaks out, it is easy to find discrimination or inequality, which can explain it after

90 RELIGIOUS MINORITIES AT RISK

the fact (e.g., Brush, 1996; Dawson, 2010, p. 5; Rule, 1988; Tilly, 1978). While we argue that the presence of a strong statistical correlation between DDI and grievances is a strong counter to this argument, we do acknowledge that causes of grievances include other factors. Accordingly, in this section we explore some of these alternative potential influences on grievance levels including the mobilization of grievances by group leaders, minority power and influence, and minority size.

Indeed, we are cautious in our engagement with "political deprivation," given the potential logical fallacies of conflating relative absence of political mobilization and/or representation of minority groups with grievance. Whereas much of the aforementioned literature tends to assume that political exclusion should significantly influence the expression of collective political grievances, groups that are more politically mobilized (often measured by their organized participation in elections or representation in legislature), should also be those most capable of mobilizing to express these grievances. We therefore are also very careful in terms of which such indicators are most likely to engender grievances versus primarily serve as vehicles for their expression.

As discussed in Chapter 2, we take a conservative approach, in which both extra-parliamentary political organization by religious minority groups as well as representation in legislative bodies are treated, first and foremost, as indicators of collective capacity. And indeed, we assert that both political organization and enjoyment of political representation should be closely associated with greater rather than lesser expression of collective grievances of any kind. Access to and influence over policy decisions, whether at the subnational or national level, however, should not only indicate a very high level of organizational capacity but also reflect a diminished need to publicly express collective grievances (e.g., Grzymala-Busse, 2015). As such, greater policy power should be associated with significantly diminished expression of any and all forms of collective grievance. We discuss these reservations and theoretical implications in the following section.

The Mobilization of Grievances

The traditional mobilization perspective has it that collective interests, which include grievances, lead to group organization, which can lead to various forms of mobilization, political action conflict, and violence (e.g., Gurr,

1993a, 1993b, 2000a; Mcarthy & Zald, 1977; Tarrow, 1989; Tilly, 1978). That is, this literature considers grievances a precursor to or motive for mobilization. This argument has been applied specifically to mobilization via religious institutions and groups (e.g., Billings & Scott, 1994; Birnir & Overos, 2019; Harris, 1994; Muchlinski, 2014). This literature focuses on how religious institutions, leaders, and ideologies can be effective at mobilizing people for political action. We discuss this literature in more detail in Chapter 4.

We do not dispute this argument that grievances are a cause of political mobilization. However, we argue that grievances themselves can also be mobilized. That is, that leaders can "construct" them (e.g., Aspinall, 2007 on ethnic and resource related grievances in the Indonesian province of Aceh). As we discuss earlier in this chapter, at the individual-level, objective DDI does not always lead to grievances but at the group level the two are more strongly connected. We argue one of the reasons this is true is because group organizations and leaders can often activate or create group-level grievances. That is, left to their own devices, many individuals may not choose to actively and publicly express grievances over objective DDI much less become politically active over these issues. However, they are more likely to do so when group leaders actively seek to convince them to express these grievances and become politically active. In addition, we argue that it is possible for group leaders and organizations to mobilize group-level grievances even in the absence of objective DDI.

Fox et al. (2019) explicitly argue that one of the reasons that objective DDI is often not correlated with individually expressed grievances is because of the influence of mobilization by group leaders and organizations. They argue specifically that "group leaders mobilize grievances. That is, grievances are collectively formed in a group when members are convinced by the group's leadership that they ought to be upset over an issue . . . [However] the presence of objective discrimination could make the task of mobilization easier for group leaders" (Fox et al., 2019, p. 511).

If one views the classic mobilization literature from this perspective, a first step in the mobilization process is to convince members of a group that they have a collective interest or ought to have grievances. Only when this motivation is created or activated can the resources be mobilized for conflict. This is an aspect of the mobilization process that is undertheorized. Yet there is some isolated discussion of this argument in the literature, usually in passing while addressing other central arguments. These disparate reflections can be used to build a more robust theory of mobilization of grievances.

For example, Sweijs et al. (2015) argue that "tensions between groups are further fueled when religious differences are politicized by public figures such as political and/or religious leaders in public discourse." Wald et al. (2005, p. 132) argue that religious ideas are an important aspect of mobilization. This is because religion influences how we perceive the world, and religion can cause people to interpret situations in a certain way. Hoffman and Jamal (2014, p. 596) argue that religion facilitates communication among members, which can facilitate mobilization. Omelicheva and Ahmed (2018, p. 8) similarly argue that "when religious issues with direct implications for the lives and livelihood of the faithful enter the local or national political agendas, they can provide a powerful motive for political participation, especially if they appear on the backdrop of religion discrimination, under-representation on religious grounds or existing inter-religious tensions." We argue that these aspects of religion can also be important in grievance activation and creation. Beyerlein and Chaves (2003, p. 30) argue that religious congregations can be co-opted into political action on issues not central to religious doctrine. More specifically, "clergy sometimes attempt to mobilize congregations by organizing political discussion and action groups within congregations, discussing political issues from the pulpit, and requesting that parishioners vote in elections, take part on other political actions, and back certain candidates and positions." We argue that such activities often serve to activate grievances among congregants.

De Juan and Hasenclever (2015, p. 202) argue,

> [R]eligions have the potential to transform secular conflicts . . . into a cosmic struggle between good and evil. Under these conditions, the conflict issues turn indivisible, the related positional differences are made into absolutes, and compromise is no longer an option for the belligerents. A clear distinction between us and them emerges together with a corresponding strong tendency to demonize the opponent as one who cannot be trusted and who has to be defeated with all available means.

Put differently, they argue that religious elites and organizations can facilitate the formation of religious grievances.

The religious "outbidding" literature also suggests that religious organizations and leaders have an interest in activating grievances. This literature argues that religious organizations and leaders will "outbid" each other, each seeking to be the most strict, radical, or hardline on a religious issue. The

DEPRIVATION, DISCRIMINATION, INEQUALITY TO GRIEVANCES 93

purpose of this outbidding is to mobilize group members into their particular organization and defect from their competitors (Basedau & Koos, 2016; Buckley & Wilcox, 2017; Henne et al., 2020; Isaacs, 2017; Toft, 2007). We argue that in doing so they effectively create expectations of policy change that are akin to grievances. Also, this literature certainly supports the argument that group organizations and leaders can manufacture or activate latent policy yearnings.

Finally, securitization theory focuses on treatment of minorities by a majority group but also involves the concept of leaders creating grievances. Securitization theory was developed to explain how many Western democracies behave in an undemocratic and illiberal manner to minorities including religious minorities. Essentially it argues that group leaders manufacture a fear of that minority, which leads to public grievances against them. More specifically, it posits that when group leaders successfully portray a minority as a security threat, this justifies discrimination against them. This "securitization" of a minority is driven by the leaders' "speech acts" which "securitize" the group. This shift in perception—which we argue can be described as the manufacturing of grievances against the group—allows normality to be superseded by an extraordinary circumstance where actions that would otherwise violate democratic norms become not only allowed but expected (Buzan et al., 1998; Cesari, 2013; Donnelly, 2007; Fox & Akbaba, 2015a; Gearty, 2007; Mabee, 2007; Razack, 2008; Waever, 1995, 2011). Whether one accepts our argument that this process involves leaders manufacturing or activating grievances, a central argument in this literature is that leaders can have a profound impact on attitudes in a conflict setting.

It is important to note that while group leaders and organizations can mobilize grievances, this is a choice, and they can also do the opposite. For example, when Marx argues religion is the opiate of the masses, he is specifically arguing that religion is used by those who control society to prevent the masses from forming grievances or at least to cause them to ignore grievances against their rulers. This is an argument that remains current in the literature today. For example, Lu and Yang (2018, p. 196) argue that "religion discourages social mobilization by shifting people's attention from sufferings in this world to the hoped-for life in another world." Koesel (2014) similarly argues that under authoritarian regimes religious organizations often make a deal with the government to support the government in return for religious freedom. Finally, Arkiran and Ben-Nun Bloom (2018, p. 5) argue that "we suggest that, all else being equal, the belief component of

94 RELIGIOUS MINORITIES AT RISK

religiosity will generally serve to justify the status quo and depress political protest because religious belief is strongly connected to values that promote the conservation of social order, such as tradition and conformity to social rules and norms." This concept of religion supporting the status quo is also a central element of many theories of religion and conflict (e.g., Fox, 1999a, 2002a; Lincoln, 2003).

Another argument on the mobilization of grievances refers to the opportunity or capacity of the group. It has long been argued that the conflict literature tends to focus on motivation-oriented variables and neglects the capacity or opportunity to voice dissatisfaction, let alone actual protest or rebellion (e.g., Collier and Hoeffler, 2002, 2004). However, not only willingness but also capacity informs action (see also Gurr, 1993a, 1993b, 2000a; Tilly, 1978). It seems likely that groups that have more organizational resources will also have more capacity to voice their interest and might have an interest to actively mobilize. While the size of the minority might be a proxy variable, its organizational resources might better capture the political and other mobilization potential of the group (Basedau et al., 2017).

Summing up, we argue that there exists a sufficient theoretical foundation to argue that grievances can be mobilized by group leaders, or other actors such as organizations, and we test this proposition in this chapter. We formalize this in the following hypothesis:

H3.8: The presence of minority political organizations will increase minorities' capacities to express higher levels of political, economic, and religious grievances.

Group Power and Opportunity

The religious rational choice literature was founded on the assumption that religious leaders and organizations act based on the existing opportunity structure. For example, Iannaccone (1995, p. 77) argues that "the actions of church and clergy are thus modeled as rational responses to the constraints and opportunities found in the religious marketplace." While Iannaccone is discussing how churches recruit members, others like Gill (2008), Koesel (2014), and Sarkissian (2015) apply this to religion and politics. However, this literature does not directly address how opportunity structures, including group power, might influence grievances expressed by religious minorities.

DEPRIVATION, DISCRIMINATION, INEQUALITY TO GRIEVANCES   95

Following the larger premises of this literature, we argue that a minority's power and influence in a country can have a profound impact on grievance formation. However, it is unclear in what direction group power influences the grievance formation process.

On one hand a more powerful group may have more opportunity to express and address grievances. That is, a group may feel safer and more effective to express grievances when they are sufficiently powerful. Put differently, power increases the expectation that the grievances will be addressed and makes it less likely that the expression of grievances will instigate negative consequences and retaliation. From this perspective, it is more rational for powerful groups to express grievances and for weaker groups to refrain from expressing them.

This argument is also consistent with aspects of the mobilization literature. Tilly (1978) classically argues that the mobilization process is heavily influenced by the opportunity structure present in a country. While Tilly's argument focuses on opportunities for resource mobilization, we argue that this concept also applies to the mobilization of grievances. When stronger organizations and leaders are present, they will be more able to mobilize grievances than groups with weaker organizations and leaders. In particular, we expect that when groups are represented in legislative bodies, this should tend to amplify rather than diminish expression of collective grievances of any kind.

We formalize this in the following hypothesis:

H3.9: Minority political representation will increase levels of political, economic, and religious grievances, by offering a more prominent platform for their expression.

On the other hand, groups with access to the government's decision-making process may express less grievances publicly. Arguably, a group whose leaders are well placed within a government or have access to policymakers and can influence policy has less need to publicly express grievances and challenge the government. Rather, the more effective rout to addressing group interests would be through that existing political access.

Grzymala-Busse (2015) argues that some of the most influential political efforts by religious organizations occur behind closed doors. That is, religious groups which have access to power can more effectively influence policy through the quiet behind the scenes lobbying of government officials

96 RELIGIOUS MINORITIES AT RISK

than through traditional processes such as party politics and the politics of grievance and political mobilization. She argues that when Churches get involves in open politics this undermines moral authority in society because this makes them seem no better than ordinary politicians. This, in the long term, decreases their political and social influence. In contrast remaining publicly neutral on political issues and publicly supporting the government in a nonpartisan manner builds credibility and can increase their ability to influence policy behind the scenes. Thus, churches with this kind of access to power would be likely to discourage or at least fail to encourage public expression of grievances.

Knill and Preidel (2015) similarly argue that religions with more social influence in a country will have more influence on policy. While their argument focuses more on the extent to which a denomination is dominant in a society and the religiosity of a population, their arguments are consistent with the argument that religions with influence have less need of a grievance formation and mobilization process to get their way.

Given this, group power and access can be an important element in the formation and expression of collective group grievances. Factors that influence group power include the following. Group unity and cohesion can increase a group's power (Basedau et al., 2016; Gurr, 1993a). Larger groups and wealthier groups, all other things being equal, will also be more powerful. Also, groups whose leaders are not only present in government bodies but are among those who directly influence the policy-making process will certainly be politically powerful.

We formalize this argument in the following hypothesis:

H3.10: Minority influence on policymaking will decrease levels of economic, religious, and political grievances.

Group Similarity and Other Determinants of Grievances

There is an ongoing debate about whether groups that are more similar or more different are more likely to engage in conflict. We argue that this debate is relevant also to grievance formation. On one hand, group difference leads to deep psychological distrust. It can inhibit effective communication and understanding between groups (Gartzke & Gleditsch 2006). Some, like Huntington (1993, 1996) argue that the basis for conflict will be between

DEPRIVATION, DISCRIMINATION, INEQUALITY TO GRIEVANCES 97

different cultural groupings. Based on this one would expect grievances to be higher when the two groups involved are more religiously different.

However, many dispute this assertion. For example, Horowitz (1985, p. 135) argues that "there has been no shortage of offhanded assertions that cultural differences engender ethnic conflict. But systematic statements of the relationship are more difficult to find." Some of the most violent conflicts have been within the same religion over issues of doctrine (Fox, 2018). In essence, this argument applies Henry Kissinger's famous explanation for the nastiness of academic politics to religious conflict. It can become extremely intense because "so little is at stake." Thus, it is also arguable that the more similar two religious groups, the higher the resentment and grievances.

Given this debate we propose no hypothesis but, rather, simply test the relationship between religious similarity and grievances. The list of potential other determinants can include more variables—which we also do not theorize in formal hypotheses.

Other general influences on the opportunity structure include stronger states, which can provide greater opportunities to achieve religious goals (Buckley & Mantilla, 2013) but are also capable of repressing them (Sarkissian, 2015; Koesel, 2014; Gurr, 1988). Democratic regimes are more likely to be accommodative of grievances and less likely to repress them (Gurr, 1993a, 2000a; Muchlinski, 2019). Periods of instability and transition can create an environment where change is more possible at the same time as inequality is increasing, thus increasing grievances (Buckley & Wilcox, 2017; Gurr, 1993a; Muchlinski, 2014). But it also can reduce the perceived costs of repression by political elites (Henne & Klocek, 2019, p. 120).

Data Analysis

Dependent Variables

In the models that follow, we test the extent to which GRD, SRD, and objective deprivation (altogether DDI) experienced by religious minorities influence the likelihood and intensity with which they will express political, religious, and/or economic grievances. As we argue earlier in the chapter, grievances indicate the explicitly verbalized subjective feeling of being marginalized, particularly as expressed by recognized members of aggrieved groups. While we theorize that both discrimination and objective deprivation experienced

98 RELIGIOUS MINORITIES AT RISK

by said groups should increase the likelihood they will express grievance, these are distinct phenomena whose influence, one on the other, we seek to model here.

Our first set of dependent variables dichotomously measures whether surveyed religious minorities in each country in the RMAR data express grievances in any given year from 2000 to 2014. This general variable is constructed from the aggregation of three separate dichotomous variables measuring whether said minority groups express either a political, religious, or economic grievance which we discuss in more detail in Chapter 2.

Our second set of dependent variables measures the intensity of these expressed grievances. Here, each of our three specific dichotomous indicators is accompanied by an intensity measure on an ordinal scale of 0–3, where 0 indicates no observed grievance, 1 a mild level of discontent, 2 an explicit collective demand for change, and 3 actual actions including legal recourse by the group to press for said change. We also include a general grievance intensity measure as a sum of the intensity scores for each of the three component grievance types, therefore ranging from 0, indicating no observed grievance of any kind, to 9, where a group expresses all three grievance types at maximum intensity.

Explanatory and Control Variables

Our primary independent variables include the RASM measures for aggregate governmental and societal religious discrimination (GRD and SRD, respectively) and the RCDC-sourced ordinal measures for religious minority group representation, minority policy power, and relative economic status. Each of these have been explored in considerable detail in the previous chapter and their inclusion represents our theoretical inference that both group-based discrimination and objective deprivation should increase the likelihood and intensity of expressed grievances. It must be noted that although we have near-universal coverage for most discrimination and objective deprivation variables, we were only able to collect data on religious minority economic status for approximately 30 percent of our cases. In order to avoid making empirical inferences from absent data while not overly constraining our otherwise complete case coverage, we use the economic status variable only in models examining the likelihood and intensity of *economic* grievance. We include an additional set of models examining

DEPRIVATION, DISCRIMINATION, INEQUALITY TO GRIEVANCES   99

the likelihood and intensity of economic grievances excluding the economic status variable, demonstrating the extent to which some of the previous findings may have been an artifact of the aforementioned limited case selection.

We also test for the extent to which group political organization influence grievance expression. This measure is a dichotomous measure of whether minority groups have politically active organizations, such as political parties and associations, which ostensibly represent their interests. As discussed in the previous section, the social-movements literature widely acknowledges the critical role played by such organizations and leadership inherent in their constitution in enabling collective mobilization and giving voice to communal grievance or perhaps even generating grievance where such concerns were not previously apparent. In short, the existence of minority group organizations should increase their capacity to express grievance. To this end, as a control, we have also included a measure of the population percentage of each religious minority group on the intuition that larger groups should also have greater capacity and opportunity to express grievance. We also include a measure for religious similarity between the minority group and a state's majority religion, where 0 indicates no shared religion (e.g., Muslims and Christians), 1 indicates a shared major religion but not a shared major denomination (e.g., Sunni vs. Shi'a Muslims), and 2 indicates a shared major religion and major denomination.

Further controls include a logarithmically scaled measure of state population size and GDP per capita, the Varieties of Democracy (V-Dem) project's polyarchy index, a continuous zero-to-one scale where one indicates a fully procedural democracy (Pemstein et al., 2019), and the PolityIV project's regime durability measure, indicating the number of years since the last significant change in a regime's authority pattern (Marshall & Jaggers, 2009). Our "mixing" of regime measure data sources is somewhat unconventional. Recent moves away from the PolityIV project in conflict research have been motivated by concerns that its composite democracy scores are themselves partially determined by whether states are engaged in armed conflict. The substitution of the V-Dem Polyarchy Index therefore avoids this potential endogeneity problem while still employing a reliable, continuous, fine-grained, and widely cited measure of democracy (Boese, 2019; Coppedge et al., 2015). By the same token, V-Dem and PolityIV's relevant democracy indices are highly correlated in our data (83.17 percent). Therefore, although V-Dem is ostensibly the more precise measure of democratic quality, the

Methods and Models

When analyzing the likelihood of minority grievance expression, either in the general or specific (political, religious, economic) varieties, we employ correlated random-effects logit models, clustering standard errors by either country or country group. In turn, when analyzing grievance intensity, of both the general and specific varieties, we employ correlated random effects–ordered logit models, again clustering standard errors by either country or country group. Country-clustered models formally assume that "assignment to treatment" occurs on the country level. In very simple terms, this assumes variation between cases is most critically mediated by the states in which each surveyed group is found. Our country-group clustered analyses, in turn, assume that findings can rather be better explained by religious minority group-level factors (see Abadie et al., 2017). We suspect the latter should offer the most directly relevant tests of our hypotheses; however, we still include the former to demonstrate robustness.

In turn, correlated random effects models (correlated because they include time-invariant predictors of key independent variable effects via group-level means) have distinct advantages on more "simple" random effects or fixed effects models alone. While random effects models tend to be more efficient than fixed effects models, the assumption that individual-specific effects are uncorrelated with the independent variables is frequently violated. Fixed effects models assume this correlation and therefore, in simple terms, eliminate all invariant or single-time period (here year level) cases, given predefined clustering, from analysis. The inclusion of time-invariant mean predictors of key independent variables within a random-effects framework, however, allows for the differentiation of within- and between-effects without the often dramatic reduction in analyzed cases inherent to fixed-effects models (Bell & Jones, 2015).

Our data analyses are presented as follows. Table 3.1 provides an overview of our correlated random effects logit and ordered logit models for expression and intensity of expressed grievances respectively, each with country and country-group clustered variants. We follow this same pattern

Table 3.1 Determinants of General Grievance and Intensity, 2000–2014

	Grievance Expressed		Grievance Intensity	
	(1a)	(2a)	(1b)	(2b)
	Correlated RE Logit	Correlated RE Logit	Correlated RE Ordered Logit	Correlated RE Ordered Logit
GRD (1 year lag)	0.091***	0.105*	0.077***	0.102*
	(0.021)	(0.052)	(0.018)	(0.042)
SRD (1 year lag)	0.148***	0.089*	0.107***	0.084**
	(0.022)	(0.037)	(0.017)	(0.029)
Minority Political	1.339***	1.840***	1.278***	1.735***
Organization	(0.183)	(0.231)	(0.178)	(0.212)
Minority	0.629***	0.322[†]	0.734***	0.356**
Representation	(0.156)	(0.187)	(0.160)	(0.138)
Minority	−0.329**	−0.374***	−0.210[†]	−0.304***
Policy Power	(0.126)	(0.113)	(0.124)	(0.085)
Religious Similarity	0.287	0.542*	0.270[†]	0.547*
to Majority	(0.200)	(0.238)	(0.163)	(0.216)
Minority Population	0.049***	0.060***	0.034***	0.046***
%	(0.010)	(0.011)	(0.009)	(0.009)
Log Country	0.195*	0.212***	0.197**	0.221***
Population	(0.077)	(0.060)	(0.070)	(0.055)
Log GDP/capita	0.125	0.069	0.129	0.080
	(0.095)	(0.083)	(0.087)	(0.075)
Polyarchy Score	0.032	0.524	−0.130	0.190
(V-Dem)	(0.461)	(0.437)	(0.426)	(0.364)
Regime Durability	−0.003	−0.002	−0.002	−0.000
	(0.003)	(0.004)	(0.003)	(0.003)
Mean GRD	−0.060[†]		−0.048[†]	
Country Level	(0.032)		(0.028)	
Mean SRD	−0.002		−0.002	
Country Level	(0.043)		(0.043)	
Mean GRD		−0.049		−0.052
Group Level		(0.056)		(0.045)
Mean SRD		0.116**		0.085*
Group Level		(0.044)		(0.034)
Constant/Cuts	Omitted	Omitted	Omitted	Omitted
Observations	9355	9355	9355	9355
Year Effects	Yes	Yes	Yes	Yes
Clustering	Country	Country-Group	Country	Country-Group

Robust standard errors are in parentheses

*** $p < 0.001$, ** $p < 0.01$, * $p < 0.05$, [†] $p < 0.10$

in Tables 3.2–3.5, discussing specific results for political, religious, and economic grievances, respectively. These results are complemented by reported odds ratios for each covariate, found in full in data tables in this book's appendix. We discuss select odds ratio results below to highlight the substantive significance of particular findings. Finally, we pair these findings with Figures 3.1–3.10, reporting marginal effects for increasing GRD and SRD on the likelihood of each kind of grievance expression by country and country-group clusters. The overlapping display of effects for GRD and SRD was accomplished through rescaling to their respective minimum and maximum observed values, with 95 percent confidence intervals reported.

Our findings in Table 3.1 confirm our key theoretical inferences that both GRD and SRD are closely correlated with increased expressions of grievance and intensity thereof among religious minorities. Odds ratio results further suggest that for every one unit increase in either discrimination measure all else being equal, we should expect an approximate 10 percent greater chance of any grievance being expressed or being expressed more intensively. These trends are clearly illustrated in Figures 3.1 and 3.2 at both the country and group-level, with each discrimination type having roughly similar degrees of influence upon grievance expression.

So, too, even as increased levels of minority group political organization and representation tend to increase grievance expression, this is substantially

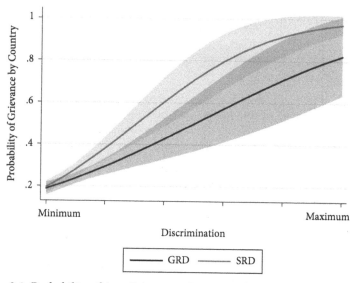

Figure 3.1 Probability of Any Grievance, Country-Clustered, 95 percent CIs

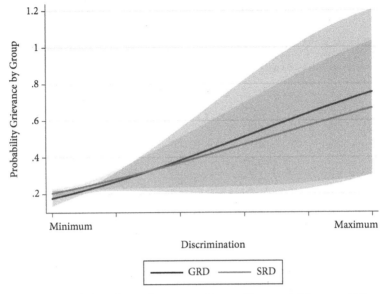

Figure 3.2 Probability of Any Grievance, Group-Clustered, 95 percent CIs

alleviated when religious minorities have a seat at the table in terms of determining relevant governmental policy. These results are replicated in odds ratio analyses as follows in group-clustered models. The presence of group political organization is associated with an about six times greater likelihood of expressing any grievance or expressing grievances more intensively than in their absence. Minority representation is in turn associated with about 1.5 times greater likelihood of expressing more intense grievances. Finally, increasing levels of minority policy power are associated with between two-thirds to three-quarters lesser likelihood of expressing grievances or expressing more intense grievances of any kind respectively.[5] Religious similarities between the minority and dominant groups also seems to increase grievance expression within group-clusters, as does having a larger minority population.

Table 3.2 confirms similar patterns for political grievance especially at the level of country clusters, but also for more intense political grievances at the level of country-group clusters (Figures 3.3 and 3.4). As important is

---

[5] Substantively similar odds ratios to those reported here for GRD and SRD, as well as minority political organization, representation, and policy power are replicated for each individual grievance type and grievance type intensity when base covariates are significant. See the Appendix for full details.

Table 3.2 Determinants of Political Grievance and Intensity, 2000–2014

	Grievance Expressed		Grievance Intensity	
	(3a)	(4a)	(3b)	(4b)
	Correlated RE Logit	Correlated RE Logit	Correlated RE Ordered Logit	Correlated RE Ordered Logit
GRD (1 year lag)	0.082***	0.080	0.068***	0.107*
	(0.021)	(0.051)	(0.019)	(0.050)
SRD (1 year lag)	0.101***	0.087[†]	0.099***	0.091*
	(0.024)	(0.045)	(0.021)	(0.038)
Minority Political	1.363***	1.874***	1.262***	1.722***
Organization	(0.216)	(0.219)	(0.203)	(0.201)
Minority	0.634***	0.351[†]	0.680***	0.395*
Representation	(0.154)	(0.188)	(0.142)	(0.167)
Minority	−0.174	−0.288*	-0.145	−0.260**
Policy Power	(0.125)	(0.116)	(0.126)	(0.100)
Religious Similarity	0.198	0.518*	0.234	0.510*
to Majority	(0.180)	(0.242)	(0.177)	(0.225)
Minority Population	0.026[†]	0.030**	0.027*	0.028**
%	(0.014)	(0.011)	(0.011)	(0.010)
Log Country	0.166*	0.164**	0.180**	0.172**
Population	(0.068)	(0.059)	(0.064)	(0.055)
Log GDP/capita	0.054	−0.046	0.061	−0.037
	(0.097)	(0.081)	(0.093)	(0.075)
Polyarchy Score	0.333	0.816	0.089	0.523
(V-Dem)	(0.533)	(0.484)	(0.499)	(0.425)
Regime Durability	−0.002	0.000	0.000	0.002
	(0.004)	(0.004)	(0.004)	(0.004)
Mean GRD	−0.052		−0.040	
Country Level	(0.033)		(0.029)	
Mean SRD	0.011		−0.010	
Country Level	(0.052)		(0.049)	
Mean GRD		−0.018		−0.054
Group Level		(0.055)		(0.053)
Mean SRD		0.073		0.055
Group Level		(0.050)		(0.043)
Constant/Cuts	Omitted	Omitted	Omitted	Omitted
Observations	9355	9355	9355	9355
Year Effects	Yes	Yes	Yes	Yes
Clustering	Country	Country-Group	Country	Country-Group

Robust standard errors are in parentheses

*** $p < 0.001$, ** $p < 0.01$, * $p < 0.05$, [†] $p < 0.10$

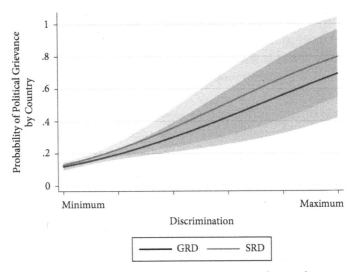

Figure 3.3 Probability of Political Grievance, Country-Clustered, 95 percent CIs

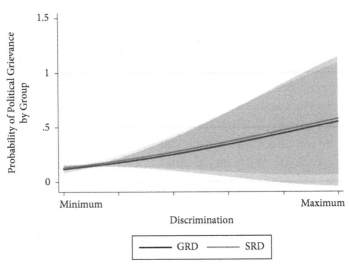

Figure 3.4 Probability of Political Grievance, Group-Clustered, 95 percent CIs

106 RELIGIOUS MINORITIES AT RISK

the replication of our general finding that although increased group capacity measured in terms of political organization, representation, and population size strongly correlate with increased political grievances, minority policy power still diminishes this propensity and intensity.

Regarding Table 3.3, it is interesting to note that although increased GRD increases likelihood and intensity of religious grievance for both country and country-group clusters, SRD only has this effect at the country level (Figure 3.5). Coupled with sustained findings that increased policy power reduces the expression of grievance for country-group clusters, this suggests that minority religious groups are both more likely to express grievance in response to GRD and more likely to have their grievances assuaged via governmental-institutional solutions than they are given rising SRD. This pattern is especially pronounced in Figure 3.6. Contra political grievances, having greater political representation does not seem to increase the likelihood or intensity of expressing religious grievances. The implications of these finding will become more clear when examining actual minority mobilization in response to these grievances in Chapter 5.

As mentioned above regarding economic grievances, we take a dual approach. In our first set of models in Table 3.4, we include our measure of religious minority economic status vis-a-vis the religious majority on the theoretical inference that economically disadvantaged groups should be more likely to express economic grievances. Given limited empirical evidence positively confirming these groups' economic statuses, however, models including this variable only analyze some 30 percent of our total cases. In the second set of models in Table 3.5, consistent with our previous models, we exclude the economic status variable and examine the likelihood and intensity of economic grievances on the entire data set. These dueling approaches offer some conflicting evidence.

In Table 3.4, we observe that economic grievances are much more likely to be stimulated by SRD rather than GRD. This is particularly true for country-level clusters as evident in Figure 3.7 contra Figure 3.8. However, in Table 3.5 we observe that while both GRD and SRD may account for economic grievance when examining country-level clusters (see Figure 3.9), SRD may only weakly explain economic grievance intensity for group-level clusters (see Figure 3.10). In turn, whereas Table 3.4 observes no effect for minority political organization or representation, Table 3.5 offers patterns that match those observed for all other grievance types. A more consistent effect across both sets of models is found for increased minority policy power, reducing

Table 3.3 Determinants of Religious Grievance and Intensity, 2000–2014

	Grievance Expressed		Grievance Intensity	
	(5a)	(6a)	(5b)	(6b)
	Correlated RE Logit	Correlated RE Logit	Correlated RE Ordered Logit	Correlated RE Ordered Logit
GRD (1 year lag)	0.075***	0.114*	0.067***	0.094*
	(0.021)	(0.051)	(0.019)	(0.042)
SRD (1 year lag)	0.082***	0.038	0.076***	0.034
	(0.021)	(0.031)	(0.018)	(0.024)
Minority Political	1.125***	1.619***	1.087***	1.536***
Organization	(0.197)	(0.265)	(0.180)	(0.244)
Minority	0.571*	0.341	0.565**	0.299†
Representation	(0.226)	(0.217)	(0.211)	(0.173)
Minority	−0.216	−0.297*	−0.172	−0.261*
Policy Power	(0.136)	(0.128)	(0.132)	(0.121)
Religious Similarity	0.302	0.559*	0.268	0.502*
to Majority	(0.200)	(0.259)	(0.168)	(0.237)
Minority Population	0.038***	0.053***	0.031***	0.047***
%	(0.011)	(0.011)	(0.009)	(0.010)
Log Country	0.171*	0.225***	0.164*	0.218***
Population	(0.084)	(0.068)	(0.077)	(0.062)
Log GDP/capita	0.100	0.041	0.088	0.037
	(0.099)	(0.100)	(0.093)	(0.090)
Polyarchy Score	0.137	0.505	0.019	0.341
(V-Dem)	(0.518)	(0.544)	(0.466)	(0.444)
Regime Durability	−0.006	−0.005	−0.003	−0.001
	(0.004)	(0.005)	(0.004)	(0.004)
Mean GRD	−0.023		−0.018	
Country Level	(0.032)		(0.030)	
Mean SRD	0.013		0.021	
Country Level	(0.049)		(0.044)	
Mean GRD		−0.046		−0.031
Group Level		(0.055)		(0.045)
Mean SRD		0.096*		0.094**
Group Level		(0.040)		(0.031)
Constant/Cuts	Omitted	Omitted	Omitted	Omitted
Observations	9355	9355	9355	9355
Year Effects	Yes	Yes	Yes	Yes
Clustering	Country	Country-Group	Country	Country-Group

Robust standard errors are in parentheses

*** $p < 0.001$, ** $p < 0.01$, * $p < 0.05$, † $p < 0.10$

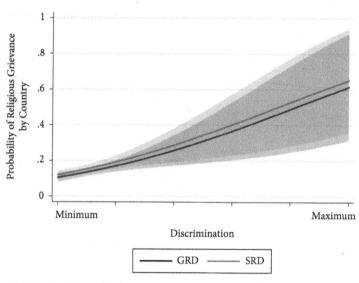

Figure 3.5 Probability of Religious Grievance, Country-Clustered, 95 percent CIs

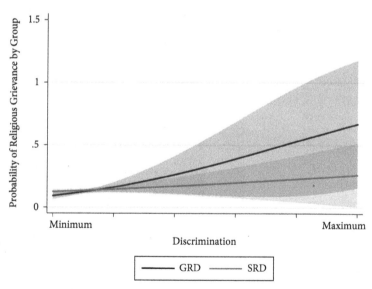

Figure 3.6 Probability of Religious Grievance, Group-Clustered, 95 percent CIs

Table 3.4 Determinants of Economic Grievance and Intensity, Constrained Models, 2000–2014

	Grievance Expressed		Grievance Intensity	
	(7a)	(8a)	(7b)	(8b)
	Correlated RE Logit	Correlated RE Logit	Correlated RE Ordered Logit	Correlated RE Ordered Logit
GRD (1 year lag)	−0.004	0.159	−0.002	0.175
	(0.051)	(0.141)	(0.043)	(0.142)
SRD (1 year lag)	0.152***	0.111[†]	0.140***	0.137*
	(0.034)	(0.064)	(0.031)	(0.063)
Minority Political	0.453	0.900	0.549	0.899
Organization	(0.663)	(0.711)	(0.608)	(0.616)
Minority	0.302	0.472	0.344	0.415
Representation	(0.272)	(0.341)	(0.229)	(0.272)
Minority	−0.333	−0.509*	−0.262	−0.432*
Policy Power	(0.208)	(0.228)	(0.168)	(0.184)
Minority Economic	−0.713*	−0.576[†]	−0.598*	−0.480[†]
Status	(0.305)	(0.321)	(0.244)	(0.286)
Religious Similarity	0.523	0.093	0.457	0.103
to Majority	(0.546)	(0.614)	(0.509)	(0.554)
Minority Population	0.012	0.065*	0.013	0.055*
%	(0.026)	(0.028)	(0.024)	(0.023)
Log Country	0.328	0.116	0.241	0.088
Population	(0.236)	(0.158)	(0.196)	(0.145)
Log GDP/capita	0.338	0.289	0.261	0.271
	(0.273)	(0.218)	(0.229)	(0.197)
Polyarchy Score	−1.320	−1.451	−1.019	−1.469
(V-Dem)	(1.776)	(1.302)	(1.429)	(1.080)
Regime Durability	0.008	0.006	0.009	0.008
	(0.008)	(0.009)	(0.008)	(0.008)
Mean GRD	0.026		0.031	
Country Level	(0.067)		(0.061)	
Mean SRD	−0.121		−0.106	
Country Level	(0.110)		(0.099)	
Mean GRD		−0.149		−0.167
Group Level		(0.146)		(0.147)
Mean SRD		0.027		−0.008
Group Level		(0.075)		(0.073)
Constant/Cuts	Omitted	Omitted	Omitted	Omitted
Observations	2949	2949	2949	2949
Year Effects	Included	Included	Included	Included
Clustering	Country	Country-Group	Country	Country-Group

Robust standard errors are in parentheses

*** $p < 0.001$, ** $p < 0.01$, * $p < 0.05$, [†] $p < 0.10$

Table 3.5 Determinants of Economic Grievance and Intensity, Full Models, 2000–2014

	Grievance Expressed		Grievance Intensity	
	(7a1)	(8a1)	(7b1)	(8b1)
	Correlated RE Logit	Correlated RE Logit	Correlated RE Ordered Logit	Correlated RE Ordered Logit
GRD (1 year lag)	0.056*	0.092	0.051*	0.109
	(0.026)	(0.104)	(0.023)	(0.104)
SRD (1 year lag)	0.076*	0.074	0.077*	0.101[†]
	(0.033)	(0.061)	(0.032)	(0.060)
Minority Political	1.013**	1.508***	0.949**	1.438***
Organization	(0.347)	(0.447)	(0.320)	(0.415)
Minority	0.754*	0.568[†]	0.751**	0.514[†]
Representation	(0.328)	(0.337)	(0.290)	(0.277)
Minority	−0.321[†]	−0.550**	−0.323[†]	−0.484**
Policy Power	(0.185)	(0.202)	(0.174)	(0.171)
Religious Similarity	0.409	0.481	0.400	0.497
to Majority	(0.323)	(0.428)	(0.301)	(0.403)
Minority Population	0.046*	0.052**	0.042*	0.046**
%	(0.019)	(0.018)	(0.017)	(0.016)
Log Country	0.321**	0.226*	0.314**	0.219*
Population	(0.123)	(0.113)	(0.118)	(0.106)
Log GDP/capita	0.338*	0.327*	0.322*	0.322*
	(0.153)	(0.165)	(0.145)	(0.155)
Polyarchy Score	−0.541	−1.012	−0.572	−1.047
(V-Dem)	(0.926)	(0.945)	(0.899)	(0.848)
Regime Durability	0.004	0.005	0.005	0.006
	(0.006)	(0.006)	(0.006)	(0.006)
Mean GRD	−0.037		−0.035	
Country Level	(0.041)		(0.039)	
Mean SRD	−0.034		−0.032	
Country Level	(0.092)		(0.088)	
Mean GRD		−0.078		−0.099
Group Level		(0.107)		(0.107)
Mean SRD		0.065		0.035
Group Level		(0.067)		(0.066)
Constant/Cuts	Omitted	Omitted	Omitted	Omitted
Observations	9355	9355	9355	9355
Year Effects	Included	Included	Included	Included
Clustering	Country	Country-Group	Country	Country-Group

Robust standard errors are in parentheses

*** $p < 0.001$, ** $p < 0.01$, * $p < 0.05$, [†] $p < 0.10$

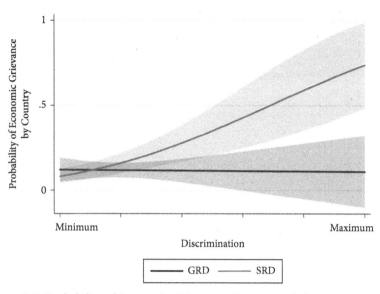

Figure 3.7 Probability of Economic Grievance, Constrained, Country-Clustered, 95 percent CIs

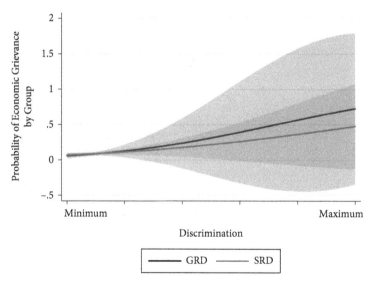

Figure 3.8 Probability of Economic Grievance, Constrained, Group-Clustered, 95 percent CIs

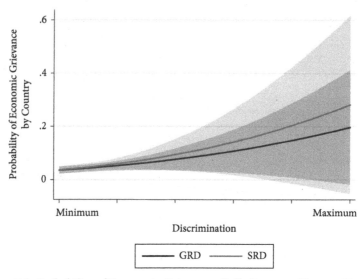

Figure 3.9 Probability of Economic Grievance, Full, Country-Clustered, 95 percent CIs

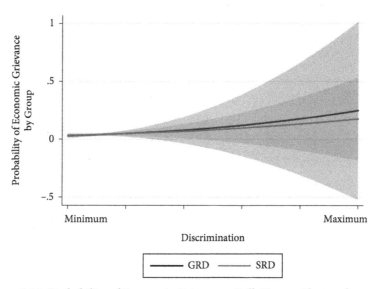

Figure 3.10 Probability of Economic Grievance, Full, Group-Clustered, 95 percent CIs

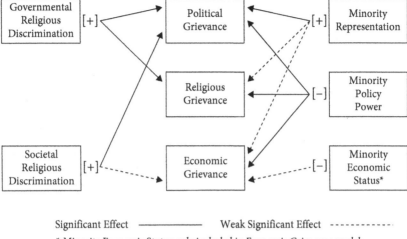

Figure 3.11 Summary of Major Causes of Minority Grievance by Type

economic grievances in all instances. It is also encouraging that where we include the minority economic status variable, we find status improvements indeed correlate with lesser expressions of economic grievance. Given the paring of these two sets of analyses, we surmise that economic status improvement and increased minority policy power should consistently reduce expressions of economic grievance. Yet GRD and SRD are likely of less direct importance. As we will see in the next chapter, however, this does not imply economic grievance does not significantly contribute to religious minority mobilization. We provide a summary of major contributions of specific elements of DDI to each specified grievance type in Figure 3.11. A somewhat more detailed summary of these findings is found in Table 3.6.

Implications and Conclusions

The most important result presented in this chapter from the perspective of our central model is that, at the collective level, objective DDI is a cause of grievances expressed by religious minorities. This is consistent with previous findings for ethnic minorities (Gurr, 1993a, 1993b, 2000a) and ethnoreligious minorities (Fox, 2002a). Because this is the first study to

114 RELIGIOUS MINORITIES AT RISK

Table 3.6 Summary of Major Findings, Country-Group Clustered Results

	General Grievances		Political Grievances		Religious Grievances		Economic Grievances	
	(A)	(B)	(A)	(B)	(A)	(B)	(A)	(B)
DDI Variables								
GRD (1 year lag)	+*	+*		+*	+*	+*		
SRD (1 year lag)	+*	+**	+†	+*				+†
Minority Policy Power	–***	–***	–*	–**	–*	–*	–**	–**
Minority Economic Status[1]	X	X	X	X	X	X	–†	–†
Other Minority-Based Variables								
Political Organization	+***	+***	+***	+***	+***	+***	+***	+***
Political Representation	+†	+**	+†	+*		+†	+†	+†
Minority Population %	+***	+***	+**	+**	+***	+***	+**	+**
Religious Similarity to Majority	+*	+*	+*	+*	+*	+*		
County Level Controls								
Log GDP per capita							+*	+*
Polyarchy Score								
Regime Durability								
Population size	+***	+***	+**	+**	+***	+***	+*	+*

(A) Models examining dichotomous grievance expression use correlated RE logits

(B) Models examining grievance intensity use correlated RE ordered logits

*** $p < 0.001$, ** $p < 0.01$, * $p < 0.05$, † $p < 0.10$, X N/A

[1] Minority Economic Status variable included in only economic grievance models due to missing data, all other variable significance levels reported from models excluding this variable.

examine this relationship for religious minorities, which includes all relevant cases from its potential universe of analysis, this in and of itself is important.

This study also provides some nuance to this finding. Whereas both GRD and SRD are strong and consistent predictors of grievance expression and intensity in general, whether examining country-level or group-level clusters, these patterns vary considerably when considering different levels of aggregation and different forms of grievance. GRD and SRD are generally reliable predictors of each grievance type (political, religious, and economic) when examining country-level clusters, with the possible exception of economic grievances in our case-constrained model. In turn, political grievance intensity is associated with both increasing GRD and SRD at the group-level, offering support for H3.1 and H3.4. Religious grievance is, however, primarily associated with increasing GRD, confirming H3.2, but not SRD, challenging H3.5. Our findings for economic grievance intensity are less determinate, however they appear to be driven by SRD and not GRD, confirming both H3.3 and H3.6. We can also generally confirm H3.7, with reservations given significant missing data, that minority groups of relatively lower economic status are more likely to express economic grievances and with greater intensity than those minorities who enjoy relatively privileged economic status.

A second major contribution is that, unlike previous group-level studies, this study examines the potential influence of group organization and leadership on the grievance-formation process. While previous studies have theorized that leaders and organizations can mobilize grievances (Fox et al., 2019), this has not been previously tested at the group level of analysis. We find that the presence of group organizations as well as minority political representation as predicted by H3.8 and H3.9 facilitates grievance formation and expression for all three types of grievances examined here. However, as predicted by H3.10, when minorities have influence on policy, grievances drop. These findings strongly suggest that group organization and political representation are instrumental to the expression of grievances. However, when group representatives have the ability to influence policy outcomes to their benefit, the motivation to express these grievances is significantly reduced.

In short, our findings suggest that increased discrimination substantially increases the likelihood that religious minorities will express a variety of grievances, enabled to no small degree by political organization and representation. If conventional accounts are correct that greater grievance leads to greater political mobilization, then our finding that having a seat at the table decreases the motivation for such grievances should also predict decreased chances of collective mobilization. In the pages that follow, we explore these inferences, finding not only that such empowerment rarely diminishes mobilization, but that different forms of grievance translate to variable nonviolent versus violent collective mobilization. How and why this is the case is the focus of our next two chapters.

On a broader level, these findings provide some perspective on the larger literature on DDI, grievances, and conflict and how this literature relates to our study. They support our contention that if one wants to understand conflict processes, the appropriate level of analysis to examine is the group-level rather than the individual-level. They also demonstrate that while grievances are related to DDI, the two are not the same and cannot be conflated either theoretically or empirically, as many past studies do. Finally, these findings demonstrate that rather than being competing theories, only one of which can be correct, both DDI and group organization are key elements of the grievance formation process. In demonstrating this we also show that the conscious mobilization of grievances is an essential element of the group-level grievance formation process.

4

Religious Minorities, Mobilization, Protest, Conflict, and Violence in Theory

In this chapter we discuss the theory that grievances lead to mobilization, protest, conflict, and violence by religious minorities. While the literature on this topic is intended to explain all of these types of behavior, most of it focuses on violent conflict. Yet some studies in this literature use other subsets of this broader set of behavior as their dependent variable. For the sake of efficiency, in this chapter we often use simplified terms such as "conflict" rather than list all these types of behavior. The intent, however, is to discuss the causes of this larger set of behaviors.

We draw from two sometimes overlapping literatures, which we consider relevant to the conflict behavior of religious minorities: the grievance literature and the religion and conflict literature. Both literatures are broader than our topic of empirical inquiry. In both cases we focus on the empirical literature and the theories that drive these empirical inquiries.

First, the grievance literature predates the religion and conflict literature. It applies to a broad array of conflicts. While some of this literature focuses on ethnic minorities (e.g., Gurr, 1993a, 1993b, 2000a), much of the relevant literature looks at a broader array of conflicts. One of its central propositions is that grievances are a potential cause of conflict, particularly with regard to minorities opposing the state. We argue that this is also applicable to religious minorities. In Chapter 5 we present the empirical tests of this model as well as discuss the differences in the processes that cause violent and nonviolent conflict.

Second, the religion and conflict literature, as a whole, addresses many types of religious conflict, which includes not only those involving religious minorities but also intrareligious conflict, such as between religious militants and governments that the militants deem insufficiently religious. Many within this literature argue that grievances are a potential cause of conflict by religious groups including religious minorities.

Religious Minorities at Risk. Matthias Basedau, Jonathan Fox, and Ariel Zellman, Oxford University Press.
© Oxford University Press 2023. DOI: 10.1093/oso/9780197693940.003.0004

118 RELIGIOUS MINORITIES AT RISK

We critically discuss these literatures with the goals of drawing from them to build our model for understanding the link between grievances and conflict and situating our study within the ongoing debates in these literatures. This involves outlining debates within these literatures as well as identifying what we consider to be flaws and inefficiencies in some of the arguments presented in these debates.

Previous empirical results are also an essential part of this discussion for several reasons. First, while discussion of grievances as a cause of conflict are common, empirical tests which actually measure grievances are rare. This applies to both the grievance literature and the religion and conflict literature. Thus, this study's empirical tests in Chapter 5 are a significant contribution. Second, a full discussion of previous empirical results allows us to better situate our findings within the larger literature. Third, these previous results provide an essential contribution to the conflict model we present in this study.

This chapter proceeds as follows. We first discuss the grievance argument. We present its central model and discuss grievance theory's critics. It is particularly important to address these critiques because, as our study is firmly within this literature, it is likely many of the grievance argument's critics would apply these critiques to our study. Thus, our arguments that these critiques are invalid or do not apply to the study at hand are critical to substantiate our study.

This discussion also highlights the contribution of our study and situates it within previous empirical work. We posit that despite much discussion of the proposition that grievances are a potential cause of conflict, relatively few studies have empirically tested this theory. Those few that have tested the theory tend to support it, but we are aware of no tests that compare the impact of grievances to deprivation, discrimination, and inequality (DDI) on conflict. That is, most studies test the impact of either grievances or DDI on conflict but do not compare the impact of these two related factors. This is true of the grievance literature as well as of the religion and conflict literature. This is an important comparison as it allows us, based on the results presented in Chapters 3 and 5, to establish that DDI leads to conflict in a two-stage model where DDI influences grievances that in turn influence conflict. However, DDI's direct influence on conflict is far weaker than that of grievances.

We then discuss the growing number of empirical studies of religion and conflict. While studies that use identity-based variables provide mixed results, studies that use DDI variables or variables measuring religious grievances, content, ideology, issues, or motivations tend to show a link between religion and conflict. This helps to demonstrate both the appropriateness of examining the impact of grievances and other factors on conflict behavior by religious minorities and how our study advances the religion and conflict literature.

From Grievances to Mobilization, Protest, Conflict, and Violence

The argument that groups who express grievances against their government are more likely to in some manner mobilize politically seems like an obvious path to conflict. In fact, much of the literature on religion and conflict as well as conflict in general assumes this is a potential path to conflict. Yet many contest this proposition. We evaluate the theoretical debate and empirical results surrounding this argument to situate both our theoretical arguments and empirical results within this literature.

In this part of the discussion, we focus on the general argument that grievances cause conflict in some manner. The arguments in this literature are important because they inform the grievances-to-conflict aspect of our model. Also, that this literature, with some important exceptions, generally fails to test the grievances-to-conflict relationship with sufficient precision, and in many cases at all, helps to both highlight the novelty of our results and understand why the tests in this literature produce inconsistent results.

While this literature focuses on violent conflict, it is intended to predict both violent conflict as well as other peaceful forms of mobilization and protest. That is, grievances are posited to cause people to seek redress from their governments in both a peaceful and nonpeaceful manner. One aspect of the literature that deserves special emphasis is that while discussion of whether grievances cause mobilization and conflict is common, actual tests of this proposition are rare. As we discuss in more detail below, this is because most studies which address this issue in their theoretical discussions do not include variables measuring grievances in their analysis. Rather, they use variables that measure DDI as surrogates for grievances. In some studies, demographic variables are used as surrogates that, essentially, makes them surrogates for DDI, which, in turn, is a surrogate for grievances. Their assumption is that when DDI is present, so too must grievances be present. This

120 RELIGIOUS MINORITIES AT RISK

makes this relationship a form of common wisdom that is often assumed but rarely tested.

While our findings support this common wisdom on a general level, the details and nuance of our findings show that the DDI to grievances to conflict relationship is sufficiently complex that these details are critically important. In fact, they are sufficiently important that any common wisdom that conflates these three distinct variables presents an overly simplistic view of the conflict process.

Specifically, as we demonstrate in Chapter 3 this DDI to grievances assumption is generally correct for religious minorities. However, as we demonstrate in Chapters 3 and 5, the evidence for the assumption that DDI is an accurate surrogate for grievances is weak at best for two reasons. First, we show in Chapter 3 that the path between DDI and grievances is complex with each type of DDI leading to a different set of types of grievances. Thus, the results of empirical tests of a DDI-grievance link are dependent upon what types of DDI and grievances are measured.

Second, our tests in Chapter 5, which use both DDI and grievances as independent variables that predict mobilization, protest, and conflict show that grievances are far better predictors of these dependent variables than is DDI. This implies that previous studies, which use DDI as a surrogate for grievances and found no relationship or a weak relationship between DDI and protest, mobilization, or conflict, may have found such a relationship between grievances and these dependent variables had these previous studies measured grievances rather than DDI or a DDI surrogate. Consequently, this scarcity of grievance variables in empirical studies of conflict and the use of DDI as a surrogate is a significant lacuna.

That is, these studies, at least in their empirical portions, miss that the link between DDI and conflict is multi-stage, with grievances as a critical intervening variable. Accordingly, we argue that while DDI significantly contributes to collective expressions of grievance, grievances themselves are a more accurate predictor of collective mobilization, whether nonviolent or violent. Put differently, while DDI and grievances are related, they are not interchangeable. Each is an important and separate link in the process, which leads to mobilization and conflict by religious minorities.

We also posit that Gurr's (1993a, 1993b, 2000a) original tests of this proposition on ethnic minorities constitute one of the very few actual tests of this multi-stage model. Accordingly, following Gurr (1993a, 1993b, 2000a), we argue that the manner in which grievances are understood and

RELIGIOUS MINORITIES, MOBILIZATION, PROTEST, CONFLICT 121

operationalized are crucial to this model. They must be understood and operationalized as collectively held grievances that are articulated and mobilized by group leaders and organizations.

The Basic Grievances Model

The core grievances model, which is the basis for our study, is quite simple. DDI causes grievances. These grievances, in turn, cause mobilization and conflict. This conflict can manifest in a variety of manners including peaceful protests, violent riots, organized terror, and rebellion. We discuss the first step, DDI to grievances, in Chapter 3. In this discussion we focus on how grievances cause mobilization, protest, and conflict.

Gurr's (1993a, 1993b, 2000a) Minorities at Risk (MAR) model is perhaps the best-known articulated version of this argument and focuses on ethnic minorities. It also provides the basic prototype for our model and his arguments with regard to the nuances of this model largely apply to the model we use in this study. However, it is important to emphasize that Gurr never argued that grievances alone determine levels of conflict, though he did argue they were a core cause. His model also takes into account state power, the role of group leaders and organization, state expansion, regime, regime change, international support, economic development, group identity, group cohesion, group demographic traits, group conflict with nonstate groups, past autonomy of the groups, and that conflicts often cross borders in various ways.

Within this myriad of factors, group leaders and organization are crucial. "Whenever these sentiments can be organized and focused by group leaders who give plausible expression to members' grievances and aspirations, they animate powerful political movements and protracted communal conflicts" (Gurr, 1993b, p. 167). In fact, Gurr (1993b) describes grievances and the potential for mobilization as the two most important factors in his conflict model. For example, Gurr (1993b, pp. 166–167) argues that "the model's most basic theoretical premise is that protest and rebellion by communal groups are jointly motivated by deep-seated grievances about group status *and* by the situationally determined pursuit of political interests, as formulated by group leaders and political entrepreneurs." Put differently, "the general hypothesis is that the greater a group's relative disadvantage . . . the greater the sense of grievance and, consequently, the greater its potential for political mobilization" (Gurr, 1993b, p. 174). This group-level grievance component is important because "communal grievances are not likely to come to the attention of government or outside observers until they are given expression by leaders of political movements who claim to represent group interest" (Gurr, 1993a, p. 68).

Thus, Gurr focuses not only on collectively held grievances but on grievances that are both given expression by group leaders and used to mobilize group members to political action. That is, as we discuss in Chapter 3, grievances collectively held by many individuals within the group are not sufficient. To be politically relevant, they must also be articulated on a group level and be the basis for group political organization. This is important because "collective interests are not unitary. There are diverse individual and segmented interests within every communal group" (Gurr, 1993a, p. 68). The key is whether group leaders can convince members that there is some collective interest or good which requires group unity on the issue. Though, obviously, it is easier to convince members to do so if many of them already hold grievances on an individual level.

Group leaders and organization are essential to this process. Thus, survey-based studies, which show a large number of group members are upset over an issue when asked, do not necessarily mean these grievances have become collectively expressed (let alone redress pursued) in this manner. Rather, grievances become politically relevant when group leaders and organizations express grievances, and there are signs of group backing for this expression of grievances. This is what we mean in this study by group-level grievances.

Gurr's (1993a, 1993b, 2000a) grievance variables are based explicitly on this conception of grievances. The MAR project measured grievances over economic, social, and political issues as well as demands for political autonomy as expressed publicly by group leaders, organizations, and representatives. Gurr's tests based on this data show a strong correlation between grievances and various forms of conflict behavior including mobilization, protest, and rebellion.

There is considerable support for this group-level grievances argument in the general literature as well as the religion and conflict literature. In a review of this literature, Asal and Deloghery (2017, p. 17) argue,

[B]oth rebels and theorist/rebels claim in their literature that oppression and injury is a key motivator for turning to violence . . . We should note that this connection is not one that is simply a product of the Age of Enlightenment and its aftermath. Speaking of the [Jewish-Israeli] rebellion against the Romans, Josephus identifies not only religious grievances but also unfair taxation as one of the key factors leading to the revolt.

Van Stekelenberg and Klandermans (2013, p. 887) similarly present this literature as arguing "that people participate in protest to express their grievances stemming from relative deprivation, frustration, or perceived injustice."

Applying this model to religious minorities is uncontroversial in the religion, politics, and conflict literature. The majority of this literature that addresses grievances posits grievances are a potential cause of religious conflict. Most references to grievances within the religion and conflict literature are made in passing but tend to argue that grievances in some manner are important to the conflict process. Hibbard (2015, p. 105) argues that the grievances which drive religious conflict are not religious but tend to be general economic and political grievances. Almond et al. (2003, pp. 130–131) argue that religious fundamentalists take advantage of economic grievances to recruit members. Demerath (2001, p. 116) similarly argues that the Christian right in the United States uses grievances over "secularity, poverty, political disenfranchisement, abortion, sexual orientation, and family values" to mobilize. Some just make general references to religious grievances causing various forms of conflict (Finnbogason & Svensson, 2018, pp. 98–99) or terror (Henne, 2012, 2019; Saiya, 2017, 2015b, 2019a, 2019b). Feuer (2018) looks at it from the government's perspective and argues that if a government's opposition frames grievances in the form of religion that government has two options. It can co-opt religion by supporting state-controlled religious organizations or repress it. We discuss how this fits into the empirical religion and conflict literature later in this chapter.

Critics of the Grievance Argument

Grievance theory has been heavily criticized. We identify five arguments made by these critics. First, they claim the original Gurr (1993a, 1993b, 2000a) studies are methodologically flawed. Second, they suggest that grievances are ubiquitous to the extent that they can be found everywhere. Thus, grievances cannot explain conflict. Third, they posit that some factor other than grievances is the true driving factor behind conflict. Fourth, they maintain that grievances can cause conflict but are not sufficient to cause conflict on their own (Muchlinski, 2019). Fifth, they provide new data and analyses which they claim refute the grievances argument.

124 RELIGIOUS MINORITIES AT RISK

As these critiques are likely be applied to our study by these critics, it is important to assess their validity. Below we discuss each of these critiques in more detail and argue that multiple aspects of these critiques themselves are problematic and that none of these critiques apply to the present study. We address these critiques by category rather than by the study or critic in question. It is also important to note, that most of these critiques focus on Gurr's (1993a, 1993b, 2000a) original work and not the studies using his Minorities at Risk (MAR) data set, which expanded upon his original data and empirical tests and generally support his original findings.

Methodological Issues

As we discuss in Chapter 3, a major methodological critique of Gurr's (1993a, 1993b, 2000a) original studies is one of selection bias. Basically, as the original MAR data set included only politically active ethnic groups, this meant that the groups included in the data set were selected based on the dependent variables—mobilization, protest, and rebellion. This, Gurr's critics argue, biases the results (Cederman et al., 2013; Fearon, 2003; Fearon & Laitin, 1996, 2003; Hug, 2003; 2013). As we note in Chapter 3, this is not necessarily a critical fault and subsequent studies of newer versions of MAR, which eliminate the selection bias issues confirm the results that grievances lead to conflict (Birnir et al., 2015; Sorens, 2009).

More importantly, this critique focuses on Gurr's methodology rather than his theory. Thus, it is not applicable to a new study that can link group-level grievances to conflict if that study uses new data which does not have this methodological issue. The RMAR data we use in this study includes all religious minorities that meet a 0.2 percent population threshold as well as a sampling of smaller minorities. Levels of DDI and grievances as well as levels of political mobilization were in no way part of the selection criteria. That, as shown in Chapter 2, the RMAR problem set includes a large number of minorities that are not coded as politically active either as expressing group-level grievances or engaging in mobilization confirms this. Accordingly, this critique is not applicable to the RMAR data.[1]

---

[1] Robustness checks for all models examined in this book confirm that excluding groups below this 0.2 percent threshold has no significant impact upon neither our variables of interest nor our analyses.

The Ubiquity of Grievances

The argument that grievances are so common that they cannot predict conflict is based on the principle that if a "cause" has no variation, it cannot predict an outcome. For example, it would be correct to say that conflict only occurs where people breathe oxygen. It is true, but this does little to tell us where conflict will occur. This is similar to the classic critique of relative deprivation theory, which posits that since one can always find perceived DDI, it is not useful as an explanation for violence and conflict (Rule, 1988, p. 205; McCarthy & Zald, 1977, p. 1215).

Collier et al. (2004) and Collier and Hoeffler (2002, 2004) make precisely this argument. They argue that if "subjective grievance is indeed widespread across societies, it cannot explain why some societies experience civil wars whereas most do not" (Collier et al., 2004, p. 256) and "that groups with grievances are sufficiently common that differences in the supply of such groups between societies are not an important influence on the risk of conflict initiation" (Collier & Hoeffler, 2002, p. 17). Thus they "see grievance as being so prevalent that it is of secondary importance, if any" (Asal & Deloughery, 2017, p. 22).

We posit that there are at least two counters to this critique. First, when grievances are in fact measured, their expression and intensity vary considerably both by group and over time. Gurr's (1993a, 1993b, 2000a) coding of grievances shows considerable variation across ethnic minorities. Even if one assumes there is selection bias in the MAR data, if grievances are ubiquitous and uniform, all groups should express them and their intensity should be similar. This is not the case. In addition, as we demonstrate in Chapter 2, both the presence and intensity of grievances also vary across religious minorities, as does DDI. As the basis for the ubiquity of grievances argument is a lack of variation, proof of variation in the presence and intensity of grievances undermines the critique's central assumption. Because the studies that make this critique do not measure grievances, we know of no cross-national empirical results which counter our findings that group-level grievances vary considerably both in their presence and intensity.

Second, we concede that if one looks at the individual level, it is unlikely that there is a minority of any kind anywhere in the world that does not include members who feel and even express grievances. However, the form of grievances that we, along with Gurr (1993a, 1993b, 2000a), posit to be relevant are group-level grievances expressed publicly by group organizations,

126 RELIGIOUS MINORITIES AT RISK

leaders, and representatives and backed by the collective feelings of the group they represent. Discontent is likely as common, though not as uniform, as Collier and Hoeffler (2002, 2004), among others, posit. In contrast, grievances mobilized by group representatives may be common, but the extent of their expression still varies from minority to minority.

The various discussions of the ubiquity of grievances critique tend to be imprecise on the types of grievances they discuss and generally do not address grievance intensity at all. In fact, there seems to be an implicit assumption that either intensity is similar across groups or that it does not matter. To the extent that can be determined, their use of the term tends to be in the context of general discontent or motivations rather than group leaders explicitly making the issue a political one. For example, Collier and Hoeffler (2004, p. 564) describe the grievance theory as follows: "Political science offers an account of conflict in terms of motive: rebellion occurs when grievances are sufficiently acute that people want to engage in violent protest." In fact, they focus on how individuals perceive their grievances: "Misperceptions of grievances may be very common: all societies have groups with exaggerated grievances" (Collier & Hoeffler, 2004, p. 564). Thus, their arguments seem to focus more on grievances held individually by group members rather than grievances expressed by group leaders and organizations.

Some Factors Other than Grievances Causes Conflict

Perhaps one of the most common critiques of any theory in the social sciences is that another theory is better. Grievance theory is no exception. While any theory of conflict that is not grievance theory implicitly makes this form of critique, two bodies of theory that compete with grievance theory explicitly argue that their explanation for conflict is superior to grievances. The first argues that conflict is driven by capacity, opportunities, and mobilization. The second argues that it is driven by greed.

Those who focus on capacity, opportunities, and mobilization tend to address grievances but mostly to dismiss them as the real explanation for mobilization. Charles Tilly (1978) is among the most important figures in the capacity, opportunities, and mobilization school. He criticizes grievance arguments for "their strong emphasis on grievances and states of mind as opposed to organizational and tactical problems . . . all movement organizations, whatever the grievances to which they respond, face the common,

RELIGIOUS MINORITIES, MOBILIZATION, PROTEST, CONFLICT   127

pressing problems of acquiring enough resources to do their work" (Tilly, 1978, p. 29). Tilly assumes collective interests exist among most groups, but conflict occurs when group leaders can mobilize sufficient resources and the political opportunity structure is conducive to pursuing their claims.

McCarthy and Zald (1977) argue that there is always enough discontent in any society to supply support for a movement if it is well organized and has at its disposal the power and capacity of some of the group's elite. However, they accept that grievances and discontent may be defined and manipulated by issue entrepreneurs.

Fearon and Laitin (2003, pp. 75–76) focus on opportunity and argue:

> The main factors determining both the secular trend and the cross-sectional variation in civil violence in this period are not ethnic or religious differences or broadly held grievances but, rather, conditions that favor *insurgency*. . . . We hypothesize that financially, organizationally, and politically weak central governments render insurgency more feasible and attractive . . . On the rebel side, insurgency is favored by rough terrain, rebels with local knowledge of the population superior to the government's, and a large population.

They further argue that "grievance may favor rebellion by leading nonactive rebels to help in hiding the active rebels. But all the guerrillas really need is superior local knowledge which enables them to threaten reprisal for denunciation" (Fearon & Laitin, 2003, p. 88).

Some within this school leave more room for grievances within the conflict process. For example, Tarrow (1989) argues that protests begin with grievances, but these grievances must be mobilized by group leaders and social movement organizations. Mobilization applies a general interpretive framework to the grievances thereby defining them and broadening the range of their potential supporters. Thus, for Tarrow, both grievances and mobilization are necessary for large social movements.

As noted above, proponents of the greed argument also explicitly make the ubiquity of grievances argument (Collier et al., 2004; Collier & Hoeffler, 2002, 2004; Murshed & Tadhoeddin, 2009). Their basic argument is that the leaders of rebellions financially benefit from the rebellion, and this is the incentive for conflict. Potential benefits include a new division of the national financial pie, control of state revenue, graft, patronage, looting, foreign support, rents, and revenues from natural resources. Even when they are still

128 RELIGIOUS MINORITIES AT RISK

rebel groups many of these benefits can apply if they control territory. Rebel groups can even, without control of territories, loot and receive foreign and local support.

On a more general level, Collier and Hoeffler (2002, 2004; Collier et al., 2004) are to some extent unclear about what they mean by "greed." On one hand, they discuss the financial benefit that can accrue to rebel groups, both during the rebellion and after it if the rebellion is successful. On the other hand, using economic rationale, they assume that where there is opportunity greed will automatically kick in. Thus, greed can be seen both as a motive and as part of the opportunity structure.

While some proponents of both of these schools of thought argue that it is an "either-or" proposition where if one explanation is correct, the other must be wrong, we conceptualize the causes of conflict differently. We argue that it is possible for both grievances and greed to motivate conflict and for mobilization, capacity, and opportunity to influence how conflict manifests. In fact, the mobilization, capacity, and opportunity argument primarily focuses on how one organizes for conflict and does not address its motivations other than to assume such motivations are omnipresent. We also posit that, other than the claims of the ubiquity of grievances in the greed literature, there is nothing in either the grievances or greed literature which argues that motivations other than the theory's preferred motivation cannot also influence conflict.

Even some of the strongest proponents of the greed argument acknowledge this possibility. For example, Collier and Hoeffler (2002, p. 14) acknowledge the alternative theory that conflict

> might be motivated purely by grievance-the opposition to perceived or actual injustice. The costs of rebellion are the labor force and equipment needed for a rebel army that can survive against the military threat posed by government forces. Because these costs must be met, even if the rebellion is motivated entirely by grievance, it must generate revenue. Hence, the circumstances that determine financial viability are potentially important regardless of the motivation for rebellion.

Thus, they concede that at least in theory both motivations and mobilization—including opportunity and capacity—are relevant and that grievances can be a motivation for conflict. However, they argue that these nongreed influences are minimal in comparison to the greed motivation.

RELIGIOUS MINORITIES, MOBILIZATION, PROTEST, CONFLICT 129

The grievances literature also explicitly acknowledges this mixed-theory approach. Gurr's MAR model (1993a, 1993b, 2000a) explicitly includes mobilization for conflict as one of the steps in its conflict model, explicitly drawing from Tilly's (1978) theories to build the theoretical and empirical foundations for this model. Also, as noted, Gurr's conception of grievances itself includes elements of mobilization in that, for Gurr, grievances are publicly expressed by group leaders, representatives, and organizations seeking to mobilize group members. Also, Gurr (2000a, pp. 79–92) acknowledges the importance of group capacity and opportunity structure factors such as regime, state power, and external support and includes them in his conflict model. Regan and Norton (2005) use the MAR data to explicitly integrate the grievances and greed models and test them. While their tests more strongly support the grievances model, they build a theoretical foundation for a conception of conflict where multiple motivations including both grievances and greed is possible.

Some within both of these opposing schools similarly leave room of a multicause model. Tarrow (1989) does so for the opportunity, mobilization, and resources school. Murshed and Tadhoeddin (2009) argue that greed is the preferred model but acknowledge that other mechanisms such as grievance might be present and that combining greed and grievance would likely make for a superior model.

Finally, both these schools of thought explicitly base their critique of grievance theory on the ubiquity of grievances argument. This has two important implications. First, all counterarguments to the ubiquity of grievances argument apply. Second, these schools implicitly accept that grievances are a part of the conflict process. Thus if, in fact, grievances are not as uniform as they claim, this means that at the very least, grievances can be part of a conflict process which also includes capacity, opportunity, mobilization, and greed.

Grievances Are Necessary but Not Sufficient

Tarrow's (1989) argument is that grievances can cause conflict, but they are not sufficient. This is because these grievances must be mobilized by social movement organizations, and in this process leadership, resources, and opportunities become a factor. Muchlinski (2019) similarly argues that "while grievances are indeed a crucial factor in explaining religious violence, emerging research suggests that they are necessary but perhaps not sufficient

130   RELIGIOUS MINORITIES AT RISK

for such violence to emerge." He echoes the mobilization, resources, and opportunity argument and notes that a sufficiently repressive regime can prevent any expression of opposition no matter how high grievances.

Yet this type of argument does not fully contradict Gurr's (1993a, 1993b, 2000a) core arguments. While Gurr does argue that spontaneous violence such as riots are possible even in the absence of mobilization, the mobilization process is a central element of his MAR model. In addition, both in his discussion of this model and elsewhere (e.g., Gurr, 1988) he explicitly acknowledges that regime is part of the opportunity structure. Nor does this type of argument contradict our model, which also accounts for mobilization.

Empirical Critiques

Several studies make the claim that their empirical results disprove the grievance argument. However, when one examines the "grievance" variables used in these studies, in nearly all cases these variables do not measure grievance. Rather, they measure some form of DDI and assume this DDI will lead to grievances or even conflate DDI with grievances.

For example, Collier and Hoeffler (2002) test the impact of finance, "grievance," military advantage, and history on violent conflict in Africa. However, their grievance measures actually measure "inequality, political repression, and social divisions" (Collier & Hoeffler, 2002, p. 17). Interestingly, they nevertheless find some evidence that these grievance surrogates, which actually measure DDI, influence conflict, but the influence is weaker than the other variables. Collier and Hoeffler (2004) perform similar tests using income inequality and land inequality as their DDI-based grievance surrogate measures and find them to be insignificant. Fearon and Laitin (2003) in their critique of grievance theory in favor of opportunity structure also do not measure grievance. They do not even measure DDI. Rather they use measures of percapita GDP and both ethnic and religious fractionalization as surrogates. That is, they use surrogates for DDI, which do not actually measure DDI and assume that these DDI surrogates are the same as grievances. Muchlinski (2014) applies the grievances are not sufficient argument and finds that a combination of "grievances," regime and opportunity all influence religious violence. However, his measure for grievances focuses on restrictions on religious freedom rather than grievances.

In fact, the majority of empirical studies that in some way argue grievances influence any form of conflict do not contain any variables measure grievances. Rather, like the empirical studies we discuss above that claim to contradict the grievance argument, they tend to use measures of DDI as surrogates. As we discuss in more detail in Chapter 3, a series of publications using the EPR data set claim that grievances are a basis for ethnic conflict but test this using variables measuring DDI, which also include elements of capacity (Cederman & Girardin, 2007; Cederman et al., 2010; Cederman et al., 2011; Cederman et al., 2013; Cederman et al., 2015; Cederman et al., 2017; Wimmer et al., 2009). Also using the horizontal inequality argument but focusing on data on ethnic violence in Xinjiang, China, Cao et al. (2018, p. 765) "argue that local religious institutions decrease violence caused by local grievances." However, their grievance variable measures differential educational attainment, a measure of inequality.

While these are examples from a larger literature, they are fully representative of that literature. This is because, to our knowledge, other than the MAR and the RMAR data sets, no cross-country datasets have systematically collected variables that specifically measure grievances expressed by minorities at the group level. One interesting partial exception (as it is not a cross-country dataset) is a country-level study of Spain, which measures regional differences in demands for autonomy, which found that this type of grievance did correlate with protest (Saxton, 2005). Also, as we discuss in more detail in Chapter 3, in survey-based studies, perceived grievances are often linked to support for protest or conflict behavior (e.g., Fox et al., 2019; Shaykhutdinov & Bragg, 2011).

Given this, and that the MAR-based studies consistently confirmed the grievances argument, we maintain that no cross-country data-based study has explicitly falsified the grievance argument. All cross-national studies based on other data that purport to test grievances actually test some form of DDI and, in some cases, demographic and country-level economic development variables, as surrogates for grievances. While we agree that these factors might influence grievances, they are not themselves grievances.

That is, we follow Gurr in arguing that the conflict process is multi-stage. DDI causes grievances. When these grievances are expressed at the group level by group leaders, representatives, and organizations, and used as a basis for mobilization, conflict may occur, assuming the opportunity structure is in favor of such mobilization. Given all of these steps and influences between DDI and conflict, the absence of a direct correlation between DDI and

132 RELIGIOUS MINORITIES AT RISK

conflict found in many previous studies is not unexpected. This is why this book's research design explicitly employs a multi-step model. We demonstrate in Chapter 3 that DDI predicts grievances. In Chapter 5 we test the link between these grievances on one hand and mobilization, protest, and conflict on the other.

The Religion and Conflict Literature

The theoretical discussions of the cross-national study of religion, conflict, and violence addresses grievances as a potential cause of conflict and violence. However, cross-national empirical tests of the grievances hypothesis are rare and tend to focus only on subsets of religious minorities such as ethnoreligious minorities (e.g., Fox, 2002a, 2004). Nevertheless, this literature provides important insights on how the grievances hypothesis applies to religious minorities.

This literature is relatively young compared to the quantitative study of civil war. The first published cross-national studies that used a religion independent variable to predict some form of intrastate conflict or violence were published in 1997 (Fox, 1997; Rummel, 1997; Walter, 1997). In comparison, Gurr's (1968, 1970) first major study of relative deprivation theory and conflict was published in 1968. This was part of a larger set of studies that began to use quantitative methods to examine the causes of domestic conflict in the 1960s (e.g., Feierabend & Feierabend, 1966; Feierabend et al., 1969; Russett, 1964; Rummel, 1966). Thus, over three decades elapsed after social scientists began to use cross-national empirical methodology to examine the causes of domestic conflict before religion was considered in a cross-national empirical study as a potential cause. This is particularly important because many of the authors in the religious conflict literature are well aware of the civil war and ethnic conflict studies and integrate many insights from this literature into their discussions.

Since 1997, the quantitative literature on religion, conflict, and violence has been growing. However, while the theoretical discussion in this literature includes the proposition that grievances are a potential cause of religious conflict, the empirical tests, with a few notable exceptions, do not include religious grievance variables. Rather most independent variables quantifying religion measure religious identity, other aspects of religious demography, religious ideology, religious belief, religious motivations, religious demands, and religious discrimination as well as more vague variables such as a conflict having religious content. While there have been studies that included grievance variables, all of these studies are precursors to the present study and involve at least one of this study's authors.

Thus far in this chapter, we have addressed the argument that grievances can cause mobilization, protest, and conflict. Now we build on this foundation but focus on the empirical literature on religion and conflict. We do so in order to establish the state of the discipline and how our study of religious grievances fits into this landscape. In doing so, we discuss the mechanisms that link religion and conflict that are theorized in these studies.

In this context, we make four important arguments about this literature. First, while discussion of grievances as a cause of religious conflict are common, few of these studies actually measure grievances. Thus, this is a proposition largely untested in the empirical literature on religious conflict. Second, despite this lack of empirical testing, the religion and conflict literature provides important insights on how grievances manifest among religious minorities and influences conflict. Third, this study constitutes the most comprehensive and detailed test of the grievances to conflict argument for religious minorities. Fourth, the evidence that religious identity alone causes conflict is at best mixed. In contrast, there is ample empirical evidence that other factors such as religious ideology, beliefs, and motivations as well as deprivation, discrimination, and inequality (DDI) are causes of conflict.

Previous Quantitative Studies of Religion, Violence, and Conflict

It is difficult to generalize about the quantitative study of religion, violence, and conflict. This is because this literature is diverse in several respects. It is based on a wide variety of conflict data sets. Some data sets focus specifically on religion and violence. Others use more general terrorism, civil war, or domestic conflict data sets that include religion variables or to which religion variables were added by the studies' authors. Some studies include a wide variety of types of conflict while others focus on a specific type. The units of analysis vary and can be countries, conflicts, specific minorities, or organizations. Partially, but not exclusively, because of this, the dependent variables of these studies vary considerably. Also, the geographic areas and time periods covered also vary across studies.

134 RELIGIOUS MINORITIES AT RISK

These studies use many different dependent variables including general measures of domestic conflict, terror, conflict termination, and conflict resolution as well as mobilization, protest, and conflict by ethnic and religious minorities. The common denominator is that these studies test religious causes for these phenomena. We draw from this literature in order to assess the potential religious causes of conflict behavior by religious minorities and how this relates to our understanding of the role of grievances in mobilization and conflict behavior by religious minorities.

Accordingly, in our overview of the state of knowledge on religion conflict and violence, we discuss information on both independent and dependent variables in these studies when relevant. However, we organize our discussion along the type of independent religion variable used in the study. These include identity variables, DDI variables, variables that measure religious motivations, beliefs, ideology, issues, and content, and studies using grievance variables. Finally, we examine variables that do not fit into these four categories and the results of relevant individual-level studies.

We make two general arguments about the relationship between religious grievances, conflict, and the religion and conflict literature. First, RMAR's addition of religious grievance variables adds important elements to our knowledge of the role of religion in mobilization, protest, violence, and conflict. Second, religious grievances might be assumed to be the most relevant consideration to explain conflict behavior by religious minorities. This proposition, however, demands empirical testing against other potential nonreligious motivations.

Religious Identity and Demography

Religious identity and demography variables come in three types. First, some measure whether a conflict is between different religions or within the same religion. Second, some measure different patterns across religious denominations. For example, are conflicts involving Muslims more violent that those involving Christians? Third, some measure religious diversity in the form of a variable that in various ways account for how many different religions are present in a country and the population size of each religion or in some cases, some of them. Typical measures of diversity include fractionalization (i.e., many and smaller groups), polarization (degree of demographic concentration between groups), and dominance of one group (comprising

50 to 60 percent or more of the population). In this section, we first discuss the nature of identity-based claims then discuss the empirical results.

Identity-based variables are likely the most commonly used religion variables in studies of intrastate conflict. Perhaps this is because demographic information is most readily available. This information can be converted from other datasets with relative ease while, in comparison, most of the other types of variables require a lengthy and often expensive data collection and coding process.

However, as Fox (2018, p. 32) notes, "identity-based theories are among the most problematic in the literature on religion and politics. This is because they tend to be superficial, and provide at best an incomplete understanding of the topic." For example, if a study finds interreligious conflicts to be more violent than intrareligious conflicts, this finding does not truly explain the causal mechanism for this finding. In fact, any theory that links religion to more conflict could be used to explain this finding, but identity variables would be unable to establish which of the many potential theories is the actual explanation.

That is, identity-based variables can serve as surrogates for a wide variety of religious phenomena that are theorized to influence levels of conflict. These include the role of religious ideologies, religious-based mobilization, grievances, and a wide range of other religious phenomena that we discuss in more detail in the following discussion. In addition, it is possible the identity-based variables are measuring more basic ingroup-outgroup dynamics. This means that even if they are found to be significantly correlated with conflict, it is difficult to determine exactly how they are influencing this outcome. Thus, even if religious identity conflicts are more likely to involve a religious ideology, for example, religious identity is a poor and imperfect surrogate.

We also suggest that the theoretical arguments made in the majority of empirical studies of religion and conflict, which use identity variables, tend to implicitly concur that religious identity alone is an insufficient explanation for religious influences in conflict. This is because nearly all of them posit some factor other than identity is, at a minimum, part of the causal mechanism measured by the identity variable in question. This also raises empirical concerns. If religious identity is an imperfect surrogate for some other religious cause, this would increase the likelihood of null results. That is, a religious identity variable may show no statistically significant connection to the dependent variable when a more precise and accurate measure of the relevant phenomenon would.

136 RELIGIOUS MINORITIES AT RISK

Nevertheless, it is certainly possible to argue that inter-group differences are themselves a cause of conflict. However, if this is the case, why would intergroup differences based on religion be different from other types of intergroup differences? Some, like Collier and Hoeffler (2002, p. 17), use religious diversity variables precisely to measure general social divisions. Thus, their tests of religious identity's influence on conflict are not driven by a religion-based theory. Some use it as a control variable while focusing their tests on other religion variables (e.g., Deitch, 2022; Fox, 2004; Svensson, 2007). Others argue that religion is not the underlying cause. For example, Filote et al. (2016) argue that nationalism is the main motivation of the terror groups they study and those groups sometimes use religious cleavages because it is an effective mobilization tactic. Yet even for Filote et al. (2016) it is the use by leaders of religious cleavages for mobilization that is theoretically important, not just the presence of such cleavages.

However, most studies which use religious identity variables tend to argue that some religious factor other than identity drives the relationship either in addition to identity or instead of identity. For example, Basedau et al. (2011) discuss the religious identity issue in detail. They argue that "diverse religious identities, similar to ethnic and other social identities, form a group identity and can result in escalating inter-group dynamics. Research demonstrates that people often privilege in-group members over out-group members. As a result, violent escalation becomes likelier" (Basedau et al., 2011, p. 754). However, they also use ideology and the likelihood of mobilization as additional rationales, noting that religious ideology makes negotiation and compromise less likely, that religious combatants may be motivated by religious rewards, often in an afterlife, and it increases the likelihood that the state will impose the majority religion on its citizens, which can increase resentment and grievances. Likewise, a study by Basedau et al. (2016) looks at specific demographic constellations such as fractionalization, polarization (i.e., two big groups instead of many smaller ones), or dominance by one group (comprising around 60 percent or more of the population) and motivational factors such as grievances or calls for violence by leaders.

Ellingsen (2005) similarly combines identity-based arguments and other arguments. She references Huntington's (1993, 1996) identity-based clash of civilizations theory and argues that religion is a "deeply rooted cultural, psychological, and affective attachment to historical and ancestral ties" (Ellingsen, 2005, p. 312). However, she also makes ideology and mobilization-based arguments. Reynal-Querol (2002) argues that religion is an important identity marker because while a person can speak more than one language, for example, one can only have one religion. But she acknowledges that "faith" can also play a role.

Lai (2006), drawing on international relations security-based theory in his study of interstate conflict, makes a power-based argument. He argues that especially if there is a history of interreligious conflict or competition between religious groups, a security dilemma situation is likely to occur where each side is unable to trust the other and ascribes hostile intentions to them. Yet he too also acknowledges that ideology can play a role. Indeed, a recent study by Zellman and Brown (2022) demonstrates that interstate conflict between religiously dissimilar states is much better explained by how states treat their rivals' coreligionists than by the mere incompatibility of their respective dominant religious identities. Moreover, even states with shared religious identities will tend to militarize disputes between them when engaged in ideological competition.

Some studies place little focus on identity-based arguments but still use religious identity or demography variables as surrogates for those arguments. All of the following make nonidentity based arguments but use some form of religious identity variables to test them. Bormann et al. (2015) make a largely grievance-based argument. Satana et al. (2013) make a DDI argument positing that religious minorities are more likely to engage in terror when they are excluded from government. Karakaya (2015, p. 514) argues that a larger number of Muslims in a country increases conflict because "Islamists adhere to radical religious identities and resort to violence as a response to cultural imperialism, colonial history, and the growing influence of Western culture." She also argues that Islamic ideology makes compromise difficult and "the promise of martyrdom render bargaining and deterrence useless" (Karakaya, 2015, p. 514).

Some argue that religious identity interacts with some other religion-based factor. Maoz and Henderson (2020) argue that religious diversity combined with closely linked religious and political institutions causes both domestic and international conflict. Ives (2019) similarly argues that religious identity linkages between a state and rebel groups in another state combined with state–religion institutional linkages makes that state more likely to intervene on behalf of that rebel group.

Thus, most studies that use religious identity variables to predict violence and conflict either argue that it is a surrogate for other religious factors, interacts with other religious factors, or use it as a control when testing for

138 RELIGIOUS MINORITIES AT RISK

other factors. Given this, we posit that the literature demonstrates a tacit recognition that religious identity alone is not the optimal variable to examine the influence of religion on domestic conflict. While the most popular nonidentity argument in these studies are ideology-linked arguments, grievances and DDI-based arguments are also prominent.

Some studies do focus exclusively on identity-based arguments such as Huntington's (1993, 1996) clash of civilization argument (Roeder, 2003; Tusicisny, 2004; Walter, 1997). However, it is important to note that identity is an issue that is broader than religious identity and Huntington's concept of civilizations is not identical to religious identity (Fox, 2004). Nevertheless, it is worthwhile to examine the results of these studies.

We examine the findings of studies of religious identity and conflict according to the variable-type categorization we discuss earlier in this section. Overall, the link between religious diversity and conflict is inconsistent across these studies for all three types of religious identity variables. Several studies measure diversity using various mathematical formulas, which take into account the proportion of the population of each significant religious group in a country. Some religious diversity studies find a positive relationship between religious diversity and some form of conflict (Reynal-Querol, 2002; Rummel, 1997) but others find no statistically significant relationship (Fearon & Laitin, 2003; Henderson & Singer, 2000; Maoz & Henderson, 2020). Collier and Hoeffler (2002) find that religious diversity reduces conflict and violence.

Three studies measure religious diversity by examining the size of the religious majority. Ellingsen (2000) found conflict to be more common when the religious majority is at least 80 percent of the population. Basedau et al. (2011) find that both armed conflict and religious armed conflict in Africa increase if the majority religion is at least 60 percent of the population. This finding was supported by Basedau et al. (2016) for all developing countries, however this only holds true for armed conflicts in general, not specifically for conflicts over religious content or between religious groups. Other demographic constellations such as fractionalization or polarization do not increase conflict. Thus, while these studies find a mostly consistently positive correlation between this form of religious diversity variable and conflict, this relationship does not hold in the one study that controls for religious content in a conflict.

Studies that examine whether specific religions are more violent also provide mixed results. Fox (2000a, 2003c, 2004) found that conflicts involving

RELIGIOUS MINORITIES, MOBILIZATION, PROTEST, CONFLICT   139

Muslims are not more common or more violent compared to other religions. Deitch (2022) found that conflicts involving Muslim rebels are significantly shorter, while Basedau et al. (2022) find that Jihadist insurgencies are significantly more durable and tend to be less rather than more lethal. Collins et al. (2011) found that members of the US House of Representatives were more likely to support the Iraq war if they were mainline Protestant. Brown (2014, 2015) found Muslim-majority states are more likely to engage in international conflict.

Several studies which compare interreligious to intrareligious conflicts found that interreligious conflicts are more violent (Basedau et al., 2011; Ellingsen, 2005; Roeder, 2003; Satana et al., 2013). However, others found no statistically significant relationship (Bormann et al., 2015; Deitch, 2022; Filote et al., 2016; Karakaya, 2015; Maoz & Henderson, 2020; Svensson, 2007; Tusicisny, 2004; Walter, 1997). Fox (2004) found that interreligious ethnic conflicts had higher levels of rebellion but only among separatist ethnic minorities. In contrast, Gurses & Rost (2017) link coreligiosity to war recurrence. Zellman and Brown (2022) found that these dynamics substantially depend upon how political actors treat their rivals' coreligionists or privilege their shared religion, rather than whether these rivals belong to the same or different religious groups. Finally, two studies show that when ethnic and religious identities mix (that is, run parallel), the likelihood of armed conflicts, but not necessarily the intensity, increases (Gubler & Selway 2011; Basedau et al., 2016).

In sum, the empirical literature which examines religious identity as a cause of conflict and violence is at best ambivalent. Few even make the argument that identity alone is a cause of conflict as they tend to argue some other factor such as mobilization, grievances, religious belief, or ideology, at least in part drive this relationship. The empirical results are sufficiently mixed such that it is difficult to conclude that there is a strong relationship between religious identity and conflict.

These mixed results are likely influenced by the multitude of ways in which both religious identity and the dependent variables are conceptualized and measured as well as the use of different units of analysis and the diverse temporal and geographic coverage of the problem sets. That being said, if religious identity had a strong relationship with conflict and violence, we would expect to see more consistency across these studies.

We argue that in practice, religious identity variables, when used to measure the influence of religion on conflict, are likely surrogates for some

140 RELIGIOUS MINORITIES AT RISK

more fundamental underlying factor or, more likely, several such factors. We further posit that identity, to the extent that it is used as a measure for religion, is often an imperfect surrogate variable for the factor or factors that are actually driving the results. This is likely causing weaker statistical links and creating many false null results. This is important for the present study because it demonstrates that identity variables are inaccurate measures of religious phenomena. For this reason variables measuring more specific religious phenomena, such as grievances, are necessary to determine the impact of religion on conflict. While this study focuses on grievances, we discuss in the following sections the collective results of studies that measure a variety of such factors.

This is not to say that identity and demography do not matter. Rather, we argue that identity and demography measures are in most cases poor surrogates for other religious factors which at least partially overlap with identity. We also demonstrate that, in practice, this type of variable has produced inconsistent results in predicting conflict.

We also posit that in order to accurately determine the influence, if any, of religious identity and demography variables which overlap with religious identity on conflict requires that a study must also account for those more specific religious factors. In Chapter 5, when controlling for these factors, we find that larger religious minorities are more likely to express grievances and engage in conflict. However, we interpret minority size as a capacity variable rather than a religious one. That is, larger minorities have a greater ability to engage in conflict. We also find some evidence that when a religious minority also has an ethnicity that is distinct from that of the majority group, they are more likely to engage in violence. It is also important to note that this observation does not apply to demographic factors which do not necessarily overlap with religious identity or those which are likely to influence levels of conflict regardless of overlap with religious identity such as rapid demographic change (Horowitz, 1985, p. 587).

Religious Deprivation, Discrimination, and Inequality

Several studies test the direct impact of DDI on domestic violence, conflict, or a similar dependent variable. All of these studies address grievances as a potential mechanism for the link between DDI and conflict, but the variables they use clearly measure DDI rather than grievances. The centrality of the grievance argument in the theorization of this relationship varies across these studies and all of them address other avenues through which DDI can lead to conflict and violence. Also, most of them find at least some connection between DDI and conflict. In this respect they parallel much of the general conflict literature which either focuses on DDI or uses DDI as a surrogate for grievances and, accordingly, our arguments regarding that literature also apply to these studies. More importantly for our purposes, this literature provides important insights on the potential role of grievances on conflict behavior by religious minorities.

Akbaba and Tydas (2011) use an updated version of Fox's (2002a, 2004) religious discrimination variable to predict protest and rebellion by ethnoreligious minorities. They base their arguments on the relative deprivation (RD) literature, which we discuss in Chapter 3, and the grievance literatures we discuss earlier in this chapter as well as religious identity. Their central argument follows Gurr's (1993a, 1993b, 2000a) basic model: "religious discrimination leads to the generation of grievances, which in turn encourages ethnoreligious minorities to engage in peaceful and violent opposition against the state" (Akbaba & Tydas, 2011, p. 271). They also argue:

> Restrictions on religion create an antagonistic and divisive atmosphere in which there is lack of trust and tolerance between both sides and a great deal of religious cleavage. Ethnoreligious groups respond to this atmosphere by forming movements of religious defense. Although having a religious identity that is different from the majority group might not be enough to generate violence by itself, we argue that discriminatory policies can act as the triggering mechanism. (Akbaba & Tydas, 2011, pp. 274–275)

They find that discrimination causes more civil war and rebellion but less protest. However, as is the case with Fox's (2002a, 2004) study, the universe of cases is limited to ethnoreligious minorities.

Basedau and Schaefer-Kehnert (2019), studying a sub-Saharan sample, make an RD-based argument but acknowledge that multiple and complex interactions are likely in play. They include grievances—without measuring them directly—within these complex interactions: "Discrimination may take many forms, may or may not result in grievances and these grievances can lead to protest or not and dissent may take various violent or nonviolent forms" (Basedau & Schaefer-Kehnert, 2019, p. 34). They measure DDI using the Religion and State (RAS) data set's governmental religious discrimination (GRD) variable and conflict using the UCDP/PRIO database. They find that GRD may cause armed conflict among theological conflicts. They define theological conflicts as those where the sides "differ over the content of religion. For instance, they can hold different views on the role of religion in the state" (Basedau & Schaefer-Kehnert, 2019, p. 32). In addition, GRD does not significantly influence religious identity conflicts or conflicts in general. Looking closer at four pertinent country cases (the Comoros, the Gambia, Mali, and Mauritania) reveals that discrimination is probably not even a direct driver of "theological" conflicts. In line with Saiya and his collaborators (e.g., Saiya & Manchanda, 2020), high levels of discrimination seem to rather indicate problematic state–religion relations, especially a climate of religious intolerance. When existing ethnic or regional cleavages become mobilized along religious lines through transnational influences and geography, violence emerges. These findings concur with the study by Basedau et al. (2016) on 130 developing countries from 1990 to 2010. Results from logistic regressions show that GRD is not a cause of religious and other conflict. However, the overlap of religious and other identities, religious groups' grievances, and religious leaders' calls for violence are. Specifically, religious determinants vary in their impact according to whether conflicts are religious or not in origin.

Jazayeri (2016, p. 406) uses the EPR data set's DDI variable to measure "the percentage of ethnic and religious population excluded from legitimate political representation" in the Middle East and North Africa. Her theoretical arguments combine the concepts of DDI, grievances, and mobilization. First, she argues that political institutions often "engage in deliberate systematic exclusion of identity groups from political power" (Jazayeri, 2016, p. 403). Second, she argues that "blocked or restricted access to legitimate decision-making authority within the state results in group-level inequalities and grievances" (Jazayeri, 2016, p. 404). Third, she includes a mobilization element: "The aggrieved identity group mobilizes against the state to address intergroup disparities. When deliberate political exclusion is used by the state, inequalities and grievances bring people together in pursuit of a common goal" (Jazayeri, 2016, p. 404). She finds that increased DDI results in increased protest and rebellion.

Muchlinski (2014) also makes a grievance-based argument. He argues that "scholars of civil war have focused on the explanatory power of grievances as a primary causal factor that drives ethnic, religious, and other minority groups to rebel against states." Like Jazayeri (2016), he argues that "political office holders, especially those in weak states with weak civil societies, have institutional incentives to favor coethnics or coreligionists with the distribution of patronage whether in the form of public goods or civil service jobs" (Muchlinski, 2014, p. 688). This results in grievance formation. However, he also argues that "greed, opportunity, and state weakness" (Muchlinski, 2014, p. 5) play an important role. He uses Grim & Finke's (2011) data on societal religious regulation, a DDI variable, and finds that it significantly predicts "the number of people killed due to religious issues in a given country for the year 2008" (Muchlinski, 2014, p. 701), also taken from the Grim and Finke (2011) data.

Nilay Saiya and his collaborators examine the impact of DDI on terrorism in a series of studies. His arguments include a grievance component but focus more on other factors to explain the link between DDI and terror. Saiya's grievance argument is ambivalent. On one hand he acknowledges the classic grievance argument. Restrictions on religious practices "are dangerous because they engender grievances, facilitate collective action and, sometimes, provoke violent backlash" (Saiya & Manchanda, 2020, p. 1786). Similarly, "authoritarian states, which do not allow participation in political decision-making and freedom of expression, increase the likelihood of terrorism in that they leave violence as the only venue by which aggrieved persons can try to change the system" (Saiya & Scime, 2015, p. 489). On the other hand, he argues that resources and mobilization are also necessary for terror (Saiya & Scime, p. 2015). But, more importantly, he focuses on the role of ideas and ideology: "Indeed, political theology—the ideas a religious group holds about political authority—matters a great deal in explaining religious terrorism" (Saiya & Scime, 2015, p. 494).

Saiya focuses on how essential religion can be to the human experience. Saiya (2019a, p. 205) argues that "attempts to repress religion constitute a denial of the very essence of what it means to be human" and therefore are "likely to be interpreted by religious groups and individuals as an affront to their very existence." When discussing how veil prohibitions, which generally target Muslim women, influence terrorism in the West, Saiya and Manchanda (2020, p. 1784) posit that "veil prohibitions simultaneously target the two core identities of Muslim women living in Europe: gender and religion. Both restrictions heighten the likelihood of radicalization and terrorism." For this reason, he argues that religious terror is likely to be more violent than secular terror: "If religion really is such an intrinsic part of the human experience, it stands to reason that its restriction is bound to have especially unfortunate consequences and likely to generate violence in ways that purely secular forms of repression do not" (Saiya, 2015a, p. 372).

While acknowledging that repressing religion can lead to grievances, the theoretical argument focuses on the radicalization of religious ideology. DDI strengthens radicals who thrive when they can convincingly argue that there is an existential threat to their religion. This undermines religious moderates who tend to oppose violence and terror and increases support for extremists who are more likely to support terror. "Often embattled religious communities, perceiving their faith to be under attack, subscribe to a ubiquitous narrative of communal disillusionment, sometimes leading to violence against those perceived to be responsible for their marginalized and suppressed status" (Saiya & Scime, 2015, p. 492).

Saiya and Manchanda (2020) specifically argue that European policies banning Islamic religious practices such as women's head coverings, which are intended to oppose radicalization, do the exact opposite: "In Europe, conservative Muslim practices, such as the donning of traditional Islamic garb, are frequently seen as attempts to promote a radical political ideology of Islamism throughout the continent" (Saiya & Manchanda, 2020, p. 1785). However, in practice, this leads to feelings of isolation and stigmatization, which increase radicalism. Also, suppressing a religion can drive a religious group underground, which usually results in radicalization. It is precisely this type of radicalized group that has "given rise to the most lethal terrorist networks in history" (Saiya & Scime, 2015, p. 493). In contrast, religious freedom undermines extremists and strengthens moderates (Saiya, 2019a).

This radicalization argument is related to the grievances argument but still distinct from it. A grievances argument assumes that those who express the grievances will seek redress for them or to alter the system to one which will not behave in the manner which causes the grievances. The radicalization argument is based on the concept that those who hold a radical ideology seek to make extensive changes in society. Because ideologically committed radicals, religious or otherwise, are unlikely to be willing to compromise on their ideals, they are more likely to use violence to advance them. Fox (2018) argues that this is because radical goals are unlikely to be accepted by the majority of a country's populations, which makes change through normal political processes unlikely. This, combined with an unwillingness to compromise, leaves violence as the only available avenue for change. While the desire of radicals for change can be seen as a form of grievance, it is one driven by ideological aspirations rather than a desire to seek redress for DDI.

RELIGIOUS MINORITIES, MOBILIZATION, PROTEST, CONFLICT   145

Thus, the process is different from that of the classical DDI-grievance model. Yet DDI plays a role because it causes radicalization. Thus, for Saiya, radicalization, rather than grievances, is the primary unmeasured intermediary variable in his studies.

This radicalization argument has important implications for the DDI-grievances-conflict model used in this study. It posits that there is a significant and common cause of grievances that while potentially influenced by DDI, is not itself DDI. It also theorizes a religious cause of conflict that while akin to grievances is not grievances. This further validates our contention that it is both theoretically and empirically important to test both the DDI-grievances and the grievances–conflict relationships. It also suggests potential avenues for future data collection.

Saiya's results consistently find links between DDI and terror using multiple data sets. Saiya and Scime (2015), using the Grim and Finke (2011) and GTD data sets, show that government regulation of religion increases levels of terror among Muslims in the West. Saiya (2019a) uses the RAS GRD variable as well as a RAS variable measuring restrictions on the religious practices and institutions of the religious majority to measure DDI and the GTD data set to measure terror. He finds both variables predict increased terror in Muslim-majority countries. Henne et al. (2020) similarly use the RAS GRD variable to measure DDI and find that it increases terror as measured by the GTD dataset. Saiya and Manchanda (2020) find that veil bans in the West predict more terror attacks, casualties, fatalities, and injuries. Saiya (2015a) using the GTD and ITERATE dataset to measure terror finds that religiously restrictive states (as measured by the RAS dataset) were the targets of the majority of terror incidents because most terror groups originated from religious restrictive states. In fact, "domestic religious terrorism is more closely associated with a country's level of religious liberty rather than its level of democracy" (Saiya, 2015a, p. 373).[2]

All of this is important to our study because it demonstrates the advisability of comparing the impact of DDI and grievances on conflict for at least three interrelated reasons. First, several of these studies, especially those of Nilay Saiya and colleagues, develop a body of theory that links DDI to conflict through avenues other than grievances. Second, multiple studies—though

---

[2] Henne et al. (2020) also test the impact of DDI on terror in Muslim-majority countries. However, their argument focuses on government support for religion and they use the RAS's GRD variable as well as other variables as a measure for support for religion. For this reason we discuss this study in the following section.

146 RELIGIOUS MINORITIES AT RISK

not all—show that DDI significantly predicts religious conflict. Third, all of these studies in their theoretical discussions acknowledge that grievances can cause conflict.

Religious Motivations, Beliefs, Ideology, Issues, and Content

A quickly growing number of studies argue that it is religion itself which causes conflict and violence and, in some manner, test that proposition. They use variables that measure the presence of religious ideologies, motivations, beliefs, content, or issues in a conflict. These studies are important because they are becoming the most popular type of study using non-identity religion variables to theorize and test the relationship between religion and conflict. While some of this theory references grievances, these studies largely posit other mechanisms linking religious factors and conflict. Thus, it is important to assess the mechanisms linking religious ideology and conflict as compared to the mechanisms linking grievances and conflict. We argue that in the case of conflict behavior by religious minorities, grievances is the more appropriate mechanism to study.

Accordingly, in this section we first evaluate how these studies theorize this connection and how this relates to the grievances argument, then discuss the empirical measurements and results. In the following section we examine these types of studies and arguments in comparison to the grievances argument and why we believe the grievances argument is the more appropriate for studies focusing on religious minorities.

Many of these studies argue that religious beliefs, motivations, and ideology can increase conflict. At its most basic level, this argument has it that religious beliefs, motivation, and ideology influence behavior (Fox, 2018). This is not a highly contested proposition but often the devil is in the details.

Within this context, several of these studies focus on one or both of two arguments.[3] The first is Juergensmeyer's (2000) concept of cosmic war. A cosmic war exists when one's religion is seen to be under some form of existential threat. The enemy or target is the source of this threat and is therefore the personification of evil. This makes the enemy deserving of punishment. Under such circumstances, even forms of violence that would otherwise be prohibited by a religion are not only justified but mandated. This cosmic war

---

[3] See, for example, Abrahms & Potter (2015); Karakaya (2016).

is "an all-or-nothing struggle against an enemy one assumes to be determined to destroy. No compromise is deemed possible. The very existence of the opponent is a threat, and until the enemy is either crushed or contained, one's own existence cannot be secure" (Juergensmeyer, 2000, p. 148).

The second is Hassner's (2003, 2009) argument that religious issues, especially disputes over sacred spaces, can be "indivisible." For Hassner, a sacred space is indivisible if it meets three criteria: its value is diminished or lost if it is divided; it cannot be exchanged or substituted with something else; and it would be desecrated by allowing access to the wrong individuals, whether they be those of other faiths or those of insufficient standing within a given faith. It is not possible to compromise over something that is indivisible. Thus, for Juergensmeyer the inability to compromise is due to existential threat but for Hassner it is due to a religious space that cannot be replaced, shared, or ceded.

It is worth noting that both the cosmic war and indivisibility arguments are compatible with the grievances argument. Existential threats can be seen as a form of DDI that would cause grievances. The same is true of intrusions on indivisible sacred spaces. However, few studies of religion and conflict apply these theories in this manner.

Many expand Hassner's argument to highlight that true believers are often unwilling to compromise over not only religious spaces but also over religious issues. For example, Svensson (2007, p. 931) argues that limiting the concept of indivisibility to sacred spaces is too narrow. He argues that the first two elements of Hassner's concept of indivisibility can be applied more broadly:

> If the belligerents' demands are explicitly anchored in a religious tradition, they will perceive the conflicting issues as indivisible, and the conflict will be less likely to be settled through negotiations ... When the belligerents raise conflicting religious positions regarding the state, then the subjective value will be increased. In fact, this means that the issue at stake cannot be divided without a substantial loss of this value. Moreover, once conflict positions explicitly based in religion have been raised, it will lead to the perception that there are no substitutes of equivalent value for the disputed state. The increased subjective value and the lack of substitutes will create a perception of indivisibility, which hinders negotiated agreements. Horse trading with other issues and other typical conflict resolution mechanisms will therefore be less applicable to these types of conflicts. (Svensson, 2007, p. 931)

148 RELIGIOUS MINORITIES AT RISK

Relying on Juergensmeyer (2000) and Fox (2004), he also argues that compromising religious values in favor of secular arguments would be to capitulate to the secular point of view. In fact, "backing down on religiously based positions would imply a break with commonly long-held beliefs, sentiments, and worldviews" (Svensson, 2007, p. 934). This basic argument carries through much of Svensson's subsequent empirical work (Nilsson & Svensson 2020, 2021; Svensson, 2013; Svensson & Harding, 2011).

Henne (2012) gives primacy to the cosmic war argument but includes aspects of the indivisibility argument. He considers religious ideology "the most important factor in a group's level of suicide terrorism" (Henne, 2012, p. 40):

> The belief in the sacred nature of the attacks and desire to demonstrate the validity of their ideology leads to an emphasis on causing as much destruction as possible from the attack. Likewise, the perception of a global struggle and "other-ing" of ethnic kin who do not abide by the group's religious beliefs as enemies can lead to a lack of concern for minimizing local fatalities. (Henne, 2012, p. 43)

While individuals have their own motives, ideology is the dominant factor on the group-level because it "can influence a group's behavior in the absence of individual devotion to its precepts. Ideologies, especially religious ideologies, provide a specific meaning for a group's actions, enabling group cohesion" (Henne, 2012, p. 42). The enemy is defined in religious terms. This "'out group' includes anyone who does not follow the terrorists' particular interpretation of a religion" (Henne, 2012, p. 41). For Henne, grievances are subsidiary to this dynamic. "Even if they are motivated by political grievances, religious terrorist groups base their calculus for success and concerns about public responses on religious standards" (Henne, 2012, p. 43).

Bercovitch and Darouen (2005) argue the opposite—that religious ideological conflicts will be less violent. They argue, drawing on Regan (2000) and Kaufmann (1996) that in ethnic wars "religious or ideological identities are more easily shed and that these conflicts might be more amenable to intervention" (Bercovitch & Darouen, 2005, p. 105) than wars over autonomy and secession.

Several studies acknowledge the role of religious ideology but point out that not all groups that follow a religious ideology engage in conflict and violence. Therefore, some additional factor is needed to differentiate between the violent and nonviolent manifestations of religious ideology.

For example, Asal et al. (2017) focus on the influence of religious organizational characteristics. Many religious organizations offer social services to their membership which helps recruitment and builds capacity. However, for them the key factor is whether a religious organization wants to facilitate change in society: "Organizations that demand fundamental changes in political institutions (as opposed to simply changes in government policies or government leadership) will be more likely to use violence than those that favor incremental changes" (Asal et al., 2017, p. 812). That is, a religious extremist religious organization is one whose goal is "to transform the society to coincide with their religious values or rules set out in a religious text" (Asal et al., 2017, p. 813). They contend that while arguments that religious ideology can motivate violence are compelling, this desire to transform society is what differentiates between religious ideology-driven groups which do and do not use violence.

Toft (2007) focuses on religious outbidding. Drawing on Snyder (2000), she argues that religious "elites attempt to outbid each other to enhance their religious credentials and thereby gain the support they need to counter an immediate threat" (Toft, 2007, p. 103). Thus, religious ideologies are more likely to support violence when religious elites take more extreme positions in order to enhance their religious legitimacy and credibility. Toft's (2007) outbidding argument also includes a mobilization and capacity component positing that insurgents who are successful at this outbidding will attract more manpower and resources. Accordingly religious outbidding also makes it more likely that religious issues will be central to a conflict.

Breslawski and Ives (2019) draw on Toft (2007) and Hassner (2009) but focus on religious competition to explain the link between religion and violence. They argue that while religious ideology plays a role, competition differentiates between violent and nonviolent organizations. They theorize that the use of religious demands increases the group's visibility which increases its likelihood of gaining external support. The more radical the demands, the greater this visibility. Essentially, this is a form of religious outbidding.

Henne et al. (2020) and Saiya (2017a) focus on radicalization. These arguments draw upon and expand the radicalization arguments made in Saiya's (2015a, 2019a; Saiya & Manchanda, 2020; Saiya & Scime, 2015) DDI-based studies. However, they add the element of how extremist religious

150 RELIGIOUS MINORITIES AT RISK

groups in society respond to government religion policy. That is, they accept that religious ideology is a cause of violence and conflict but argue that this occurs when religious groups are radicalized and extremist groups are enabled by governments.

Their arguments focus on Muslim-majority countries but are applicable more widely. They argue that when governments support a majority religion and especially when they restrict minority religions and alternative interpretations of the majority religion, this has negative consequences. Radicals within the majority religion see these government policies as endorsing and enabling their radical interpretations of religious ideology. More importantly this empowerment encourages radicalized nongovernment actors to engage in harassment, discrimination, violence, and terrorism against both religious minorities and members of the majority religion seen as not being sufficiently compliant with the radicalized religious ideology. That is, "when states institutionalize religious favoritism, their beneficiaries may arrive at the reasonable conclusion that the state implicitly approves discrimination, harassment, and even violence against nonprivileged faiths" (Henne et al., 2020, p. 1950).

Saiya (2017a) makes this argument in the context of blasphemy laws. He argues that "laws against religious defamation weaken reform-minded moderate Muslims, silence members of minority faiths and political dissidents, and promote violence and terrorism" (Saiya, 2017a, p. 1088). This is because these laws "serve to coerce religious conformity, silence opposing religious views, and weaken the forces of moderation" (Saiya, 2017a: pp. 1089–1090). In effect they "legalize discrimination against minority religious groups and codify the existing reality of religious persecution in society by affording religious actors the capability to regulate political life to varying extents" (Saiya, 2017a, p. 1090). This also increased radicalism because "where laws against blasphemy exist, radicals do not have their views challenged and critiqued in the marketplace of ideas, so they are not forced to defend them from competing views" Saiya 2017a, p. 1090). This strengthens radicals and weakens moderates.

Some focus more on grievances. For example, Henne (2019, p. 71) combines the grievances and radicalization arguments:

> When governments exert control over religious institutions, they may increase the grievances of the affected communities. Members of a religious community may adopt more extreme views of their government or religion,

RELIGIOUS MINORITIES, MOBILIZATION, PROTEST, CONFLICT   151

in reaction to their inability to completely control their worship. This could lead them to join or support terrorist groups.

A common theme that runs through Asal et al. (2017), Toft (2007), Bresalwski and Ives (2017), Henne (2019), Henne et al. (2020) Saiya (2017a, 2019a), Saiya and Manchanda (2020), and Saiya and Scime (2015) is the greater the changes in society and politics demanded by a religious group or organization, the greater the likelihood of violence. The specific theorized avenues by which these demands become more radical differs across these studies, but they largely agree on the end result.

A large majority of these studies show a statistical link between religion and conflict. Several of these studies, however they are theorized, in practice measure the presence of religious issues or policy demands in a conflict. While the specific criteria for what constitutes a religious issue or policy demand differs across studies, it is arguable that these variables are quite similar to the extent that exchanging coding criteria between studies would be unlikely to cause major changes in the codings or results.

Asal et al. (2017, p. 821) using the MAROB data consider a political organization religious if it had an ideology "derived from religious sources" and sought "sociopolitical change in order to transform societies in congruence with religious precepts." Their study focuses on the Middle East so the majority of the religious organizations included in the study are Islamic. They found that while this variable predicted the organization's willingness to use violence, it was less influential than views on gender exclusion, a more specific element of many interpretations of Islamic doctrine which constitutes a good surrogate for the more radical versions of Islamic ideology.

Breslawski and Ives (2019, p. 618) "define factions as having a religious ideology when factions communicate aims or goals that are characterized by the prioritization of their religion over other religions. That is, religious factions advocate for increased benefits for members of their religion relative to other religions." They use Cunningham et al.'s (2012) dataset of factions that are seeking self-determination in Asia, Africa, and the Middle East. They find that religious (mostly Islamic) factions are more likely to use violence, and the countries with more religious factions experience more violence.

Deitch (2022, p. 9) using the PITF data and religion data collected for her study measures "religious content, which means the conflict includes religious goals or demands, such as the religious state policy or maintaining religious-sacred places." She finds it significantly increases conflict duration

152 RELIGIOUS MINORITIES AT RISK

but not conflict recurrence or whether conflicts are terminated in an agreement or victory.

Svensson (2007, p. 936) using the PRIO data set measures religious "incompatibilities" defined as "explicit aspirations to create a state, or a region within the state, governed by religious laws and legislation, or whether one specific religious tradition should be given a special role." He finds that religious incompatibilities make the peaceful settlement of conflict less likely. Much of his subsequent work uses the same variable, where he finds that religious warring groups rarely make concessions on religious demands (Svensson, 2013; Svensson & Harding, 2011).

Svensson also developed the Religion and Armed Conflict (RELAC) dataset, which uses a "religious issues" variable. This variable looks broadly at the claims and stated aspirations of the warring parties. It also codes, separately, Islamist claims, evangelical claims, secularist claims, and other religious claims. The results show that religious issues are correlated with levels of conflict (Svensson & Nilsson, 2018) and "that transnational Islamist conflicts are less likely to experience negotiations" (Nilsson & Svensson, 2020).

Toft (2007, 2021) using an original dataset, focuses on religious centrality, which "is the degree to which religious belief or practice is a cleavage in the conflict. Religion is central to civil war if the rebels fight over whether the state or a rebel-dominated region will be ruled according to a specific religious tradition" (Toft, 2021, pp. 1611–1612). She finds that religious civil wars are more violent and intractable. They are also less likely to end in a negotiated settlement. Basedau et al. (2022) using the Rebel and Religion dataset, however, find that when specific rebel religious affiliations and rebel-state religious ideological incompatibilities as well as important confounders are taken into account, this lethality effect is entirely reversed. They measure theological claims as "demands to make a certain faith a state religion or to base lawmaking on religion, which follows our basic idea that ideology should refer to an abstract idea of the political order" (Basedau et al., 2022, p. 10). The longer duration of such conflicts is, however, confirmed (see also Svensson & Nilsson, 2018), especially after the end of the Cold War (Basedau et al., 2022).

Some studies diverge from the issue perspective. For example, Henne's (2012, p. 54) measure of religious ideology "is based on the importance of religion in the group's grievances and the means through which a group justifies its actions." He finds that this predicts the number of deaths in suicide terror incidents as measured by the GTD data set.

RELIGIOUS MINORITIES, MOBILIZATION, PROTEST, CONFLICT   153

A series of studies measure government policy including government support for religion, a form of government imposition of a religious ideology on its citizens. Henne (2019) links government religion policies as measured by the RAS data set, especially those that restrict the ordination of minority religious clergy, restrict religious political parties, or enact religious requirements for holding office, to increased levels of terrorism as measured by the GTD dataset. Using the same data but focusing on Muslim-majority countries, Henne et al. (2020) find that the RAS government support for religion variable increases terrorism by Muslim religious terror groups as measured by the GTD dataset. Saiya (2017a) finds that the presence of blasphemy laws in Muslim-majority countries increases terror as measured by the GTD data set.

Other studies provide less elaboration of their coding criteria. For example, Abrahms and Potter (2015) measure "religious motivations" for terror but do not define the term in more detail and find that this variable predicts greater civilian targeting in terror attacks as measured by the MAROB database. Carter et al. (2021) code terrorist groups based on whether they self-identify as having a religious ideology and find that these self-identifying groups are more likely to use suicide terror.

While all of the aforementioned studies found some link between their religion variables and conflict, the literature has produced some studies that find no such link. Bercovitch and Darouen (2005) measure whether religion is the most important issue in an ethnic conflict. They find that in ethnic wars religious conflicts are more likely to be mediated than wars of autonomy or secession. Also, Karakaya (2016) measures two variables, one that simply measures whether a group has a religious ideology and another that measures whether organizations focus on establishing a religious state. Using the MAROB data, she finds that neither of these variables predict the use of violence by ethnoreligious organizations in the Middle East. These two exceptions both focus on ethnic conflict, which indicates that while the overall the results show a strong link between religious motivations, beliefs, ideology, issues, and content on one hand, and conflict and violence on the other, they show more mixed results only for interethnic violence and conflict.

On a more general level, these studies are important to the present study because they demonstrate that religious factors can influence conflict. This suggests that religious grievances are likely to influence conflict. However, as we discuss below, the distinctions between the variables used by these studies and grievances are important.

154 RELIGIOUS MINORITIES AT RISK

Religious Motivations, Beliefs, Ideology, Issues, and Content Versus Grievances

It is important to examine the similarities and differences between religious grievances on one hand and religious motivations, beliefs, ideology, issues, and content on the other hand both in theory and how this manifests in empirical studies. This is because the present study measures and tests religious grievances but not these other factors for both theoretical and empirical reasons. Theoretically, the distinction between these two types of religion variables is important because we maintain that the impact of grievances on religious conflict has been rarely tested and that grievances are the more appropriate variable for studies that focus on religious minorities. Thus, both the overlap and distinctions between these two types of arguments have important implications.

We argue that there are two aspects of overlap between the two. First, religious motivations, issues, and content can include grievances over religious issues or religious DDI but in practice the variables that measure these factors generally include a broader set of phenomena than grievances. Second, religious ideology, belief, and motivations may cause grievances to form. This makes them related but not the same.

To what extent religious issues, for example, include grievances depends on the definition. Henne (2012, p. 54), for example, includes "the importance of religion in the group's grievances and the means through which a group justifies its actions." Thus, grievances are clearly part of his variable but there are other parts which have little to do with grievances. Toft (2007, p. 97) takes a more general approach and looks for cases where "religious belief or practice is either a central or peripheral issue." This could potentially include grievances over restrictions on religious practice but certainly includes a wider range of issues.

Others use definitions that focus more on an ideology-driven agendas. For example, Svensson (2007, p. 936) includes cases where a religious actor expresses "explicit aspirations to create a state, or a region within the state, governed by religious laws and legislation, or whether one specific religious tradition should be given a special role." Similarly, Asal et al. (2017, p. 821) include groups with an ideology "derived from religious sources" and sought "sociopolitical change in order to transform societies in congruence with religious precepts." The religious ideology, motivation, and beliefs described in these definitions arguably do not include grievances. However, upset over

RELIGIOUS MINORITIES, MOBILIZATION, PROTEST, CONFLICT   155

the failure of the state to conform to the religious ideology in question could be construed as a grievance of sorts. Yet this conception grievances would be a consequence of this political agenda, not one that is caused by DDI.

Thus, there is sufficient overlap between grievances on one hand and religious motivations, beliefs, ideology, issues, and content on the other hand to argue that these studies demonstrate the likelihood that religious grievances may influence conflict behavior among religious minorities. However, they are sufficiently different such that it remains important to test the impact of religious grievances using variables which specifically measure this phenomenon. Also, there is a distinction between these studies and the present study that is both theoretically and empirically relevant. This study focuses specifically on religious minorities, and these other studies do not. This is important theoretically because the questions one asks when analyzing the causes of conflict are often dependent upon the types of actors involved. This is important empirically because it is often the case that different questions are operationalized with different variables.

The units of analysis—or actors—in these studies of religious motivations, beliefs, ideology, issues, and content fit into three categories. First, several focus on specific organizations (Asal et al., 2014; Breslawski & Ives, 2019; Karakaya, 2016). While some of these organizations represent minority groups, many of them are political factions within a religious majority group. The common denominator between these organizations is that they are pursuing a political agenda that can potentially be driven by a religious ideology.

Second, several focus on religious conflict (Bercovitch & Darouen, 2005; Basedau et al., 2016; Basedau et al., 2022; Deitch, 2022; Nilsson & Svenson, 2020, 2021; Svensson, 2007; 2013; Svensson & Harding, 2011; Svensson & Nilsson, 2018; Toft, 2007, 2021). In these studies groups are already involved in conflicts in and the variables are differentiating between types of conflict. Thus, examining whether religious issues or ideology are involved is appropriate. Finally, several focus on terrorism (Abrahms & Potter, 2015; Henne, 2012; Saiya, 2017a). Terror is a specific type of conflict tactic, so the variables appropriate to these studies are similar to those of the previous category. While the common denominator for conflicts and terror is violence, in most cases these types of conflicts center on organizations, rebel, and terror groups.

More importantly, all three of these types of studies include opposition from both religious majorities and minorities. Thus, they require

156 RELIGIOUS MINORITIES AT RISK

variables sufficiently general that they can be coded for both majority-based and minority-based organizations. Factors like religious motivations, beliefs, ideology, issues, and content are more appropriate to this task than grievances.

While these types of variables could be applied to a study that focuses on religious minorities, such as the RMAR project, we posit that grievances are more appropriate for at least five interrelated reasons. First, they are specific to the theoretical framework developed for the project, which predicts that DDI will cause grievance which, in turn, will cause conflict. Second, because we also examine other types of grievances, a religious grievance variable constructed similarly to variables for other types of grievances facilitates assessing the comparative impact of these different types of grievances on conflict.

Third, groups representing religious majorities and minorities make different types of political demands. For example, many majority-based religious rebel and terror organizations seek to overthrow the state and replace it with one that is more consistent with their religious views. Extreme examples of this are the Iranian revolution, the Taliban, and the Islamic State. In contrast, religious minorities tend to make different types of demands. These demands largely focus on a state altering its policy to eliminate DDI and redress grievances, though in a small minority of cases they can involve demands for self-determination.

Fourth, the RMAR framework focuses on religious minorities rather than organizations. We posit that grievances are the most appropriate and accurate measure of the religious importance factor in this context. While it is possible to say that an organization expresses an ideology, it is more difficult to assume religious minorities, who are often diverse and represented by diverse organizations, express any particular unified ideology. This is even true of a religious ideology because views on religion as well as religiosity tend to vary among most religious populations. Also, focusing on the presence of religious content or issues in a conflict presumes there is a conflict that conflates this variable with our dependent variables.

In contrast, grievances expressed over DDI are often a unifying factor. As noted earlier in this chapter, critics of grievance theory argue they are ubiquitous. While levels of grievances expressed by group representatives vary from group to group, when such grievances are expressed, they are likely shared by a majority of the group and thus represent group sentiment. They are almost certainly politically relevant.

More importantly, religious grievances are the most common and likely manifestation of religion's importance in a study measuring the conflict behavior of a religious minority as a whole. Religious grievances can be seen as a subset of the more general concepts of religious motivations, beliefs, issues, and content. We posit that using this more specific variable is the best fit to the population we seek to study. That is, because religious motivations, beliefs, issues, and content are most likely to manifest as grievances in conflicts involving religious minorities, grievances are the most appropriate religious phenomenon to measure in this study.

Fifth, the literature surrounding the MAR project recognizes this distinction. The core MAR data set measures ethnic minorities and focuses on grievances rather than issues or ideology (Gurr, 1993a, 1993b, 2000a). In order to address factors such as issues and ideology, the project developed the MAROB data set, which uses organizations that represent ethnic minorities as the unit of analysis (Asal et al., 2014; Asal et al., 2008). That is, to account for issue demands and ideology, the MAR project looked at the subgroup level of analysis. Thus, using the grievances approach when looking at a minority as a whole is consistent with the existing theoretical and empirical literature.

Given this, we draw two conclusions. First, while related to grievances, the empirical measures of religious motivation, beliefs, ideology, issues, and content are distinct from measures of religious grievances. Second, the grievance variables used in this study are the best fit for the phenomena we seek to test both theoretically and empirically.

Other Religion Variables

While the overwhelming majority of variables in cross-national conflict studies measure identity, DDI or religious belief, ideology, motivations, content, or issues, some studies measure other aspects of religion. Ellingsen (2005) finds that conflict is more common in countries with more religious populations. Issacs (2016a) finds that the use of religious rhetoric by religious organizations predicts the use of violence by those organizations.

Two studies look at alternative variables focusing on specific countries. Cao et al. (2018) in a study focusing on China find that the presence of local religious institutions decreases levels of violence. They argue that these institutions decrease grievances in two ways, "first, they provide local public

158 RELIGIOUS MINORITIES AT RISK

goods; second, they provide an 'information bridge' between the local population and the government, allowing for nonviolent management of potential discontent" (Cao et al., 2018, p. 1). Brathwaite and Park (2020) in a study of India found that religious appeals by politicians increased interreligious violence.

Grievance Studies

While many studies include grievances in their theorization of religious conflict, only a few studies of religion and conflict use and test grievance variables. All these studies involve at least one of this book's authors and can be considered precursors to this study. Thus, they constitute important steps in the intellectual history and development of this study.

Fox (2002a, 2004) in a study on the impact of religion on ethnic conflict found that religious grievances increased ethnic rebellion but only among separatist groups. It had no influence on protest. Basedau et al. (2016) found that the overlap of religious and other identities as well as grievances over discrimination and religious calls for violence all cause violence. Finally, Basedau et al. (2017) in a study of religious minorities in Asia, Latin America, the Middle East, and sub-Saharan Africa found no correlation between grievances and violence.

All of these studies were limited in some manner. Fox (2002a, 2004) focused only on ethnoreligious minorities. Basedau et al. (2016) and Basedau et al. (2017) covered a limited geographical area, focusing on developing countries only. They also used a grievance variable more general than the more specific variables used in this study. This is important because this study finds that pathways to conflict are dependent upon the specific type of grievance measured. The lack of specificity of the Basedau et al. (2017) variable is likely the reason it is not correlated with conflict.

All these studies contributed to the present study in how the variables used to test the grievances to conflict proposition are conceived and collected. Specifically, the variable structure and content from Fox (2002a, 2004) was expanded in order to create the RAS data set. Basedau et al. (2016) used the RCDC dataset whose variables provided the basis for large portions on the RMAR variables. Basedau et al. (2017) combined the RAS and RCDC datasets and was the pilot study which helped launch the RMAR data set. In particular, this study concluded that more fine-grained data on the type and intensity of both DDI and grievances as well as organizations is required, especially at the group and not just the country level.

Individual-Level Studies

While our discussion focuses on cross-national studies, given the relatively small number of previous cross-national studies on religion and conflict, it is worthwhile to also briefly review those survey-based studies which examine what religious factors make individuals willing to support political violence. Studies of individual religiosity show mixed results. One found that more religious people are more likely to support violence (Arkian & Ben-Nun Bloom, 2018) while others found no significant correlation (Acevdo & Chaudhary, 2015; Fair & Patel, 2019) or a negative correlation (Adamczyk & LaFree, 2019).

Several more specific religious factors were found to increase support for violence. These include belief in Quranic authoritativeness (Acevdo & Chaudhary, 2015), scriptural literalism (Fair & Patel, 2019), engaging in religious activities outside of worship (Adamczyk & LaFree, 2019), when people frame issues as religious (Canetti et al., 2019), and when people believe that religious leaders should play a greater role in politics (Fair & Shepard, 2006). In addition, communal prayer makes people who belong to combatant groups more likely to support arming political parties but makes people in noncombatant groups more likely to oppose militarization (Hoffman & Nugent, 2017). US evangelicals and fundamentalists are more likely to support militant internationalism (Guth, 2013).

There are some factors that make support for religious violence less likely. Belonging to a religious denomination and identity make people less likely to want to revolt (MaCulloch & Pezzibi, 2007). Also, unsurprisingly, religious leaders who "embrace secularism and are tolerant of other faiths reject religion-based violence" (Basedau & Koos, 2016, p. 770).

Conclusions

The concept that grievances are a cause of mobilization, protest, violence, and conflict has been present in the empirical conflict literature from its early years (e.g., Gurr, 1970), though the first major empirical studies focusing on grievances were not published until Gurr's (1993a, 1993b, 2000a) "Minorities at Risk" argument. Since that point, the grievance argument has been a central yardstick other theories use to establish their credibility, often by claiming these other theories are superior to the grievance argument. Yet empirical tests of the grievance argument are rare and tend to support the theory. Gurr's (1993a, 1993b, 2000a) theory has been heavily criticized, even if some of these critiques are, in our assessment, inaccurate. Also, all studies using Gurr's MAR data focus on ethnic rather than religious conflict.

Other studies use Gurr's MAR dataset and explicitly test the grievance argument for religious grievances (Fox, 2002a, 2004). However, these tests have been limited because the Fox (2002a, 2004) studies were limited to ethnic conflicts. Basedau et al. (2016) and Basedau et al. (2017), which included DDI and grievance variables, are far more basic and limited than those of the present study. They also include fewer religious minorities than the present study. Thus, the present study breaks new empirical ground.

The grievance argument also fits well into the empirical religion and conflict literature for at least two reasons. First, many of these studies theorize DDI or grievances as a part of the religious conflict process. Second, one of the major findings of the religion and conflict literature is that when religious issues are involved in a conflict this tends to increase the levels of conflict. This study accounts for this in the form of our religious grievance variable which measures complaints over restrictions on religious practices. It also adds complaints over political and economic issues allowing an unprecedented comparison between the impact of religious variables and similar nonreligious variables. In addition, unlike the MAR-based studies, the RMAR data set does not suffer from comparable selection bias.

Given this, the hypotheses and results we present in Chapter 5 provide a new and unique look at both the grievance argument and the conflict behavior of religious minorities. Combined with the results in Chapter 3, these findings both confirm the DDI–grievances–conflict argument and that religion can play a central role in domestic conflict. They also demonstrate the nuances of these relationship with an unprecedented level of specificity and detail. All of this, we argue, provides considerable support for our central contention that grievances matter.

5

An Empirical Examination of the Grievances to Mobilization Model

In this chapter we empirically examine the second stage of our two-stage model, whether grievances influence levels of mobilization for conflict. We find that grievances matter in the conflict process. More importantly we find that different types of grievances influence different types of mobilization differently. Specifically, we find that as grievances become more difficult to accommodate, they are more likely to result in violent rather than peaceful mobilization. These finding are important because much of the existing literature either dismisses the relevance of grievances in the conflict process or acknowledges grievances' relevance, but does not include variables measuring grievances on their empirical tests. Thus, this study is among the few that not only demonstrates that grievances matter, but demonstrates how and under what circumstances they matter.

In Chapters 3 and 4, we explored the dominant theories explaining patterns of minority mobilization against the state. Many argue that minority grievances are a key cause of minority mobilization, whether through peaceful or violent means. Yet we find that only a handful of scholars directly measure the extent to which group-level grievances contribute to such mobilization. We also find that most studies rely almost entirely on deprivation, discrimination, and inequality (DDI) measures, and in some cases measures that are surrogates for DDI, asserting that such conditions should contribute to grievance formation, which in turn should be a major motivation for collective mobilization. We consider these approaches to be highly problematic as they assume the presence of group-level grievances rather than seek to measure critical social phenomena, which they theorize to be the key causal mechanism translating DDI into collective mobilization. By failing to measure grievances, they also indirectly strengthen an important critique of the grievance–mobilization model—that because minorities are "almost always" aggrieved, grievance as a "constant cause" cannot explain collective mobilization.

Religious Minorities at Risk. Matthias Basedau, Jonathan Fox, and Ariel Zellman, Oxford University Press.
© Oxford University Press 2023. DOI: 10.1093/oso/9780197693940.003.0005

162 RELIGIOUS MINORITIES AT RISK

As we demonstrate in Chapter 3, DDI does in fact significantly contribute to the expression and intensity of a variety of grievances among religious minorities, the first stage in our two-stage model. In particular, we find that while governmental religious discrimination (GRD) significantly contributes to both political and religious grievances, societal religious discrimination (SRD) primarily contributes to political and economic grievances. We also find that although increased levels of minority political representation gives religious minorities greater voice to express political as well as religious and economic grievances, taking part in government policy-making significantly decreases both the likelihood and intensity of these grievances. We additionally find that improvements in the relative economic status of religious minorities significantly decreases the expression and intensity of economic grievances. These findings illustrate the empirical validity of many underlying assumptions in the grievances to mobilization literature based upon actual observation rather than assumptions of expressed collective grievances.

What remains to be tested in this chapter is the second stage of the model, whether expressed group-level grievances by religious minorities in fact better explain patterns of collective mobilization than previous scholarship, which has relied upon DDI alone as an assumed proxy for subsequent grievances. We find that while some aspects of DDI predict some aspects of mobilization, grievances are much stronger and more consistent predictors of mobilization. We argue that this demonstrates that grievances matter in mobilization and that DDI's primary influence on mobilization is through its influence on grievances. While it is likely DDI has some direct influence on mobilization for conflict in addition to its indirect influence through grievances, we argue that much of the ability of DDI to predict mobilization may be due to aspects of grievances unmeasured by this study. By demonstrating the validity of this proposition, our two-stage model substantially improves upon the empirical accuracy of previous studies and confirms the theoretical intuitions of the grievances to mobilization approach.

We not only find that group-level grievances contribute to mobilization for conflict, we find that the different types of grievances matter. That is, we find that different kinds of grievances contribute to markedly different patterns of mobilization among religious minorities, regarding their choice of nonviolent versus violent means, and in selecting between violent strategies. Especially remarkable is our finding that although political grievances significantly contribute to both nonviolent and violent mobilization, religious minorities primarily seek redress for *religious* grievances using peaceful or only limited violent means. By contrast, economically aggrieved religious minorities are significantly more likely to pursue violent over nonviolent mobilization. In addition, when testing DDI measures in conjunction with grievance, we find grievances to more significantly predict mobilization than DDI. This confirms the two-stage model originally proposed by Gurr (1993a, 1993b, 2000a).

We hypothesize based on these findings that the expected intensity of mobilization by aggrieved religious minorities, from nonviolent protest up to rebellion, is a function of the difficulty states have in redressing the sources of minority grievance. Whereas religious grievances are most easily accommodated, resulting in lower intensity, mostly peaceful political mobilization, political and particularly economic grievances are substantially more challenging, resulting in more intense and often violent mobilization. This proposition is a substantial innovation in a field that has only recently begun to consider the causes of nonviolent and violent mobilization within a unified theoretical framework. To accomplish this, we present a number of statistical tests utilizing the Religious Minorities at Risk (RMAR) data to examine the extent to which grievances contribute to both patterns of nonviolent versus violent mobilization as well as a range of specific violent mobilization types including rioting, organized violence against civilians, and rebellion.

Our results contribute to a nuanced understanding of collective mobilization by aggrieved minorities, complementing and significantly refining both more "traditional" literature on ethnic conflict and the rapidly expanding study of religion and conflict. That is, our findings contribute to the literature in several ways. First, we confirm that the two-stage model of DDI to grievances and grievances to mobilization is an accurate description of conflict processes for minority conflict behavior. Second, we confirm that this model applies to religious minorities. Third, we provide a more detailed description of how different types of grievances can lead to different types of mobilization and conflict behavior. Fourth, we further develop grievance theory, particularly explanations of which types of grievances are more likely to manifest as nonviolent versus violent mobilization.

The remainder of this chapter is organized as follows. First, we briefly discuss the emergent literature integrating the study of nonviolent and violent forms of collective action and offer prospective hypotheses regarding the extent to which different forms of grievance should contribute to said mobilization. Second, we describe in detail the outcomes under analysis, offering basic descriptive statistics examining the relative prevalence of nonviolent and violent religious minority mobilization over our period of study. Third, we explain the variables and data employed in our statistical tests, especially those that did not appear previously in Chapter 3, and outline our modeling strategies and their appropriateness for the present research. In exploring our results, we first examine causes of nonviolent versus violent mobilization by religious minorities and discuss the extent to which they match or challenge existing understandings of the relation between grievances and mobilization. Fourth, we examine how our results vary by particular violent mobilization strategies and their relation to complementary scholarship. Finally, we close with a discussion of the key implications of these findings.

Contributions of Grievance to Nonviolent and Violent Minority Mobilization

In this section, we survey recent efforts to examine the causes of nonviolent and violent collective mobilization within a single theoretical framework. While informed by theoretical intuitions that collective grievance should contribute to mobilization, these approaches remain substantially limited by the near absence of any direct empirical examination of grievances themselves, excepting early work by Gurr (1993a, 1993b, 2000a) with the Minorities at Risk Project (MAR) and more recent scholarship by the authors and their collaborators (Basedau et al., 2016; Basedau et al., 2017; Fox, 2002a, 2004), culminating in this volume.

With the advantage of new RMAR data on specific types and intensities of collective grievances, we generally hypothesize that different kinds of grievances contribute in distinct ways to variably intensive forms of collective mobilization, from peaceful protest to violent rebellion. We further hypothesize that the likelihood of more intense forms of mobilization are linked to states' willingness and ability to accommodate the particular demands that follow from particular grievances. In short order, religious grievances are relatively easy to redress and therefore are associated with lower levels of violence. Political grievances demand more costly reforms and are therefore likely to engender more intense mobilization. Finally, economic grievances are the most difficult and costly to redress, suggesting a much higher likelihood for violent outcomes.

A Unified Theory of Nonviolent and Violent Mobilization?

A reasonably large body of scholarly work, discussed at length in Chapter 4, separately examines the causes of nonviolent and violent collective action. Yet until quite recently, scholars investigating nonviolent collective protest (Collier & Hoeffler, 2002, 2004; Fearon & Laitin, 2003; Hegre & Sambanis, 2006; Kalyvas, 2006) and those interested in violent conflict (della Porta & Diani, 2006; McAdam et al., 1996; McCarthy & Zald, 1977; Schock, 1999) had developed and operated in largely separate theoretical frameworks (Tilly, 1978; Tilly & Tarrow, 2006). With the recent publication of global and regional data sets measuring peaceful as well as violent mobilization, it has become increasingly possible to engage in systematic comparative analysis to identify specific drivers behind the onset of nonviolent and violent conflict (Chenoweth & Lewis, 2013; Salehyan et al., 2012). As these two research strands have become more integrated, multiple studies have shown that factors predicting nonviolent versus violent mobilization differ considerably (Chenoweth & Lewis, 2013; Cunningham, 2013; Regan & Norton, 2005). Nonviolent "resistance" is generally more difficult to predict than more violent forms of collective action, in part due to its lower visibility. Yet Chenoweth and Ulfelder (2017) argue that peaceful mobilization is likely driven more by leaders' agency and determination to overcome adverse circumstances than more general structural factors. White et al. (2015) highlight how groups' particular claims and tactical choices evolve into nonviolent versus violent mobilization.

Recent quantitative studies in particular indicate a number of variables with clearly divergent influences on nonviolent versus violent collective opposition to the state. For example, although group size and internal disunity appear to have little influence on likelihood of nonviolent protest, they each significantly contribute to violence. In turn, prior histories of peaceful mobilization appear to increase the probability of continued or resumed peaceful rather than violent campaigns (Braithwaite, et al., 2015; Cunningham, 2013; Gleditsch & Rivera, 2017; Raleigh, 2014). Intergroup factors including both relations with the state and between competing groups, political and economic discrimination, and state-led repression all appear to contribute

166   RELIGIOUS MINORITIES AT RISK

to both nonviolent and violent mobilization onset (Cunningham, 2013; Pierskalla, 2010; Raleigh, 2014; Regan & Norton, 2005, Shellman et al., 2013). Yet while political exclusion seems to increase the likelihood of both, studies are considerably divided over the significance of this effect (Cunningham, 2013; Regan & Norton, 2005). State-level factors such as regime type and stability also appear to have systematic influences on chosen forms of collective mobilization (Cunningham, 2013; Chenoweth & Ulfelder, 2017; Fearon & Laitin, 1997). For example, more democratic regimes appear to be more likely to experience peaceful protest, but have no consistent effect on armed conflict (Chenoweth & Ulfelder, 2017). Finally, contextual factors including population density, resource lootability, rough terrain, and ethnic and religious fractionalization all appear to increase likelihood of violence but not nonviolent mobilization (Chenoweth & Ulfelder, 2013; Hegre & Sambanis, 2006).

Also as discussed in considerable detail in Chapter 4 and summarized earlier in this chapter, grievances are commonly considered a key cause of minority mobilization against states and other relevant political entities. Yet given the paucity of empirical data to date regarding their actual expression, scholars have substantially relied upon DDI and other measures to proxy these phenomena. A key implication of this absence is as follows. A growing scholarly consensus recognizes that nonviolent and violent collective mobilization may have distinct political, societal, and structural causes. However, the extent to which any particular kind of grievance should lead to nonviolent or violent outcomes remains substantially undertheorized.

Prospective Hypotheses

This aspect of our analysis is therefore primarily exploratory in nature, with the intent that our findings should enable future theorization and testing of our speculative explanations. Based upon our prior survey of the literature and our emergent understandings of the links between DDI and collective expressions of grievance, we offer several prospective hypotheses. First and foremost, we argue that expressed grievances by religious minorities more consistently and comprehensively predict patterns of collective mobilization than DDI measures alone. While DDI certainly contributes to group motivations to express collective grievances, as we have already demonstrated in Chapter 3, this relationship is hardly invariant, with particular constellations of DDI being more consistently associated with different grievances.

The forms that collective mobilization take are in turn substantially and significantly conditioned on the costs that targeted states are likely to incur in attempting to redress or suppress these grievances. This approach follows from the generally accepted understanding that more intense forms of mobilization are strong signaling mechanisms to targeted states. Groups that engage in higher levels of violence are more willing to sacrifice to achieve their desired ends (Hultman, 2017; Kydd & Walter, 2006; Wood & Kathman, 2014). Although the ability of minority groups to engage in more intense forms of mobilization is deeply dependent upon their collective material, organizational, and political capacities, violence is moreover often used to give the impression of greater collective strength (Polo & Gleditsch, 2016; Thomas et al., 2016).

Yet it is also true that states almost always prefer to limit intensely violent outcomes (Straus, 2012). As minority demands escalate, democratic states should be more willing to accommodate (Hultman, 2012; Gleditsch & Ruggeri, 2010). Autocratic states should invest in higher levels of repression and co-optation (Pierskalla, 2009; Sullivan, 2019), although this approach has been demonstrated elsewhere to be considerably less successful given more intense demands (Anisin, 2016; Bell & Murdie, 2018). This generally implies that even if state goals are purely instrumental, that is, to minimize violence and regime instability rather than to achieve more "just" or "equitable" outcomes, protest should be relatively common and rebellion particularly rare, even given high-capacity minority groups, as the former can be more easily managed by states than the latter (also see Klein & Regan, 2018). We therefore also expect that wealthier, more democratic states should be better able to avoid the most intense forms of minority mobilization, regardless of motivation.

That said, some kinds of collective grievance are more easily accommodated than others. From our analyses in Chapter 3, religious grievances are primarily a response to GRD. This suggests that although it may take low levels of mobilization, whether via peaceful protest or rioting, for religious minorities to signal their discontent regarding experiencing discrimination, it should be relatively "cheap" for states to prevent further escalation. In fact, Fox (2020) argues that GRD requires the state to commit resources to maintain GRD. Thus, reducing GRD can, in terms of resources, constitute a net gain for the state. By markedly reducing GRD, a key motivation for conflict should also

168 RELIGIOUS MINORITIES AT RISK

be substantially reduced. As such, although religious grievances should be associated with increasing levels of peaceful mobilization, we expect significantly fewer and less intense instances of violent mobilization by religiously aggrieved minorities. More formally:

H5.1: Increasing expression of religious grievance by religious minorities is significantly associated with higher levels of nonviolent but not violent mobilization.

H5.2: Increasing expression of religious grievance by religious minorities is significantly associated with only low-intensity forms of violent mobilization.

Political grievances, on the other hand, stem from both GRD and SRD, strongly suggesting that religious minorities are aggrieved owing to their perceived mistreatment by state and society at large. Effective redress then likely requires states not only to reduce levels of official discrimination, but to give religious minorities a stronger sense of political control and empowerment or even autonomy facing a hostile majority population. Such political accommodation is certainly more costly to states and should therefore require higher levels of minority resolve to demonstrate its necessity (esp. Cunningham 2013; Regan & Norton, 2005). That said, provision of greater political autonomy or share in policy control is certainly less costly in the long term than rebellion and has been demonstrated in recent work elsewhere to be remarkably common (Bormann & Savun, 2018; Gurr, 2000b; Sambanis et al., 2018). We therefore expect that political grievances should be associated with less rather than more intense forms of violent political mobilization. We formalize these hypotheses as follows:

H5.3: Increasing expression of political grievance by religious minorities is significantly associated with higher levels of both nonviolent and violent mobilization.

H5.4: Increasing expression of political grievances by religious minorities is significantly associated with less intense forms of violent mobilization.

Finally, our models in Chapter 3 suggest that economic grievances are tied not to GRD but rather SRD and relative economic deprivation. But whereas greater policy power reduces the expression and intensity of economic grievances, the meaningful redress of relative economic deprivation often requires much more than political reform or even provision of minority autonomy. Rather, what is often demanded is foundational structural reforms like income redistribution and privileged access to natural resources over "mere" political or societal accommodation (Besançon, 2005; Houle, 2018; Schock, 1996; Solt, 2008). To credibly signal resolve therefore also requires from minorities much more intense forms of collective mobilization than either religious or political grievances. Even when implemented, such policies tend to take time to have a measurable effect. In addition, because such grievances are less likely to be accommodated, they are more likely to escalate into the more violent forms of mobilization. We therefore suspect economic grievances to be associated with both nonviolent and even intensely violent forms of minority mobilization. Our formal hypotheses being as follows:

H5.5: Increasing expression of economic grievance by religious minorities is significantly associated with higher levels of both nonviolent and violent mobilization.

H5.6: Increasing expression of economic grievances by religious minorities is significantly associated with more intense forms of violent mobilization.

Dependent Variables: Nonviolent versus Violent Forms of Collective Mobilization

In the analyses that follow, we measure the likelihood that collective grievances expressed by religious minorities will result in either nonviolent or violent forms of mobilization. We operationalize them as follows:

- *Nonviolent mobilization*: activities organized by members of religious minority groups, without the use of physical violence, in a given year to voice protest. These activities include demonstrations, rallies, strikes, press conferences, campaigns, blockades, or dialogues.
- *Violent mobilization*: activities such as spontaneous riots by members of a minority group, which may or may not include fatalities, organized violence including terrorism conducted by or on behalf of a minority

170 RELIGIOUS MINORITIES AT RISK

group against civilians, and/or armed conflict/rebellion against the state by or on behalf of said minority group.

In instances where a minority is engaged in both nonviolent and violent mobilization in a given year, the codings employed here favor the more extreme action.

Recognizing that our definition for "violent" mobilization is highly sensitive to even minor forms of harm (e.g., intentional property damage), we also offer parallel models measuring mobilization events which either exclude or include at least one fatality. So defined, nonfatal events include 100 percent of annual nonviolent mobilizations and 39 percent of annual violent mobilizations recorded in the RMAR data set. We offer a more detailed summary of minority-level mobilization in Table 5.1. Of all 711 state-level religious minority groups surveyed, a majority (67.8 percent) have neither engaged in nonviolent nor violent forms of mobilization even once during the 2000–2014 period. That said, RMAR records a gradual increase in mobilization over the same period, most pronounced

Table 5.1 Most Intense Mobilization Type by Religious Minority

			2000 to 2014	
	2000	2014	All Years	At Least Once
Any Mobilization				
- # groups mobilized	43	86	922	248
- % groups mobilized	5.67	11.15	8.03	31.52
Nonviolent Mobilization				
- # groups mobilized	9	34	276	174
- % groups mobilized	1.19	4.41	2.40	22.60
Violent Mobilization				
- # groups mobilized	34	52	646	147
- % groups mobilized	4.48	6.74	5.62	19.07
* Violent Nonlethal Mobilization				
- # groups mobilized	12	17	253	114
- % groups mobilized	1.58	2.20	2.20	14.79
* Violent Lethal Mobilization				
- # groups mobilized	22	35	383	88
- % groups mobilized	2.90	4.54	3.33	11.41
# cases	759	771	11,487	771

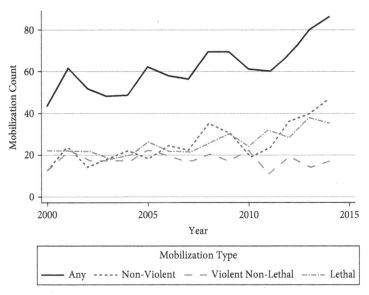

Figure 5.1 Number of Groups Mobilizing by Type, 2000–2014

for nonviolent and lethal violent events. These trends are summarized in Figure 5.1.

Our operationalization of violent mobilization follows familiar precedents in the intrastate conflict literature, differentiating between minority participation in riots, organized violence against civilian targets including terrorism, and antistate or separatist rebellion (see Bodea et al., 2017; Cunningham & Lemke, 2014; Regan & Norton, 2005). These violent phenomena are readily recognized to be of differing intensity and their choice as strategies of minority redress are commonly argued to be a complex product of group capacity, material opportunity, and the permissiveness versus repressiveness of the political regimes within which these groups find themselves. For instance, more democratic regimes are typically theorized to experience higher levels of protest, owing to their greater tolerance for free speech and assembly. Authoritarian states are expected to experience high likelihood of organized violence and rebellion, being more willing to repress lower levels of violence yet leaving aggrieved minorities with strong incentives to seek violent rather than peaceful redress when capable.

Altogether, we find that the number of religious minorities who have engaged in any kind of violent mobilization during our period of study represent a relatively small minority at 5.62 percent of overall year-level potential

172 RELIGIOUS MINORITIES AT RISK

Table 5.2 Violent Mobilization Type by Religious Minority

			2000 to 2014	
	2000	2014	All Years	At Least Once
Any Violent Mobilization				
- # groups mobilized	34	52	646	145
- % groups mobilized	4.48	6.74	5.62	18.83
Riots				
- # groups mobilized	22	31	373	130
- % groups mobilized	2.91	4.03	3.26	16.88
Organized Violence Against Civilians (incl. terrorism)				
- # groups mobilized	16	31	284	57
- % groups mobilized	2.11	4.03	2.48	7.40
Rebellion				
- # groups mobilized	5	7	83	23
- % groups mobilized	0.66	0.91	0.72	2.99
# cases	757	770	11,454	

cases. That said, nearly 19 percent of our surveyed minorities engaged in some form of violent mobilization at least once over the same time period. Of these, 16.88 percent were involved in riots, 7.40 percent in some form of organized violence including terrorism, and only 2.99 percent in rebellion. More detailed descriptions can be found in Table 5.2. While this time period saw a modest increase in the number of groups engaging in some form of violence annually, only organized violence saw a meaningful rise from 2000 to 2014. These trends are summarized in Figure 5.2.

This continues an interesting pattern that emerges from our findings on DDI and grievances in Chapter 2. While 84.82 percent of minorities experience at least some form of DDI in at least one year in the RMAR data, 55.75 percent express grievances. In turn even fewer, 32.2 percent, engaged in some form of mobilization. That said, the critique could be raised that we have operationalized our grievance measurements in such a way that predetermines that particular grievances will be associated with particular forms of mobilizations.

To empirically allay this concern, we offer Tables 5.3 and 5.4 reporting Spearman's Rho rank correlation coefficients, between each of our grievance and grievance intensity measures respectively, and each distinct form of mobilization analyzed in this chapter. Here we find, as expected, highly

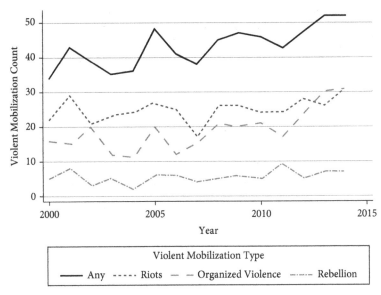

Figure 5.2 Number of Groups Violently Mobilizing in Year, 2000–2014

Table 5.3 Spearman's Rho Rank Correlation Coefficients, Grievances, and Mobilization*

	Grievances			Mobilization Type			
	Political	Religious	Economic	Nonviolent	Rioting	Violence vs. Civilians	Rebellion
Political	1.000						
Religious	0.369	1.000					
Economic	0.311	0.206	1.000				
Nonviolent	0.271	0.198	0.127	1.000			
Rioting	0.177	0.197	0.124	0.152	1.000		
Violence vs. Civilians	0.147	0.100	0.127	0.089	0.208	1.000	
Rebellion	0.092	0.070	0.076	0.081	0.083	0.211	1.000

*All correlations significant with at least 99.9% confidence

174 RELIGIOUS MINORITIES AT RISK

Table 5.4 Spearman's Rho Rank Correlation Coefficients, Grievance Intensities, and Mobilization*

	Grievance Intensities			Mobilization Type			
	Political	Religious	Economic	Nonviolent	Rioting	Violence vs. Civilians	Rebellion
Political	1.000						
Religious	0.371	1.000					
Economic	0.305	0.209	1.000				
Nonviolent	0.297	0.214	0.128	1.000			
Rioting	0.189	0.209	0.125	0.152	1.000		
Violence vs. Civilians	0.155	0.103	0.127	0.089	0.208	1.000	
Rebellion	0.100	0.072	0.077	0.081	0.083	0.211	1.000

*All correlations significant with at least 99.9% confidence

significant correlations but of very low magnitude between all forms of expressed grievance and mobilization. These correlations are most variable for nonviolent mobilization, with nonviolent mobilization being most correlated with political grievances (0.271) and political grievance intensity (0.297) and least correlated with economic grievances (0.127) and economic grievance intensity (0.128). Violent mobilization types are, however, much more consistently correlated across all grievance types and intensities, from about 0.125 to 0.200 for rioting, 0.100 to 0.150 for violence against civilians, and 0.070 to 0.100 for rebellion. In other words, just as DDI does not necessarily lead to group-level grievances, these grievances do not automatically lead to mobilization of any particular type. For this reason, we examine not only the likelihood that grievances lead to mobilization, but also other factors that likely influence these processes.

Independent Variables: Measured Influences on Mobilization and Conflict

Our primary explanatory variables include our annual measures for group-level expression and intensity of political, religious, and economic grievance described in detail in Chapter 2 and employed as dependent variables in Chapter 3. We also include as controls all previous DDI variables including GRD, SRD, and minority policy power, as well as variables we argue more appropriately proxy group capacity, including minority political organization, political representation, and minority population percentage. Owing to significant missing data problems, minority economic status and ethnic overlap variables are included in robustness checks only. To control for potential temporal endogeneity concerns, all grievance variables as well as GRD and SRD are lagged by one year. We do not lag the remainder of our DDI nor minority capacity variables, as they speak directly to minority capacity in the same year in which they are measured (in addition to collective motivation to mobilize). For the same reason, we again also control for and do not lag minority policy power as a significant indicator of religious minority capacity, even as it simultaneously represents an ordinal measure ranging from political deprivation to political empowerment.

Although DDI may still be an indirect cause of collective mobilization, there are reasons to expect that aspects of DDI may still exercise an independent influence apart from engendering grievance. While discrimination, whether GRD or SRD, should increase a group's motivation to mobilize or perhaps rebel, they may also directly influence collective capacity (Akbaba & Taydas, 2011; Ghatak & Prins, 2017; Jenkins & Schock, 2003). Whereas GRD is likely correlated with greater restrictions on minority freedoms to organize, SRD may increase collective determination to bear costs of violent rebellion.

In turn, as argued in Chapter 3 that politically organized groups are more capable of expressing grievances (and indeed are likely to organize as a means to express grievances), so too should this increase minority capacity to mobilize, whether employing nonviolent or violent means (McAdam et al., 2001; Tarrow, 1994). Greater minority political representation is similarly indicative of group capacity and, as previously demonstrated, representation is more consistently a means to express rather than reduce grievance (Alonso & Ruiz-Rufino, 2007; Wilson, 2019). We therefore expect it should also contribute to greater collective mobilization seeking redress in one form or another. Increasing degrees of minority policy power also indicate greater capacity, however given our discussion in Chapter 3 that this measure also proxies lower levels of political deprivation, we expect negative or nonsignificant influence on mobilization (Bloemraad, 2013; Hodžić & Mraović, 2015). Indeed, greater ability to influence political outcomes makes mobilization less necessary. Finally, although improved minority economic status should decrease collective motivation to mobilize, wealthier groups should also have a much greater capacity do so (Cunningham & Lemke, 2014; Koubi & Böhmelt, 2014; Piazza, 2011). Here we expect motivation to trump capacity, although acknowledge our findings are likely limited by considerable missing data on minority economic status.

In addition to DDI and minority capacity variables, we expect certain state-level conditions to be variably permissive or restrictive of religious minority nonviolent versus violent mobilization. For instance, increasing levels of per-capita GDP should indicate a greater capacity by states to suppress rebellion as well as increase the cost of violent mobilization for even relatively deprived minority groups (Jenne et al., 2007). That said, wealthier states should also be more capable of enduring and therefore more tolerant of nonviolent mobilization (Regan & Norton, 2005; Siroky et al., 2020). These divergent paths may also hold for more durable regimes and increasing levels of democracy (Gurr, 1988). The latter expectation may, however, be upset by patterns observed elsewhere that middling democracies (or anocracies) tend to experience greater levels of internal violence owing to the coupling of increasing public freedoms and more limited state capacity to engage in coercive repression (e.g., Akbaba & Taydas, 2011; Bernhard et al., 2017; Cederman et al., 2010; Gleditsch & Ruggeri, 2010; Regan & Norton, 2005).

We also consider additional background variables with potential to influence minority group and state capacity (see, e.g. Hegre & Sambanis, 2006). For instance, both states with larger populations and those with disproportionately larger minority groups should experience greater mobilization, whether nonviolent or violent, as a matter of sheer probability. It may also be that states with larger and more professional military forces are less likely to experience internal violence given both the higher level of state development and increased capacity of the state to suppress violence these indicators suggest. Greater internet access may increase minority capacity for self-organization and mobilization, however it may also indicate higher levels of development wherein protest and violence are less likely. Empirical results on cell phone coverage in Africa suggest that the availability of social media does increase violence (Pierskalla & Hollenbach, 2013). Increasing levels of youth unemployment may be reservoirs for popular discontent and therefore recruitment by aggrieved minorities and lower levels of state capacity to suppress minority mobilization (e.g., Caruso & Gavrilova, 2012). As with grievances in Chapter 3, we consider degree of religious and ethnic similarity between minority and dominant religious groups as factors that likely decrease mobilization likelihood (Basedau et al., 2016; Gubler & Selway, 2011; Reynal-Querol, 2002; Wucherpfennig et al., 2012).

These latter control variables include all previous ones employed in our grievance models in Chapter 3 (logged GDP per capita, V-Dem Polyarchy scores, regime durability, minority population percentage, logged country population, and religious and ethnic overlap variables between minority and majority groups). We also add additional state-level controls. These include the percentage share of armed forces personnel of each country's total labor force, population percentage with internet access, and youth unemployment rate for ages 15–24, drawn from the World Bank's World Development Indicators (World Bank, n.d.). Finally, in models specifically examining violent forms of mobilization, we include a measure for rugged terrain, as the average elevation in each surveyed country (Shaver et al., 2019). This follows the common observation that rebel groups are more likely to operate in territory less accessible to opponent states (Carter et al., 2019).[1]

Methods and Models

As in Chapter 3, we employ correlated random effects models clustered by country or country group to examine in our first set of models how religious minority grievances contribute to nonviolent versus violent mobilization. We again submit that country-group clustered results are those most likely to accurately measure minority group–specific effects, such that country-clustered results are provided for robustness only. This is because country-group clustered models are essentially designed to test the reasonable assumption that group-level factors (see Abadie et al., 2017), such as levels of DDI and collective grievance or even minority population percentage, better predict group-level behaviors than country-level factors, such as GDP per capita, level of democracy, or youth unemployment. Further robustness checks substitute nonlethal versus lethal mobilization outcomes. Given our ordinal dependent variables, we rely upon random effects correlated multinomial logistic regressions to examine how each explanatory variable

---

[1] We expect this variable to be of limited utility given our generalization of "ruggedness" to the state level rather than the particular geographies in which rebels operate. Nonetheless, we include this measure in deference to common practice.

contributes to the likelihood of nonviolent or violent mobilization, versus no mobilization. In our second set of models, we employ this same approach to examine how religious minority grievances contribute to three forms of violent mobilization: riots, organized violence against civilians, and rebellion.

Multinomial logistic regressions have obvious advantages over a variety of other conceivable strategies to analyze these outcomes. Unlike running separate sets of logistic regressions to examine each outcome type, whether nonviolent versus violent or each violent mobilization type, multinomial models allow us to consider each simultaneously without requiring either to be an explicit control condition of the other. Unlike multistep probits, it does not require us to assume that either conditions must temporally precede the other. Finally, unlike an ordered logit model that would assume more violent events to be a more extreme outcome of the same class of events as nonviolent or less violent ones, multinomial models allow us to discern how our explanatory variables distinctly contribute to each distinct outcome.

Models appearing in the main text are found in the following tables. For our nonviolent versus violent mobilization models, Table 5.5 offers four models that include dichotomous measures for the presence/absence of expressed political, religious, and economic grievances by minority group. Model 1a and 2a offer country and country-group clustered results respectively tested against the main explanatory and control variables, whereas Models 1b and 2b offer these tests using a constricted subset of cases for which data is available on ethnic overlap between religious majority and minority groups. Table 5.6 follows this same pattern, but substitutes measures for political, religious, and economic grievance intensity in the place of simple expression of said grievances. Robustness checks offer further constricted versions of these models including our relative economic status variable and parallel models substituting nonlethal versus lethal mobilization outcomes for nonviolent versus violent ones.

For our violent mobilization types models, we provide four tables each with (a) and (b) type models excluding and including respectively our ethnic overlap variable. Table 5.7 includes Models 5a and 5b, which employ country-clustered correlated random effects models examining our dichotomous measures of grievances by minority group. Table 5.8 includes Models 6a and 6b, which employ country-group clusters using these same variables. Table 5.9 includes Models 7a and 7b, examining our grievance intensity variables using country-clustered models, while Table 5.10 includes Models 8a and 8b employing these same variables with country-group clustered models. As in Chapter 3's reporting of odds ratios, we provide full tables of relative risk ratios for each covariate for each model (relative to nonmobilization or nonviolent mobilization as appropriate) in the appendix. We also discuss select relative risk ratios to highlight the substantive significance of key findings.

A summary table of major findings for our country-group clustered models is presented at the end of the chapter in Table 5.11. In all models, we include a year-lagged measure of our dependent variable to control for potential autocorrelation and illustrate the extent to which previous mobilization types do (or do not) influence future mobilization.

Correlates of Nonviolent Mobilization

Regarding the influence of grievance on nonviolent mobilization, found in Tables 5.5 and 5.6, our results are remarkably diverse. We find that although expressions of political grievance are significantly associated with increased likelihood of nonviolent mobilization for both country- and group-clustered results, political grievance intensity is significant only for our country-clustered results. Whereas religious grievances are associated with greater likelihood of nonviolent mobilization for both country- and group-clustered results, we find no significant results when measuring religious grievance intensity. Finally, neither expressions of economic grievance nor increased intensity therein is associated with nonviolent mobilization in any model. Turning to our odds ratios for group-clustered results, groups that express political or religious grievances are about 1.6 times more likely to engage in nonviolent mobilization than those that do not. Therefore, relying upon our group-clustered results as the most reliable test of group-relevant effects, these results suggest that although we may expect some degree of nonviolent action by politically and religiously aggrieved religious minorities, this level of mobilization is no more likely as such grievances increase and not at all likely for economic grievances.

Turning to our DDI measures, we find that GRD is not associated with nonviolent mobilization for our country or group-clustered models. SRD however is associated with greater nonviolent mobilization for country-clustered models only. Whereas minority policy power only decreases nonviolent mobilization in country-clustered models, improved relative economic status appears to correlate with decreased mobilization in robustness checks. Altogether, our findings highlight the nuanced degree to which grievances

180 RELIGIOUS MINORITIES AT RISK

contribute to nonviolent mobilization while demonstrating the insufficiency of DDI to approximate these effects let alone explain their outcome.

Regarding our other minority-level variables, we find that increased minority political organization is associated with significantly higher likelihood of nonviolent mobilization. More formally, groups that are politically organized are about 2.8 or 2 times more likely to engage in nonviolent mobilization, whether relying upon our models that measure grievance expression or grievance intensity respectively. Minority political representation, however, has no such observable effect. Increased minority share of a state's population is significantly associated with increased likelihood of nonviolent mobilization for both country- and group-clustered models. Religious similarity between minority and dominant groups in country-clustered models, as well as in group-clustered models measuring grievance intensity, reveal negative effects on nonviolent mobilization. No such effects are apparent for religious minorities' ethnic distinctiveness from dominant groups.

Finally, for our country-level measures, we find that GDP per capita, security sector size, youth unemployment, and internet access have no obvious influence suggesting little substantive role for economic development in enabling nonviolent mobilization. By contrast, it is interesting to note that while increased levels of democracy correlate with lesser mobilization, regime stability produces the opposite effect. A basic explanation may be that democracies are better able to address minority concerns, lowering the likelihood of grievance. However, more stable governments are also those that can best tolerate protest. Unsurprisingly, larger state populations also correlate with higher likelihood of nonviolent mobilization.

Correlates of Violent versus Nonviolent Mobilization

Examining these same models reveals a somewhat different set of causes for violent mobilization, again in Tables 5.5 and 5.6. Here we find that political grievance expression is significantly associated with violent outcomes for both country and group-clustered results, however grievance intensity is significant for country-clustered models only. By contrast, religious grievance expression is associated with violent outcomes for country-clustered results *only*, while religious grievance intensity is insignificant for both model types. Finally, dichotomously measured economic grievance is strongly associated with violent outcomes, although the intensity variable holds for

Table 5.5 Determinants of Nonviolent and Violent Mobilization, Grievance Types, 2000–2014

Correlated RE Multinomial Logits	(1a)		(1b)		(2a)		(2b)	
	Country-Level Clustering		Country-Level Clustering w/ Ethnic Overlap		Group-Level Clustering		Group-Level Clustering w/ Ethnic Overlap	
	Nonviolent	Violent	Nonviolent	Violent	Nonviolent	Violent	Nonviolent	Violent
Minority Grievance	0.499*	0.325[†]	0.506**	0.323[†]	0.515*	0.401*	0.534*	0.368[†]
- Political (1 year lag)	(0.195)	(0.167)	(0.189)	(0.177)	(0.221)	(0.191)	(0.218)	(0.194)
Minority Grievance	0.455[†]	0.361[†]	0.467[†]	0.367[†]	0.470*	0.132	0.478*	0.097
- Religious (1 year lag)	(0.254)	(0.219)	(0.262)	(0.213)	(0.228)	(0.207)	(0.229)	(0.215)
Minority Grievance	0.071	1.112***	0.161	1.059***	0.333	1.058***	0.407	1.094***
- Economic (1 year lag)	(0.359)	(0.264)	(0.376)	(0.263)	(0.354)	(0.252)	(0.357)	(0.257)
GRD (1 year lag)	0.004	0.009	0.002	0.015	0.028	-0.043	0.041	-0.042
	(0.020)	(0.023)	(0.020)	(0.026)	(0.069)	(0.063)	(0.061)	(0.067)
SRD (1 year lag)	0.048***	0.007	0.042**	0.017	0.022	0.110*	0.019	0.074[†]
	(0.013)	(0.014)	(0.014)	(0.016)	(0.061)	(0.052)	(0.060)	(0.045)
Minority Political	0.763***	1.597***	0.538*	1.430***	1.059***	1.692***	0.823***	1.454***
Organization	(0.231)	(0.260)	(0.237)	(0.300)	(0.248)	(0.383)	(0.254)	(0.412)
Minority	0.057	0.869***	0.168	0.778***	-0.040	1.006***	0.061	0.895***
Representation	(0.206)	(0.217)	(0.199)	(0.205)	(0.234)	(0.256)	(0.236)	(0.250)
Minority	−0.218[†]	−0.237*	−0.204[†]	−0.229[†]	−0.138	−0.247[†]	−0.103	−0.218
Policy Power	(0.120)	(0.115)	(0.115)	(0.129)	(0.154)	(0.141)	(0.149)	(0.145)

(continued)

Table 5.5 Continued

Correlated RE Multinomial Logits	(1a) Country-Level Clustering		(1b) Country-Level Clustering w/ Ethnic Overlap		(2a) Group-Level Clustering		(2b) Group-Level Clustering w/ Ethnic Overlap	
	Nonviolent	Violent	Nonviolent	Violent	Nonviolent	Violent	Nonviolent	Violent
Log GDP/capita	0.210	−0.280*	0.220	−0.295*	0.179	−0.489**	0.167	−0.530**
	(0.150)	(0.141)	(0.152)	(0.138)	(0.136)	(0.173)	(0.136)	(0.170)
Polyarchy Score	−1.441†	−1.670*	−1.576†	−1.589*	−1.264*	−1.167	−1.473*	−0.904
(V-Dem)	(0.816)	(0.762)	(0.827)	(0.765)	(0.584)	(0.737)	(0.600)	(0.765)
Regime Durability	0.010**	0.006	0.010***	0.004	0.010**	0.005	0.010**	0.004
	(0.003)	(0.005)	(0.003)	(0.005)	(0.004)	(0.006)	(0.004)	(0.006)
Security Sector %	0.043	0.064	0.030	0.056	0.043	0.117†	0.016	0.097
of Labor Force	(0.066)	(0.048)	(0.067)	(0.048)	(0.082)	(0.062)	(0.082)	(0.066)
Youth	−0.002	0.014	0.001	0.013	−0.009	0.016	−0.004	0.014
Unemployment %	(0.012)	(0.010)	(0.011)	(0.010)	(0.013)	(0.011)	(0.012)	(0.011)
Internet Use %	0.007	0.011	0.005	0.010	0.010	0.015†	0.008	0.015†
	(0.007)	(0.007)	(0.007)	(0.007)	(0.008)	(0.008)	(0.008)	(0.009)
Minority Population	0.025***	0.054***	0.026**	0.057***	0.031***	0.086***	0.031**	0.089***
%	(0.008)	(0.009)	(0.008)	(0.011)	(0.010)	(0.014)	(0.010)	(0.017)
Log Country	0.375***	0.499***	0.371***	0.532***	0.370***	0.584***	0.366***	0.585***
Population	(0.075)	(0.092)	(0.077)	(0.102)	(0.070)	(0.098)	(0.071)	(0.102)
Religious Similarity	−0.461†	−0.103	−0.628†	0.127	−0.308	−0.400	−0.370	−0.217
to Majority	(0.280)	(0.250)	(0.363)	(0.294)	(0.248)	(0.310)	(0.256)	(0.344)

	(1)	(2)	(3)	(4)	(5)	(6)	(7)	(8)
Distinct Ethnicity vs. Majority			−0.087	0.440*			0.046	0.556*
			(0.173)	(0.185)			(0.139)	(0.220)
Mean GRD Country Level	−0.058†	−0.082*	−0.056	−0.107*				
	(0.035)	(0.035)	(0.037)	(0.042)				
Mean SRD Country Level	0.056	0.102*	0.060	0.094*				
	(0.037)	(0.040)	(0.040)	(0.042)				
Mean GRD Group Level					−0.062	0.000	−0.078	−0.008
					(0.073)	(0.068)	(0.066)	(0.073)
Mean SRD Group Level					0.059	−0.033	0.060	0.009
					(0.065)	(0.060)	(0.065)	(0.054)
Mobilization Type Year Lagged Control	0.216	1.150***	0.205	1.138***	0.025	0.588***	0.000	0.601***
	(0.140)	(0.112)	(0.131)	(0.110)	(0.166)	(0.111)	(0.164)	(0.113)
Constant	−12.041***	−11.461***	−11.652***	−12.096***	−12.366***	−12.647***	−11.832***	−12.679***
	(1.512)	(2.044)	(1.562)	(2.226)	(1.450)	(2.275)	(1.490)	(2.362)
Observations	8,168		6,691		8,168		6,691	
Year Effects	Included		Included		Included		Included	
Clustering	Country		Country		Country Group		Country Group	
Correlated Intercepts	No		No		No		Yes†	

Robust standard errors are in parentheses

*** $p < 0.001$, ** $p < 0.01$, * $p < 0.05$, † $p < 0.10$

Table 5.6 Determinants of Nonviolent and Violent Mobilization, Grievance Intensity Types, 2000–2014

Correlated RE Multinomial Logits	(3a) Country-Level Clustering		(3b) Country-Level Clustering w/ Ethnic Overlap		(4a) Group-Level Clustering		(4b) Group-Level Clustering w/ Ethnic Overlap	
	Nonviolent	Violent	Nonviolent	Violent	Nonviolent	Violent	Nonviolent	Violent
Minority Grievance	0.165*	0.131	0.171*	0.158[†]	−0.009	0.087	0.000	0.089
intensity, Pol, year lag	(0.071)	(0.083)	(0.068)	(0.093)	(0.092)	(0.092)	(0.091)	(0.095)
Minority Grievance	0.109	0.137	0.110	0.113	−0.033	−0.136	−0.034	−0.165
intensity, Rel, year lag	(0.134)	(0.101)	(0.140)	(0.100)	(0.121)	(0.100)	(0.125)	(0.104)
Minority Grievance	0.024	0.468***	0.083	0.486***	0.081	0.206	0.169	0.301*
intensity, Econ year lag	(0.176)	(0.121)	(0.184)	(0.119)	(0.192)	(0.132)	(0.199)	(0.137)
GRD (1 year lag)	0.012	0.014	0.011	0.020	0.004	−0.037	0.007	−0.049
	(0.020)	(0.023)	(0.019)	(0.026)	(0.049)	(0.063)	(0.045)	(0.065)
SRD (1 year lag)	0.054***	0.011	0.046**	0.020	0.020	0.093[†]	0.019	0.059
	(0.014)	(0.014)	(0.015)	(0.016)	(0.055)	(0.051)	(0.053)	(0.043)
Minority Political	0.766***	1.626***	0.551*	1.462***	0.657**	1.259***	0.450*	0.994*
Organization	(0.227)	(0.265)	(0.231)	(0.305)	(0.220)	(0.371)	(0.225)	(0.395)
Minority	0.071	0.866***	0.190	0.775***	-0.257	0.911***	-0.133	0.834***
Representation	(0.193)	(0.211)	(0.187)	(0.203)	(0.214)	(0.241)	(0.212)	(0.236)
Minority	−0.197[†]	−0.259*	−0.183[†]	−0.245[†]	−0.174	−0.299*	−0.144	−0.278*
Policy Power	(0.113)	(0.115)	(0.110)	(0.128)	(0.142)	(0.139)	(0.137)	(0.140)

Log GDP/capita	0.181	−0.343*	0.189	−0.350**	0.173	−0.552***	0.174	−0.559***
	(0.126)	(0.137)	(0.130)	(0.136)	(0.132)	(0.173)	(0.129)	(0.170)
Polyarchy Score	−1.289†	−1.365†	−1.425*	−1.291†	−1.130*	−0.935	−1.348*	−0.787
(V-Dem)	(0.674)	(0.746)	(0.690)	(0.750)	(0.575)	(0.721)	(0.578)	(0.746)
Regime Durability	0.006*	0.003	0.006*	0.003	0.008*	−0.002	0.009*	−0.001
	(0.003)	(0.005)	(0.003)	(0.005)	(0.004)	(0.006)	(0.004)	(0.006)
Security Sector %	0.002	0.064	−0.010	0.059	0.037	0.107	0.019	0.087
of Labor Force	(0.046)	(0.049)	(0.047)	(0.050)	(0.083)	(0.074)	(0.081)	(0.078)
Youth	−0.009	0.017†	−0.006	0.016	−0.019	0.013	−0.013	0.011
Unemployment %	(0.012)	(0.010)	(0.011)	(0.010)	(0.012)	(0.011)	(0.011)	(0.011)
Internet Use %	0.005	0.011	0.004	0.010	0.009	0.016†	0.006	0.014
	(0.006)	(0.007)	(0.007)	(0.007)	(0.008)	(0.009)	(0.008)	(0.009)
Minority Population	0.024***	0.054***	0.026***	0.057***	0.018*	0.070***	0.019*	0.072***
%	(0.007)	(0.009)	(0.007)	(0.011)	(0.008)	(0.014)	(0.008)	(0.016)
Log Country	0.281***	0.493***	0.275***	0.534***	0.293***	0.535***	0.285***	0.515***
Population	(0.073)	(0.095)	(0.077)	(0.108)	(0.065)	(0.096)	(0.066)	(0.097)
Religious Similarity	−0.487†	−0.101	−0.718†	0.136	−0.394†	−0.459	−0.463†	−0.307
to Majority	(0.292)	(0.253)	(0.374)	(0.297)	(0.240)	(0.311)	(0.251)	(0.329)
Distinct Ethnicity			−0.156	0.426*			−0.025	0.356†
vs. Majority			(0.164)	(0.180)			(0.133)	(0.208)
Mean Pol grievance	1.705**	−0.295	1.670**	−0.429				
Intensity—Country	(0.559)	(0.598)	(0.561)	(0.642)				

(*continued*)

Table 5.6 Continued

Correlated RE Multinomial Logits	(3a) Country-Level Clustering		(3b) Country-Level Clustering w/ Ethnic Overlap		(4a) Group-Level Clustering		(4b) Group-Level Clustering w/ Ethnic Overlap	
	Nonviolent	Violent	Nonviolent	Violent	Nonviolent	Violent	Nonviolent	Violent
Mean Rel grievance Intensity—Country	0.158 (0.383)	0.222 (0.476)	0.225 (0.367)	0.218 (0.524)				
Mean Econ grievance Intensity—Country	1.608[†] (0.965)	2.503[†] (1.311)	1.433 (0.973)	2.096 (1.365)				
Mean GRD Country Level	−0.058[†] (0.032)	−0.077* (0.033)	−0.057[†] (0.033)	−0.100* (0.041)				
Mean SRD Country Level	−0.069[†] (0.037)	0.072[†] (0.041)	−0.058 (0.039)	0.072 (0.045)				
Mean Pol grievance Intensity—Group					1.340*** (0.219)	0.349 (0.440)	1.331*** (0.210)	0.436 (0.456)
Mean Rel grievance Intensity—Group					0.863*** (0.210)	1.295*** (0.310)	0.842*** (0.205)	1.314*** (0.315)
Mean Econ grievance Intensity—Group					−0.185 (0.558)	1.910** (0.621)	−0.157 (0.536)	1.731** (0.639)
Mean GRD Group Level					−0.048 (0.055)	−0.017 (0.068)	−0.047 (0.050)	−0.003 (0.071)
Mean SRD Group Level					−0.004 (0.060)	−0.067 (0.062)	−0.007 (0.059)	−0.037 (0.057)

Mobilization Type	0.219	1.127***	0.212	1.111***	0.085	0.614***	0.075	0.636***
Year Lagged Control	(0.152)	(0.115)	(0.141)	(0.112)	(0.174)	(0.118)	(0.174)	(0.122)
Constant	−10.258***	−11.072***	−9.763***	−11.868***	−10.649***	−11.069***	−10.128***	−10.756***
	(1.393)	(2.032)	(1.470)	(2.253)	(1.427)	(2.098)	(1.470)	(2.177)
Observations	8,168		6,691		8,168		6,691	
Year Effects	Included		Included		Included		Included	
Clustering	Country		Country		Country Group		Country Group	
Correlated Intercepts	No		No		No		No	

Robust standard errors are in parentheses

*** $p < 0.001$, ** $p < 0.01$, * $p < 0.05$, † $p < 0.10$

188   RELIGIOUS MINORITIES AT RISK

country-clustered results alone. Examined in terms of relative risk ratios for group-clustered models, politically aggrieved minorities are about 1.5 times more likely to violently mobilize whereas economically aggrieved minorities are nearly 3 times more likely to violently mobilize than nonaggrieved groups.

So, in contrast with our nonviolent mobilization results, whereas religious grievances are seemingly irrelevant for violent outcomes, both political and economic grievances strongly are. These results are almost exactly replicated in robustness checks for nonlethal versus lethal outcomes, paralleling our nonviolent versus violent main models. Altogether, our results suggest that although aggrieved religious minorities certainly do organize violently, such violent mobilization may have relatively little to do with religious grievances, even if religiously motivated armed groups frame their agendas as such (see Basedau et al., 2022).

This does not imply, however, that treatment of religious minorities via DDI exercises no meaningful effects. While we find no significant influence for GRD, we do find that SRD independently contributes to violent mobilization in group-clustered models with dichotomous grievance indicators. That this effect weakens when accounting for grievance intensity confirms our intuition that SRD's influence on mobilization is more likely motivational rather than capacity oriented. Minority policy power remains weakly negatively associated with violent mobilization for country- and group-clustered models, while robustness checks confirm that improved relative economic status are strongly associated with decreased propensity for violent mobilization.

Regarding our remaining group-level variables, it is highly interesting that both minority political organization and political representation are strongly and significantly associated with violent outcomes in all models. This again suggests representation indeed captures group capacity more than motivation in our mobilization models. Likewise, larger religious minority groups are also more likely to engage in violent mobilization. Ethnic distinctiveness, although only available in a smaller sample, appears to increase violent mobilization in country-clustered models, partially confirming findings on armed conflict elsewhere (Basedau et al., 2016; Selway, 2011). All these results are replicated in our lethality models.

In terms of our country-level controls, we find no significant effects for regime durability for either country- or group-clustered tests. Diminishing levels of democracy and higher levels of youth unemployment appear correlated with violent mobilization, but only for country-clustered models.

AN EMPIRICAL EXAMINATION 189

Higher percentage employment in the security sector and greater internet access weakly correlate with higher likelihood of violent mobilization, but only for group-clustered models. The former finding clashes with suggestions elsewhere that states with larger and more professional military forces should experience less internal violence given their higher levels of development and capacity to suppress violence. Yet larger military forces may also indicate more repressive states, which may itself encourage minority violence. Finally, while increasing GDP per capita strongly predict lower likelihood of violent mobilization, confirming common understandings that wealthier states experience less minority violence, larger state populations predict greater violence likelihood. Major effects from these models examining nonviolent versus violent mobilization are summarized in Figure 5.3.

The contrasting experiences of Jewish and Muslim minorities in Canada offers a particularly salient example of how different configurations of grievances contribute to nonviolent versus violent mobilization within the same country. There we observe almost yearly examples of peaceful protest

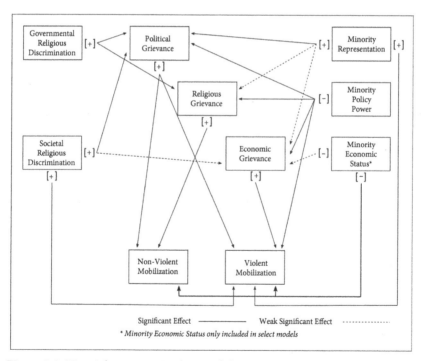

Figure 5.3 Nonviolent versus Violent Mobilization, Summary of Significant Effects

190 RELIGIOUS MINORITIES AT RISK

by Jews yet both peaceful and low-intensity violent mobilization by Muslims. What can account for these differences?

Regarding minority-specific capacity variables, Jews and Muslims represent on average 1 percent and 2.5 percent, respectively, of the population from 2000 to 2014. Both groups were also consistently politically organized and represented during this period. In terms of DDI, neither group experienced any degree of GRD while Canadian Jews actually experienced significantly higher levels of SRD on average than Canadian Muslims (~10 versus ~7), although both experienced significantly higher SRD than the Canadian average (~2.5). Muslims, however, were not observed to have been explicitly included in political decision-making at the local nor national level, whereas Jews consistently were. A more meaningful contrast arises in relative socioeconomic status, with Jews being collectively wealthier and Muslims collectively poorer than the average Canadian.

As we have consistently argued, however, while increasing levels of DDI certainly predict higher levels of grievance, this relationship is not invariant. Indeed, both Muslims and Jews, despite the latter's lower levels of explicit inclusion in the policy-making process, consistently expressed grievances at similar average intensities (2.2 for Muslims versus 2.6 for Jews). So, too, although Jewish minorities experienced "objectively" higher levels of SRD, Muslims expressed more frequently and more intense religious grievances than Jews (1.67 versus 0.8). Finally, while neither group consistently expressed economic grievances, these tended to be more intense for Muslims than Jews (0.8 versus 0.2).

For both groups, the almost yearly incidence of nonviolent mobilization is certainly consistent for the observed levels of political and religious grievance, whereas the markedly higher incidence of violent mobilization by Canadian Muslims is correlated with lower relative socioeconomic status, increased levels of economic grievance, and de facto exclusion from government policy-making, at least at higher levels during the period under investigation. These findings closely mirror Huber and Basedau's (2018) analysis. Based upon an earlier version of the RMAR data, they argue that the patterns observed here are motivated by a combined internal and external motivation structure. While Muslims' "value-based incompatibilities with liberal Canadian society" and "imported radicalization" certainly contribute to greater likelihood of violence, their "subjectively disappointing integration status" magnifies these discontents and grievances, leading to a substantially higher likelihood to rely upon violent forms of collective mobilization (Huber & Basedau, 2018, p. 16).

Correlates of Varieties of Violent Mobilization

These analyses show that grievances influence both violent and nonviolent mobilization among religious minorities. However, the types of grievances that influence nonviolent and violent mobilization differ. In short order, our findings are as follows:

- *Political grievances* appear to predict both nonviolent and violent actions.
- *Religious grievances* only lead to nonviolent mobilization.
- *Economic grievances* appear only to generate violent outcomes.
- *Minority relative economic deprivation, minority organization,* and *minority population share* are strongly and consistently related to both nonviolent and violent mobilization, whereas increased minority policy power appears to somewhat diminish the likelihood of violent mobilization.
- *SRD* is associated with violent outcomes even when controlling for expressions of minority grievance.

Given our rather broad definition of violent mobilization however, these results offer an altogether incomplete picture of when and why religious minorities turn to violence. Whereas participation in a riot is certainly a more extreme action than a peaceful protest, riots are themselves fairly commonplace when compared against terrorism against civilians or outright rebellion. The following analyses, drawn from results which appear in Tables 5.7, 5.8, 5.9, and 5.10, are therefore critical to understand to what extent collective grievances drive spontaneous, or at least unorganized, mayhem versus concerted collective actions intended to cause mass casualties in service of political, religious, and/or economic objectives.

Riots and Other Forms of Spontaneous Violence

As the least intense form of collective violence we measure, we find that nearly every form of grievance significantly contributes in some manner to the likelihood of riots by religious minorities targeting state and social institutions (ostensibly controlled by the religious majority). Both expression and increasing intensity of political grievances are linked to riots—or

Table 5.7 Determinants of Violent Mobilization Types, Grievance Types, 2000–2014, Country-Clustered Models

	(5a)			(5b)		
	Correlated RE Multinomial Logit			**Correlated RE Multinomial Logit**		
	(a) Rioting	**(b) Violence v. Civilians**	**(c) Rebellion**	**(a) Rioting**	**(b) Violence v. Civilians**	**(c) Rebellion**
Minority Grievance	0.516**	0.657*	−0.963*	0.489*	0.628*	−1.332**
- Political (1 year lag)	(0.181)	(0.286)	(0.472)	(0.192)	(0.303)	(0.517)
Minority Grievance	0.657**	0.020	0.787*	0.634**	−0.051	0.677[†]
- Religious (1 year lag)	(0.223)	(0.321)	(0.352)	(0.212)	(0.323)	(0.367)
Minority Grievance	0.701*	1.803***	1.295[†]	0.551[†]	1.748***	1.709**
- Economic (1 year lag)	(0.277)	(0.465)	(0.706)	(0.285)	(0.464)	(0.645)
GRD (1 year lag)	0.018	−0.001	−0.057	0.038	0.003	−0.098[†]
	(0.028)	(0.041)	(0.041)	(0.031)	(0.045)	(0.052)
SRD (1 year lag)	0.022	−0.020	0.024	0.030	−0.001	0.064
	(0.020)	(0.037)	(0.049)	(0.023)	(0.034)	(0.062)
Minority Political	1.053***	3.948***	1.520[†]	0.746*	3.475***	1.411[†]
Organization	(0.323)	(0.861)	(0.828)	(0.355)	(0.778)	(0.824)
Minority	0.620*	1.168**	1.447**	0.587*	0.983**	1.233**
Representation	(0.276)	(0.386)	(0.489)	(0.271)	(0.345)	(0.443)
Minority	−0.067	−0.169	−0.361	−0.043	−0.129	−0.420
Policy Power	(0.102)	(0.215)	(0.267)	(0.116)	(0.198)	(0.294)
Log GDP/capita	−0.335[†]	−0.031	−0.752*	−0.322[†]	−0.057	−0.820*
	(0.175)	(0.319)	(0.362)	(0.165)	(0.323)	(0.355)

Polyarchy Score	−0.893	−0.702	−1.711	−0.821	−0.338	−2.051
(V-Dem)	(0.884)	(1.920)	(1.616)	(0.865)	(1.813)	(1.494)
Regime Durability	0.002	−0.004	0.011	−0.004	−0.004	0.017
	(0.005)	(0.013)	(0.016)	(0.005)	(0.013)	(0.017)
Security Sector %	−0.026	0.061	0.187**	−0.026	0.057	0.163*
of Labor Force	(0.081)	(0.098)	(0.069)	(0.080)	(0.089)	(0.075)
Youth	0.002	−0.007	0.027	0.000	−0.005	0.024
Unemployment %	(0.013)	(0.024)	(0.021)	(0.013)	(0.022)	(0.022)
Internet Use %	0.015*	0.006	0.018	0.014†	0.007	0.014
	(0.007)	(0.014)	(0.017)	(0.008)	(0.014)	(0.018)
Minority Population	0.037***	0.068**	0.090***	0.042***	0.076**	0.088***
%	(0.010)	(0.025)	(0.018)	(0.011)	(0.026)	(0.022)
Log Country	0.329***	1.162***	0.805***	0.379***	1.103***	0.941***
Population	(0.102)	(0.270)	(0.211)	(0.106)	(0.263)	(0.241)
Religious Similarity	−0.279	0.792	0.005	−0.178	1.179*	0.707
to Majority	(0.300)	(0.483)	(0.552)	(0.380)	(0.486)	(0.734)
Distinct Ethnicity				0.382*	0.542†	1.027*
vs. Majority				(0.163)	(0.326)	(0.424)
Rough Terrain	−0.002	−0.007†	0.004	−0.001	−0.006	0.002
(avg elevation)	(0.002)	(0.004)	(0.003)	(0.001)	(0.004)	(0.003)
Mean GRD	−0.053	−0.136*	0.014	−0.118*	−0.112	0.046
Country Level	(0.044)	(0.066)	(0.101)	(0.050)	(0.076)	(0.111)

(*continued*)

Table 5.7 Continued

	(5a)			(5b)		
	Correlated RE Multinomial Logit			**Correlated RE Multinomial Logit**		
	(a) Rioting	**(b) Violence v. Civilians**	**(c) Rebellion**	**(a) Rioting**	**(b) Violence v. Civilians**	**(c) Rebellion**
Mean SRD	0.079	0.199*	−0.265*	0.082	0.139	−0.410**
Country Level	(0.051)	(0.099)	(0.121)	(0.055)	(0.095)	(0.160)
Mobilization Type	0.924***	1.571***	1.778***	0.899***	1.546***	1.846***
Year Lagged Control	(0.185)	(0.225)	(0.287)	(0.181)	(0.231)	(0.289)
Constant	−8.229***	−29.202***	−17.271***	−9.130***	−28.412***	−19.442***
	(2.194)	(5.763)	(4.793)	(2.151)	(5.674)	(5.205)
Observations		8,119			6,642	
Year Effects		Included			Included	
Clustering		Country			Country	
Correlated Intercepts	(a)–(b)	(a)–(c)	(b)–(c)	(a)–(b)[†]	(a)–(c)	(b)–(c)[†]

Robust standard errors are in parentheses

*** $p < 0.001$, ** $p < 0.01$, * $p < 0.05$, [†] $p < 0.10$

Table 5.8 Determinants of Violent Mobilization Types, Grievance Types, 2000–2014, Country-Group Clustered Models

	(6a)			(6b)		
	Correlated RE Multinomial Logit			Correlated RE Multinomial Logit		
	(a) Rioting	(b) Violence v. Civilians	(c) Rebellion	(a) Rioting	(b) Violence v. Civilians	(c) Rebellion
Minority Grievance	0.633***	0.699*	−1.026[†]	0.618**	0.648*	−1.386*
- Political (1 year lag)	(0.199)	(0.311)	(0.544)	(0.201)	(0.309)	(0.562)
Minority Grievance	0.438*	−0.499	−0.166	0.358[†]	−0.518	−0.080
- Religious (1 year lag)	(0.217)	(0.332)	(0.513)	(0.218)	(0.335)	(0.523)
Minority Grievance	0.553*	1.934***	1.263[†]	0.441[†]	2.037***	1.834***
- Economic (1 year lag)	(0.256)	(0.545)	(0.657)	(0.250)	(0.550)	(0.533)
GRD (1 year lag)	−0.149[†]	−0.218	0.353*	−0.125	−0.201	0.355[†]
	(0.083)	(0.151)	(0.180)	(0.085)	(0.152)	(0.187)
SRD (1 year lag)	0.152*	0.093	0.128	0.121*	0.078	0.117
	(0.065)	(0.058)	(0.131)	(0.057)	(0.055)	(0.156)
Minority Political	1.175***	4.206***	1.413	0.949**	3.498**	1.196
Organization	(0.313)	(1.110)	(1.631)	(0.335)	(1.112)	(1.581)
Minority	0.803**	1.980***	2.546**	0.740**	1.697***	1.951**
Representation	(0.264)	(0.391)	(0.854)	(0.261)	(0.367)	(0.721)
Minority	−0.099	−0.166	−0.445	−0.082	−0.108	−0.397
Policy Power	(0.138)	(0.295)	(0.339)	(0.141)	(0.291)	(0.373)

(*continued*)

Table 5.8 Continued

	(6a)			(6b)		
	Correlated RE Multinomial Logit			Correlated RE Multinomial Logit		
	(a) Rioting	(b) Violence v. Civilians	(c) Rebellion	(a) Rioting	(b) Violence v. Civilians	(c) Rebellion
Log GDP/capita	−0.437*	−0.339	−1.469*	−0.469**	−0.404	−1.594*
	(0.182)	(0.388)	(0.642)	(0.176)	(0.396)	(0.637)
Polyarchy Score	−0.476	−0.412	−3.956*	−0.050	−0.034	−3.792*
(V-Dem)	(0.767)	(1.575)	(2.012)	(0.799)	(1.639)	(1.906)
Regime Durability	−0.001	−0.003	0.032	−0.004	−0.003	0.032
	(0.005)	(0.013)	(0.029)	(0.005)	(0.013)	(0.027)
Security Sector %	−0.023	0.192	0.351*	−0.032	0.132	0.278
of Labor Force	(0.077)	(0.145)	(0.168)	(0.081)	(0.152)	(0.171)
Youth	−0.001	−0.002	0.066†	−0.007	0.002	0.052
Unemployment %	(0.013)	(0.026)	(0.039)	(0.013)	(0.026)	(0.036)
Internet Use %	0.016†	0.010	0.030	0.015†	0.010	0.028
	(0.008)	(0.017)	(0.027)	(0.008)	(0.016)	(0.026)
Minority Population	0.059***	0.104***	0.191***	0.064***	0.111***	0.181***
%	(0.013)	(0.030)	(0.043)	(0.016)	(0.032)	(0.043)
Log Country	0.436***	1.100***	1.491***	0.443***	1.069***	1.456***
Population	(0.092)	(0.220)	(0.381)	(0.095)	(0.221)	(0.382)
Religious Similarity	−0.374	−0.319	−0.779	−0.315	0.396	0.116
to Majority	(0.319)	(0.750)	(0.951)	(0.364)	(0.729)	(1.126)

Distinct Ethnicity				0.477*	0.814[†]	1.681*
vs. Majority				(0.200)	(0.448)	(0.813)
Rough Terrain	−0.001	−0.008*	0.005	−0.001	−0.009*	0.004
(avg elevation)	(0.001)	(0.004)	(0.004)	(0.001)	(0.004)	(0.003)
Mean GRD	0.129	0.173	−0.516*	0.091	0.177	−0.542*
Group Level	(0.087)	(0.164)	(0.207)	(0.089)	(0.170)	(0.213)
Mean SRD	−0.092	−0.005	−0.274[†]	−0.055	0.008	−0.273
Group Level	(0.071)	(0.072)	(0.141)	(0.066)	(0.071)	(0.176)
Mobilization Type	0.445*	0.603**	0.949***	0.436*	0.647**	1.108***
Year Lagged Control	(0.181)	(0.232)	(0.255)	(0.184)	(0.238)	(0.249)
Constant	−10.029***	−28.616***	−28.444***	−10.185***	−27.847***	−27.514***
	(2.079)	(5.777)	(8.029)	(2.107)	(5.801)	(8.328)
Observations		8,119			6,642	
Year Effects		Included			Included	
Clustering		Country Group			Country Group	
Correlated Intercepts	(a)–(b)***	(a)–(c)*	(b)–(c)**	(a)–(b)***	(a)–(c)*	(b)–(c)*

Robust standard errors are in parentheses

*** $p < 0.001$, ** $p < 0.01$, * $p < 0.05$, [†] $p < 0.10$

Table 5.9 Determinants of Violent Mobilization Types, Grievance Intensities, 2000–2014, Country-Clustered Models

	(7a)			(7b)		
	Correlated RE Multinomial Logit			Correlated RE Multinomial Logit		
	(a) Rioting	(b) Violence vs. Civilians	(c) Rebellion	(a) Rioting	(b) Violence vs. Civilians	(c) Rebellion
Minority Grievance	0.149	0.246*	−0.246	0.158	0.267*	−0.283
intensity, Pol, year lag	(0.094)	(0.121)	(0.183)	(0.102)	(0.133)	(0.214)
Minority Grievance	0.310***	0.091	0.238†	0.274**	0.050	0.131
intensity, Rel, year lag	(0.090)	(0.119)	(0.138)	(0.087)	(0.123)	(0.138)
Minority Grievance	0.323**	0.704***	0.665†	0.296*	0.698***	0.938***
Intensity, Econ year lag	(0.117)	(0.183)	(0.390)	(0.122)	(0.184)	(0.198)
GRD (1 year lag)	0.026	0.008	−0.047	0.045	0.013	−0.092†
	(0.028)	(0.040)	(0.038)	(0.030)	(0.045)	(0.055)
SRD (1 year lag)	0.028	−0.017	0.017	0.034	0.001	0.046
	(0.019)	(0.038)	(0.043)	(0.023)	(0.035)	(0.054)
Minority Political	1.086***	3.873***	1.466†	0.780*	3.460***	1.326†
Organization	(0.318)	(0.844)	(0.816)	(0.346)	(0.781)	(0.792)
Minority	0.610*	1.148***	1.523**	0.581*	0.977**	1.309***
Representation	(0.260)	(0.350)	(0.481)	(0.259)	(0.321)	(0.400)
Minority	−0.086	−0.217	−0.411	−0.064	−0.166	−0.470†
Policy Power	(0.104)	(0.220)	(0.253)	(0.117)	(0.196)	(0.269)
Log GDP/capita	−0.429**	−0.084	−0.660†	−0.401**	−0.109	−0.697†
	(0.161)	(0.313)	(0.396)	(0.156)	(0.320)	(0.367)

Polyarchy Score (V-Dem)	−1.755 (1.494)	−0.136 (1.774)	−0.459 (0.862)	−1.385 (1.594)	−0.544 (1.848)
Regime Durability	0.014 (0.017)	−0.006 (0.014)	−0.006 (0.006)	0.007 (0.016)	−0.006 (0.014)
Security Sector % of Labor Force	0.148* (0.075)	0.053 (0.094)	−0.018 (0.081)	0.169* (0.077)	0.053 (0.101)
Youth Unemployment %	0.019 (0.024)	−0.002 (0.024)	0.005 (0.013)	0.020 (0.022)	−0.003 (0.025)
Internet Use %	0.008 (0.018)	0.005 (0.014)	0.014† (0.008)	0.013 (0.018)	0.004 (0.014)
Minority Population %	0.090*** (0.021)	0.075** (0.026)	0.042*** (0.011)	0.092*** (0.017)	0.066** (0.025)
Log Country Population	0.960*** (0.241)	1.142*** (0.279)	0.376*** (0.106)	0.824*** (0.221)	1.164*** (0.278)
Religious Similarity to Majority	0.773 (0.661)	1.209* (0.503)	−0.184 (0.385)	0.077 (0.535)	0.745 (0.506)
Distinct Ethnicity vs. Majority	0.977* (0.424)	0.523† (0.302)	0.326* (0.157)		
Rough Terrain (avg elevation)	0.002 (0.002)	−0.006 (0.004)	−0.001 (0.002)	0.003 (0.002)	−0.006 (0.004)
Mean Pol grievance	0.684 (1.840)	0.902 (1.598)	−0.138 (0.685)	1.283 (1.809)	0.590 (1.623)
Intensity—Country					

(continued)

Table 5.9 Continued

	(7a)			(7b)		
	Correlated RE Multinomial Logit			Correlated RE Multinomial Logit		
	(a) Rioting	(b) Violence vs. Civilians	(c) Rebellion	(a) Rioting	(b) Violence vs. Civilians	(c) Rebellion
Mean Rel grievance	0.056	−1.695	−0.766	−0.004	−1.844	−0.807
Intensity—Country	(0.621)	(1.433)	(1.159)	(0.602)	(1.464)	(1.338)
Mean Econ grievance	3.252*	2.800	0.531	2.719[†]	2.123	−0.044
Intensity—Country	(1.478)	(2.508)	(3.386)	(1.494)	(2.371)	(3.445)
Mean GRD	−0.052	−0.134*	0.015	−0.110*	−0.111	0.048
Country Level	(0.041)	(0.065)	(0.091)	(0.048)	(0.077)	(0.101)
Mean SRD	0.039	0.183	-0.302*	0.048	0.119	-0.404**
Country Level	(0.053)	(0.124)	(0.129)	(0.059)	(0.120)	(0.157)
Mobilization Type	0.884***	1.549***	1.755***	0.865***	1.507***	1.814***
Year Lagged Control	(0.185)	(0.234)	(0.287)	(0.181)	(0.237)	(0.307)
Constant	−7.765***	−28.531***	−18.153***	−8.683***	−28.457***	−20.220***
	(2.127)	(5.773)	(4.853)	(2.088)	(5.769)	(5.051)
Observations		8,119			6,642	
Year Effects		Included			Included	
Clustering		Country			Country	
Correlated Intercepts	(a)–(b)	(a)–(c)	(b)–(c)	(a)–(b)	(a)–(c)	(b)–(c)

Robust standard errors are in parentheses

*** $p < 0.001$, ** $p < 0.01$, * $p < 0.05$, [†] $p < 0.10$

Table 5.10 Determinants of Violent Mobilization Types, Grievance Intensities, 2000–2014, Country Group Clustered Models

	(8a)			(8b)		
	Correlated RE Multinomial Logit			Correlated RE Multinomial Logit		
	(a) Rioting	(b) Violence vs. Civilians	(c) Rebellion	(a) Rioting	(b) Violence vs. Civilians	(c) Rebellion
Minority Grievance	0.203*	0.181	−0.337[†]	0.221*	0.172	−0.353[†]
intensity, Pol, year lag	(0.100)	(0.131)	(0.193)	(0.099)	(0.135)	(0.201)
Minority Grievance	0.032	−0.293*	−0.480*	−0.010	−0.307*	−0.469*
intensity, Rel, year lag	(0.097)	(0.138)	(0.218)	(0.098)	(0.144)	(0.233)
Minority Grievance	0.028	0.563*	0.183	0.048	0.612**	0.544**
Intensity, Econ year lag	(0.109)	(0.228)	(0.329)	(0.116)	(0.234)	(0.210)
GRD (1 year lag)	−0.132	−0.201	0.359*	−0.121	−0.184	0.322[†]
	(0.083)	(0.148)	(0.163)	(0.085)	(0.149)	(0.177)
SRD (1 year lag)	0.133*	0.080	0.110	0.104[†]	0.066	0.094
	(0.063)	(0.058)	(0.130)	(0.054)	(0.054)	(0.144)
Minority Political	0.914**	3.524**	0.407	0.668*	2.779*	0.338
Organization	(0.313)	(1.150)	(1.700)	(0.329)	(1.155)	(1.559)
Minority	0.708**	1.851***	2.581**	0.675**	1.584***	2.075**
Representation	(0.243)	(0.396)	(0.824)	(0.241)	(0.369)	(0.704)
Minority	−0.131	−0.213	−0.569[†]	−0.124	−0.156	−0.519
Policy Power	(0.137)	(0.292)	(0.345)	(0.139)	(0.285)	(0.360)
Log GDP/capita	−0.544**	−0.401	−1.428*	−0.542***	−0.441	−1.474*
	(0.174)	(0.395)	(0.695)	(0.168)	(0.403)	(0.655)

(continued)

Table 5.10 Continued

	(8a)			(8b)		
	Correlated RE Multinomial Logit			**Correlated RE Multinomial Logit**		
	(a) Rioting	**(b) Violence vs. Civilians**	**(c) Rebellion**	**(a) Rioting**	**(b) Violence vs. Civilians**	**(c) Rebellion**
Polyarchy Score	−0.216	−0.312	−3.008	0.077	0.097	−3.000
(V-Dem)	(0.714)	(1.615)	(2.044)	(0.748)	(1.671)	(1.992)
Regime Durability	−0.008	−0.011	0.006	−0.009[†]	−0.009	0.012
	(0.005)	(0.016)	(0.026)	(0.005)	(0.016)	(0.024)
Security Sector %	−0.006	0.174	0.337	−0.017	0.136	0.268
of Labor Force	(0.080)	(0.153)	(0.214)	(0.085)	(0.157)	(0.199)
Youth	0.001	−0.006	0.052	−0.004	−0.001	0.044
Unemployment %	(0.012)	(0.027)	(0.042)	(0.012)	(0.025)	(0.040)
Internet Use %	0.018*	0.007	0.021	0.016[†]	0.006	0.018
	(0.009)	(0.017)	(0.028)	(0.009)	(0.017)	(0.027)
Minority Population	0.048***	0.083**	0.170***	0.052***	0.094**	0.155***
%	(0.013)	(0.031)	(0.042)	(0.015)	(0.033)	(0.041)
Log Country	0.407***	1.028***	1.401***	0.396***	0.983***	1.311***
Population	(0.087)	(0.230)	(0.406)	(0.089)	(0.235)	(0.369)
Religious Similarity	−0.401	−0.423	−0.677	−0.398	0.294	0.061
to Majority	(0.325)	(0.755)	(0.874)	(0.371)	(0.714)	(0.991)
Distinct Ethnicity				0.296	0.644	1.136
vs. Majority				(0.195)	(0.453)	(0.708)

Rough Terrain	−0.001	−0.009*	0.004	−0.001	−0.010*	0.003
(avg elevation)	(0.001)	(0.004)	(0.004)	(0.001)	(0.004)	(0.004)
Mean Pol grievance	−0.205	1.345[†]	1.326	−0.175	1.612*	0.947
Intensity—Group	(0.378)	(0.747)	(0.918)	(0.395)	(0.703)	(1.006)
Mean Rel grievance	1.004***	0.778	1.808[†]	1.040***	0.591	1.712[†]
Intensity—Group	(0.297)	(0.692)	(1.002)	(0.295)	(0.705)	(1.003)
Mean Econ grievance	2.202***	2.549[†]	4.115*	1.990***	2.523[†]	3.601*
Intensity—Group	(0.511)	(1.354)	(1.876)	(0.510)	(1.373)	(1.816)
Mean GRD	0.105	0.149	−0.516**	0.087	0.176	−0.480*
Group Level	(0.085)	(0.163)	(0.171)	(0.088)	(0.165)	(0.189)
Mean SRD	−0.100	−0.073	−0.405*	−0.072	−0.077	−0.373*
Group Level	(0.071)	(0.075)	(0.173)	(0.066)	(0.072)	(0.189)
Mobilization Type	0.406*	0.615**	0.900***	0.403*	0.656**	1.022***
Year Lagged Control	(0.177)	(0.224)	(0.237)	(0.182)	(0.232)	(0.243)
Constant	−8.657***	−26.303***	−26.855**	−8.477***	−25.479***	−24.808**
	(1.789)	(5.747)	(8.543)	(1.810)	(5.958)	(8.102)
Observations		8,119			6,642	
Year Effects		Included			Included	
Clustering		Country Group			Country-Group	
Correlated Intercepts	(a)–(b)**	(a)–(c)[†]	(b)–(c)**	(a)–(b)**	(a)–(c)*	(b)–(c)**

Robust standard errors are in parentheses

*** $p < 0.001$, ** $p < 0.01$, * $p < 0.05$, [†] $p < 0.10$

other unorganized, spontaneous forms of violence—for country- and group-clustered models, or about 1.9 and 1.2 times more likely given expression and increasing intensity of political grievances respectively for group-clustered models. So too, both religious and economic grievances are associated with significantly higher chance of riots for both country and group-clustered models, although intensity of these grievances is associated with riots only for country-clustered models. The expression of religious and economic grievances, in turn, translate to about a 1.5 and 1.7 times greater likelihood of riots for group-clustered models. These findings are consistent with our earlier ones for political and economic grievances as linked to violent outcomes, while demonstrating that religious grievances too may be linked to violence, albeit on a less extreme level.

We also find some interesting effects for our DDI variables. Country-clustered tests reveal no significant influence for DDI on likelihood of riots whatsoever. However, our country-group clustered models reveal a weak negative influence of GRD on rioting, but a significantly increased likelihood of rioting with rising SRD. Increasing minority policy influence has no observable influence while, again owing to our missing data problem, comparable examination of limited violence-type models including our minority economic status variable was computationally infeasible. That SRD encourages riots again suggests that societal repression does increase collective motivation to fight. However, our much stronger and more significant findings for political, religious, and economic grievances further strengthen our contention that DDI absent expressed grievance is altogether insufficient to explain collective mobilization.

Regarding our group-level capacity variables, as with the previous general violence mobilization analysis, group organization, political representation, and relative population size are significantly associated with riots in both country and country-group clustered analyses. No effect is found for minority religious similarity to the majority, however distinct ethnicity does appear to contribute to riot likelihood in robustness checks. These results suggest several important phenomena are at work, particularly that minority group capacity does significantly contribute to their ability to engage in less formally organized violent opposition.

In terms of our country-level control variables, neither democracy, regime durability, security sector size, nor youth unemployment influences riot likelihood in either country or country-group clustered models. Although increased GDP per capita makes riots less likely, greater internet access has the opposite effect, suggesting an ambivalent effect for economic development on this level of violent mobilization. It also indirectly suggests that riots may be influenced by internet-based mobilization. Finally, states with larger populations are more likely to experience riots while rough terrain measures, as expected, have no significant effect.

Despite only a relatively small number of religious minorities engaging in violent mobilization of any kind during our period of analysis, rioting is certainly the most prevalent. Our data observes rioting across nearly all conceivable religious minorities, whether Animists, Buddhists, Christians, Hindus, Jews, Muslims, or Sikhs, as well as in countries ranging from the highly democratic (e.g., Canada, Denmark, France) to the deeply authoritarian (e.g., China, Myanmar, Syria). Every minority group we survey that engaged in any more severe form of violent mobilization, whether organized violence against civilians or rebellion, also engaged in rioting at some point between 2000 and 2014. As such, rioting can be but is far from always a first step toward more severe forms of violent mobilization.

What then differentiates religious minorities that riot from those that escalate to more violent means? Our results earlier in this chapter, especially compared to significant predictors for peaceful mobilization previously and more violent forms of mobilization explored later, offer some tantalizing hints. First, while all forms of grievance are strongly correlated with rioting, only religious grievances are not also positively associated with more severe violence. Second, of all our DDI measures, only SRD independently contributes to rioting. This is particularly interesting given our finding in Chapter 3 that only GRD and not SRD significantly predicts religious grievances. Taken together, this implies that societal discrimination is an important trigger to move religiously aggrieved minorities from peaceful tactics, observed in the previous section, to more (albeit not particularly severely) violent ones.

Here we offer the illustrative example of the Egyptian Copts, the largest and among the oldest Christian communities in the Arab world. Today, Copts comprise between 10 and 15 percent of the Egyptian population and reside primarily in urban areas, especially metropolitan Cairo. Although sharing a common ethnicity, history, spoken language, and national identity with Egyptian Muslims, they tend to be more educated and wealthier than the population average (Mohamoud et al., 2013).

Despite the Egyptian constitution formally guaranteeing freedom of religion, Copts also faced nontrivial levels of GRD (scores between 21 and

206 RELIGIOUS MINORITIES AT RISK

23) only outmatched by the Baha'i (with a consistent GRD score of 27) between 2000 and 2014. They also endured unparalleled levels of societal discrimination during the same period (SRD scores between 43 and 47 contra Baha'i and Jewish Egyptians at a maximum SRD score of 6), an unfortunately common experience of relatively large religious minorities in religiously discriminatory societies (Fox, 2020).

While Copts have long been excluded from meaningful influence over policy-making, 2006 saw the first appointment of a Copt provincial governor in more than 30 years, while two Christians also held appointed positions in the national government's 32-member cabinet during this period.[2] By 2011, Christians again complained of discrimination in government hiring and underrepresentation in senior government leadership positions, both elected and appointed.[3] Following the deposition of Mohamed Morsi's brief Muslim Brotherhood–aligned government (2012–2103) by coup, General Abdel Fattah el-Sisi issued legislation in 2014 mandating that a minimum of 24 Christians must be elected through party lists in the first parliamentary elections after the new constitution's ratification, an increase over the previous parliament, which included 13 Christians.[4]

It follows that while Egyptian Copts have very rarely expressed collective economic grievances of any kind, political grievances are apparent in the RMAR data for nine of the fifteen years covered by our study, six being at the highest measured intensity: 2001, and 2004 to 2005, but most notably between 2010 and 2012 amid the collapse of Hosni Mubarak's rule. Religious grievances have, in turn, been consistently expressed by the Coptic community, for eleven of the fifteen years surveyed, with nine being at the highest intensity: 2000, 2003 to 2006, 2008, 2010 to 2011, and 2014. These religious grievances correlated with highly significant instances of societal violence targeting Copts ranging from attacks on Coptic priests and community leaders, desecration of Coptic cemeteries, bombings of Coptic Churches, and other sectarian "clashes" often instigated by fallacious attribution of unsolved crimes to Coptic suspects (Gabbay, 2018; Tadros & Habib, 2022; Yefet, 2019). And indeed, Coptic political mobilization in response to these collective affronts follow much as expected by our

---

[2] US State Department Report on International Religious Freedom, 2001–2014, https://2009-2017.state.gov/j/drl/rls/irf//index.htm.
[3] US State Department Report on International Religious Freedom, 2001–2014.
[4] US State Department Report on International Religious Freedom, 2001–2014.

models. While Copts engaged in peaceful protests in 2003 through 2005, they participated in riots in all years included in RMAR excepting 2002 to 2003 and 2007.

Altogether then, the case of Egyptian Copts well illustrates our findings regarding the causes of religious minority participation in riots. Consistently high levels of GRD meaningfully contribute to collective expression of both political and religious grievances. And indeed, we see that efforts by the Egyptian government to redress political grievances by giving Copts a seat at the policy-making table have likely been instrumental in preventing these grievances from translating into more intense forms of violence. However, consistent failures to reign in societal discrimination has contributed to continued Coptic marginalization and religious grievance. It has also likely triggered low-intensity spontaneous violence, namely riots, by Copts who view peaceful recourse to have been clearly insufficient to prevent these increasingly regularized instances of societal repression.

Organized Violence against Civilians

Turning to more intense forms of violent mobilization, under the category of organized violence against civilians, we include acts that fall under many conventional definitions of terrorism, namely violence employed by groups targeting noncombatants. However, we recognize that many competing definitions exist, which exceed our specific notion by including attacks on security forces or focusing on the intention to spread fear and intimidate (e.g., Byman, 2020). In order to avoid confusion, we therefore prefer the label "organized violence against civilians."

In any case, organized violence against civilians represents a significant escalation from riots, suggesting that this phenomenon should also be driven by distinct factors. We find this to be partially true. Here we find that although political grievance expression and intensity are significantly correlated with violence against civilians for country-clustered models, only political grievance expression is significant for group-clustered models, with relative risk ratios predicting about two times greater likelihood of such violence than when political grievances are not expressed. While religious grievances produce no significant effects in country-clustered models, more intense religious grievances are associated with significantly *lower* likelihood of organized violence for group-clustered models. This translates in relative

208 RELIGIOUS MINORITIES AT RISK

risk ratios to about a three-quarters lesser likelihood of such violence as religious grievances increase in intensity.

By contrast, economic grievance expression and intensity are strongly and consistently associated with greater likelihood of violence for both country- and group-clustered models. For group-clustered models, relative risk ratios include a nearly seven times greater likelihood of organized violence against civilians when economic grievances are expressed and about 1.8 times greater likelihood of such violence as economic grievances increase in intensity relative to their absence. These divergent trends further strengthen our earlier findings that although religious grievances do influence religious minority mobilization, they do not tend to encourage violence. Again, it appears that violence by religious minorities is rarely religiously motivated, at least not by grievances over religious discrimination.

Regarding our DDI variables, contrary to our findings for riots, we observe no significant effects whatsoever for either country or country-group clustered tests. Group capacity variables however reveal nearly identical effects to those found for riots. Greater organizational capacity as measured by political organization, representation, and population share again increases the likelihood that a religious minority will be involved in organized violence against civilians. The sole exception is that in robust country-clustered models including our distinct ethnicity variable, we find that religious similarity between minorities and majorities significantly increases the likelihood of organized violence. State-level controls also reveal fewer significant effects than for riots, with only state population and rough terrain positively and negatively correlated, respectively, with organized violence for both country and country-group clustered models. Altogether, we are left with the strong inference that grievances, not DDI, are the critical predictors of civilian-targeted organized violence by religious minorities.

To illustrate these factors, we examine the escalation of mobilization by religious minorities from nonviolent protest to rioting to organized violence targeting civilians in Bahrain. Since achieving formal independence from the United Kingdom in 1971, Bahrain has been politically dominated by Sunni Islam despite its near population parity with (or perhaps slight majority for) Shi'a. Its ruling al-Khalifa royal family has often been criticized for its human rights abuses and its political suppression of Shi'as. That said, over the period of our study, collective mobilization by Shi'a Muslims has varied from nonviolent particularly in the early 2000s to an escalation to regular rioting by

2007 to the emergence of organized violence by Shi'a terror groups against Sunni civilian targets by 2011.

Regarding Shi'a collective capacity, the RMAR data is quite consistent from 2000 to 2014. On average, Shi'a Muslims constituted some 45 percent of the Bahraini population, observed as politically organized from 2001 until the present. Lacking consistent political representation until 2006, Shi'a collective mobilization was largely nonviolent in nature, escalating to riots only in 2004. Political representation however only granted a brief reprieve with a return to more violent forms of mobilization in 2007. In terms of DDI, the level of GRD experienced by Shi'a hovered at a middling level, with RAS's GRD index registering scores from 6 to 8 from 2000 to 2009, and then substantially increasing in parallel with increasingly violent group mobilization to 9 in 2010, 13 in 2011, and 14 in 2013. SRD followed a similar pattern, remaining at 8 from 2000 to 2010, rising to 11 in 2011 and remaining at 10 from 2012 to 2014. Thus, while there was a rise in violence and both GRD and SRD with the beginning of the events of the Arab Spring, the general pattern predates these events. Finally, Shi'as have been consistently and explicitly excluded from governmental decision-making as well as suffering relative economic deprivation vis-a-vis the dominant Sunni majority for RMAR's entire temporal range.

Observed violent escalation of Shi'a mobilization, from nonviolence to riots to organized violence against Sunni civilian targets, is better explained by shifts in expressed grievances. Until the outbreak of sustained violent mobilization in 2007, collective political grievance expression initially preceded the achievement of group political representation in 2004 and 2005, while religious grievances were consistently moderately expressed from 2000 to 2007. Economic grievances were never expressed, however, until 2010.

The sustained turn to riots as a means of collective mobilization began in 2007, correlating with an intense rise in Shi'a political grievances, while political and religious grievances ceased to be openly expressed altogether in 2008 and 2009. The transition from rioting to organized violence, between 2010 and 2011, correlated with a steep and sustained rise in political grievance intensity, the first sustained and intense emergence of economic grievances, but only brief and relatively mild expressions of religious grievance. These patterns closely mirror our statistical models, wherein shifts from nonviolent to more intensively violent mobilization strategies are most closely associated with changes in degree of expressed grievances rather than other background conditions.

210 RELIGIOUS MINORITIES AT RISK

Rebellion

Finally, the most extreme and rare iteration of collective violence by religious minorities we measure is rebellion. Our definition is identical to that provided by the UCDP/PRIO armed conflict data set as "a contested incompatibility that concerns government and/or territory where the use of armed force between two parties, of which at least one is a government of a state, results in at least 25 battle-related deaths in a calendar year" (Pettersson, 2020). As described previously in Figure 5.2, our data includes 83 case-years of rebellion, encompassing 23 of 770 unique state-level minority groups identified by the RMAR data. Of these identified groups, 18 are Muslim, 1 is Christian, and 4 represent indigenous religions that can be described as animist or Christian syncretic depending upon the case.

The apparent rarity of religiously defined minority rebellion is unsurprising. Recent scholarship concurrently examining ethnic, linguistic, and religious divisions defining rebel groups in civil war strongly suggests intrastate conflict is more likely to occur between incompatible linguistic rather than religious dyads (Bormann et al., 2015). Typically the most diffuse and populous cultural units to which individuals can claim collective allegiance, religion should moreover less often translate into high-order social and political cleavages than ethnicity (McCauley, 2019). So too, although religiously defined ideological incompatibilities between states and rebels demonstrably contribute to the protraction of intrastate conflict more than between more ideologically neutral adversaries (Keels & Wiegand, 2020), so-defined ideological armed conflicts actually contribute to substantially fewer casualties than otherwise expected (Basedau et al., 2022).

Turning back to our results, we see three distinct patterns for political, religious, and economic grievances. In contrast to our findings regarding riots and organized violence, political grievances appear to weakly contribute to the *reduction* rather than escalation of rebellion among religious minorities. Although these findings only reach 95 percent significance in country-clustered models employing our dichotomous measure of political grievance expression versus 90 percent significance in group-clustered models measuring either political grievance expression or intensity, results of reduced significance are hardly surprising in the case of rare outcomes. Relative risk ratios for group-clustered models, in turn, suggest a just over one third and nearly three quarters reduced likelihood of rebellion when grievances are expressed or their intensity increases respectively. These results also match our theoretical inferences regarding our nonviolent versus violent mobilization models that states likely prefer political accommodation of religious minorities to religious insurgency.

Regarding religious grievances, we observe a mismatch between our country-clustered and country group–clustered models. In the former, greater religious grievance appears to support rebellion, whereas in the latter, rebellion likelihood drops significantly—by nearly two-thirds likelihood via relative risk ratios—as religious grievances become more intense. These opposed results highlight the methodological importance of accurate measurement of hypothesized causal conditions. Because country-clustered models assume that most relevant variation occurs on the country rather than group level, it is highly likely that our positive significant finding here is an artifact of overlooking critical within-group variation. For instance, empirical confirmation of the assumption that the Israeli-Palestinian conflict is driven by religious incompatibilities would be less likely using group-clustered models, which would observe considerable within-group (Israeli and Palestinian) religionization over time but rather consistent dyadic ethnolinguistic incompatibilities. That said, religionization may better explain increasing conflict intensity from the first to second Palestinian Intifada (see Abulof, 2014; Fox & Sandler, 2004; Litvak, 1998; Mellor, 2017; Peled & Peled, 2019). Altogether, then, our negative significant finding for the country-group model is more reliable.

Finally, regarding economic grievances, we observe a consistent if weak positive effect of grievance expression in both country and country-group clustered models and grievance intensity in country-clustered models on rebellion likelihood. To clarify the influence of economic grievances on rebellion, we turn now to relative risk ratios for our group-clustered model 6a in Table 5.8. Here we find an over 3.5 greater likelihood of rebellion compared to where economic grievances are absent (to say nothing of a highly significant 6.3 greater likelihood in our constrained model 6b, which includes consideration of religious minority ethnicity). As with the observed relatively low significance of political grievances, these results confirm our hypothesis that economic grievances are associated with more intense forms of violent mobilization, despite rebellion being a particularly rare outcome.

These findings suggest several critical inferences. First and foremost, when religious minorities engage in rebellion, they appear not to be motivated by religious or even political grievances. Moreover, although economic grievances appear to play a significant role, that increasing intensity of these

212 RELIGIOUS MINORITIES AT RISK

grievances does not reliably predict rebellion suggests that even this may be insufficient.

Taken together with findings for our DDI variables, an even more nuanced picture is revealed. No DDI measures significantly influence rebellion in country-clustered models. In country group–clustered models, however, we observe that higher levels of GRD are significantly positively associated with rebellion whereas SRD is not. This finding may be a statistical artifact of a very limited set of observed religious rebellions. However, to the extent that GRD measures targeted government repression of religious minorities, this result certainly complements earlier scholarship which finds that whereas concentrated repression may successfully crush more minor forms of collective disobedience, it may encourage more violent outcomes (Regan & Norton, 2005; Cunningham & Lemke, 2014; Koos, 2016; Schatzman, 2005).

In terms of our group-level capacity variables, we again witness patterns that substantially replicate our findings for both riots and organized violence against civilians. Although minority political organization only significantly contributes to rebellion in country-clustered models, increased minority political representation, larger minority share of state populations, and ethnic differentiation from the dominant religion group all predict greater rebellion likelihood in both country and country-group clustered models. State-level control variables also follow predictable patterns, with higher per-capita GDP and increased levels of democracy associated with lower likelihood of rebellion and larger security sectors, higher youth unemployment, and larger state populations predict a greater chance of rebellion. Major effects from these models examining violent mobilization types are summarized in Figure 5.4.

Given our very small number of identified "religious" rebellions and our previously asserted caveats regarding the difficulty of using RMAR data to appropriately identify such rebellions as "mass mobilizations" on par with other mobilization types, we remain cautious in our interpretation of these results. While it may be true that such rebellions are most likely to occur when religious minorities are economically, rather than politically or religiously aggrieved, we also expect religiously motivated rebels to co-opt such grievances to advance their own agendas. As it has been argued elsewhere, religious fundamentalists often take advantage of nonreligious grievances to recruit members and mobilize constituent publics (Almond et. al., 2003; Demerath, 2001). Governments may also attempt to simultaneously

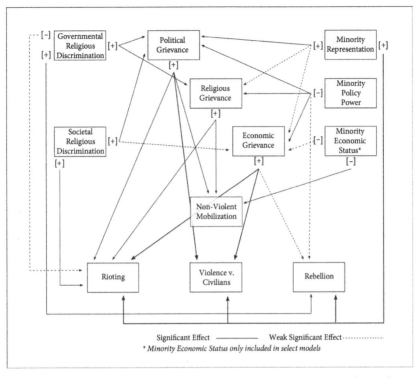

Figure 5.4 Nonviolent and Violent Mobilization Types, Summary of Significant Effects

co-opt and control these trends by both increasing government control of religious institutions and actively suppressing religious dissent (Feuer, 2018; Finnbogason & Svensson, 2015).

So just as religious rebel actors may effectively transform nonreligious conflicts into seemingly "religious rebellions," states may successfully redress "actual" religious grievances while failing to minimize others, particularly economic or political. As such, "religious rebellion" identified by RMAR by Shi'a (e.g., Hezbollah in Lebanon and Houthi in Yemen), Sunni (e.g., Jundullah in Iran and NLA in Macedonia), and Christian Animist (e.g., anti-Balaka in Central African Republic, SSLM in South Sudan) armed actors, unsurprisingly, mirror deep existing political and economic inequalities experienced by religious groups rather than necessarily distinct religious collective ambitions. That religious actors can profit from these trends does not imply that religion does not matter. Rather, it suggests a more nuanced understanding of the conditions under which religious minorities at risk rebel.

214   RELIGIOUS MINORITIES AT RISK

Although having mostly taken place prior to the temporal period covered by RMAR, we offer the First and Second Sudanese Civil Wars from 1955 to 1972 and 1983 to 2005, respectively, culminating in the 2011 independence of South Sudan, as a highly recognizable example of these dynamics. These conflicts were marked by significant and sustained religious grievances harbored by the predominantly Animist and Christian "Black African" south against the Sunni Muslim Arab dominated north. Yet they also serve as exceptions that prove the rule that religious grievances tend not to lead to armed rebellion. Despite imposition of Shari'a law being an immediate trigger for the second civil war in particular, neither would have occurred had it not been for decades if not centuries of political and economic exploitation of South Sudan by Khartoum.

Although domination of the north over the south far predated joint Egyptian-British colonial rule, which formally began in 1896, British authorities maintained and exacerbated the administrative and economic divisions between the two regions. First investing heavily in the modernization and liberalization of the northern economy, historians have argued the British also encouraged controlled Islamization of the north, in an effort to counteract the indigenous religious authority of the messianic Mahdists (who briefly overthrew Ottoman-Egyptian rule of Sudan from 1882 to 1889; El-Baatahani, 2001; Collins, 2008). With the 1919 Egyptian Revolution, however, the British reversed course, seeking to exclude potentially rebellious Western-educated elite. This involved not only turning to more traditional religious leaders in the north, but empowering local, tribal leaders in the south. They also sought to stem the spread of Islam southward through support of Christian missionaries and adoption of English in the place of Arabic as the language of administration (Lobban, 2010). After decades of British failures to quash growing (Northern) Sudanese nationalism, colonial authorities moved in the 1940s to extract themselves from Sudan, building a political and administrative infrastructure that would again control the South, leaving it politically marginalized and economically impoverished (Collins 1976).

Following Sudan's declaration of independence in 1955, its new leadership refused to establish a federal system of governance, contributing to a chain of mutinies by Southern Sudanese army officers and the outbreak of the first Sudanese Civil War. The conflict finally ended nearly seventeen years later with the Addis Ababa peace agreement, promising to establish the south as a united autonomous region, redressing its economic and political marginalization.[5] Multiple factors, including persistent regional underdevelopment, poor governance, sustained North-South and intertribal southern rivalries, coupled with the shifting political fortunes of northern political elite in Khartoum, combined to render these promises aspirational at best, and they were never seriously implemented (Beswick, 1991; Kasfir, 1977; Wakoson, 1990).

Indeed, the increasingly assertive Sudanese Muslim Brotherhood were relentless in using the opportunity afforded by the settlement to undermine the credibility of Sudan's ostensibly secular leadership (for having accepted a "humiliating" agreement) and to divide the southern leadership against itself. When by 1983, Sudanese President Jaafar Nimeiry had survived his fifteenth coup attempt, he realigned himself with the Brotherhood, decreed shari'a as the law of the land for both north and south, and abrogated the Addis Ababa Agreement, including eliminating any remaining vestige of southern autonomy (Wakoson, 1990; Beswick, 1991). The immediate consequence was a reactivation of the North-South civil war, a conflict that lasted until 2005 with roughly two million casualties (direct and indirect) and four million displaced persons.

The salience of religion varied widely over two decades of conflict, particularly as the political and military leadership of Khartoum has fluctuated between overtly Islamist to secular authoritarian (Toft, 2007). Feelings of religious and cultural marginalization among South Sudan's many non-Muslim ethnic groups have undoubtedly been important to motivating popular calls to arms and in defining the South Sudanese main rebel groups' expressly secular political aims (Breilid, 2013; Jok, 2015; Tounsel, 2021). Nonetheless, it can hardly be underestimated the extent to which the religious grievances that have characterized this long and bloody conflict, are situated within larger structural contexts of political and economic deprivation, which render them salient.

Implications and Conclusions

The results presented in this chapter demonstrate that not only are grievances a critical cause of religious minority mobilization, whether nonviolent or

---

[5] Although religious grievances were a relatively marginal aspect of the settlement, the World Council of Churches was instrumental in bringing the Sudanese government and southern rebels to the negotiating table (Wakoson, 1990).

216 RELIGIOUS MINORITIES AT RISK

violent, but also their direct measurement provides a much more nuanced understanding of their influence on conflict patterns than those that rely solely on DDI. Indeed, by collecting data on diverse expressions of grievance by religious minorities and examining their particular contributions to collective mobilization, we are able to paint a much clearer picture as to the role that grievances play in motivating conflict. So too, we are able to demonstrate the extent to which some DDI measures, especially policy power, may in fact be capturing contributions to conflict entirely unrelated to collective grievance, especially including but not limited to minority organizational capacity and minority leaders' likely avenues of social influence. These major results are summarized in Table 5.11.

Our results are also important for demonstrating the extent to which religious groups, despite being a distinct subset of minority groups, share interests and motivations that rather complement those of more commonly identified groups, whether ethnic or linguistic. Indeed, we find that religious grievances themselves rarely if ever directly contribute to especially violent forms of mobilization, even by religious minority groups. This finding suggests researchers and practitioners should be extraordinarily cautious in dismissing claims by aggrieved religious groups as intangible, ephemeral, or "merely" symbolic. If anything, our results demonstrate that religious minorities fight most intensely for the same rights and resources as other "nonideological" groups, apparently prioritizing political and economic objectives over religious ones.

Finally, we propose an innovative explanation for observed patterns of mobilization intensity by religious minorities, summarized in Table 5.12. Once accounting for minority group collective capacities and state-level background conditions, we argue that the particular intensity of observed minority mobilization, from peaceful protest to violent rebellion, largely depend upon the kinds of reforms demanded by distinct forms of minority grievance. Religious grievances can be relatively easily and effectively assuaged by reducing the level of governmental discrimination experienced by minorities. To signal these demands generally requires only low levels of mobilization, which present only weak challenges to state authority. Accommodation and high-intensity violence avoidance is therefore entirely realistic. Political grievances are more challenging, requiring both policy and institutional reforms such as minority representation, greater policy control, and collective autonomy. These concessions are much more costly to the state, requiring greater demonstrations of collective resolve to convince

Table 5.11 Summary of Major Findings, Country-Group Clustered Results

Correlated Random Effects Multinomial Logits	Nonviolent		Violent		Rioting		Violence vs. Civilians		Rebellion	
	(A)	(B)	(A)	(B)	(A)	(B)	(A)	(B)	(A)	(B)
Grievance Variables										
Political	+*		+*		+***	+*	+*		−†	−†
Religious	+*				+*			−*		−*
Economic			+***		+*		+***	+*	+†	
DDI Variables										
GRD (1 year lag)					−†				+*	+*
SRD (1 year lag)			+*	+†	+*	+*				
Minority Policy Power			−†							−†
Minority Economic Status[1]	−***	−*	−***	−**	X	X	X	X	X	X
Other Minority-Based Variables										
Political Organization	+***	+**	+***	+***	+***	+**	+***	+**		
Political Representation			+***	+***	+**	+**	+***	+***	+**	+**
Minority Population %	+***	+*	+***	+***	+***	+***	+***	+**	+***	+***
Religious Similarity to Majority		−†								
Distinct Ethnicity vs. Majority[1]					+*		+†		+*	

(*continued*)

Table 5.11 Continued

Correlated Random Effects Multinomial Logits	Nonviolent		Violent		Rioting		Violence vs. Civilians		Rebellion	
	(A)	(B)	(A)	(B)	(A)	(B)	(A)	(B)	(A)	(B)
County Level Controls										
Log GDP per capita			− **	− ***	− *	− **			− *	− *
Polyarchy Score	− *	− *							− *	
Regime Durability	+**	+*								
Security Sector Size			+ †						+ *	
Youth Unemployment									+ †	
Internet Use %			+ †	+ †	+ †	+*				
Population size	+***	+***	+***	+***	+***	+***	+***	+***	+***	+***
Rough Terrain[1]							− *	− *		

(A) Models including dichotomous grievance measures, (B) Models including grievance intensity measures

*** $p < 0.001$, ** $p < 0.01$, * $p < 0.05$, † $p < 0.10$, X N/A

[1] Variable included in only select models

Table 5.12 Grievance to Mobilization Summary

Grievances Type	Reforms Demanded	Mobilization Intensity
Religious	Policy/Political *Reduction of GRD*	Nonviolent, Riots
Political	Institutional *Policy Input, Autonomy*	Nonviolent, Riots, Violence vs. Civilians
Economic	Structural *Economic Redistribution*	Riots, Violence vs. Civilians, Rebellion

leaders of the need for reform. As such, collective mobilization is more likely to rise to the level of organized violence before states credibly commit to political accommodation. Economic grievances present the most substantial challenges in that their redress may demand structural as well as policy and institutional reforms well beyond what the state is willing or capable of accommodating. More violent mobilization including rebellion therefore becomes a more likely outcome. We discuss these ideas in more detail in the context of the results from the entire study in the following chapter.

6

Conclusions

This study combines two bodies of research. The first delves into the links between religion and conflict. The second focuses on the role of grievances in conflict behavior by minorities. Both bodies of work are part of the larger literature on civil wars and domestic conflict. Despite being part of these research traditions, this study benefits from data which includes a confluence of factors which allow us to examine minority conflict behavior in a manner that has not previously been possible.

Overall, we find that grievances matter in explaining the conflict behavior of religious minorities but not just religious grievances. Our two-stage model, originally proposed by Gurr (1993a, 1993b, 2000a), where deprivation, discrimination, and inequality (DDI) leads to grievances, which in turn leads to conflict, all of which is mediated by other factors including group capacity, shows that this conflict process is a complex one. In this process, grievances are a critical intermediate variable between DDI experienced by religious minorities, and the mobilization patterns they select to redress these grievances. The neglect, and in some cases dismissal, of this intermediary condition by more recent scholarship is consequential. Also, as we discuss in this chapter, it can result in both potentially misinterpreting group capacity as grievance and disregarding how even well-organized, relatively deprived groups may still prefer peaceful over violent mobilization.

Religion, in the form of religious DDI and religious grievances, plays an important role but not a dominant one in the conflict process. Religious grievances, for example, are among the least robust predictors of violent mobilization by religious minorities, but these grievances do strongly correlate with peaceful protest and rioting. Rather, it is political and especially economic grievances as well as group capacity that predict more violent behavior, including organized violence against civilians and rebellion. In this regard, behavior by religious minorities may be substantially similar to more commonly studied ethnolinguistic minorities.

Religious Minorities at Risk. Matthias Basedau, Jonathan Fox, and Ariel Zellman, Oxford University Press.
© Oxford University Press 2023. DOI: 10.1093/oso/9780197693940.003.0006

222 RELIGIOUS MINORITIES AT RISK

This has several interrelated implications. First, the observed importance of accounting for collective expressions of grievance is relevant for understanding the conflict behaviors of all minority groups, not just religious ones. Second, different types of grievances have a different impact on both peaceful and violent forms of mobilization. Third, we posit that in many ways religious minorities behave like other types of minorities. Finally, given all of this, we posit that it is not possible to understand the conflict behavior of religious minorities without taking religious factors into account but nor can such behavior be explained by religious factors alone.

In this chapter we discuss all of this with an emphasis on what this study has to add to the religion and conflict, minority conflict, and general domestic conflict and civil war literatures. We first discuss the comparative advantages of the Religion and State-Minorities (RMAR) data set over previous data sets. Second, we examine what our findings can add to the literature on minority conflict as well as the general domestic conflict and civil war literature with a special focus on the role of grievances and our two-stage model in conflict involving minorities. In this section we also explore linkages with broader discussions of minority grievance, mobilization, and intrastate conflict. Third, we evaluate what our findings contribute to the religion and conflict literature. Finally, we discuss how all of this might influence future research.

The Comparative Advantage of the RMAR Data

As we discuss throughout this book the RMAR data set represents a confluence of factors that are present in no previous data collection. That is, while any one of the characteristics of the data are present individually in other data sets, and a portion of them can be found combined in some other conflict data sets, there is no other data set that includes all of the following characteristics:

- It uses the religious minority rather than the state as the unit of analysis.
- It includes all relevant minorities and is therefore not subject to selection bias critiques.
- It includes multiple variables measuring different types and intensities of DDI including both religious and nonreligious DDI.

- It includes multiple variables measuring different types and intensities of group-level grievances including both religious and nonreligious grievances.
- It includes multiple variables measuring group capacity and influence.
- It includes variables measuring both peaceful and violent mobilization as well as acts of violence.

While Gurr's (1993a, 1993b, 2000a) Minorities at Risk (MAR) dataset was the first to use the minority as the unit of analysis, it focused on ethnic minorities. Fox (2002a, 2004) collected additional data on the 105 ethnoreligious minorities included in this collection. However, both collections are incomplete. Gurr included only politically relevant ethnic minorities based on two criteria, one of which was sufficient for inclusion. First, the group experienced significant discrimination. Second, the group was politically active. The Ethnic Power Relations (EPR) dataset which also used the ethnic minority as the unit of analysis uses similar criteria for including only "politically relevant" ethnic groups and has a far more limited range of variables than MAR and RMAR, which includes an absence of grievance variables.

All other datasets that measure conflict by ethnic or religious minorities use countries, conflicts, or organizations rather than the minority as the unit of analysis. The religion-based conflict data sets include comprehensive lists of conflicts or religious organizations, some of which involve religious minorities and some of which do not. They also do not examine the behavior of religious minorities not engaged in conflict. This is also true of the more general conflict and terror data sets which include cases of religious conflict or terror.

In contrast RMAR includes all religious minorities which meet a cutoff of 0.2 percent of a country's population as well as some minorities below this cutoff. None of them were selected based on either levels of DDI or political mobilization. Thus, while RMAR does not include all minorities in a country as it does not include, for example, ethnic minorities that are not religiously distinct from the majority, it does include a reasonably complete list of all but the smallest religious minorities. Thus, no previous conflict data set has been based on religious minorities, and the RMAR data is more complete within its defined universe of analysis than previous minority-based datasets. This quality also means that selection bias issues raised with previous minority-based data collections do not apply to RMAR, as we discuss in more detail in

224 RELIGIOUS MINORITIES AT RISK

Chapters 3 and 4.[1] This, in and of itself, makes it an unprecedented opportunity to delve into the dynamics of minority group-based conflict.

The breadth of the variables available in RMAR is similar to that of MAR, though, as noted, the two data sets cover different types of minorities. This has at least three important implications. First, as we demonstrate in Chapters 3 and 4, there is a substantial theoretical discussion in both the general conflict literature and the religion and politics literature on the role of grievances on conflict, particularly in conflict involving minority groups. Testing these propositions is central to this study. As we discuss in more detail in this chapter the role of grievances is central to understanding the process which leads to conflict involving religious minorities.

Second, the inclusion of multiple types of grievances and DDI as well as other important independent variables measuring factors such as group capacity and group political influence, and demographic factors helps to demonstrate the complexity of the conflict process for religious minorities. Third, the inclusion of multiple dependent variables measuring both peaceful and violent mobilization and conflict, as well as different types of violent conflict, allows us to demonstrate that different antecedents lead to different types of conflict. That is, not only can we analyze what types of factors lead to conflict behavior by religious minorities, we can also isolate which factors lead to different types of conflict behavior.

All of this demonstrates that RMAR is a unique and unprecedented data collection. This study demonstrates and realizes RMAR's potential to provide new insights into the causes and manifestations of conflict by religious minorities. We posit these insights are also relevant to other types of conflict and have important implications for conflict theory. RMAR's focus on religious minorities also provides important insights for the religion and politics literature. In the rest of this chapter we discuss these findings and their implications.

Implications for General Conflict Theory

We posit that this study's most important finding with respect to the conflict literature is that grievances matter. We are not the first to make this argument,

---

[1] Also, in order to assure that there are no issues of selection bias we ran robustness checks for all tests excluding all minorities below the 0.2 percent cutoff. These tests, found in the Appendix, produced substantially the same results as the primary tests, which included all groups found in RMAR.

but we posit that we provide the strongest proof for this contention to date. As we discuss in more detail in Chapters 3 and 4, there is considerable debate over this issue. On one hand, there seems to be wide acceptance that grievances are potentially part of the conflict process, especially for conflicts involving minorities. On the other hand, grievances-based models are heavily criticized on both theoretical and methodological grounds. In addition, several key studies purport to falsify the grievances argument, a contention we dispute on the grounds that none of these studies actually measured grievances, among others. RMAR is designed in a manner that the methodological critiques against previous grievance-based studies do not apply. Our findings clearly support the theoretical argument that grievances matter.

More specifically we find considerable support for a two-stage model whose core is similar to and inspired by the core of Gurr's (1993a, 1993b, 2000a) original MAR model, where DDI makes grievances more likely and grievances, in turn, are associated with higher levels of conflict. However, the particulars matter, and some of our findings on specific relationships diverge from Gurr's MAR model. We discuss this along with our other important empirical findings in more detail in the following sections.

From DDI to Grievances

As we discuss in Chapter 3, despite many theoretical claims that DDI causes grievances, few studies empirically test the link between the two. The few exceptions that use cross-national data find support for a DDI-grievances link. A brief analysis by Gurr (1993b, pp. 178–179) using the Minorities at Risk (MAR) data set found that DDI predicts political, economic, cultural, and autonomy-based grievances by ethnic minorities. Fox (2002a) similarly found that religious DDI causes religious grievances among 105 ethnoreligious minorities included in the MAR data set. Finally, in a precursor to the present study, Basedau et al. (2017) found that religious DDI predicts a general grievances variable among religious minorities.

In this study we provide a similar but more detailed analysis for religious minorities examining the impact of three DDI variables along group capacity and other controls. Overall, we find a clear and strong link between DDI and grievances, but the analysis also reveals that the process is complex. We argue that many of the details of this complex process have important implications for our understanding of the grievance formation process.

226 RELIGIOUS MINORITIES AT RISK

Our findings on the statistical links between DDI and grievances show that all forms of DDI predict at least one form of grievance and all forms of grievances are predicted by at least one form of DDI. However not all forms of DDI predict all forms of grievances. In fact, no form of DDI that we measure predicts all three types of grievance included in the study. Thus, on one hand we establish the larger principle that DDI does predict grievances but, on the other hand, the specifics matter.

The grievance formation process is complex and influenced by multiple factors (e.g., Aspinall, 2007). Economic grievances are weakly influenced by DDI and not only by economic DDI. It is important to reiterate that there is a considerable amount of missing data on the economic status variable but there is sufficient data to provide results. That being said, economic status predicts economic grievances as one would expect—minorities that have a higher economic status are less likely to express economic grievances. Societal religious discrimination (SRD) has a similar impact in that higher SRD predicts higher economic grievances. Minority representation also increases economic grievances. Governmental religious discrimination (GRD) has no significant impact on economic grievances.

Yet the most important predictor of economic grievances is not a form of DDI. Rather, it is capacity-based variables such as minority organization, minority representation, minority policy power, and minority size. Thus, for example, as a minority has more influence over policy in a country, they are less likely to express economic grievances. This implies that even in cases of economic inequality, when religious minorities have the ability to seek redress through influencing policy, they feel less need to express grievances over economic issues. On the other hand, the simple presence of minority organizations, representation, and larger minorities increase economic grievances. Here too, it is the organizations with the capacity to express grievances and a minority's numbers which influence the grievance process in addition to economic DDI.

Thus, while influenced by economic DDI, economic grievances are connected more strongly to noneconomic factors. This, in combination with other factors, has profound implications for our understanding of the influence of economic factors on the conflict process. As we discuss in more detail later in this chapter, this result is part of a complex relationship between economic factors and conflict that possibly illuminates the inconsistent results in previous studies attempting to link economic factors and conflict.

CONCLUSIONS 227

Political grievances are similarly influenced both by DDI and group capacity. In addition to being significantly influenced by both SRD and GRD, minority representation and minority policy power both influence grievances in a manner similar to their influence on economic grievances.

Religious grievances are influenced by GRD but not SRD. This in and of itself is interesting. This means that grievances expressed over religious issues are influenced by the treatment of religious minorities by governments but not their treatment by society. This highlights an important finding: that the impact on grievances of societal DDI (as measured by SRD) differs from that of governmental DDI (as measured by GRD).

It is important to recall that all forms of grievances measured here are public group-level expressions of upset over their status and a desire for redress aimed at governments. Thus, this examination of the data reveals links, or the lack thereof, between objective DDI and the types of complaints for which minority organizations and representatives seek redress from the government. Given this, it is unsurprising that religious grievances—a measure of whether the groups feels discriminated against or marginalized on issues regarding religious practices—is predicted by GRD, which measures governmental restrictions on exactly these issues. It is also not surprising that GRD—DDI by governments—also results in political grievances which, more specifically, measure complaints over discrimination on issues of political inclusion.

However, it is somewhat surprising that SRD does not predict religious grievances. The SRD variable includes components that measure violence and harassment of religious minorities, and much of this violence and harassment is against clergy. Similarly, many of the attacks against property included in the SRD variable are against religious property. Yet SRD is associated with representatives of religious minorities expressing political but not religious grievances. This indicates that rather than responding to SRD in religious terms, religious minorities respond to it in terms of complaints over political exclusion.

This finding that both SRD and GRD are associated with complaints over political exclusion but only GRD predicts complaints over religious issues is a profoundly important finding on how minorities respond to societal-level DDI as opposed to government-level DDI. From the perspective of religious minorities, poor behavior by a government raises both religious issues and issues of inclusion. Again, this is not surprising. That societal-level DDI, as measured by SRD, raises issues of inclusion is also not surprising. It would

228 RELIGIOUS MINORITIES AT RISK

be surprising if discrimination, negative speech acts, harassment, violence, and property crimes perpetrated by members of a religious majority against a religious minority did not cause feelings of exclusion among that minority.

However, that SRD is not associated with religious complaints is unexpected. When a religious minority is targeted as a religious minority one would expect this to also raise religious issues. While we cannot rule out that individual members of religious minorities feel religiously slighted over SRD, we found no evidence that this manifests in efforts to seek redress over religious issues from the government.

Rather SRD's impact on grievances manifests in two ways. First, as noted, it increases political and economic grievances. Second, as we discuss in more detail below, it increases the potential for rioting. This indicates that when governments restrict religious practices and institutions (GRD) religious minorities see this as a religious and political issue. However, when religious minorities experience SRD, they respond in two manners. First, with respect to the government they see political inclusion and influence as the solution. Second, with respect to society they can react with violent frustration. As will be recalled, the SRD variable includes acts of violence and harassment against religious minorities as well as speech acts that most would consider incitement. Given this, a direct and relatively spontaneous form of violent response to SRD such as rioting is not surprising and could be considered an informal expression of general grievances and frustration in a manner similar to the frustration-anger mechanism included in relative deprivation (RD) theory. We address this in more detail later in the chapter.

Given that grievances, as we measure them, are a form of seeking redress, it is not surprising that the RMAR variables for group capacity which measure aspects of political inclusion and political power influence the grievance formation process. Minority representation, which measures whether the religious minority members or organizations are included in government, increases political grievances and to a lesser extent religious and economic grievances. However, minority policy power, which measures whether minority members or organizations influence government policy, decreases all three types of grievances.

This interaction is important. It highlights the distinction between representation and power. Minority representation measures whether a minority has a voice within the government. We posit that this represents a minority that has a greater capacity to publicly seek redress from its government on issues important to it but not necessarily the power to influence policy. That

CONCLUSIONS 229

is, an opposition party in a government, for example, can make itself heard, but its power to influence policy is limited. However, actual power in setting policy reduces the need to express grievances. This is because grievances are essentially a form of request or demand for change in government policy. Minorities which have the power to influence that policy have less of a need to publicly demand such changes.

Grievances, DDI, and Mobilization

As we discuss in Chapter 4, while a large plurality of the literature argues that grievances lead to conflict, there is a substantial contingent that disagrees with this proposition. Our findings show that grievances influence conflict behavior by religious minorities. However, we find that this relationship is complex and mediated by other factors. We show that DDI also matters, but less so than grievances. Thus, while the two-stage model of DDI to grievances and grievances to conflict is supported by the evidence, the data also shows a lesser direct influence by DDI on conflict that occurs in tandem.

Political, religious, and economic factors are all associated with increased levels of nonviolent mobilization. For the political and religious component, it is grievances and not DDI that prompt increased nonviolent mobilization. However, it is a minority's relative economic deprivation rather than economic grievances themselves that appear to influence nonviolent mobilization. Thus, while poorer minorities are more likely to express grievances over economic issues, it is this status of being poor that directly influences nonviolent mobilization rather than these grievances.

All three types of grievances are positively associated with rioting, as is SRD. Rioting is the most spontaneous form of violence measured in this study. The other forms involve organization, purpose, and premeditated decisions.

We posit that SRD leads to rioting because, as noted, all but four of the 27 acts included in SRD are themselves violent, a form of incitement, or otherwise not too far removed from violence. Specifically, four of the components are negative public speech acts against the minority that can be considered forms of incitement. Saying the wrong thing can often lead to rioting as occurred in the Charlie Hebdo riots in 2015, which were incited when the French satirical newspaper Charlie Hebdo published what many Muslims considered an inappropriate picture of the prophet Muhammed. In this case

230 RELIGIOUS MINORITIES AT RISK

the rioting occurred worldwide, not just in France. Three are classified as property crimes such as graffiti and vandalism which can also raise feelings of insecurity, anger, and frustration. Six measure nonviolent harassment. Yet there is no shortage of examples where harassment escalates into violence. Finally, eight are classified as violence against the minority. Thus, as violence begets violence, that SRD can provoke spontaneous violence is not surprising.

In contrast, no form of DDI significantly influence levels of organized violence against civilians (most of which would be classified by most scholars as terror incidents). Political and economic grievances, but not religious grievances make this type of organized violence more likely. In fact, religious grievances decrease the intensity of organized violence against civilians. Unlike riots, organized violence is, by definition, organized. It involves organized groups and premeditated decisions. This implies that the direct link between DDI and conflict is far more likely to inspire spontaneous violence but not premeditated organized violence. Group-level grievances, however, can inspire both.

As noted, the incidence of rebellion is low, which has two consequences for our analysis. First, the results must be considered tentative due to low levels of variation. Second, we accept marginally significant results as sufficiently valid to include in our analysis. Grievances have crosscutting influences on levels of rebellion. Economic grievances (based on marginal significance) are associated with higher levels of rebellion. However, political grievances (based on marginal significance) are associated with lower levels of rebellion. Religious grievances do not influence the likelihood of rebellion but decrease the intensity of rebellion. Conversely, GRD is directly associated with higher incidence of rebellion.

While we discuss our more general explanation for these findings on rebellion later in this chapter in the context of all the results, there is one issue we address here since it is related specifically to rebellion. We argue that GRD's direct influence on rebellion is because it indirectly measures repression. If the effect was more directly related to religion, we believe that the negative influence of religious grievances on rebellion intensity would not be present. Sufficiently repressive states can often suppress nonviolent mobilization and lower levels of violence such as rioting and even organized violence. Thus, when repression is sufficiently high, the only form of conflict likely is the more intense types such as rebellion (Gurr, 1988; Regan & Norton, 2005).

CONCLUSIONS 231

Group Capacity

Group capacity consistently predicts levels of conflict for all four variables. We examine three group capacity variables. *Group organization* measures the presence of political parties or advocacy groups for the minority but does not address whether these groups have representatives in the government. *Political representation* measures whether the minority has representatives in the (legislative branch of) government but not whether those representatives influence government policy. Finally, *policy power* measures whether group representatives influence policy.

The policy power variable has some ambiguities as to whether it truly measures DDI or group capacity. It has four values. First, the minority group dominates government decision-making. Second, the group has power over policy along with the religious majority and, potentially, other minority groups. Third, the minority exercises no power over policy but there is no official bar to such power. For example, the group could have elected representatives in a country's legislative body but be in the opposition. Fourth, the group is completely excluded from political power. Altogether then, even as this variable is an important marker of group capacity, it also represents a reversed scaled form of DDI (political deprivation), which we demonstrate in Chapter 3 to have a significant impact upon the expression and intensity of grievances.

We find that all forms of both nonviolent and violent mobilization are significantly influenced by capacity. Political organization increases the incidence of all our dependent variables other than rebellion. Political representation influences all the dependent variables other than nonviolent mobilization. As political organizations both with and without representatives in government bodies are, at least in theory, both roughly equally capable of organizing, we posit these findings mean that groups with organizational capacity are more likely to engage in both violent and nonviolent organized mobilization and conflict.

The results for policy power are intriguing. While only marginally significant, they indicate that groups with a higher influence on government policy are less likely to rebel, but the variable has no influence on the other three outcomes we examine. That groups which influence policy are less likely to rebel shows some nuance to the concept of capacity. That is, if the group's capacity is sufficiently significant that it can get results based on capacity alone, conflict, or at least its most violent manifestations, become less desirable. In fact, organized violence might undermine the group's ability to influence

232 RELIGIOUS MINORITIES AT RISK

policy so it would be counterproductive. This result is also consistent with expectations if we treat policy power as a DDI variable, because it predicts that groups that are less excluded from power, rebel less. Nevertheless, the variable's primary influence is through its influence on grievances.

Other Influences

The two most important influences that are not DDI, grievance, or capacity measures are demographic. Larger minorities engage in all forms of mobilization more often and more intensely. Also, conflict is more common and intense in more populous countries. Minority size can also be seen as a capacity variable. That is, larger minorities have more resources, even if these resources are only manpower related, and more influence. Also, because not all members of a minority need participate in nonviolent mobilization or violence for such phenomena to occur, a larger number of people increases the chances that at least some will participate in these activities. The results for the country's population size similarly indicate that when there is more opportunity for an event to occur, as measured by the number of people that could potentially participate, it is more likely to occur.

The other results are of less importance to our central theoretical arguments and are discussed in more detail in Chapter 5.

The Bigger Picture: The Dynamics of Conflicts by Religious Minorities

While we consider the finding that grievances matter to be the most important finding of this study, of near similar importance is our finding that conflict behavior by religious minorities is complex and influenced by multiple simultaneous mechanisms. For this reason, we feel that arguments focusing on which theory or mechanism is the primary influence on conflict are asking the wrong question. Rather than asking which theory is correct, we should ask which combination of theories or mechanisms drive conflict and under which circumstances?

We posit there are at least four theoretically important mechanisms. First, as noted, grievances matter. The mechanism first articulated by Gurr (1993a, 1993b, 2000a) where DDI causes group-level grievances and these group-level

CONCLUSIONS 233

grievances, in turn, predict conflict is confirmed by our study. However, this process is complex because not all types of DDI cause all kinds of group-level grievances and not all types of group-level grievances cause all types of conflict. Thus, the specifics and nuances of these grievances also matter.

A second mechanism is the government's ability to accommodate grievances. As we argue in Chapter 5, some types of grievances are easier to accommodate than others. Political and religious grievances can be accommodated through policies of inclusion or, conversely, repealing policies of exclusion. Economic grievances, however, are more difficult to accommodate even in cases where a government is willing in principle to do so. This accommodation often involves policies of affirmative action and income redistribution, which can be politically unpopular and often fail (Holzer & Neumark, 2006; also see Besançon, 2005; Houle, 2018, Schock, 1996; Solt, 2008).

A third mechanism involves DDI and grievances. Our findings show that SRD influences rioting only among types of conflict behavior. As will be recalled from our discussions in Chapters 3 and 4, many argue that DDI will nearly always result in grievances to the extent that one need only measure DDI and some even conflate the two empirically (e.g., Cederman et al., 2013; Collier & Hoeffler, 2002, 2004; Fearon & Laitin, 2003). We argue that the evidence shows that while there is a correlation between the two, DDI does not automatically cause grievances in exact proportion to levels of DDI, especially with regard to group-level grievances.

The grievance variables we measure in this study are group-level and measure whether group representatives and organizations publicly express these grievances as part of an agenda-seeking public redress. However, the dynamics of SRD and conflict imply the presence of a different type of grievance: individual-level grievances. These grievances are similar to those implied in RD theory. RD theory, as formulated by Gurr (1970), posits that perceived DDI results in frustration, which results in anger which, in turn results in aggression and violence. The theory is drawn from conceptions of RD in the psychology literature, which is intended to explain the behavior of individuals rather than collective behavior. Thus, in its essence it is an individual-level theory used to explain collective behavior (Rule, 1988, p. 202).

However, if we accept that individuals can feel grievances, irrespective of whether they are expressed at the group level, individual-level grievances can also inspire conflict behavior. However, because there is no group-level element to these grievances, the behavior that is inspired by individual-level grievances most likely would be spontaneous collective violence, such as

234 RELIGIOUS MINORITIES AT RISK

riots. That is, riots are rarely purposeful and planed in advance. Rather they occur when many individuals spontaneously choose to join a riot event perhaps due to their anger and frustration, though this does not rule out other motives for joining, such as a desire to loot.

This also explains why it is SRD and not GRD that directly influences rioting. GRD is a government policy that is relatively constant, especially when compared to SRD. While GRD does change over time, this change is slow and does not occur often in a particular country (Fox, 2016, 2020). While a constant, mostly unchanging form of DDI can in theory spark a spontaneous event such as a riot, we posit that riots tend to be sparked over discreet events. In the case of GRD this would be relatively rare events such as a government imposing a new form of GRD or a particularly public and harsh act of enforcement of an existing GRD policy.

SRD, on the other hand, is a series of events. If SRD is at high levels in a country, this is because there are multiple discreet SRD events in any given year. A clergy member from the majority publicly denigrates the minority, perhaps in a manner that strikes a nerve. A place of worship is vandalized or perhaps set on fire. Members of the majority are harassed, attacked, or killed. Each of these is a distinct event that can not only cause frustration and anger on its own but also may awaken preexisting deep-seated frustration and anger. As these events become more common and severe, this frustration and anger builds and each new event has an increased likelihood of being the straw that breaks the camel's back and provoking a riot.

Thus, riots are about deep-seated, systemic DDI that builds frustration and anger over time. But they are also usually sparked by a specific discrete event and are perpetrated by a group of unorganized individuals who are each individually frustrated and angry.

Based on this we theorize that there are at least two different types of grievances that are relevant to conflict behavior by religious minorities, individual-level grievances and group-level grievances. While individual-level grievances can spark events such as riots, group-level grievances are the more influential of the two. This is because group-level grievances are an important step in organizing for more purposeful political action such as organized protest, lobbying the government, and organized violence such as terrorism and rebellion. All of these activities have in common that they are not spontaneous and their purpose is to seek to influence governments or perhaps replace them, in order to achieve a policy goal that serves group interests which is often the redress of grievances.

CONCLUSIONS 235

We acknowledge that there is an alternative mechanism that can explain this result. It is possible that the DDI variables are capturing unmeasured group-level grievances. That is, our group-level grievance measures are imperfect in that they capture some but not all activities that would be considered group-level grievance expression, and the DDI variables are acting as surrogates for this. We consider this the less likely explanation but cannot rule it out. Further research that includes the measurement of both individual-level grievances and group-level grievances is necessary in order to provide evidence to confirm or falsify our arguments regarding individual-level grievances.

The final theoretically important mechanism is group capacity. We follow Gurr (1993a, 1993b, 2000a) and Tarrow (1989) in arguing that both grievances and capacity matter. It is not an either-or type of proposition as suggested by advocates of capacity and mobilization arguments such as Tilly (1978), McCarthy and Zald (1977), and Fearon and Laitin (2003), among others. Rather, capacity works in conjunction with other factors including but not limited to grievances to influence levels of conflict. It is also worth emphasizing that capacity influences both stages of our two-stage model. It influences grievance formation as well as conflict behavior once grievances have been formed.

We specifically rebut the arguments by McCarthy and Zald (1977), Collier et al. (2004), and Collier and Hoeffler (2002, 2004), among others, that grievances are sufficiently ubiquitous that they do not matter. Rather we demonstrate, as did Gurr (1993a, 1993b, 2000a) and Fox (2002a, 2004), that group-level grievances vary, and this variation is an important influence on conflict. Because we do not measure individual-level grievances we cannot directly disprove claims that such grievances have this level of ubiquity, but we argue that our results showing SRD influences riots imply that individual-level grievances vary at least in part based on levels of certain types of DDI.

Thus, we posit that grievances provide the motivation, or at least one of them, for conflict behavior by religious minorities. However, capacity provides the explanation for how groups organize for conflict behavior. Each is an important part of the conflict process and it is important to understand how they work in conjunction. While, as we discuss in Chapter 5, other factors also influence levels of conflict behavior by religious minorities, these are those on which we focus theoretically. We also allow that it is possible other unmeasured motivations such as "greed" or other forms of opportunity (e.g., Collier & Hoeffler, 2004) may influence the conflict process.

Some Implications

Our findings have some significant implications for the study of domestic conflict and civil wars beyond the presence of a complex conflict process for religious minorities that involves both grievances and capacity. In fact, we posit that this complex relationship sheds some light on the inconsistent findings found in the original RD literature as well as the ongoing debates over whether grievances influence conflict.

RD theory essentially predicted there is a link between DDI and conflict; however, as we discuss in more detail in Chapters 3 and 4, studies based on RD theory found inconsistent results when testing this relationship. We posit that these inconsistent findings are due to the complex relationship between DDI and conflict behavior that is different from the complex multistep process predicted by RD theory. In fact, our findings show that, when looking at the conflict behavior of religious minorities, the influence of DDI on conflict is complex in at least four ways.

First, the primary influence of DDI on conflict is mediated through group-level grievances. Few of the event-based, cross-national RD-based studies measured grievances of any kind, and the survey-based studies rarely measured objective DDI. Thus, these studies did not account for the two-stage process that we argue causes conflict behavior by religious minorities. Put differently, when A causes B and B causes C there will sometimes be a statistical correlation between A and C, but in most cases any correlation will be weaker than those found in each of the two stages of this process and often the direct correlation will not be significant. Thus, studies which do not use grievances in their models, which characterizes nearly all cross-national RD studies, will often find no relationship between their DDI and conflict variables.

Second, different DDI measures behave differently. Thus, when measuring the direct impact of DDI on conflict, each type of DDI has a different pattern of influence on the conflict process as well as different influences on different dependent variables. This means the specific type of DDI measured in a study as well as the specific type of conflict variable will influence the results. This is particularly relevant to economic DDI variables which, as discussed in detail earlier in this chapter, have a complex relationship with grievances and conflict behavior. Because most early, cross-national, RD-based studies used economic variables, this complex relationship helps explain the lack of consistent results in these studies.

CONCLUSIONS   237

Third, the non-DDI and grievance variables are important. The presence or absence of different independent variables in addition to the DDI variables can influence results. This manifestation of the complexity of the relationships tested in this study likely influenced many RD studies.

Fourth, all the dynamics found in this study apply to religious minorities. It is likely that the details of this complexity are different for other types of minorities. For example, Gurr (1993a, 1993b, 2000a), when testing the links between DDI and grievances for ethnic minorities found results similar to this study in that different forms of DDI had different influences on his several grievance variables, and these grievance variables had different influences on his several conflict behavior variables. However, these specifics differ from the specifics of our study. For example, Gurr (1993b, p. 180) found that economic, social, and political grievances all influenced mobilization for protest but only political grievances influenced rebellion. Thus, the population of a study is also important. It is also worth noting that both this study and studies based on Gurr's MAR project focus on minorities. Studies that seek to explain conflicts that are not minority-based likely also have different dynamics.

In sum, the complexity of our results illuminates both the conflict process as well the challenges to any such study due to this complexity. They not only explain the widely diverging results of previous studies, they also demonstrate that much future work needs to be done examining the complex relationship between DDI, grievances, and conflict among problem sets other than religious minorities. Our results also demonstrate that true understanding of conflict processes is not possible without accounting for grievances in addition to DDI, and that the type of DDI and grievance examined matters. While we establish this in the specific case of religious minorities, it is reasonable to believe that this finding will travel to other contexts, and our findings certainly provide a basis for a mandate to test this proposition for other problem sets. Because other than a small number of studies based on our data and the MAR data, no cross-national study includes true grievance variables, this future research is essentially a reevaluation of nearly everything we think we know about civil wars and domestic conflicts, particularly those involving minorities.

Implications for the Religion and Conflict Literature

The results of this study provide a number of important insights that are specific to the religion and conflict literature. These insights, while adding

238 RELIGIOUS MINORITIES AT RISK

to what we know about religion and conflict, also highlight some things we do not know and suggest avenues for future research. We highlight three takeaways for the religion and conflict literature. First, religious minorities in many ways behave similarly to other types of minorities. Second, religious grievances contribute to protest and rioting but not organized violence. Third, measurements and definitions matter.

Religious Minorities Behave Much Like Other Minorities

Perhaps this study's most important finding with regard to the religion and conflict literature is that when examining the conflict behavior of religious minorities, the "minorities" aspect is more important than the "religion" aspect. While religious DDI (as measured by GRD and SRD) and grievances are important aspects of the conflict process, so are political and economic DDI and grievances as well as the minority's level of organization, representation in government, and power over policy. That is, religious DDI is just one among many forms of DDI that might be placed on a religious minorities and grievances expressed over religious issues are one among several forms of grievances expressed by these minorities.

This is not to say that religious DDI and grievances are not important. As we discuss in more detail, they are. Nevertheless, religious DDI and grievances are part of the larger picture, which involves many secular factors and the dynamics of religious DDI; causing grievances that influence conflict is a pattern that is comparable to other types of DDI and grievances for religious and other minorities. Taking a step back, the larger takeaway from this aspect of the study is that not all conflict involving religious minorities is about religion. While religion can be important, that is not always the case, and even when it is, other nonreligious factors are generally in play. Thus, it is important to remember that religious minorities are minorities that are in many ways comparable and similar to other types of minorities.

Religious Grievances among Religious Minorities Do Not Cause Organized Violence

When looking at religious minorities *as a whole*—a qualification that we posit is quite important—religious grievances are associated with protest

CONCLUSIONS 239

and rioting by the minority but lower levels of organized violence including organized violence against civilians and terror. This contrasts strongly with the existing literature on religious violence and conflict, which largely finds a link between the presence of religious motivations, beliefs, ideology, issues, and content on one hand and violence conflict on the other. We believe there are three reasons for these diverging results.

First, we argue that the behavior of religious minorities is often different from those of religious conflicts within the same religious group. Conflicts between religious minorities and the state are, by definition, interreligious. Religious minorities tend to be seeking political inclusion or an end to DDI because they are treated differently. In contrast, religious conflicts within the same religion usually involve differences within the same group over the role religion should play in politics and government or differences over theology itself. These demands generally are not the removal of restrictions on religion but, rather, demands for privileging the majority religion and perhaps state enforcement of the majority religion.

The few previous studies that include religious grievances are consistent with this finding. Fox (2002a, 2004) found that religious grievances could only enhance levels of violence in the presence of grievances over autonomy among ethnoreligious minorities but in the absence of autonomy grievances, had little effect. Basedau et al. (2017) in a study of religious minorities in Asia, Latin America, the Middle East, and sub-Saharan Africa found no correlation between grievances and violence. Basedau et al. (2016) do find a link between grievances and conflict but used the country rather than the minority as the unit of analysis and the grievances variable measures grievances over DDI in general and is not religion-specific.

In contrast, the studies that find a link between violence and religious motivations, beliefs, ideology, issues, and content do not focus on religious minorities. While these variables are not identical to our religious grievance variable which measures expression of grievances over restrictions on religious practices and institutions—an expression that is essentially seeking redress for these grievances—as we argue in Chapter 4, they are sufficiently similar to make the results comparable. That is, while most do not include grievances specifically in their variable definitions, they include some form of demand that involves a change in how a government deals with religion or perhaps to replace the current government with one that will deal with religion differently. This includes variables which measure whether opposition groups of various kinds seek change in government religion laws or policy

(Asal et al., 2014; Svensson, 2007; Svensson, 2013; Svensson & Harding, 2011), seek to prioritize their preferred religion over others (Breslawski & Ives, 2017; Svensson, 2007; Svensson, 2013; Svensson & Harding, 2011), seek to establish a religious state (Karakaya, 2016), or have religious goals or demands (Deitch, 2022). Henne (2012) includes religious grievances in his definition but also other aspects of religion. Other variables are more general and just measure the presence of religious ideologies, motivations or issues (Abrahms & Potter, 2015; Bercovitch & Darouen, 2005; Carter et al., 2020; Toft, 2007, 2021; Karakaya, 2016) which could include grievances or something similar but the specifics are unspecified.

All these studies other than Bercovitch and Darouen (2005) and Karakaya (2016) found a significant link between their religion variable and conflict. These previous studies which use this type of variable focus on one of two types of units of analysis. The first is conflicts or civil wars (Deitch, 2022; Svensson 2007; Svensson, 2013; Svensson & Harding, 2011; Toft, 2007, 2021). The second is political organizations and factions (Abrahms & Potter, 2015; Asal et al., 2014; Breslawski & Ives, 2017; Carter et al., 2020). Thus, they include problem sets, which involve both conflicts within the religious majority and interreligious conflict. This implies that these significant findings are being driven more by the intrareligious conflicts than the interreligious conflicts. Put differently, our findings compared with those of previous studies indicates that religious issues, grievances, motivations, ideology, and beliefs are likely to cause organized violence in interreligious conflicts but not intrareligious conflicts. Future research specifically comparing the impact of the same religion variable on interreligious and intrareligious conflict would be necessary to fully test this proposition.

Second, while our study looks at the behavior of religious minorities as a whole, nearly all of the previous religion and conflict studies focus on either political organizations or conflicts. Thus, they largely focus on religious armed groups who are a subset of all members of the relevant group. This is less important for the dependent variable than the independent variable. Our grievance variables measure grievances expressed by all representative of the group. The religious motivations, beliefs, ideology, issues, and content variables in these other studies are largely those expressed by violent organizations and combatants. This implies who among a religious group expresses religious grievances, motivations, beliefs, ideology, and issues is important. It also implies that much of what determines the link between religion and conflict occurs at the organizational level.

CONCLUSIONS 241

Third, most previous studies do not differentiate among different types of violence as we do in our study. However, this is only a partial explanation because, as shown in Chapter 5, even when looking at violence in general without differentiating between types, there is no significant relationship between religious grievances and violence. Given this, future studies of religion and conflict would benefit from developing variables that allow for testing different types of conflict behavior.

Measurement and Definitions Matter

Our results using religious grievances, GRD, and SRD reveal a complex relationship between religion and conflict behavior by religious minorities. Each of these variables has a different influence on conflict behavior. All of them are likely better predictors than religious identity variables which remain common as independent variables in the religious conflict literature. All of them are also more specific than, for example, a variable measuring whether "religious issues" are present in a conflict, an organization has a "religious ideology," or a conflict has "religious content." Both religious grievances and GRD would both constitute religious issues or content, as would many forms of SRD. Thus, the extent to which we are more specific and detailed about how we define and measure religion is important.

Given this, we argue that studies of religion and conflict would benefit from more detailed and specific variables. Religious issues, motivations, and content, for example, can be divided into more specific types with separate variables measuring each. It is likely that different manifestations of religion and different types of religion-based demands will have different influences of conflict. For example, as noted, demands to create a theocracy likely influences conflict differently than grievances expressed over religious discrimination. Future studies of religion and conflict, as well as the impact of religion in other social, political, and economic phenomena should take this onto account. The few existing studies which do so demonstrate the utility of this research strategy. These include Saiya's (2017a) study of the impact of blasphemy laws on terror, Saiya and Manchanda's (2020) study of the impact of veil prohibitions on terror in Europe, and Asal et al.'s (2014) variable for ideologies of gender exclusion.

Our results also show that it is important to match one's variables to one's theory. For example, many previous studies argue that the mechanism which

242 RELIGIOUS MINORITIES AT RISK

links DDI to conflict is grievances. Yet very few of these studies measure grievances and rely on DDI variables and, in some cases, variables that can only be described as surrogates for DDI. As we demonstrate, setting aside the complex relationship between DDI and grievances including that the specific types of DDI and grievances measured matter, the direct influence of DDI and grievances on conflict can be quite different. Thus, the match between theory and measurement is critical if one wishes to accurately evaluate a theory.

Policy Implications

Our study is not intended as a policy paper. Rather it is intended to delve into the complex causes of conflict behavior by religious minorities. Nevertheless, our findings do have some implications for policy.

While this policy recommendation is not novel, our findings show that reducing DDI and increasing the political inclusion of religious minorities contributes to greater domestic peace. While policymakers are unlikely to find this revelation to be surprising, our findings do provide some novel information on how to go about this process. First, in addition to reducing DDI, it is important that minorities feel they have an avenue to influence policy. Minorities who have this type of access express fewer grievances and engage in less violence.

Second, grievances are important. While for many reasons it is good policy to reduce the levels of DDI even in the absence of grievances, the presence of organized groups expressing grievances is a sign that conflict behavior is more imminent.

Third, grievances can be accommodated, and when they are accommodated violence is reduced. Our results imply that political and religious grievances are most often accommodated well before levels of violence reach relatively extreme levels. Accommodating them before they escalate will in the long run likely be less costly and more effective in reducing violence and instability.

Fourth, economic DDI and grievances are the most difficult to accommodate in the short term and require long-term policies that will take time to show results. This underlines our recommendation to address DDI and grievances as early as possible.

Fifth, DDI encourages the formation of identity-based political organizations to represent the aggrieved minority. Identity politics is inherently destabilizing so policies intended to remove the impetus for the formation of these types of organizations will likely be beneficial for stability and national unity. This is not a new observation. For example, *The Ethics of the Fathers* (2:4 and 4:5) twice warns of the dangers of separating oneself from the community.

Some Final Thoughts

This study provides new data and insight into a long-standing discussion. We would like to conclude by highlighting some general thoughts about how to have that discussion rather than what conclusions that discussion ought to reach. First, the minority level of analysis is important. Countries do not treat all minorities the same, and each minority in the country is in its own way unique. This means that when examining conflict in a country that involves minorities, the research design needs to account for this. This is not intended to discount country-level factors such as regime type and economic performance. Rather, we believe that we have demonstrated that the subnational level of analysis is a critical part of the conflict process and should be included in future research.

Second, we support a multitheory approach. Just as the multimethod approach argues that each method of research has advantages and disadvantages, we argue the same is true of theory. No theory has a monopoly on insight. Thus, while grievances can influence conflict behavior, so can capacity as well as other approaches such as greed. In this context, we do not see our findings as the triumph of grievance theory over its competitors in the academic marketplace. Rather, our results show that multiple factors, including but not limited to grievances, influence conflict. While all theories should be tested rigorously, we suggest that research designs that focus on which combination of theories and factors influence conflict will be more productive than research designs intended to prove that a single theoretical approach is the correct one.

Finally, that being said, grievances matter. Grievances are often discussed but rarely tested in the cross-national conflict literature, including the religion and conflict literature. While we make no claim that grievances are the only influence on conflict, we believe we have established that they are sufficiently important to be explicitly included into future empirical work and theorizing.

APPENDIX

Supplementary Analyses and Robustness Checks

Chapter 3

Table 3.1A Determinants of General Grievance and Intensity, 2000–2014, Odds Ratios

	Grievance Expressed		Grievance Intensity	
	(1a)	(2a)	(1b)	(2b)
	Correlated RE Logit	Correlated RE Logit	Correlated RE Ordered Logit	Correlated RE Ordered Logit
GRD (1 year lag)	1.095***	1.111*	1.080***	1.108*
	(0.023)	(0.057)	(0.019)	(0.046)
SRD (1 year lag)	1.160***	1.093*	1.113***	1.087**
	(0.025)	(0.040)	(0.019)	(0.031)
Minority Political	3.816***	6.297***	3.591***	5.667***
Organization	(0.698)	(1.456)	(0.639)	(1.201)
Minority	1.875***	1.381[†]	2.082***	1.428**
Representation	(0.293)	(0.258)	(0.332)	(0.196)
Minority	0.720**	0.688***	0.810[†]	0.738***
Policy Power	(0.091)	(0.078)	(0.101)	(0.063)
Religious Similarity	1.333	1.719*	1.310[†]	1.727*
to Majority	(0.266)	(0.410)	(0.214)	(0.373)
Minority Population	1.051***	1.061***	1.034***	1.047***
%	(0.011)	(0.012)	(0.010)	(0.010)
Log Country	1.215*	1.236***	1.218**	1.247***
Population	(0.094)	(0.074)	(0.085)	(0.069)
Log GDP/capita	1.134	1.072	1.138	1.083
	(0.107)	(0.089)	(0.099)	(0.081)
Polyarchy Score	1.032	1.688	0.878	1.209
(V-Dem)	(0.476)	(0.738)	(0.375)	(0.441)

(continued)

246 APPENDIX

Table 3.1A Continued

	Grievance Expressed		Grievance Intensity	
	(1a)	(2a)	(1b)	(2b)
	Correlated RE Logit	Correlated RE Logit	Correlated RE Ordered Logit	Correlated RE Ordered Logit
Regime Durability	0.998	0.998	0.998	1.000
	(0.003)	(0.004)	(0.003)	(0.003)
Mean GRD	0.942[†]		0.953[†]	
Country Level	(0.030)		(0.027)	
Mean SRD	0.998		0.998	
Country Level	(0.042)		(0.042)	
Mean GRD		0.953		0.949
Group Level		(0.053)		(0.043)
Mean SRD		1.123**		1.089*
Group Level		(0.049)		(0.038)
Constant/Cuts	Omitted	Omitted	Omitted	Omitted
Observations	9355	9355	9355	9355
Year Effects	Yes	Yes	Yes	Yes
Clustering	Country	Country Group	Country	Country Group

Robust standard errors are in parentheses

*** $p < 0.001$, ** $p < 0.01$, * $p < 0.05$, [†] $p < 0.10$

APPENDIX   247

Table 3.1B Determinants of General Grievance and Intensity, 2000–2014, Minorities at or above 0.2% Population Cutoff

	Grievance Expressed		Grievance Intensity	
	(1a)	(2a)	(1b)	(2b)
	Correlated RE Logit	Correlated RE Logit	Correlated RE Ordered Logit	Correlated RE Ordered Logit
GRD (1 year lag)	0.099***	0.068	0.069**	0.085†
	(0.028)	(0.050)	(0.023)	(0.047)
SRD (1 year lag)	0.167***	0.067†	0.117***	0.072*
	(0.031)	(0.041)	(0.023)	(0.032)
Minority Political	1.460***	1.895***	1.457***	1.802***
Organization	(0.218)	(0.260)	(0.212)	(0.238)
Minority	0.681***	0.492*	0.757***	0.443***
Representation	(0.185)	(0.198)	(0.184)	(0.137)
Minority	−0.400**	−0.419***	−0.248†	−0.325***
Policy Power	(0.141)	(0.118)	(0.140)	(0.087)
Religious Similarity	0.530*	0.706**	0.383*	0.671**
to Majority	(0.210)	(0.257)	(0.184)	(0.230)
Minority Population	0.046***	0.056***	0.030**	0.043***
%	(0.012)	(0.012)	(0.011)	(0.009)
Log Country	0.189*	0.260***	0.183**	0.255***
Population	(0.082)	(0.067)	(0.071)	(0.061)
Log GDP/capita	0.159	0.145	0.156	0.133
	(0.099)	(0.092)	(0.087)	(0.081)
Polyarchy Score	0.069	0.345	−0.162	0.045
(V-Dem)	(0.498)	(0.483)	(0.453)	(0.394)
Regime Durability	−0.003	−0.003	−0.002	−0.000
	(0.003)	(0.004)	(0.003)	(0.004)
Mean GRD	−0.072†		−0.045	
Country Level	(0.037)		(0.032)	
Mean SRD	−0.025		−0.010	
Country Level	(0.061)		(0.054)	
Mean GRD		−0.023		−0.047
Group Level		(0.055)		(0.051)
Mean SRD		0.137**		0.091*
Group Level		(0.048)		(0.038)

(*continued*)

248 APPENDIX

Table 3.1B Continued

	Grievance Expressed		Grievance Intensity	
	(1a)	(2a)	(1b)	(2b)
	Correlated RE Logit	Correlated RE Logit	Correlated RE Ordered Logit	Correlated RE Ordered Logit
Constant/Cuts	Omitted	Omitted	Omitted	Omitted
Observations	7211	7211	7211	7211
Year Effects	Yes	Yes	Yes	Yes
Clustering	Country	Country Group	Country	Country Group

Robust standard errors are in parentheses

*** $p < 0.001$, ** $p < 0.01$, * $p < 0.05$, [†] $p < 0.10$

APPENDIX 249

Table 3.2A Determinants of Political Grievance and Intensity, 2000–2014, Odds Ratios

	Grievance Expressed		Grievance Intensity	
	(3a)	(4a)	(3b)	(4b)
	Correlated RE Logit	Correlated RE Logit	Correlated RE Ordered Logit	Correlated RE Ordered Logit
GRD (1 year lag)	1.085***	1.084	1.071***	1.113*
	(0.023)	(0.055)	(0.020)	(0.055)
SRD (1 year lag)	1.106***	1.091[†]	1.104***	1.095*
	(0.026)	(0.049)	(0.023)	(0.042)
Minority Political	3.908***	6.514***	3.531***	5.598***
Organization	(0.846)	(1.427)	(0.717)	(1.125)
Minority	1.885***	1.421[†]	1.974***	1.484*
Representation	(0.289)	(0.267)	(0.280)	(0.247)
Minority	0.840	0.750*	0.865	0.771**
Policy Power	(0.105)	(0.087)	(0.109)	(0.077)
Religious Similarity	1.219	1.679*	1.263	1.665*
to Majority	(0.220)	(0.406)	(0.223)	(0.375)
Minority Population	1.027[†]	1.030**	1.027*	1.028**
%	(0.014)	(0.011)	(0.011)	(0.010)
Log Country	1.180*	1.179**	1.197**	1.188**
Population	(0.080)	(0.070)	(0.076)	(0.066)
Log GDP/capita	1.055	0.955	1.063	0.964
	(0.102)	(0.077)	(0.099)	(0.073)
Polyarchy Score	1.396	2.262[†]	1.093	1.687
(V-Dem)	(0.744)	(1.096)	(0.546)	(0.717)
Regime Durability	0.998	1.000	1.000	1.002
	(0.004)	(0.004)	(0.004)	(0.004)
Mean GRD	0.949		0.961	
Country Level	(0.032)		(0.028)	
Mean SRD	1.011		0.990	
Country Level	(0.052)		(0.048)	
Mean GRD		0.982		0.948
Group Level		(0.054)		(0.051)
Mean SRD		1.076		1.057
Group Level		(0.054)		(0.046)

(*continued*)

Table 3.2A Continued

	Grievance Expressed		Grievance Intensity	
	(3a)	(4a)	(3b)	(4b)
	Correlated RE Logit	Correlated RE Logit	Correlated RE Ordered Logit	Correlated RE Ordered Logit
Constant/Cuts	Omitted	Omitted	Omitted	Omitted
Observations	9355	9355	9355	9355
Year Effects	Yes	Yes	Yes	Yes
Clustering	Country	Country Group	Country	Country Group

Robust standard errors are in parentheses

*** $p < 0.001$, ** $p < 0.01$, * $p < 0.05$, † $p < 0.10$

APPENDIX 251

Table 3.2B Determinants of Political Grievance and Intensity, 2000–2014, Minorities at or above 0.2% Population Cutoff

	Grievance Expressed		Grievance Intensity	
	(3a)	(4a)	(3b)	(4b)
	Correlated RE Logit	Correlated RE Logit	Correlated RE Ordered Logit	Correlated RE Ordered Logit
GRD (1 year lag)	0.087**	0.067	0.068**	0.091
	(0.028)	(0.058)	(0.022)	(0.055)
SRD (1 year lag)	0.098***	0.057	0.096***	0.066
	(0.031)	(0.055)	(0.027)	(0.046)
Minority Political	1.588***	2.010***	1.487***	1.841***
Organization	(0.274)	(0.253)	(0.254)	(0.231)
Minority	0.704***	0.488*	0.761***	0.542***
Representation	(0.182)	(0.201)	(0.175)	(0.170)
Minority	−0.231	−0.300*	−0.182	−0.263*
Policy Power	(0.145)	(0.127)	(0.144)	(0.108)
Religious Similarity	0.469*	0.702**	0.464*	0.688**
to Majority	(0.197)	(0.265)	(0.208)	(0.244)
Minority Population	0.024	0.030**	0.024*	0.028**
%	(0.016)	(0.012)	(0.012)	(0.010)
Log Country	0.150*	0.188**	0.162*	0.187**
Population	(0.072)	(0.067)	(0.066)	(0.061)
Log GDP/capita	0.051	−0.018	0.065	−0.020
	(0.101)	(0.093)	(0.095)	(0.084)
Polyarchy Score	0.446	0.829	0.060	0.419
(V-Dem)	(0.632)	(0.569)	(0.591)	(0.489)
Regime Durability	−0.001	0.001	0.001	0.003
	(0.005)	(0.004)	(0.004)	(0.004)
Mean GRD	−0.062		−0.044	
Country Level	(0.040)		(0.032)	
Mean SRD	0.014		−0.019	
Country Level	(0.073)		(0.062)	
Mean GRD		−0.011		−0.045
Group Level		(0.062)		(0.060)
Mean SRD		0.090		0.064
Group Level		(0.060)		(0.050)

(continued)

252 APPENDIX

Table 3.2B Continued

	Grievance Expressed		Grievance Intensity	
	(3a)	(4a)	(3b)	(4b)
	Correlated RE Logit	Correlated RE Logit	Correlated RE Ordered Logit	Correlated RE Ordered Logit
Constant/Cuts	Omitted	Omitted	Omitted	Omitted
Observations	7211	7211	7211	7211
Year Effects	Yes	Yes	Yes	Yes
Clustering	Country	Country Group	Country	Country Group

Robust standard errors are in parentheses

*** $p < 0.001$, ** $p < 0.01$, * $p < 0.05$, † $p < 0.10$

APPENDIX 253

Table 3.3A Determinants of Religious Grievance and Intensity, 2000–2014, Odds Ratios

	Grievance Expressed		Grievance Intensity	
	(5a)	(6a)	(5b)	(6b)
	Correlated RE Logit	Correlated RE Logit	Correlated RE Ordered Logit	Correlated RE Ordered Logit
GRD (1 year lag)	1.077***	1.121*	1.069***	1.098*
	(0.023)	(0.058)	(0.021)	(0.046)
SRD (1 year lag)	1.085***	1.038	1.079***	1.035
	(0.023)	(0.032)	(0.020)	(0.025)
Minority Political	3.079***	5.049***	2.964***	4.646***
Organization	(0.606)	(1.337)	(0.534)	(1.135)
Minority	1.770*	1.407	1.760**	1.349†
Representation	(0.400)	(0.305)	(0.371)	(0.234)
Minority	0.805	0.743*	0.842	0.770*
Policy Power	(0.109)	(0.095)	(0.111)	(0.094)
Religious Similarity	1.353	1.748*	1.308	1.652*
to Majority	(0.271)	(0.453)	(0.219)	(0.391)
Minority Population	1.039***	1.055***	1.032***	1.048***
%	(0.011)	(0.012)	(0.009)	(0.011)
Log Country	1.187*	1.252***	1.178*	1.244***
Population	(0.099)	(0.085)	(0.091)	(0.077)
Log GDP/capita	1.106	1.042	1.092	1.038
	(0.110)	(0.105)	(0.101)	(0.093)
Polyarchy Score	1.147	1.656	1.020	1.406
(V-Dem)	(0.594)	(0.901)	(0.475)	(0.624)
Regime Durability	0.994	0.995	0.997	0.999
	(0.004)	(0.005)	(0.004)	(0.004)
Mean GRD	0.977		0.982	
Country Level	(0.031)		(0.029)	
Mean SRD	1.013		1.022	
Country Level	(0.050)		(0.045)	
Mean GRD		0.955		0.970
Group Level		(0.052)		(0.043)
Mean SRD		1.101*		1.099**
Group Level		(0.044)		(0.034)

(continued)

254 APPENDIX

Table 3.3A Continued

	Grievance Expressed		Grievance Intensity	
	(5a)	(6a)	(5b)	(6b)
	Correlated RE Logit	Correlated RE Logit	Correlated RE Ordered Logit	Correlated RE Ordered Logit
Constant/Cuts	Omitted	Omitted	Omitted	Omitted
Observations	9355	9355	9355	9355
Year Effects	Yes	Yes	Yes	Yes
Clustering	Country	Country Group	Country	Country Group

Robust standard errors are in parentheses

*** $p < 0.001$, ** $p < 0.01$, * $p < 0.05$, † $p < 0.10$

APPENDIX   255

Table 3.3B Determinants of Religious Grievance and Intensity, 2000–2014, Minorities at or above 0.2% Population Cutoff

	Grievance Expressed		Grievance Intensity	
	(5a)	(6a)	(5b)	(6b)
	Correlated RE Logit	Correlated RE Logit	Correlated RE Ordered Logit	Correlated RE Ordered Logit
GRD (1 year lag)	0.060*	0.096[†]	0.053*	0.082[†]
	(0.027)	(0.051)	(0.024)	(0.046)
SRD (1 year lag)	0.100***	0.048	0.089***	0.041[†]
	(0.027)	(0.032)	(0.023)	(0.025)
Minority Political	1.278***	1.578***	1.254***	1.511***
Organization	(0.234)	(0.280)	(0.207)	(0.259)
Minority	0.590*	0.417[†]	0.604**	0.357[†]
Representation	(0.252)	(0.233)	(0.236)	(0.188)
Minority	−0.176	−0.321*	−0.139	−0.288*
Policy Power	(0.136)	(0.132)	(0.133)	(0.126)
Religious Similarity	0.295	0.618*	0.230	0.535*
to Majority	(0.223)	(0.269)	(0.182)	(0.243)
Minority Population	0.035**	0.048***	0.029***	0.043***
%	(0.012)	(0.012)	(0.009)	(0.010)
Log Country	0.171[†]	0.284***	0.163*	0.272***
Population	(0.089)	(0.073)	(0.081)	(0.067)
Log GDP/capita	0.163	0.119	0.143	0.108
	(0.107)	(0.108)	(0.097)	(0.096)
Polyarchy Score	0.126	0.550	−0.010	0.372
(V-Dem)	(0.580)	(0.596)	(0.517)	(0.485)
Regime Durability	−0.007[†]	−0.007	−0.005	−0.003
	(0.004)	(0.005)	(0.004)	(0.005)
Mean GRD	−0.011		−0.008	
Country Level	(0.038)		(0.034)	
Mean SRD	0.009		0.023	
Country Level	(0.059)		(0.051)	
Mean GRD		−0.041		−0.032
Group Level		(0.055)		(0.050)
Mean SRD		0.091*		0.091**
Group Level		(0.043)		(0.033)

(continued)

256 APPENDIX

Table 3.3B Continued

	Grievance Expressed		Grievance Intensity	
	(5a)	(6a)	(5b)	(6b)
	Correlated RE Logit	Correlated RE Logit	Correlated RE Ordered Logit	Correlated RE Ordered Logit
Constant/Cuts	Omitted	Omitted	Omitted	Omitted
Observations	7211	7211	7211	7211
Year Effects	Yes	Yes	Yes	Yes
Clustering	Country	Country Group	Country	Country Group

Robust standard errors are in parentheses

*** $p < 0.001$, ** $p < 0.01$, * $p < 0.05$, † $p < 0.10$

APPENDIX   257

Table 3.4A Determinants of Economic Grievance and Intensity, Constrained Models, 2000–2014, Odds Ratios

	Grievance Expressed		Grievance Intensity	
	(7a)	(8a)	(7b)	(8b)
	Correlated RE Logit	Correlated RE Logit	Correlated RE Ordered Logit	Correlated RE Ordered Logit
GRD (1 year lag)	0.996	1.173	0.998	1.191
	(0.051)	(0.165)	(0.043)	(0.169)
SRD (1 year lag)	1.165***	1.117†	1.150***	1.147*
	(0.040)	(0.072)	(0.036)	(0.072)
Minority Political	1.573	2.460	1.732	2.457
Organization	(1.043)	(1.750)	(1.054)	(1.514)
Minority	1.353	1.603	1.411	1.514
Representation	(0.368)	(0.547)	(0.323)	(0.413)
Minority	0.717	0.601*	0.770	0.649*
Policy Power	(0.149)	(0.137)	(0.129)	(0.119)
Minority Economic	0.490*	0.562†	0.550*	0.619†
Status	(0.150)	(0.181)	(0.134)	(0.177)
Religious Similarity	1.687	1.097	1.579	1.108
to Majority	(0.922)	(0.673)	(0.803)	(0.614)
Minority Population	1.013	1.067*	1.013	1.056*
%	(0.026)	(0.030)	(0.024)	(0.024)
Log Country	1.388	1.123	1.272	1.092
Population	(0.327)	(0.178)	(0.249)	(0.158)
Log GDP/capita	1.402	1.335	1.299	1.311
	(0.383)	(0.291)	(0.298)	(0.258)
Polyarchy Score	0.267	0.234	0.361	0.230
(V-Dem)	(0.474)	(0.305)	(0.516)	(0.249)
Regime Durability	1.008	1.006	1.009	1.008
	(0.008)	(0.009)	(0.008)	(0.008)
Mean GRD	1.027		1.031	
Country Level	(0.069)		(0.063)	
Mean SRD	0.886		0.899	
Country Level	(0.097)		(0.089)	
Mean GRD		0.862		0.846
Group Level		(0.126)		(0.125)

(continued)

Table 3.4A Continued

	Grievance Expressed		Grievance Intensity	
	(7a)	(8a)	(7b)	(8b)
	Correlated RE Logit	Correlated RE Logit	Correlated RE Ordered Logit	Correlated RE Ordered Logit
Mean SRD		1.027		0.992
Group Level		(0.077)		(0.072)
Constant/Cuts	Omitted	Omitted	Omitted	Omitted
Observations	2949	2949	2949	2949
Year Effects	Included	Included	Included	Included
Clustering	Country	Country Group	Country	Country Group

Robust standard errors are in parentheses

*** $p < 0.001$, ** $p < 0.01$, * $p < 0.05$, † $p < 0.10$

APPENDIX 259

Table 3.4B Determinants of Economic Grievance and Intensity, Constrained Models, 2000–2014, Minorities at or above 0.2% Population Cutoff

	Grievance Expressed		Grievance Intensity	
	(7a)	(8a)	(7b)	(8b)
	Correlated RE Logit	Correlated RE Logit	Correlated RE Ordered Logit	Correlated RE Ordered Logit
GRD (1 year lag)	−0.027	0.172	−0.022	0.183
	(0.056)	(0.137)	(0.045)	(0.137)
SRD (1 year lag)	0.168***	0.115†	0.156***	0.137*
	(0.042)	(0.064)	(0.038)	(0.062)
Minority Political	1.083	1.405†	1.137†	1.335*
Organization	(0.700)	(0.721)	(0.638)	(0.615)
Minority	0.145	0.283	0.193	0.268
Representation	(0.273)	(0.317)	(0.228)	(0.261)
Minority	−0.271	−0.474*	−0.210	−0.405*
Policy Power	(0.198)	(0.214)	(0.165)	(0.175)
Minority Economic	−0.603†	−0.331	−0.481*	−0.254
Status	(0.308)	(0.314)	(0.236)	(0.281)
Religious Similarity	0.522	−0.024	0.436	−0.013
to Majority	(0.560)	(0.608)	(0.518)	(0.545)
Minority Population	−0.001	0.049†	0.001	0.042†
%	(0.028)	(0.028)	(0.026)	(0.024)
Log Country	0.307	0.108	0.222	0.085
Population	(0.248)	(0.163)	(0.203)	(0.148)
Log GDP/capita	0.421	0.435†	0.349	0.419*
	(0.288)	(0.223)	(0.235)	(0.197)
Polyarchy Score	−1.953	−1.979	−1.457	−1.905†
(V-Dem)	(1.775)	(1.331)	(1.379)	(1.090)
Regime Durability	0.006	0.001	0.006	0.003
	(0.009)	(0.009)	(0.008)	(0.008)
Mean GRD	0.035		0.039	
Country Level	(0.071)		(0.063)	
Mean SRD	−0.145		−0.136	
Country Level	(0.124)		(0.111)	
Mean GRD		−0.182		−0.194
Group Level		(0.144)		(0.144)

(continued)

260 APPENDIX

Table 3.4B Continued

	Grievance Expressed		Grievance Intensity	
	(7a)	(8a)	(7b)	(8b)
	Correlated RE Logit	Correlated RE Logit	Correlated RE Ordered Logit	Correlated RE Ordered Logit
Mean SRD		0.032		−0.001
Group Level		(0.076)		(0.073)
Constant/Cuts	Omitted	Omitted	Omitted	Omitted
Observations	2479	2479	2479	2479
Year Effects	Included	Included	Included	Included
Clustering	Country	Country Group	Country	Country Group

Robust standard errors are in parentheses

*** $p < 0.001$, ** $p < 0.01$, * $p < 0.05$, † $p < 0.10$

Table 3.5A Determinants of Economic Grievance and Intensity, full models, 2000–2014, Odds Ratios

	Grievance Expressed		Grievance Intensity	
	(7a1)	(8a1)	(7b1)	(8b1)
	Correlated RE Logit	Correlated RE Logit	Correlated RE Ordered Logit	Correlated RE Ordered Logit
GRD (1 year lag)	1.058*	1.096	1.053*	1.115
	(0.027)	(0.114)	(0.024)	(0.116)
SRD (1 year lag)	1.079*	1.077	1.080*	1.107[†]
	(0.036)	(0.066)	(0.035)	(0.067)
Minority Political	2.753**	4.519***	2.584**	4.212***
Organization	(0.955)	(2.021)	(0.828)	(1.746)
Minority	2.126*	1.766[†]	2.120**	1.671[†]
Representation	(0.698)	(0.595)	(0.614)	(0.464)
Minority	0.725[†]	0.577**	0.724[†]	0.616**
Policy Power	(0.134)	(0.116)	(0.126)	(0.105)
Religious Similarity	1.506	1.617	1.491	1.644
to Majority	(0.487)	(0.692)	(0.449)	(0.663)
Minority Population	1.047*	1.054**	1.043*	1.047**
%	(0.020)	(0.019)	(0.018)	(0.017)
Log Country	1.378**	1.254*	1.369**	1.245*
Population	(0.170)	(0.142)	(0.162)	(0.132)
Log GDP/capita	1.402*	1.387*	1.379*	1.379*
	(0.214)	(0.229)	(0.200)	(0.214)
Polyarchy Score	0.582	0.364	0.565	0.351
(V-Dem)	(0.539)	(0.344)	(0.507)	(0.298)
Regime Durability	1.004	1.005	1.005	1.006
	(0.006)	(0.006)	(0.006)	(0.006)
Mean GRD	0.964		0.966	
Country Level	(0.039)		(0.038)	
Mean SRD	0.967		0.968	
Country Level	(0.089)		(0.086)	
Mean GRD		0.925		0.906
Group Level		(0.099)		(0.097)
Mean SRD		1.067		1.035
Group Level		(0.071)		(0.068)

(continued)

Table 3.5A Continued

	Grievance Expressed		Grievance Intensity	
	(7a1)	(8a1)	(7b1)	(8b1)
	Correlated RE Logit	Correlated RE Logit	Correlated RE Ordered Logit	Correlated RE Ordered Logit
Constant/Cuts	Omitted	Omitted	Omitted	Omitted
Observations	9355	9355	9355	9355
Year Effects	Included	Included	Included	Included
Clustering	Country	Country Group	Country	Country Group

Robust standard errors are in parentheses

*** $p < 0.001$, ** $p < 0.01$, * $p < 0.05$, † $p < 0.10$

APPENDIX 263

Table 3.5B Determinants of Economic Grievance and Intensity, Full Models, 2000–2014, Minorities at or above 0.2% Population Cutoff

	Grievance Expressed		Grievance Intensity	
	(7a1)	(8a1)	(7b1)	(8b1)
	Correlated RE Logit	Correlated RE Logit	Correlated RE Ordered Logit	Correlated RE Ordered Logit
GRD (1 year lag)	0.027	0.048	0.024	0.065
	(0.035)	(0.124)	(0.031)	(0.123)
SRD (1 year lag)	0.131***	0.076	0.130***	0.103
	(0.037)	(0.065)	(0.036)	(0.064)
Minority Political	1.265***	1.848***	1.190***	1.697***
Organization	(0.377)	(0.498)	(0.337)	(0.446)
Minority	0.521[†]	0.472	0.530*	0.441
Representation	(0.273)	(0.329)	(0.241)	(0.277)
Minority	−0.455*	−0.545**	−0.449*	−0.480**
Policy Power	(0.208)	(0.197)	(0.192)	(0.166)
Religious Similarity	0.470	0.464	0.464	0.471
to Majority	(0.403)	(0.456)	(0.368)	(0.423)
Minority Population	0.037[†]	0.047*	0.033[†]	0.040*
%	(0.020)	(0.019)	(0.018)	(0.016)
Log Country	0.357*	0.234[†]	0.348**	0.222[†]
Population	(0.141)	(0.125)	(0.134)	(0.115)
Log GDP/capita	0.455**	0.514**	0.432**	0.491**
	(0.175)	(0.177)	(0.162)	(0.162)
Polyarchy Score	−0.899	−1.470	−0.890	−1.463
(V-Dem)	(1.060)	(1.054)	(0.995)	(0.926)
Regime Durability	0.005	0.002	0.005	0.003
	(0.007)	(0.007)	(0.007)	(0.007)
Mean GRD	−0.034		−0.032	
Country Level	(0.052)		(0.049)	
Mean SRD	−0.099		−0.096	
Country Level	(0.099)		(0.095)	
Mean GRD		−0.063		−0.083
Group Level		(0.127)		(0.126)
Mean SRD		0.082		0.047
Group Level		(0.072)		(0.071)

(continued)

264 APPENDIX

Table 3.5B Continued

	Grievance Expressed		Grievance Intensity	
	(7a1)	(8a1)	(7b1)	(8b1)
	Correlated RE Logit	Correlated RE Logit	Correlated RE Ordered Logit	Correlated RE Ordered Logit
Constant/Cuts	Omitted	Omitted	Omitted	Omitted
Observations	7211	7211	7211	7211
Year Effects	Included	Included	Included	Included
Clustering	Country	Country Group	Country	Country Group

Robust standard errors are in parentheses

*** $p < 0.001$, ** $p < 0.01$, * $p < 0.05$, † $p < 0.10$

Chapter 5 Appendix Materials

Table 5.5A Determinants of Nonviolent and Violent Mobilization, Grievance Types, 2000–2014, Relative Risk Ratios

Correlated RE Multinomial Logits	(1a) Country-Level Clustering		(1b) Country-Level Clustering w/ Ethnic Overlap		(2a) Group-Level Clustering		(2b) Group-Level Clustering w/ Ethnic Overlap	
	Nonviolent	Violent	Nonviolent	Violent	Nonviolent	Violent	Nonviolent	Violent
Minority Grievance	1.646*	1.384[†]	1.658**	1.382[†]	1.673*	1.493*	1.706*	1.445[†]
- Political (1 year lag)	(0.322)	(0.231)	(0.313)	(0.245)	(0.370)	(0.285)	(0.371)	(0.280)
Minority Grievance	1.576[†]	1.435[†]	1.596[†]	1.443[†]	1.601*	1.141	1.613*	1.101
- Religious (1 year lag)	(0.400)	(0.314)	(0.418)	(0.307)	(0.366)	(0.236)	(0.369)	(0.236)
Minority Grievance	1.074	3.039***	1.174	2.882***	1.396	2.881***	1.502	2.985***
- Economic (1 year lag)	(0.385)	(0.801)	(0.442)	(0.757)	(0.494)	(0.725)	(0.536)	(0.766)
GRD (1 year lag)	1.004	1.009	1.002	1.015	1.029	0.958	1.042	0.959
	(0.020)	(0.023)	(0.020)	(0.027)	(0.071)	(0.061)	(0.064)	(0.064)
SRD (1 year lag)	1.049***	1.007	1.043**	1.018	1.023	1.117*	1.020	1.077[†]
	(0.014)	(0.014)	(0.015)	(0.017)	(0.062)	(0.058)	(0.061)	(0.048)
Minority Political	2.144***	4.937***	1.713*	4.180***	2.883***	5.428***	2.277***	4.281***
Organization	(0.496)	(1.283)	(0.406)	(1.255)	(0.714)	(2.078)	(0.578)	(1.765)
Minority	1.059	2.385***	1.182	2.177***	0.960	2.734***	1.063	2.446***
Representation	(0.218)	(0.517)	(0.235)	(0.446)	(0.224)	(0.699)	(0.251)	(0.612)

(continued)

Table 5.5A Continued

Correlated RE Multinomial Logits	(1a) Country-Level Clustering		(1b) Country-Level Clustering w/ Ethnic Overlap		(2a) Group-Level Clustering		(2b) Group-Level Clustering w/ Ethnic Overlap	
	Nonviolent	Violent	Nonviolent	Violent	Nonviolent	Violent	Nonviolent	Violent
Minority Policy Power	0.804[†]	0.789*	0.815[†]	0.796[†]	0.871	0.781[†]	0.902	0.804
	(0.096)	(0.091)	(0.094)	(0.103)	(0.134)	(0.110)	(0.134)	(0.116)
Log GDP/capita	1.233	0.755*	1.246	0.744*	1.196	0.613**	1.181	0.589**
	(0.185)	(0.106)	(0.189)	(0.103)	(0.162)	(0.106)	(0.161)	(0.100)
Polyarchy Score (V-Dem)	0.237[†]	0.188*	0.207[†]	0.204*	0.282*	0.311	0.229*	0.405
	(0.193)	(0.143)	(0.171)	(0.156)	(0.165)	(0.229)	(0.138)	(0.310)
Regime Durability	1.010**	1.006	1.010***	1.004	1.010**	1.005	1.010**	1.004
	(0.003)	(0.005)	(0.003)	(0.005)	(0.004)	(0.006)	(0.004)	(0.006)
Security Sector % of Labor Force	1.044	1.067	1.030	1.057	1.044	1.124[†]	1.016	1.102
	(0.069)	(0.051)	(0.069)	(0.051)	(0.085)	(0.070)	(0.083)	(0.073)
Youth Unemployment %	0.998	1.014	1.001	1.013	0.991	1.017	0.996	1.014
	(0.012)	(0.010)	(0.011)	(0.010)	(0.013)	(0.011)	(0.012)	(0.011)
Internet Use %	1.007	1.011	1.005	1.010	1.010	1.015[†]	1.008	1.015[†]
	(0.007)	(0.007)	(0.007)	(0.007)	(0.008)	(0.008)	(0.008)	(0.009)
Minority Population %	1.025***	1.055***	1.026**	1.058***	1.032***	1.090***	1.032**	1.093***
	(0.008)	(0.010)	(0.008)	(0.012)	(0.010)	(0.015)	(0.010)	(0.018)
Log Country Population	1.455***	1.648***	1.449***	1.702***	1.448***	1.794***	1.442***	1.795***
	(0.109)	(0.152)	(0.112)	(0.174)	(0.102)	(0.176)	(0.102)	(0.183)

Religious Similarity	0.631†	0.902	0.534†	1.136	0.735	0.670	0.691	0.805
to Majority	(0.176)	(0.226)	(0.194)	(0.333)	(0.182)	(0.208)	(0.177)	(0.277)
Distinct Ethnicity			0.917	1.553*			1.047	1.743*
vs. Majority			(0.158)	(0.287)			(0.146)	(0.383)
Mean GRD	0.944†	0.922*	0.945	0.899*				
Country Level	(0.033)	(0.032)	(0.035)	(0.038)				
Mean SRD	1.058	1.108*	1.062	1.098*				
Country Level	(0.039)	(0.045)	(0.042)	(0.047)				
Mean GRD					0.940	1.000	0.925	0.992
Group Level					(0.068)	(0.068)	(0.061)	(0.072)
Mean SRD					1.061	0.968	1.062	1.009
Group Level					(0.069)	(0.058)	(0.069)	(0.055)
Mobilization Type	1.241	3.159***	1.227	3.120***	1.025	1.801***	1.000	1.823***
Year Lagged Control	(0.174)	(0.354)	(0.161)	(0.343)	(0.170)	(0.199)	(0.164)	(0.206)
Constant	0.000***	0.000***	0.000***	0.000***	0.000***	0.000***	0.000***	0.000***
	(0.000)	(0.000)	(0.000)	(0.000)	(0.000)	(0.000)	(0.000)	(0.000)
Observations	8,168		6,691		8,168		6,691	
Year Effects	Included		Included		Included		Included	
Clustering	Country		Country		Country Group		Country Group	
Correlated Intercepts	No		No		No		Yes†	

Robust standard errors are in parentheses

*** $p < 0.001$, ** $p < 0.01$, * $p < 0.05$, † $p < 0.10$

Table 5.5B Determinants of Nonviolent and Violent Mobilization, Grievance Types, 2000–2014, Minorities at or above 0.2% Population Cutoff

Correlated RE Multinomial Logits	(1a) Country-Level Clustering		(1b) Country-Level Clustering w/ Ethnic Overlap		(2a) Group-Level Clustering		(2b) Group-Level Clustering w/ Ethnic Overlap	
	Nonviolent	Violent	Nonviolent	Violent	Nonviolent	Violent	Nonviolent	Violent
Minority Grievance	0.383	0.375*	0.397[†]	0.363*	0.420[†]	0.409*	0.442[†]	0.355[†]
- Political (1 year lag)	(0.236)	(0.171)	(0.215)	(0.181)	(0.252)	(0.197)	(0.250)	(0.199)
Minority Grievance	0.363	0.314	0.393	0.306	0.442[†]	0.143	0.451[†]	0.098
- Religious (1 year lag)	(0.282)	(0.219)	(0.292)	(0.214)	(0.250)	(0.209)	(0.252)	(0.217)
Minority Grievance	−0.144	1.116***	0.009	1.037***	0.276	1.006***	0.352	1.028***
- Economic (1 year lag)	(0.365)	(0.270)	(0.381)	(0.274)	(0.368)	(0.256)	(0.370)	(0.258)
GRD (1 year lag)	−0.007	−0.009	−0.011	−0.003	0.038	−0.037	0.058	−0.039
	(0.023)	(0.025)	(0.024)	(0.025)	(0.080)	(0.063)	(0.068)	(0.066)
SRD (1 year lag)	0.051**	0.003	0.041*	0.017	−0.051	0.072	−0.048	0.060
	(0.016)	(0.012)	(0.018)	(0.015)	(0.066)	(0.045)	(0.065)	(0.044)
Minority Political	1.004***	1.547***	0.773**	1.424***	1.237***	1.623***	1.002***	1.369***
Organization	(0.265)	(0.266)	(0.280)	(0.308)	(0.285)	(0.370)	(0.298)	(0.394)
Minority	−0.031	0.838***	0.096	0.732***	−0.072	0.941***	0.038	0.814***
Representation	(0.206)	(0.209)	(0.202)	(0.198)	(0.251)	(0.246)	(0.258)	(0.237)
Minority	−0.223[†]	−0.203[†]	−0.212[†]	−0.208	−0.149	−0.224[†]	−0.113	−0.206
Policy Power	(0.129)	(0.116)	(0.125)	(0.127)	(0.164)	(0.134)	(0.161)	(0.137)
Log GDP/capita	0.223	−0.253[†]	0.239	−0.260[†]	0.181	−0.444**	0.174	−0.473**
	(0.169)	(0.141)	(0.172)	(0.135)	(0.146)	(0.170)	(0.145)	(0.165)

Polyarchy Score	−1.525†	−1.493*	−1.656†	−1.344†	−1.245*	−0.918	−1.531*	−0.657
(V-Dem)	(0.896)	(0.755)	(0.916)	(0.757)	(0.627)	(0.757)	(0.648)	(0.763)
Regime Durability	0.008*	0.002	0.008*	0.001	0.007†	0.000	0.008*	−0.002
	(0.004)	(0.004)	(0.004)	(0.005)	(0.004)	(0.006)	(0.004)	(0.006)
Security Sector %	0.092	0.067	0.075	0.061	0.100	0.138*	0.068	0.122*
of Labor Force	(0.057)	(0.044)	(0.058)	(0.046)	(0.078)	(0.060)	(0.079)	(0.062)
Youth	−0.002	0.014	0.002	0.012	−0.007	0.019†	−0.002	0.017
Unemployment %	(0.012)	(0.010)	(0.012)	(0.010)	(0.015)	(0.011)	(0.014)	(0.011)
Internet Use %	0.011	0.014*	0.008	0.012†	0.013	0.019*	0.010	0.018*
	(0.009)	(0.007)	(0.009)	(0.007)	(0.008)	(0.008)	(0.008)	(0.009)
Minority Population	0.027**	0.049***	0.028**	0.051***	0.027**	0.070***	0.027*	0.070***
%	(0.009)	(0.009)	(0.010)	(0.011)	(0.010)	(0.013)	(0.010)	(0.015)
Log Country	0.402***	0.486***	0.400***	0.528***	0.392***	0.586***	0.396***	0.599***
Population	(0.084)	(0.089)	(0.088)	(0.099)	(0.077)	(0.096)	(0.078)	(0.099)
Religious Similarity	−0.802*	−0.416	−0.977*	−0.166	−0.515*	−0.750*	−0.585*	−0.531
to Majority	(0.330)	(0.274)	(0.466)	(0.294)	(0.262)	(0.305)	(0.270)	(0.325)
Distinct Ethnicity			−0.122	0.449*			0.084	0.476*
vs. Majority			(0.225)	(0.200)			(0.156)	(0.219)
Mean GRD	−0.054	−0.058	−0.050	−0.085*				
Country Level	(0.043)	(0.035)	(0.045)	(0.041)				
Mean SRD	0.061	0.122***	0.065	0.105*				
Country Level	(0.046)	(0.038)	(0.050)	(0.041)				

(*continued*)

Table 5.5B Continued

Correlated RE Multinomial Logits	(1a) Country-Level Clustering		(1b) Country-Level Clustering w/ Ethnic Overlap		(2a) Group-Level Clustering		(2b) Group-Level Clustering w/ Ethnic Overlap	
	Nonviolent	Violent	Nonviolent	Violent	Nonviolent	Violent	Nonviolent	Violent
Mean GRD					−0.083	−0.009	−0.109	−0.017
Group Level					(0.084)	(0.068)	(0.072)	(0.071)
Mean SRD					0.135†	0.011	0.131†	0.028
Group Level					(0.071)	(0.054)	(0.070)	(0.054)
Mobilization Type	0.179	1.096***	0.174	1.078***	0.046	0.611***	0.013	0.621***
Year Lagged Control	(0.151)	(0.109)	(0.143)	(0.107)	(0.178)	(0.109)	(0.176)	(0.111)
Constant	−12.839***	−11.248***	−12.477***	−12.164***	−12.830***	−12.509***	−12.487***	−12.655***
	(1.617)	(1.971)	(1.707)	(2.187)	(1.527)	(2.222)	(1.592)	(2.309)
Observations	6252		5095		6252		5095	
Year Effects	Included		Included		Included		Included	
Clustering	Country		Country		Country Group		Country Group	
Correlated Intercepts	No		No		No		No	

Robust standard errors are in parentheses

*** $p < 0.001$, ** $p < 0.01$, * $p < 0.05$, $^\dagger p < 0.10$

Table 5.6A Determinants of Nonviolent and Violent Mobilization, Grievance Intensity Types, 2000–2014, Relative Risk Ratios

	(3a)		(3b)		(4a)		(4b)	
Correlated RE Multinomial Logits	Country-Level Clustering		Country-Level Clustering w/ Ethnic Overlap		Group-Level Clustering		Group-Level Clustering w/ Ethnic Overlap	
	Nonviolent	Violent	Nonviolent	Violent	Nonviolent	Violent	Nonviolent	Violent
Minority Grievance	1.180*	1.140	1.187*	1.171[†]	0.991	1.091	1.000	1.093
intensity, Pol, year lag	(0.083)	(0.095)	(0.081)	(0.108)	(0.091)	(0.101)	(0.091)	(0.103)
Minority Grievance	1.115	1.146	1.116	1.120	0.968	0.873	0.967	0.848
intensity, Rel, year lag	(0.149)	(0.116)	(0.156)	(0.112)	(0.117)	(0.087)	(0.121)	(0.088)
Minority Grievance	1.024	1.596***	1.086	1.626***	1.084	1.229	1.184	1.351*
intensity, Econ year lag	(0.181)	(0.194)	(0.199)	(0.194)	(0.208)	(0.162)	(0.236)	(0.185)
GRD (1 year lag)	1.012	1.014	1.011	1.020	1.004	0.963	1.007	0.952
	(0.020)	(0.023)	(0.019)	(0.026)	(0.049)	(0.061)	(0.045)	(0.062)
SRD (1 year lag)	1.056***	1.011	1.047**	1.020	1.021	1.098[†]	1.019	1.060
	(0.015)	(0.014)	(0.016)	(0.016)	(0.056)	(0.056)	(0.055)	(0.046)
Minority Political	2.152***	5.082***	1.735*	4.313***	1.930**	3.522***	1.568*	2.703*
Organization	(0.489)	(1.345)	(0.401)	(1.314)	(0.424)	(1.306)	(0.353)	(1.069)
Minority	1.073	2.377***	1.209	2.171***	0.773	2.488***	0.875	2.302***
Representation	(0.207)	(0.501)	(0.226)	(0.441)	(0.165)	(0.600)	(0.186)	(0.543)
Minority	0.821[†]	0.772*	0.833[†]	0.783[†]	0.840	0.742*	0.865	0.757*
Policy Power	(0.093)	(0.089)	(0.092)	(0.100)	(0.119)	(0.103)	(0.119)	(0.106)
Log GDP/capita	1.198	0.710*	1.208	0.704**	1.189	0.576***	1.190	0.571***
	(0.151)	(0.097)	(0.157)	(0.096)	(0.157)	(0.100)	(0.153)	(0.097)

(continued)

Table 5.6A Continued

Correlated RE Multinomial Logits	(3a) Country-Level Clustering		(3b) Country-Level Clustering w/ Ethnic Overlap		(4a) Group-Level Clustering		(4b) Group-Level Clustering w/ Ethnic Overlap	
	Nonviolent	Violent	Nonviolent	Violent	Nonviolent	Violent	Nonviolent	Violent
Polyarchy Score	0.275[†]	0.255[†]	0.241*	0.275[†]	0.323*	0.393	0.260*	0.455
(V-Dem)	(0.186)	(0.190)	(0.166)	(0.206)	(0.186)	(0.283)	(0.150)	(0.339)
Regime Durability	1.006*	1.003	1.006*	1.003	1.008*	0.998	1.009*	0.999
	(0.003)	(0.005)	(0.003)	(0.005)	(0.004)	(0.006)	(0.004)	(0.006)
Security Sector %	1.002	1.066	0.990	1.061	1.038	1.112	1.019	1.091
of Labor Force	(0.046)	(0.052)	(0.047)	(0.053)	(0.086)	(0.082)	(0.083)	(0.085)
Youth	0.991	1.017[†]	0.994	1.016	0.982	1.013	0.987	1.011
Unemployment %	(0.011)	(0.010)	(0.011)	(0.010)	(0.012)	(0.011)	(0.011)	(0.011)
Internet Use %	1.005	1.011	1.004	1.010	1.009	1.016[†]	1.006	1.014
	(0.006)	(0.007)	(0.007)	(0.007)	(0.008)	(0.009)	(0.008)	(0.009)
Minority Population	1.024***	1.055***	1.026***	1.058***	1.019*	1.073***	1.019*	1.075***
%	(0.007)	(0.010)	(0.008)	(0.012)	(0.008)	(0.015)	(0.008)	(0.017)
Log Country	1.324***	1.638***	1.317***	1.705***	1.341***	1.708***	1.329***	1.673***
Population	(0.096)	(0.155)	(0.101)	(0.184)	(0.087)	(0.163)	(0.087)	(0.163)
Religious Similarity	0.614[†]	0.904	0.488[†]	1.146	0.674[†]	0.632	0.629[†]	0.736
to Majority	(0.179)	(0.228)	(0.182)	(0.341)	(0.162)	(0.196)	(0.158)	(0.242)

	1	2	3	4	5	6	7	8
Distinct Ethnicity vs. Majority			0.855 (0.140)	1.532* (0.275)			0.975 (0.130)	1.427† (0.297)
Mean Pol grievance Intensity—Country	5.504** (3.076)	0.745 (0.446)	5.310** (2.979)	0.651 (0.418)				
Mean Rel grievance Intensity—Country	1.171 (0.449)	1.248 (0.594)	1.252 (0.460)	1.244 (0.652)				
Mean Econ grievance Intensity—Country	4.994† (4.818)	12.222† (16.020)	4.193 (4.078)	8.134 (11.101)				
Mean GRD Country Level	0.943† (0.030)	0.926* (0.031)	0.944† (0.031)	0.905* (0.037)				
Mean SRD Country Level	0.933† (0.035)	1.074† (0.044)	0.944 (0.037)	1.075 (0.048)				
Mean Pol grievance Intensity—Group					3.819*** (0.838)	1.417 (0.623)	3.783*** (0.795)	1.547 (0.705)
Mean Rel grievance Intensity—Group					2.371*** (0.498)	3.651*** (1.131)	2.321*** (0.476)	3.719*** (1.172)
Mean Econ grievance Intensity—Group					0.831 (0.463)	6.750** (4.194)	0.855 (0.458)	5.648** (3.609)
Mean GRD Group Level					0.953 (0.052)	0.983 (0.067)	0.954 (0.048)	0.997 (0.071)
Mean SRD Group Level					0.996 (0.060)	0.935 (0.058)	0.993 (0.059)	0.963 (0.055)

(*continued*)

Table 5.6A Continued

Correlated RE Multinomial Logits	(3a) Country-Level Clustering		(3b) Country-Level Clustering w/ Ethnic Overlap		(4a) Group-Level Clustering		(4b) Group-Level Clustering w/ Ethnic Overlap	
	Nonviolent	Violent	Nonviolent	Violent	Nonviolent	Violent	Nonviolent	Violent
Mobilization Type	1.245	3.087***	1.237	3.039***	1.089	1.847***	1.078	1.888***
Year Lagged Control	(0.190)	(0.356)	(0.174)	(0.339)	(0.190)	(0.219)	(0.188)	(0.229)
Constant	0.000***	0.000***	0.000***	0.000***	0.000***	0.000***	0.000***	0.000***
	(0.000)	(0.000)	(0.000)	(0.000)	(0.000)	(0.000)	(0.000)	(0.000)
Observations	8,168		6,691		8,168		6,691	
Year Effects	Included		Included		Included		Included	
Clustering	Country		Country		Country Group		Country Group	
Correlated Intercepts	No		No		No		No	

Robust standard errors are in parentheses

*** $p < 0.001$, ** $p < 0.01$, * $p < 0.05$, [†] $p < 0.10$

Table 5.6B Determinants of Nonviolent and Violent Mobilization, Grievance Intensity Types, 2000–2014, Minorities at or above 0.2% Population Cutoff

Correlated RE Multinomial Logits	(3a) Country-Level Clustering		(3b) Country-Level Clustering w/ Ethnic Overlap		(4a) Group-Level Clustering		(4b) Group-Level Clustering w/ Ethnic Overlap	
	Nonviolent	Violent	Nonviolent	Violent	Nonviolent	Violent	Nonviolent	Violent
Minority Grievance	0.143†	0.177*	0.146*	0.203*	−0.071	0.088	−0.054	0.088
intensity, Pol, year lag	(0.082)	(0.089)	(0.074)	(0.098)	(0.104)	(0.094)	(0.103)	(0.096)
Minority Grievance	0.083	0.122	0.091	0.100	−0.030	−0.097	−0.027	−0.123
intensity, Rel, year lag	(0.144)	(0.101)	(0.148)	(0.100)	(0.131)	(0.097)	(0.135)	(0.101)
Minority Grievance	−0.113	0.415***	−0.033	0.426***	0.021	0.181	0.111	0.271*
intensity, Econ year lag	(0.177)	(0.115)	(0.183)	(0.114)	(0.188)	(0.129)	(0.193)	(0.132)
GRD (1 year lag)	−0.001	−0.004	−0.002	0.002	−0.009	−0.036	0.002	−0.049
	(0.023)	(0.025)	(0.024)	(0.025)	(0.054)	(0.062)	(0.048)	(0.063)
SRD (1 year lag)	0.063***	0.010	0.048**	0.022	−0.043	0.062	−0.036	0.052
	(0.016)	(0.012)	(0.018)	(0.015)	(0.058)	(0.043)	(0.057)	(0.043)
Minority Political	0.914***	1.553***	0.692**	1.428***	0.775**	1.230***	0.553*	0.957*
Organization	(0.260)	(0.264)	(0.269)	(0.306)	(0.248)	(0.363)	(0.265)	(0.383)
Minority	−0.053	0.821***	0.080	0.711***	−0.364	0.843***	−0.230	0.754***
Representation	(0.194)	(0.205)	(0.190)	(0.199)	(0.225)	(0.232)	(0.229)	(0.224)
Minority	−0.205†	−0.228*	−0.191	−0.226†	−0.190	−0.271*	−0.158	−0.258†
Policy Power	(0.125)	(0.115)	(0.122)	(0.125)	(0.148)	(0.132)	(0.147)	(0.132)

(*continued*)

Table 5.6B Continued

Correlated RE Multinomial Logits	(3a)		(3b)		(4a)		(4b)	
	Country-Level Clustering		Country-Level Clustering w/ Ethnic Overlap		Group-Level Clustering		Group-Level Clustering w/ Ethnic Overlap	
	Nonviolent	Violent	Nonviolent	Violent	Nonviolent	Violent	Nonviolent	Violent
Log GDP/capita	0.230	−0.320*	0.247[†]	−0.328*	0.207	−0.493**	0.215	−0.492**
	(0.147)	(0.133)	(0.150)	(0.130)	(0.138)	(0.168)	(0.136)	(0.163)
Polyarchy Score	−1.336[†]	−1.109	−1.503*	−0.950	−1.246*	−0.738	−1.491*	−0.570
(V-Dem)	(0.736)	(0.719)	(0.763)	(0.722)	(0.587)	(0.727)	(0.608)	(0.733)
Regime Durability	0.004	0.000	0.005	-0.001	0.006	−0.007	0.007[†]	−0.006
	(0.003)	(0.005)	(0.003)	(0.005)	(0.004)	(0.006)	(0.004)	(0.006)
Security Sector %	0.037	0.076[†]	0.022	0.075	0.079	0.120[†]	0.055	0.103
of Labor Force	(0.046)	(0.046)	(0.044)	(0.048)	(0.088)	(0.072)	(0.087)	(0.072)
Youth	−0.012	0.018[†]	−0.008	0.016	−0.020	0.014	−0.013	0.013
Unemployment %	(0.012)	(0.010)	(0.011)	(0.010)	(0.014)	(0.011)	(0.012)	(0.011)
Internet Use %	0.006	0.014*	0.004	0.012[†]	0.011	0.019*	0.008	0.016[†]
	(0.008)	(0.007)	(0.008)	(0.007)	(0.008)	(0.009)	(0.008)	(0.009)
Minority Population	0.024***	0.049***	0.026***	0.051***	0.015[†]	0.058***	0.015[†]	0.058***
%	(0.007)	(0.009)	(0.008)	(0.011)	(0.008)	(0.013)	(0.008)	(0.015)
Log Country	0.291***	0.497***	0.285**	0.549***	0.310***	0.534***	0.309***	0.530***
Population	(0.084)	(0.090)	(0.091)	(0.102)	(0.070)	(0.094)	(0.072)	(0.094)

	(1)	(2)	(3)	(4)	(5)	(6)	(7)	(8)
Religious Similarity to Majority	−0.795*	−0.396	−1.080*	−0.141	−0.624*	−0.765*	−0.716**	−0.553[†]
	(0.336)	(0.273)	(0.466)	(0.296)	(0.250)	(0.308)	(0.269)	(0.316)
Distinct Ethnicity vs. Majority			−0.219	0.452*			−0.013	0.284
			(0.207)	(0.193)			(0.153)	(0.208)
Mean Pol grievance Intensity—Country	2.020***	−0.598	1.999***	−0.783				
	(0.604)	(0.608)	(0.559)	(0.658)				
Mean Rel grievance Intensity—Country	0.362	0.010	0.399	−0.024				
	(0.441)	(0.601)	(0.408)	(0.669)				
Mean Econ grievance Intensity—Country	1.409	2.458[†]	1.191	2.119				
	(0.930)	(1.293)	(0.906)	(1.336)				
Mean GRD Country Level	−0.053	−0.052	−0.054	−0.077[†]				
	(0.039)	(0.035)	(0.041)	(0.041)				
Mean SRD Country Level	−0.092*	0.103**	−0.073[†]	0.100*				
	(0.044)	(0.040)	(0.042)	(0.044)				
Mean Pol grievance Intensity—Group					1.523***	0.420	1.478***	0.431
					(0.246)	(0.436)	(0.235)	(0.449)
Mean Rel grievance Intensity—Group					0.857***	1.060***	0.846***	1.043***
					(0.240)	(0.319)	(0.235)	(0.320)
Mean Econ grievance Intensity—Group					−0.537	1.492*	−0.490	1.339*
					(0.577)	(0.603)	(0.569)	(0.615)

(continued)

Table 5.6B Continued

Correlated RE Multinomial Logits	(3a) Country-Level Clustering		(3b) Country-Level Clustering w/ Ethnic Overlap		(4a) Group-Level Clustering		(4b) Group-Level Clustering w/ Ethnic Overlap	
	Nonviolent	Violent	Nonviolent	Violent	Nonviolent	Violent	Nonviolent	Violent
Mean GRD					−0.045	−0.017	−0.052	−0.004
Group Level					(0.060)	(0.066)	(0.055)	(0.068)
Mean SRD					0.057	−0.025	0.047	−0.018
Group Level					(0.064)	(0.055)	(0.064)	(0.056)
Mobilization Type	0.185	1.073***	0.183	1.047***	0.119	0.628***	0.097	0.648***
Year Lagged Control	(0.160)	(0.112)	(0.152)	(0.105)	(0.191)	(0.119)	(0.191)	(0.122)
Constant	−10.945***	−11.066***	−10.374***	−12.121***	−11.130***	−11.022***	−10.823***	−10.884***
	(1.535)	(1.934)	(1.666)	(2.186)	(1.458)	(2.052)	(1.515)	(2.129)
Observations	6252		5095		6252		5095	
Year Effects	Included		Included		Included		Included	
Clustering	Country		Country		Country Group		Country Group	
Correlated Intercepts	No		No		No		No	

Robust standard errors are in parentheses

*** $p < 0.001$, ** $p < 0.01$, * $p < 0.05$, † $p < 0.10$

Table 5.7A Determinants of Violent Mobilization Types, Grievance Types, 2000–2014, Country-Clustered Models, Relative Risk Ratios

	(5a)			(5b)		
	Correlated RE Multinomial Logit			**Correlated RE Multinomial Logit**		
	(a) Rioting	**(b) Violence vs. Civilians**	**(c) Rebellion**	**(a) Rioting**	**(b) Violence vs. Civilians**	**(c) Rebellion**
Minority Grievance	1.675**	1.929*	0.382*	1.631*	1.874*	0.264**
- Political (1 year lag)	(0.303)	(0.552)	(0.180)	(0.313)	(0.568)	(0.137)
Minority Grievance	1.929**	1.021	2.198*	1.884**	0.950	1.969[†]
- Religious (1 year lag)	(0.430)	(0.328)	(0.774)	(0.400)	(0.307)	(0.722)
Minority Grievance	2.016*	6.070***	3.653[†]	1.735[†]	5.741***	5.522**
- Economic (1 year lag)	(0.559)	(2.823)	(2.579)	(0.495)	(2.665)	(3.563)
GRD (1 year lag)	1.018	0.999	0.945	1.038	1.003	0.907[†]
	(0.029)	(0.041)	(0.038)	(0.032)	(0.045)	(0.047)
SRD (1 year lag)	1.022	0.980	1.025	1.030	0.999	1.066
	(0.020)	(0.037)	(0.050)	(0.024)	(0.034)	(0.066)
Minority Political	2.865***	51.839***	4.571[†]	2.108*	32.312***	4.100[†]
Organization	(0.926)	(44.619)	(3.786)	(0.748)	(25.132)	(3.380)
Minority	1.858*	3.217**	4.250**	1.799*	2.672**	3.431**
Representation	(0.513)	(1.241)	(2.077)	(0.487)	(0.922)	(1.520)
Minority	0.935	0.845	0.697	0.957	0.879	0.657
Policy Power	(0.095)	(0.182)	(0.186)	(0.111)	(0.174)	(0.193)

(*continued*)

Table 5.7A Continued

	(5a)			(5b)		
	Correlated RE Multinomial Logit			Correlated RE Multinomial Logit		
	(a) Rioting	(b) Violence vs. Civilians	(c) Rebellion	(a) Rioting	(b) Violence vs. Civilians	(c) Rebellion
Log GDP/capita	0.715[†]	0.970	0.472*	0.725[†]	0.944	0.440*
	(0.125)	(0.310)	(0.171)	(0.120)	(0.305)	(0.156)
Polyarchy Score	0.409	0.496	0.181	0.440	0.713	0.129
(V-Dem)	(0.362)	(0.952)	(0.292)	(0.380)	(1.293)	(0.192)
Regime Durability	1.002	0.996	1.011	0.996	0.996	1.017
	(0.005)	(0.013)	(0.016)	(0.005)	(0.013)	(0.017)
Security Sector %	0.974	1.063	1.205**	0.974	1.059	1.177*
of Labor Force	(0.079)	(0.104)	(0.083)	(0.078)	(0.095)	(0.089)
Youth	1.002	0.993	1.027	1.000	0.995	1.024
Unemployment %	(0.013)	(0.024)	(0.022)	(0.013)	(0.022)	(0.023)
Internet Use %	1.015*	1.006	1.018	1.014[†]	1.007	1.014
	(0.008)	(0.014)	(0.017)	(0.008)	(0.014)	(0.018)
Minority Population	1.038***	1.070**	1.095***	1.043***	1.079**	1.092***
%	(0.010)	(0.027)	(0.020)	(0.011)	(0.029)	(0.024)
Log Country	1.389***	3.195***	2.237***	1.461***	3.015***	2.562***
Population	(0.142)	(0.862)	(0.471)	(0.154)	(0.793)	(0.617)
Religious Similarity	0.757	2.208	1.005	0.837	3.250*	2.028
to Majority	(0.227)	(1.067)	(0.555)	(0.318)	(1.579)	(1.489)

Distinct Ethnicity				1.466*	1.719†	2.793*
vs. Majority				(0.239)	(0.561)	(1.185)
Rough Terrain	0.998	0.993†	1.004	0.999	0.994	1.002
(avg elevation)	(0.002)	(0.004)	(0.003)	(0.001)	(0.004)	(0.003)
Mean GRD	0.948	0.873*	1.015	0.889*	0.894	1.047
Country Level	(0.042)	(0.057)	(0.103)	(0.044)	(0.068)	(0.116)
Mean SRD	1.082	1.220*	0.767*	1.086	1.150	0.664**
Country Level	(0.055)	(0.121)	(0.093)	(0.060)	(0.109)	(0.106)
Mobilization Type	2.519***	4.810***	5.920***	2.458***	4.693***	6.337***
Year Lagged Control	(0.466)	(1.080)	(1.698)	(0.446)	(1.086)	(1.831)
Constant	0.000***	0.000***	0.000***	0.000***	0.000***	0.000***
	(0.001)	(0.000)	(0.000)	(0.000)	(0.000)	(0.000)
Observations		8,119			6,642	
Year Effects		Included			Included	
Clustering		Country			Country	
Correlated Intercepts	(a)–(b)	(a)–(c)	(b)–(c)	(a)–(b)†	(a)–(c)	(b)–(c)†

Robust standard errors are in parentheses

*** $p < 0.001$, ** $p < 0.01$, * $p < 0.05$, † $p < 0.10$

Table 5.7B Determinants of Violent Mobilization Types, Grievance Types, 2000–2014, Country-Clustered Models, Minorities at or above 0.2% Population Cutoff

	(5a)			(5b)		
	Correlated RE Multinomial Logit			Correlated RE Multinomial Logit		
	(a) Rioting	(b) Violence vs. Civilians	(c) Rebellion	(a) Rioting	(b) Violence vs. Civilians	(c) Rebellion
Minority Grievance	0.574**	0.652*	−0.913[†]	0.527**	0.626[†]	−1.279*
- Political (1 year lag)	(0.182)	(0.317)	(0.470)	(0.188)	(0.333)	(0.517)
Minority Grievance	0.581**	−0.037	0.741*	0.530*	−0.138	0.651[†]
- Religious (1 year lag)	(0.220)	(0.324)	(0.344)	(0.210)	(0.331)	(0.370)
Minority Grievance	0.717*	1.927***	1.215[†]	0.523[†]	1.833***	1.646*
- Economic (1 year lag)	(0.287)	(0.468)	(0.701)	(0.284)	(0.463)	(0.644)
GRD (1 year lag)	0.006	−0.026	−0.088[†]	0.019	−0.015	−0.116*
	(0.021)	(0.047)	(0.048)	(0.023)	(0.049)	(0.052)
SRD (1 year lag)	0.020	−0.036	0.029	0.033	−0.012	0.065
	(0.020)	(0.038)	(0.046)	(0.023)	(0.034)	(0.062)
Minority Political	1.034**	4.031***	1.384[†]	0.715[†]	3.815***	1.463[†]
Organization	(0.344)	(0.814)	(0.801)	(0.378)	(0.779)	(0.880)
Minority	0.525*	1.313***	1.534**	0.466[†]	1.109***	1.259**
Representation	(0.268)	(0.364)	(0.503)	(0.266)	(0.337)	(0.454)
Minority	−0.042	−0.124	−0.351	−0.029	−0.116	−0.408
Policy Power	(0.094)	(0.235)	(0.265)	(0.104)	(0.210)	(0.293)

Log GDP/capita	−0.314†	0.008	−0.727*	−0.294†	−0.033	−0.786*
	(0.181)	(0.330)	(0.355)	(0.168)	(0.334)	(0.345)
Polyarchy Score	−0.649	−0.332	−1.676	−0.485	0.184	−1.755
(V-Dem)	(0.881)	(2.044)	(1.559)	(0.861)	(1.981)	(1.474)
Regime Durability	−0.002	−0.006	0.008	−0.008	−0.005	0.014
	(0.005)	(0.014)	(0.016)	(0.005)	(0.014)	(0.017)
Security Sector %	−0.014	0.078	0.197**	−0.015	0.066	0.170*
of Labor Force	(0.079)	(0.122)	(0.069)	(0.078)	(0.110)	(0.074)
Youth	0.002	−0.012	0.026	−0.001	−0.010	0.023
Unemployment %	(0.014)	(0.026)	(0.021)	(0.013)	(0.025)	(0.022)
Internet Use %	0.018*	0.008	0.021	0.016*	0.008	0.016
	(0.008)	(0.015)	(0.017)	(0.008)	(0.015)	(0.018)
Minority Population	0.030**	0.064*	0.084***	0.034***	0.074**	0.079***
%	(0.010)	(0.026)	(0.018)	(0.011)	(0.028)	(0.022)
Log Country	0.320**	1.122***	0.795***	0.376***	1.090***	0.906***
Population	(0.104)	(0.261)	(0.216)	(0.104)	(0.253)	(0.245)
Religious Similarity	−0.594†	0.437	−0.172	−0.460	0.821	0.537
to Majority	(0.335)	(0.560)	(0.537)	(0.383)	(0.513)	(0.728)
Distinct Ethnicity				0.370*	0.668†	0.985*
vs. Majority				(0.166)	(0.399)	(0.439)
Rough Terrain	−0.002	−0.007	0.004	−0.001	−0.006	0.002
(avg elevation)	(0.002)	(0.004)	(0.003)	(0.001)	(0.004)	(0.003)

(continued)

Table 5.7B Continued

	(5a)			(5b)		
	Correlated RE Multinomial Logit			Correlated RE Multinomial Logit		
	(a) Rioting	(b) Violence vs. Civilians	(c) Rebellion	(a) Rioting	(b) Violence vs. Civilians	(c) Rebellion
Mean GRD	−0.034	−0.093	0.048	−0.091*	−0.073	0.072
Country Level	(0.039)	(0.065)	(0.108)	(0.041)	(0.076)	(0.110)
Mean SRD	0.095[†]	0.238*	−0.251*	0.090	0.163[†]	−0.402**
Country Level	(0.057)	(0.101)	(0.118)	(0.059)	(0.097)	(0.157)
Mobilization Type	0.863***	1.479***	1.691***	0.839***	1.450***	1.765***
Year Lagged Control	(0.179)	(0.222)	(0.284)	(0.173)	(0.234)	(0.291)
Constant	−8.098***	−29.116***	−17.024***	−9.092***	−29.143***	−18.965***
	(2.241)	(5.732)	(4.840)	(2.205)	(5.538)	(5.305)
Observations		6224			5067	
Year Effects		Included			Included	
Clustering		Country			Country	
Correlated Intercepts	(a)–(b)	(a)–(c)	(b)–(c)	(a)–(b)	(a)–(c)	(b)–(c)[†]

Robust standard errors are in parentheses

*** $p < 0.001$, ** $p < 0.01$, * $p < 0.05$, [†] $p < 0.10$

Table 5.8A Determinants of Violent Mobilization Types, Grievance Types, 2000–2014, Country Group Clustered Models, Relative Risk Ratios

	(6a)			(6b)		
	Correlated RE Multinomial Logit			Correlated RE Multinomial Logit		
	(a) Rioting	(b) Violence vs. Civilians	(c) Rebellion	(a) Rioting	(b) Violence vs. Civilians	(c) Rebellion
Minority Grievance	1.884***	2.011*	0.358[†]	1.856**	1.911*	0.250*
- Political (1 year lag)	(0.375)	(0.625)	(0.195)	(0.373)	(0.591)	(0.141)
Minority Grievance	1.550*	0.607	0.847	1.431[†]	0.596	0.923
- Religious (1 year lag)	(0.336)	(0.201)	(0.434)	(0.312)	(0.200)	(0.483)
Minority Grievance	1.738*	6.917***	3.537[†]	1.554[†]	7.669***	6.257***
- Economic (1 year lag)	(0.445)	(3.770)	(2.325)	(0.388)	(4.219)	(3.338)
GRD (1 year lag)	0.862[†]	0.804	1.424*	0.883	0.818	1.426[†]
	(0.072)	(0.121)	(0.256)	(0.075)	(0.124)	(0.267)
SRD (1 year lag)	1.164*	1.098	1.137	1.129*	1.081	1.124
	(0.075)	(0.063)	(0.149)	(0.065)	(0.059)	(0.175)
Minority Political	3.238***	67.117***	4.109	2.584**	33.064**	3.307
Organization	(1.012)	(74.501)	(6.701)	(0.866)	(36.757)	(5.231)
Minority	2.233**	7.245***	12.761**	2.096**	5.460***	7.039**
Representation	(0.590)	(2.831)	(10.897)	(0.547)	(2.002)	(5.077)
Minority	0.905	0.847	0.641	0.922	0.898	0.672
Policy Power	(0.125)	(0.250)	(0.217)	(0.130)	(0.261)	(0.251)

(*continued*)

Table 5.8A Continued

	(6a)			(6b)		
	Correlated RE Multinomial Logit			Correlated RE Multinomial Logit		
	(a) Rioting	(b) Violence vs. Civilians	(c) Rebellion	(a) Rioting	(b) Violence vs. Civilians	(c) Rebellion
Log GDP/capita	0.646*	0.713	0.230*	0.626**	0.668	0.203*
	(0.117)	(0.276)	(0.148)	(0.110)	(0.264)	(0.129)
Polyarchy Score	0.621	0.662	0.019*	0.951	0.967	0.023*
(V-Dem)	(0.477)	(1.043)	(0.039)	(0.760)	(1.584)	(0.043)
Regime Durability	0.999	0.997	1.033	0.996	0.997	1.033
	(0.005)	(0.013)	(0.030)	(0.005)	(0.013)	(0.028)
Security Sector %	0.977	1.211	1.421*	0.968	1.141	1.320
of Labor Force	(0.075)	(0.175)	(0.239)	(0.078)	(0.173)	(0.226)
Youth	0.999	0.998	1.068[†]	0.993	1.002	1.053
Unemployment %	(0.013)	(0.026)	(0.041)	(0.013)	(0.026)	(0.038)
Internet Use %	1.016[†]	1.010	1.031	1.015[†]	1.010	1.029
	(0.008)	(0.017)	(0.027)	(0.009)	(0.017)	(0.027)
Minority Population	1.060***	1.109***	1.210***	1.066***	1.117***	1.198***
%	(0.014)	(0.033)	(0.051)	(0.017)	(0.036)	(0.051)
Log Country	1.547***	3.005***	4.442***	1.557***	2.911***	4.287***
Population	(0.142)	(0.661)	(1.692)	(0.147)	(0.645)	(1.639)
Religious Similarity	0.688	0.727	0.459	0.730	1.486	1.123
to Majority	(0.220)	(0.545)	(0.436)	(0.265)	(1.083)	(1.265)

Distinct Ethnicity				1.611*	2.256†	5.373*
vs. Majority				(0.323)	(1.012)	(4.369)
Rough Terrain	0.999	0.992*	1.005	0.999	0.991*	1.004
(avg elevation)	(0.001)	(0.004)	(0.004)	(0.001)	(0.004)	(0.003)
Mean GRD	1.138	1.189	0.597*	1.095	1.193	0.581*
Group Level	(0.099)	(0.195)	(0.124)	(0.097)	(0.203)	(0.124)
Mean SRD	0.912	0.995	0.760†	0.946	1.008	0.761
Group Level	(0.065)	(0.072)	(0.107)	(0.063)	(0.072)	(0.134)
Mobilization Type	1.561*	1.828**	2.584***	1.546*	1.909**	3.030***
Year Lagged Control	(0.283)	(0.424)	(0.660)	(0.285)	(0.454)	(0.753)
Constant	0.000***	0.000***	0.000***	0.000***	0.000***	0.000***
	(0.000)	(0.000)	(0.000)	(0.000)	(0.000)	(0.000)
Observations		8,119			6,642	
Year Effects		Included			Included	
Clustering		Country Group			Country Group	
Correlated Intercepts	(a)–(b)***	(a)–(c)*	(b)–(c)**	(a)–(b)***	(a)–(c)*	(b)–(c)*

Robust standard errors are in parentheses

*** $p < 0.001$, ** $p < 0.01$, * $p < 0.05$, † $p < 0.10$

Table 5.8B Determinants of Violent Mobilization Types, Grievance Types, 2000–2014, Country Group Clustered Models, Minorities at or above 0.2% Population Cutoff

	(6a)			(6b)		
	Correlated RE Multinomial Logit			**Correlated RE Multinomial Logit**		
	(a) Rioting	**(b) Violence vs. Civilians**	**(c) Rebellion**	**(a) Rioting**	**(b) Violence vs. Civilians**	**(c) Rebellion**
Minority Grievance	0.650**	0.703*	−0.968†	0.600**	0.640*	−1.340*
- Political (1 year lag)	(0.206)	(0.320)	(0.560)	(0.207)	(0.320)	(0.578)
Minority Grievance	0.425†	−0.504	−0.098	0.328	−0.542	−0.033
- Religious (1 year lag)	(0.219)	(0.345)	(0.524)	(0.218)	(0.353)	(0.542)
Minority Grievance	0.520†	1.888***	1.168†	0.392	1.977***	1.719**
- Economic (1 year lag)	(0.267)	(0.538)	(0.642)	(0.253)	(0.544)	(0.542)
GRD (1 year lag)	−0.140	−0.218	0.328†	−0.111	−0.198	0.326†
	(0.090)	(0.160)	(0.173)	(0.090)	(0.164)	(0.180)
SRD (1 year lag)	0.116*	0.072	0.102	0.113†	0.068	0.101
	(0.058)	(0.057)	(0.132)	(0.059)	(0.057)	(0.158)
Minority Political	1.167***	4.104***	1.320	0.923**	3.369**	1.145
Organization	(0.310)	(1.123)	(1.627)	(0.326)	(1.107)	(1.601)
Minority	0.714**	1.888***	2.495**	0.627*	1.599***	1.906**
Representation	(0.258)	(0.378)	(0.846)	(0.251)	(0.357)	(0.721)
Minority	−0.076	−0.146	−0.416	−0.065	−0.094	−0.373
Policy Power	(0.132)	(0.284)	(0.337)	(0.133)	(0.283)	(0.374)

Log GDP/capita	−0.383*	−0.252	−1.415*	−0.401*	−0.331	−1.513*
	(0.183)	(0.378)	(0.618)	(0.178)	(0.381)	(0.615)
Polyarchy Score	−0.306	−0.047	−3.726[†]	0.116	0.363	−3.545[†]
(V-Dem)	(0.797)	(1.668)	(2.060)	(0.808)	(1.710)	(1.927)
Regime Durability	−0.006	−0.009	0.025	−0.010[†]	−0.008	0.025
	(0.006)	(0.014)	(0.029)	(0.005)	(0.014)	(0.027)
Security Sector %	−0.006	0.241[†]	0.385*	−0.012	0.194	0.315[†]
of Labor Force	(0.074)	(0.140)	(0.167)	(0.076)	(0.145)	(0.172)
Youth	0.001	0.002	0.068[†]	−0.004	0.005	0.054
Unemployment %	(0.013)	(0.026)	(0.040)	(0.013)	(0.025)	(0.037)
Internet Use %	0.018*	0.013	0.036	0.016[†]	0.013	0.033
	(0.008)	(0.017)	(0.027)	(0.008)	(0.017)	(0.027)
Minority Population	0.046***	0.085**	0.171***	0.049***	0.093***	0.159***
%	(0.012)	(0.028)	(0.039)	(0.014)	(0.029)	(0.040)
Log Country	0.433***	1.119***	1.524***	0.453***	1.104***	1.501***
Population	(0.091)	(0.222)	(0.372)	(0.092)	(0.222)	(0.387)
Religious Similarity	−0.659*	−0.960	−1.182	−0.545	−0.255	−0.391
to Majority	(0.323)	(0.743)	(0.943)	(0.349)	(0.715)	(1.079)
Distinct Ethnicity				0.401*	0.802[†]	1.582[†]
vs. Majority				(0.201)	(0.465)	(0.817)
Rough Terrain	−0.001	−0.007[†]	0.005	0.000	−0.007[†]	0.004
(avg elevation)	(0.001)	(0.004)	(0.004)	(0.001)	(0.004)	(0.003)

(continued)

Table 5.8B Continued

	(6a)			(6b)		
	Correlated RE Multinomial Logit			Correlated RE Multinomial Logit		
	(a) Rioting	(b) Violence vs. Civilians	(c) Rebellion	(a) Rioting	(b) Violence vs. Civilians	(c) Rebellion
Mean GRD	0.116	0.169	−0.497*	0.070	0.162	−0.525*
Group Level	(0.094)	(0.174)	(0.201)	(0.093)	(0.183)	(0.208)
Mean SRD	−0.051	0.024	−0.232†	−0.042	0.028	−0.239
Group Level	(0.064)	(0.075)	(0.139)	(0.067)	(0.076)	(0.174)
Mobilization Type	0.468**	0.613**	0.916***	0.455*	0.658**	1.071***
Year Lagged Control	(0.181)	(0.240)	(0.246)	(0.184)	(0.247)	(0.241)
Constant	−9.978***	−28.943***	−28.758***	−10.290***	−28.379***	−28.111***
	(2.069)	(5.774)	(7.861)	(2.099)	(5.765)	(8.440)
Observations		6224			5067	
Year Effects		Included			Included	
Clustering		Country Group			Country Group	
Correlated Intercepts	(a)–(b)**	(a)–(c)†	(b)–(c)**	(a)–(b)**	(a)–(c)*	(b)–(c)*

Robust standard errors are in parentheses

*** $p < 0.001$, ** $p < 0.01$, * $p < 0.05$, † $p < 0.10$

Table 5.9A Determinants of Violent Mobilization Types, Grievance Intensities, 2000–2014, Country-Clustered Models, Relative Risk Ratios

	(7a)			(7b)		
	Correlated RE Multinomial Logit			**Correlated RE Multinomial Logit**		
	(a) Rioting	**(b) Violence vs. Civilians**	**(c) Rebellion**	**(a) Rioting**	**(b) Violence vs. Civilians**	**(c) Rebellion**
Minority Grievance	1.160	1.279*	0.782	1.171	1.307*	0.753
intensity, Pol, year lag	(0.110)	(0.155)	(0.143)	(0.119)	(0.173)	(0.161)
Minority Grievance	1.364***	1.095	1.268[†]	1.316**	1.052	1.140
intensity, Rel, year lag	(0.122)	(0.130)	(0.175)	(0.114)	(0.129)	(0.157)
Minority Grievance	1.381**	2.021***	1.944[†]	1.345*	2.009***	2.554***
Intensity, Econ year lag	(0.162)	(0.370)	(0.759)	(0.164)	(0.370)	(0.505)
GRD (1 year lag)	1.026	1.008	0.954	1.046	1.013	0.912[†]
	(0.028)	(0.041)	(0.037)	(0.032)	(0.045)	(0.050)
SRD (1 year lag)	1.029	0.984	1.017	1.034	1.001	1.047
	(0.020)	(0.038)	(0.044)	(0.024)	(0.035)	(0.057)
Minority Political	2.962***	48.065***	4.332[†]	2.181*	31.810***	3.766[†]
Organization	(0.943)	(40.555)	(3.536)	(0.754)	(24.855)	(2.982)
Minority	1.840*	3.153***	4.586**	1.787*	2.656**	3.702***
Representation	(0.478)	(1.102)	(2.207)	(0.463)	(0.853)	(1.481)
Minority	0.917	0.805	0.663	0.938	0.847	0.625[†]
Policy Power	(0.095)	(0.177)	(0.168)	(0.110)	(0.166)	(0.168)
Log GDP/capita	0.651**	0.920	0.517[†]	0.670**	0.897	0.498[†]
	(0.105)	(0.288)	(0.205)	(0.104)	(0.287)	(0.183)

(continued)

Table 5.9A Continued

	(7a)			(7b)		
	Correlated RE Multinomial Logit			Correlated RE Multinomial Logit		
	(a) Rioting	(b) Violence vs. Civilians	(c) Rebellion	(a) Rioting	(b) Violence vs. Civilians	(c) Rebellion
Polyarchy Score	0.608	0.580	0.250	0.632	0.873	0.173
(V-Dem)	(0.528)	(1.072)	(0.399)	(0.544)	(1.548)	(0.258)
Regime Durability	0.998	0.994	1.007	0.994	0.994	1.014
	(0.005)	(0.014)	(0.016)	(0.006)	(0.014)	(0.017)
Security Sector %	0.983	1.054	1.184*	0.982	1.054	1.160*
of Labor Force	(0.080)	(0.107)	(0.091)	(0.079)	(0.099)	(0.086)
Youth	1.007	0.997	1.020	1.005	0.998	1.019
Unemployment %	(0.014)	(0.025)	(0.023)	(0.013)	(0.024)	(0.025)
Internet Use %	1.015*	1.004	1.013	1.014[†]	1.005	1.008
	(0.008)	(0.014)	(0.018)	(0.008)	(0.015)	(0.018)
Minority Population	1.038***	1.068**	1.097***	1.042***	1.078**	1.095***
%	(0.010)	(0.027)	(0.019)	(0.011)	(0.028)	(0.023)
Log Country	1.384**	3.203***	2.281***	1.457***	3.133***	2.611***
Population	(0.142)	(0.890)	(0.503)	(0.154)	(0.875)	(0.629)
Religious Similarity	0.750	2.107	1.080	0.832	3.351*	2.167
to Majority	(0.228)	(1.065)	(0.578)	(0.320)	(1.686)	(1.433)
Distinct Ethnicity				1.386*	1.686[†]	2.657*
vs. Majority				(0.218)	(0.510)	(1.127)

Rough Terrain	0.998	0.994	1.003	0.999	0.994	1.002
(avg elevation)	(0.002)	(0.004)	(0.002)	(0.002)	(0.004)	(0.002)
Mean Pol grievance	0.832	1.804	3.606	0.871	2.464	1.981
Intensity—Country	(0.571)	(2.928)	(6.522)	(0.597)	(3.936)	(3.645)
Mean Rel grievance	1.058	0.184	0.465	0.996	0.158	0.446
Intensity—Country	(0.657)	(0.263)	(0.539)	(0.600)	(0.232)	(0.597)
Mean Econ grievance	25.842*	16.442	1.701	15.165†	8.356	0.957
Intensity—Country	(38.198)	(41.235)	(5.759)	(22.661)	(19.813)	(3.297)
Mean GRD	0.950	0.875*	1.015	0.896*	0.895	1.050
Country Level	(0.039)	(0.057)	(0.093)	(0.043)	(0.069)	(0.106)
Mean SRD	1.040	1.201	0.739*	1.049	1.127	0.668**
Country Level	(0.055)	(0.149)	(0.095)	(0.062)	(0.136)	(0.105)
Mobilization Type	2.422***	4.708***	5.784***	2.375***	4.513***	6.138***
Year Lagged Control	(0.447)	(1.100)	(1.659)	(0.430)	(1.068)	(1.884)
Constant	0.000***	0.000***	0.000***	0.000***	0.000***	0.000***
	(0.001)	(0.000)	(0.000)	(0.000)	(0.000)	(0.000)
Observations		8,119			6,642	
Year Effects		Included			Included	
Clustering		Country			Country	
Correlated Intercepts	(a)–(b)	(a)–(c)	(b)–(c)	(a)–(b)	(a)–(c)	(b)–(c)

Robust standard errors are in parentheses

*** $p < 0.001$, ** $p < 0.01$, * $p < 0.05$, † $p < 0.10$

Table 5.9B Determinants of Violent Mobilization Types, Grievance Intensities, 2000–2014, Country-Clustered Models, Minorities at or above 0.2% Population Cutoff

	(7a)			(7b)		
	Correlated RE Multinomial Logit			**Correlated RE Multinomial Logit**		
	(a) Rioting	**(b) Violence vs. Civilians**	**(c) Rebellion**	**(a) Rioting**	**(b) Violence vs. Civilians**	**(c) Rebellion**
Minority Grievance	0.200*	0.271*	−0.208	0.204*	0.307*	−0.242
intensity, Pol, year lag	(0.094)	(0.134)	(0.191)	(0.099)	(0.147)	(0.220)
Minority Grievance	0.278**	0.090	0.206	0.241**	0.040	0.106
intensity, Rel, year lag	(0.089)	(0.114)	(0.139)	(0.086)	(0.122)	(0.140)
Minority Grievance	0.294*	0.675***	0.598	0.259*	0.658***	0.878***
Intensity, Econ year lag	(0.120)	(0.179)	(0.371)	(0.123)	(0.180)	(0.201)
GRD (1 year lag)	0.015	−0.016	−0.086[†]	0.026	−0.004	−0.118[†]
	(0.021)	(0.048)	(0.048)	(0.023)	(0.050)	(0.064)
SRD (1 year lag)	0.029	−0.031	0.026	0.038[†]	−0.009	0.049
	(0.020)	(0.037)	(0.039)	(0.022)	(0.034)	(0.052)
Minority Political	1.045**	3.726***	1.313[†]	0.717[†]	3.506***	1.366
Organization	(0.339)	(0.735)	(0.791)	(0.369)	(0.708)	(0.867)
Minority	0.509*	1.279***	1.638***	0.454[†]	1.077***	1.376**
Representation	(0.257)	(0.338)	(0.492)	(0.256)	(0.316)	(0.452)
Minority	−0.062	−0.165	−0.396	−0.046	−0.141	−0.460[†]
Policy Power	(0.097)	(0.234)	(0.250)	(0.104)	(0.207)	(0.267)
Log GDP/capita	−0.406*	−0.027	−0.575	−0.380*	−0.073	−0.597
	(0.164)	(0.321)	(0.373)	(0.155)	(0.324)	(0.365)

Polyarchy Score	−0.143	−0.234	−1.477	−0.029	0.360	−1.569
(V-Dem)	(0.867)	(1.883)	(1.467)	(0.839)	(1.844)	(1.414)
Regime Durability	−0.006	−0.006	0.004	−0.010†	−0.006	0.009
	(0.005)	(0.014)	(0.015)	(0.005)	(0.014)	(0.015)
Security Sector %	0.000	0.052	0.176*	0.000	0.053	0.156*
of Labor Force	(0.080)	(0.122)	(0.077)	(0.077)	(0.104)	(0.071)
Youth	0.008	−0.009	0.018	0.005	−0.009	0.017
Unemployment %	(0.014)	(0.027)	(0.021)	(0.013)	(0.025)	(0.023)
Internet Use %	0.018*	0.009	0.015	0.016*	0.009	0.009
	(0.008)	(0.015)	(0.018)	(0.008)	(0.015)	(0.019)
Minority Population	0.030***	0.062*	0.084***	0.034***	0.073**	0.080***
%	(0.009)	(0.026)	(0.018)	(0.010)	(0.027)	(0.021)
Log Country	0.326**	1.157***	0.794***	0.385***	1.174***	0.911***
Population	(0.104)	(0.280)	(0.231)	(0.104)	(0.276)	(0.246)
Religious Similarity	−0.581†	0.368	−0.070	−0.449	0.849	0.652
to Majority	(0.336)	(0.569)	(0.520)	(0.387)	(0.518)	(0.713)
Distinct Ethnicity				0.337*	0.694†	0.943*
vs. Majority				(0.163)	(0.364)	(0.457)
Rough Terrain	−0.001	−0.005	0.003	0.000	−0.004	0.002
(avg elevation)	(0.002)	(0.004)	(0.002)	(0.001)	(0.004)	(0.002)
Mean Pol grievance	−0.481	0.293	0.989	−0.538	0.619	0.340
Intensity—Country	(0.681)	(1.603)	(1.806)	(0.661)	(1.540)	(1.853)

(*continued*)

Table 5.9B Continued

	(7a)			(7b)		
	Correlated RE Multinomial Logit			Correlated RE Multinomial Logit		
	(a) Rioting	(b) Violence vs. Civilians	(c) Rebellion	(a) Rioting	(b) Violence vs. Civilians	(c) Rebellion
Mean Rel grievance	0.101	−4.298	−0.524	−0.006	−4.408	−0.671
Intensity—Country	(0.756)	(3.024)	(1.255)	(0.725)	(2.750)	(1.526)
Mean Econ grievance	3.400*	2.509	0.309	2.899[†]	1.908	−0.234
Intensity—Country	(1.525)	(2.668)	(3.248)	(1.525)	(2.442)	(3.277)
Mean GRD	−0.032	−0.089	0.054	−0.083*	−0.080	0.077
Country Level	(0.036)	(0.064)	(0.099)	(0.039)	(0.076)	(0.103)
Mean SRD	0.057	0.310*	−0.285*	0.064	0.231[†]	−0.384*
Country Level	(0.062)	(0.143)	(0.127)	(0.063)	(0.134)	(0.157)
Mobilization Type	0.823***	1.475***	1.681***	0.801***	1.417***	1.753***
Year Lagged Control	(0.180)	(0.229)	(0.291)	(0.173)	(0.234)	(0.329)
Constant	−7.834***	−28.437***	−17.839***	−8.839***	−29.332***	−19.814***
	(2.162)	(5.833)	(4.782)	(2.141)	(5.583)	(4.984)
Observations		6224			5067	
Year Effects		Included			Included	
Clustering		Country			Country	
Correlated Intercepts	(a)–(b)	(a)–(c)	(b)–(c)	(a)–(b)	(a)–(c)	(b)–(c)[†]

Robust standard errors are in parentheses

*** $p < 0.001$, ** $p < 0.01$, * $p < 0.05$, [†] $p < 0.10$

Table 5.10A Determinants of Violent Mobilization Types, Grievance Intensities, 2000–2014, Country Group Clustered Models, Relative Risk Ratios

	(8a)			(8b)		
	Correlated RE Multinomial Logit			**Correlated RE Multinomial Logit**		
	(a) Rioting	**(b) Violence vs. Civilians**	**(c) Rebellion**	**(a) Rioting**	**(b) Violence vs. Civilians**	**(c) Rebellion**
Minority Grievance	1.225*	1.198	0.714[†]	1.247*	1.188	0.703[†]
intensity, Pol, year lag	(0.123)	(0.157)	(0.138)	(0.124)	(0.160)	(0.141)
Minority Grievance	1.033	0.746*	0.619*	0.990	0.736*	0.625*
intensity, Rel, year lag	(0.100)	(0.103)	(0.135)	(0.097)	(0.106)	(0.146)
Minority Grievance	1.028	1.755*	1.201	1.050	1.845**	1.724**
Intensity, Econ year lag	(0.112)	(0.400)	(0.395)	(0.121)	(0.431)	(0.362)
GRD (1 year lag)	0.876	0.818	1.432*	0.886	0.832	1.380[†]
	(0.072)	(0.121)	(0.233)	(0.075)	(0.124)	(0.245)
SRD (1 year lag)	1.142*	1.083	1.116	1.109[†]	1.068	1.098
	(0.072)	(0.063)	(0.145)	(0.060)	(0.058)	(0.158)
Minority Political	2.493**	33.932**	1.502	1.950*	16.098*	1.402
Organization	(0.779)	(39.012)	(2.553)	(0.642)	(18.587)	(2.185)
Minority	2.031**	6.369***	13.211**	1.964**	4.872***	7.964**
Representation	(0.493)	(2.524)	(10.887)	(0.473)	(1.800)	(5.607)
Minority	0.878	0.808	0.566[†]	0.883	0.856	0.595
Policy Power	(0.120)	(0.236)	(0.195)	(0.123)	(0.244)	(0.214)
Log GDP/capita	0.581**	0.670	0.240*	0.582***	0.643	0.229*
	(0.101)	(0.265)	(0.167)	(0.098)	(0.259)	(0.150)

(*continued*)

Table 5.10A Continued

	(8a)			(8b)		
	Correlated RE Multinomial Logit			Correlated RE Multinomial Logit		
	(a) Rioting	(b) Violence vs. Civilians	(c) Rebellion	(a) Rioting	(b) Violence vs. Civilians	(c) Rebellion
Polyarchy Score	0.806	0.732	0.049	1.080	1.102	0.050
(V-Dem)	(0.575)	(1.182)	(0.101)	(0.809)	(1.842)	(0.099)
Regime Durability	0.992	0.989	1.006	0.991[†]	0.991	1.012
	(0.005)	(0.016)	(0.026)	(0.005)	(0.015)	(0.024)
Security Sector %	0.994	1.190	1.401	0.983	1.146	1.308
of Labor Force	(0.080)	(0.182)	(0.300)	(0.084)	(0.180)	(0.260)
Youth	1.001	0.994	1.053	0.996	0.999	1.045
Unemployment %	(0.012)	(0.027)	(0.045)	(0.012)	(0.025)	(0.042)
Internet Use %	1.018*	1.007	1.021	1.016[†]	1.006	1.018
	(0.009)	(0.017)	(0.028)	(0.009)	(0.017)	(0.027)
Minority Population	1.049***	1.087**	1.185***	1.053***	1.098**	1.168***
%	(0.014)	(0.034)	(0.049)	(0.016)	(0.036)	(0.048)
Log Country	1.503***	2.797***	4.060***	1.485***	2.671***	3.711***
Population	(0.131)	(0.643)	(1.650)	(0.133)	(0.628)	(1.370)
Religious Similarity	0.670	0.655	0.508	0.672	1.342	1.062
to Majority	(0.217)	(0.495)	(0.444)	(0.249)	(0.958)	(1.053)
Distinct Ethnicity				1.345	1.904	3.114
vs. Majority				(0.263)	(0.862)	(2.204)

Rough Terrain	0.999	0.991*	1.004	0.999	0.990*	1.003
(avg elevation)	(0.001)	(0.004)	(0.004)	(0.001)	(0.004)	(0.004)
Mean Pol grievance	0.814	3.838†	3.766	0.840	5.011*	2.577
Intensity—Group	(0.308)	(2.866)	(3.457)	(0.332)	(3.522)	(2.594)
Mean Rel grievance	2.730***	2.177	6.099†	2.828***	1.806	5.543†
Intensity—Group	(0.810)	(1.506)	(6.111)	(0.835)	(1.273)	(5.558)
Mean Econ grievance	9.043***	12.790†	61.245*	7.314***	12.466†	36.653*
Intensity—Group	(4.625)	(17.322)	(114.917)	(3.733)	(17.121)	(66.549)
Mean GRD	1.110	1.160	0.597**	1.090	1.192	0.619*
Group Level	(0.094)	(0.189)	(0.102)	(0.096)	(0.197)	(0.117)
Mean SRD	0.905	0.929	0.667*	0.931	0.926	0.688*
Group Level	(0.065)	(0.069)	(0.116)	(0.061)	(0.067)	(0.130)
Mobilization Type	1.502*	1.850**	2.460***	1.496*	1.928**	2.778***
Year Lagged Control	(0.266)	(0.414)	(0.583)	(0.272)	(0.447)	(0.676)
Constant	0.000***	0.000***	0.000***	0.000***	0.000***	0.000**
	(0.000)	(0.000)	(0.000)	(0.000)	(0.000)	(0.000)
Observations		8,119			6,642	
Year Effects		Included			Included	
Clustering		Country Group			Country Group	
Correlated Intercepts	(a)–(b)**	(a)–(c)†	(b)–(c)**	(a)–(b)**	(a)–(c)*	(b)–(c)**

Robust standard errors are in parentheses

*** $p < 0.001$, ** $p < 0.01$, * $p < 0.05$, † $p < 0.10$

Table 5.10B Determinants of Violent Mobilization Types, Grievance Intensities, 2000–2014, Country Group Clustered Models, Minorities at or above 0.2% Population Cutoff

	(8a)			(8b)		
	Correlated RE Multinomial Logit			Correlated RE Multinomial Logit		
	(a) Rioting	(b) Violence vs. Civilians	(c) Rebellion	(a) Rioting	(b) Violence vs. Civilians	(c) Rebellion
Minority Grievance	0.204*	0.203	−0.298	0.214*	0.193	−0.315
intensity, Pol, year lag	(0.103)	(0.135)	(0.206)	(0.102)	(0.140)	(0.215)
Minority Grievance	0.057	−0.250[†]	−0.417[†]	0.016	−0.264[†]	−0.410[†]
intensity, Rel, year lag	(0.095)	(0.140)	(0.221)	(0.094)	(0.147)	(0.237)
Minority Grievance	0.027	0.538*	0.152	0.042	0.585**	0.492*
Intensity, Econ year lag	(0.107)	(0.222)	(0.322)	(0.115)	(0.228)	(0.213)
GRD (1 year lag)	−0.122	−0.189	0.330*	−0.106	−0.170	0.293[†]
	(0.088)	(0.159)	(0.157)	(0.089)	(0.162)	(0.169)
SRD (1 year lag)	0.102[†]	0.057	0.084	0.100[†]	0.056	0.075
	(0.053)	(0.057)	(0.130)	(0.054)	(0.056)	(0.146)
Minority Political	0.909**	3.510**	0.415	0.655*	2.731*	0.377
Organization	(0.313)	(1.160)	(1.706)	(0.322)	(1.140)	(1.576)
Minority	0.635**	1.778***	2.519**	0.585*	1.493***	2.037**
Representation	(0.237)	(0.390)	(0.820)	(0.232)	(0.365)	(0.707)
Minority	−0.106	−0.175	−0.526	−0.103	−0.119	−0.481
Policy Power	(0.130)	(0.285)	(0.343)	(0.130)	(0.282)	(0.359)
Log GDP/capita	−0.493**	−0.304	−1.352*	−0.483**	−0.365	−1.386*
	(0.172)	(0.387)	(0.670)	(0.166)	(0.392)	(0.631)

Polyarchy Score	−0.085	0.008	−2.782	0.221	0.489	−2.745
(V-Dem)	(0.729)	(1.672)	(2.073)	(0.749)	(1.713)	(2.003)
Regime Durability	−0.012*	−0.014	0.000	−0.013*	−0.012	0.005
	(0.005)	(0.016)	(0.026)	(0.005)	(0.016)	(0.024)
Security Sector %	0.006	0.211	0.366[†]	−0.001	0.178	0.302
of Labor Force	(0.077)	(0.148)	(0.208)	(0.078)	(0.152)	(0.192)
Youth	0.002	−0.003	0.052	−0.001	0.001	0.045
Unemployment %	(0.012)	(0.027)	(0.043)	(0.012)	(0.025)	(0.041)
Internet Use %	0.020*	0.011	0.026	0.017*	0.010	0.023
	(0.009)	(0.018)	(0.028)	(0.009)	(0.018)	(0.027)
Minority Population	0.037**	0.073*	0.155***	0.039**	0.085**	0.139***
%	(0.012)	(0.029)	(0.040)	(0.014)	(0.030)	(0.039)
Log Country	0.398***	1.074***	1.435***	0.402***	1.056***	1.367***
Population	(0.086)	(0.229)	(0.402)	(0.085)	(0.236)	(0.374)
Religious Similarity	−0.658*	−1.021	−1.041	−0.596[†]	−0.274	−0.362
to Majority	(0.322)	(0.786)	(0.846)	(0.348)	(0.720)	(0.949)
Distinct Ethnicity				0.223	0.758	1.072
vs. Majority				(0.196)	(0.488)	(0.720)
Rough Terrain	−0.001	−0.007[†]	0.005	0.000	−0.008[†]	0.004
(avg elevation)	(0.001)	(0.004)	(0.004)	(0.001)	(0.004)	(0.004)
Mean Pol grievance	−0.194	1.335[†]	1.272	−0.214	1.552*	0.822
Intensity—Group	(0.375)	(0.751)	(0.917)	(0.386)	(0.727)	(1.024)

(*continued*)

Table 5.10B Continued

	(8a)			(8b)		
	Correlated RE Multinomial Logit			Correlated RE Multinomial Logit		
	(a) Rioting	(b) Violence vs. Civilians	(c) Rebellion	(a) Rioting	(b) Violence vs. Civilians	(c) Rebellion
Mean Rel grievance	0.915**	0.061	1.299	0.911**	−0.186	1.181
Intensity—Group	(0.307)	(0.707)	(0.954)	(0.306)	(0.713)	(0.951)
Mean Econ grievance	1.894***	2.222[†]	3.843*	1.679***	2.141	3.355[†]
Intensity—Group	(0.492)	(1.298)	(1.787)	(0.478)	(1.327)	(1.753)
Mean GRD	0.094	0.143	−0.482**	0.069	0.158	−0.454*
Group Level	(0.091)	(0.174)	(0.165)	(0.091)	(0.178)	(0.182)
Mean SRD	−0.064	−0.025	−0.349*	−0.061	−0.030	−0.315[†]
Group Level	(0.062)	(0.074)	(0.168)	(0.065)	(0.075)	(0.187)
Mobilization Type	0.424*	0.615**	0.867***	0.418*	0.660**	0.985***
Year Lagged Control	(0.178)	(0.233)	(0.232)	(0.183)	(0.243)	(0.238)
Constant	−8.472***	−27.284***	−27.352***	−8.467***	−26.947***	−25.701**
	(1.763)	(5.717)	(8.446)	(1.772)	(5.957)	(8.179)
Observations		6224			5067	
Year Effects		Included			Included	
Clustering		Country Group			Country Group	
Correlated Intercepts	(a)–(b)**	(a)–(c)	(b)–(c)**	(a)–(b)**	(a)–(c)[†]	(b)–(c)**

Robust standard errors are in parentheses

*** $p < 0.001$, ** $p < 0.01$, * $p < 0.05$, [†] $p < 0.10$

References

Abadie, A., Athey, S., Imbens, G. W., & Wooldridge, J. (2017). When should you adjust standard errors for clustering? *National Bureau of Economic Research, Working Paper 24003*. https://doi.org/10.3386/w24003.

Abrahms, M., & Potter, P. B. K. (2015). Explaining terrorism: Leadership deficits and militant group tactics. *International Organization, 69*(2), 311–342. https://doi.org/10.1017/S0020818314000411.

Abulof, U. (2014). The roles of religion in national legitimation: Judaism and Zionism's elusive quest for legitimacy. *Journal for the Scientific Study of Religion, 53*(3), 515–533. https://www.jstor.org/stable/24644225.

Acevdo, G. A., & Chaudhary, A. R. (2015). Religion, cultural clash, and Muslim attitudes about politically motivated violence. *Journal for the Scientific Study of Religion, 54*(2), 242–260. https://doi.org/10.1111/jssr.12185.

Adamczyk, A., & LaFree, G. (2019). Religion and support for political violence among Christians and Muslims in Africa. *Sociological Perspectives, 62*(6), 948–979. https://doi.org/10.1177/0731121419866813.

Akbaba, Y., & Tydas, Z. (2011). Does religious discrimination promote dissent? A quantitative analysis. *Ethnopolitics, 10*(3), 271–295.

Almond, G., Appleby, R. S., & Sivan, E. (2003). *Strong religion: The rise of fundamentalism around the world*. University of Chicago Press.

Alonso, S., & Ruiz-Rufino, R. (2007). Political representation and ethnic conflict in new democracies. *European Journal of Political Research, 46*(2), 237–267. https://doi.org/10.1111/j.1475-6765.2007.00693.x.

Anisin, A. (2016). Violence begets violence: Why states should not lethally repress popular protest. *International Journal of Human Rights, 20*(7), 893–913. https://doi.org/10.1080/13642987.2016.1192536.

Arikan, G., & Bloom, P. B.-N. (2018). Religion and political protest: A cross country analysis. *Comparative Political Studies, 52*(2), 246–276. https://doi.org/10.1177/0010414018774351.

Asal, V., & Deloughery, K. (2017). Grievance: The nexus between grievances and conflict. In M. Stohl, M. I. Lichbach, & P. N. Grabosky (Eds.), *States and peoples in conflict: Transformations of conflict studies* (pp. 17–21). Routledge.

Asal, V., Johnson, C., & Wilkenfeld, J. (2008). Ethnopolitical violence and terrorism in the Middle East. In J. J. Hewitt, J. Wilkenfeld, & T. R. Gurr (Eds.), *Peace and conflict 2008* (pp. 55–66). Paradigm.

Asal, V., Schulzke, M., & Pate, A. (2017). Why do some organizations kill while others do not: An examination of Middle Eastern organizations. *Foreign Policy Analysis. 13*(4), 811–831. https://doi.org/10.1111/fpa.12080.

Aspinall, E. (2007). The construction of grievance: Natural resources and identity in a separatist conflict. *Journal of Conflict Resolution, 51*(6), 950–972. https://doi.org/10.1177/0022002707307.

304 REFERENCES

Ayres, R. W., & Saideman, S. (2000). Is separatism as contagious as the common cold or as cancer? Testing international and domestic explanations. *Nationalism and Ethnic Politics, 6*(3), 91–113. https://doi.org/10.1080/13537110008428605.

Basedau, M., Deitch, M., & Zellman, A. (2022). Rebels with a cause: Does ideology make armed conflicts longer and bloodier? *Journal of Conflict Resolution, 66*(10), 1826–1853. https://doi.org/10.1177/00220027221108222.

Basedau, M., Fox, J., Pierskalla, J., Strüver, G., & Vüllers, J. (2017). Does discrimination breed grievances and do grievances breed violence? New evidence from and analysis of religious minorities in developing countries. *Conflict Management and Peace Science, 31*(3), 217–239. https://doi.org/10.1177/0738894215581329.

Basedau, M., Fox, J., Huber, C., Pieters, A., Konzack, T., & Deitch, M. (2019). Introducing the "Religious Minorities at Risk" dataset. *Peace Economics, Peace Science, and Public Policy.* https://doi.org/10.1515/peps-2019-0028.

Basedau, M., Gobien, S., & Hoffman, L. (2022). Identity threats and ideas of superiority as drivers of religious violence? Evidence from a survey experiment in Dar es Salaam, Tanzania. *Journal of Peace Research, 59*(3), 395–408. https://doi.org/10.1177/002234 33211035234.

Basedau, M., & Koos, C. (2016). When do religious leaders support faith-based violence? Evidence from a survey poll in Sudan. *Political Research Quarterly, 68*(4), 760–772. https://doi.org/10.1177/1065912915603128.

Basedau, M., Pfeiffer, B., & Vüllers, J. (2016). Bad religion? Religion, collective action, and the onset of armed conflict in developing countries. *Journal of Conflict Resolution, 60*(2), 226–255. https://doi.org/10.1177/0022002714541853.

Basedau, M., & Schaefer-Kehnert, J. (2019). Religious discrimination and religious armed conflict in sub-Saharan Africa: An obvious relationship? *Religion, State & Society, 47*(1), 30–47. https://doi.org/10.1080/09637494.2018.1531617.

Basedau, M., Strüver, G., Vüllers, J., & Wegenast, T. (2011). Do religious factors impact armed conflict? Empirical evidence from sub-Saharan Africa. *Terrorism and Political Violence, 23*(5), 752–779. https://doi.org/10.1080/09546553.2011.619240.

Bell, A., & Jones, K. (2015). Explaining fixed effects: Random effects modeling of time-series cross-sectional and panel data. *Political Science Research and Methods, 3*(1), 133–153. https://doi.org/10.1017/psrm.2014.7.

Bell, S. R., & Murdie, A. (2018). The apparatus for violence: Repression, violent protest, and civil war in a cross-national framework. *Conflict Management and Peace Science, 35*(4), 336–354. https://doi.org/10.1177/0738894215626848.

Ben-Nun Bloom, P. (2015). State-level restriction of religious freedom and women's rights: A global analysis. *Political Studies, 64*(4), 832–853. https://doi.org/10.1111/1467-9248.12212.

Bercovitch, J., & Darouen, Jr., K. (2005). Managing ethnic civil wars: Assessing the determinants of successful mediation. *Civil Wars, 7*(1), 98–116. https://doi.org/10.1080/13698280500074453.

Bernhard, M., Örsün, Ö. F., & Reşat Bayer, R. (2017). Democratization in conflict research: How conceptualization affects operationalization and testing outcomes. *International Interactions, 43*(6), 941–966. https://doi.org/10.1080/03050629.2017.1257489.

Besançon, M. L. (2005). Relative resources: Inequality in ethnic wars, revolutions, and genocides. *Journal of Peace Research, 42*(4), 393–415. https://doi.org/10.1177/002234 3305054.

REFERENCES 305

Beswick, S. F. (1991). The Addis Ababa Agreement: 1972–1983 harbinger of the second civil war in the Sudan. *Northeast African Studies, 13*(2/3), 191–215. https://www.jstor.org/stable/43660097.

Bettiza, G. (2019). *Finding faith in American foreign policy: Religion and American diplomacy in a postsecular World.* Oxford University Press.

Beyerlein, K., & Chaves, M. (2003). The political activities of religious congregations in the US. *Journal for the Scientific Study of Religion, 42*(2), 229–246. https://doi.org/10.1111/1468-5906.00175.

Billings, D. B., & Scott, S. L. (1994). Religion and political legitimation. *Annual Review of Sociology, 20,* 173–201. https://www.annualreviews.org/doi/abs/10.1146/annurev.so.20.080194.001133.

Birnir, J. K., & Overos, H. D. (2019). Religion and political mobilization. In W. R. Thompson (Ed.), *Oxford Research Encyclopedia of Politics* (pp. 1–24). Oxford University Press. https://doi.org/10.1007/978-981-13-0242-8_22-1.

Birnir, J. K., & Satana, N. S. (2013). Religion and coalition politics. *Comparative Political Studies, 46*(1), 3–30. https://doi.org/10.1177/0010414012453.

Birnir, J. K., Wilkenfeld, J., Fearon, D. D., Laitin, D. D., Gurr, T. R., Brancati, D., Saideman, S. M., Pate, M., & Hultquist, A. S. (2015). Socially relevant groups, ethnic structure, and AMAR. *Journal of Peace Research, 52*(1), 110–115. https://doi.org/10.1177/0022343314536915.

Bloemraad, I. (2013). Accessing the corridors of power: Puzzles and pathways to understanding minority representation. *West European Politics, 36*(3), 652–670. https://doi.org/10.1080/01402382.2013.773733.

Bodea, C., Elbadawi I., & Houle, C. (2017). Do civil wars, coups and riots have the same structural determinants? *International Interactions, 43*(3), 537–561. https://doi.org/10.1080/03050629.2016.1188093.

Boese, V. A. (2019). How (not) to measure democracy. *International Area Studies Review, 22*(2), 95–107. https://doi.org/10.1177/2233865918815571.

Bormann, N.-C., Cederman, L.-E., & Vogt, M. (2015). Language, religion, and ethnic civil war. *Journal of Conflict Resolution, 61*(4), 774–771. https://doi.org/10.1177/0022002715600755.

Bormann, N.-C., & Savun, B. (2018). Reputation, concessions, and territorial civil war: Do ethnic dominoes fall, or don't they? *Journal of Peace Research, 55*(5), 671–686. https://doi.org/10.1177/0022343318767499.

Braithwaite, A., Braithwaite, J. M., & Kucik, J. (2015). The conditioning effect of protest history on the emulation of nonviolent conflict. *Journal of Peace Research, 52*(6), 697–711. https://doi.org/10.1177/0022343315593993.

Brathwaite, R., & Park, B. (2020). Measurement and conceptual approaches to religious violence: The use of natural language processing to generate religious violence event data. *Politics and Religion, 12*(1), 81–22.

Breilid, A. (2013). The role of education in Sudan's civil war. *Prospects, 43,* 35–47.

Breskaya, O., Giordan, G., & Richardson, J. T. (2018). Human rights and religion: A sociological perspective. *Journal for the Scientific Study of Religion, 57*(3), 419–431. https://doi.org/10.1111/jssr.12544.

Breslawski, J., & Ives, B. (2019). Killing for God? Factional violence on the transnational stage. *Journal of Conflict Resolution, 63*(3), 617–643. https://doi.org/10.1177/0022002718763632.

306 REFERENCES

Brown, D. (2014). Christian and Muslim population and first use of force by states 1946–2001. *Politcs and Religion Journal, 8*(2), 327–360. https://doi.org/10.54561/prj0 802327b.

Brown, D. (2015). The permissive nature of the Islamic war ethic. *Journal of Religion and Violence, 2*(3), 460–483. https://doi.org/10.5840/jrv20153173.

Brush, S. G. (1996). Dynamics of theory change in the social sciences: Relative deprivation and collective violence. *Journal of Conflict Resolution, 40*(4), 523–545. https://doi.org/10.1177/0022002796040004001.

Buckley, D. T., & Mantilla, L. F. (2013). God and governance: Development, state capacity, and the regulation of religion. *Journal for the Scientific Study of Religion, 52*(2), 328–348. https://doi.org/10.1111/jssr.12025.

Buckley, D. T., & Wilcox, C. (2017). Religious change, political incentives, and explaining religious-secular relations in the United States and the Philippines. *Politics & Religion, 10*(3), 543–566. https://doi.org/10.1017/S1755048317000050.

Buzan, B., Waever, O., & de Wilde, J. (1998). *Security: A new framework for analysis.* Lynne Rienner.

Byman, D. (2022). Understanding, and misunderstanding, state sponsorship of terrorism. *Studies in Conflict & Terrorism, 45*(12), 1031–1049. https://doi.org/10.1080/10576 10X.2020.1738682.

Canetti, D., Rubin, A., Khatib, I., & Wayne, C. (2019). Framing and fighting the impact of conflict frames on political attitudes. *Journal of Peace Research, 56*(6), 737–752. https://doi.org/10.1177/0022343319826324.

Cao, X., Duan, H., Liu, C., & Wei, Y. (2018). Local religious institutions and the impact of interethnic inequality on conflict. *International Studies Quarterly, 62*(4), 765–781. https://doi.org/10.1093/isq/sqy035.

Carnevale, D. N. (2019). A context-grounded approach to religious freedom: The case of orthodoxy in the Moldovan Republic. *Religions, 10*(5), 1–18. https://doi.org/10.3390/rel10050314.

Carter, B., Van Nuys, M., & Albayrak, C. (2021). State sponsorship of religiously motivated terrorism: A deadly combination. *Democracy and Security, 17*(2), 181–209. https://doi.org/10.1080/17419166.2020.1848558.

Carter, D. B., Shaver, A. C., & Wright, A. L. (2019). Places to hide: Terrain, ethnicity, and civil conflict. *Journal of Politics, 81*(4), 1446–1465. https://www.journals.uchicago.edu/doi/10.1086/704597.

Caruso, R., & Gavrilova, E. (2012). Youth unemployment, terrorism and political violence, evidence from the Israeli/Palestinian conflict. *Peace Economics, Peace Science and Public Policy, 18*(2). https://doi.org/10.1515/1554-8597.1254.

Cederman, L.-E., & Girardin, L. (2007). Beyond fractionalization: Mapping ethnicity onto nationalist insurgencies. *American Political Science Review, 101*(1), 173–185.

Cederman, L.-E., Gleditsch, K. S., & Buhaug, H. (2013). *Inequality, grievances, and civil war.* Cambridge University Press.

Cederman, L.-E., Gleditsch, K. S., & Wucherpfennig, J. (2017). Predicting the decline of ethnic civil War: Was Gurr right and for the right reasons? *Journal of Peace Research, 54*(2), 262–274. https://doi.org/10.1177/0022343316684191.

Cederman, L.-E., Hug, S., & Krebs, L. F. (2010). Democratization and civil war: Empirical evidence. *Journal of Peace Research, 47*(4), 377–394. https://doi.org/10.1177/00223 43310368336.

REFERENCES 307

Cederman, L.-E., Weidmann, N. B., & Bormann, N. C. (2015). Triangulating horizontal inequality: Toward an improved conflict analysis. *Journal of Peace Research, 52*(6), 806–821. https://doi.org/10.1177/0022343315597969.

Cederman, L.-E., Weidmann, N. B., & Gleditsch, K. S. (2011). Horizontal inequalities and ethnonationalist civil wars: A global comparison. *American Political Science Review, 105*(3), 478–495.

Cederman, L.-E., Wimmer, A., & Min, B. (2010). Why do ethnic groups rebel? A new data analysis *World Politics, 62*(1), 87–119.

Cesari, J. (2013). *Why the West fears Islam: An exploration of Islam in liberal democracies.* Palgrave Macmillan.

Chenoweth, E., & Lewis, O. A. (2013). Unpacking nonviolent campaigns: Introducing the NAVCO 2.0 dataset. *Journal of Peace Research, 50*(3), 415–423. https://doi.org/10.1177/0022343312471551.

Chenoweth, E., & Ulfelder, J. (2017). Can structural conditions explain the onset of nonviolent uprisings? *Journal of Conflict Resolution, 61*(2), 298–324. https://doi.org/10.1177/0022002715576574.

Clark, E. A. (2013). Liberalism in decline: Legislative trends limiting religious freedom in Russia and Central Asia. *Transnational Law & Contemporary Problems, 22* (2), 297–342.

Collier, P. (1998). On economic causes of civil war. *Oxford Economic Papers, 50*(4), 563–557. https://doi.org/10.1093/oep/50.4.563.

Collier, P., & Hoeffler, A. (2002). On the incidence of civil war in Africa. *Journal of Conflict Resolution, 46*(1), 13–28. https://doi.org/10.1177/0022002702046001002.

Collier, P., & Hoeffler, A. (2004). Greed and grievance in civil war. *Oxford Economic Papers, 56*, 563–595. https://doi.org/10.1093/oep/gpf064.

Collier, P., Hoeffler, A., & Söderbom, M. (2004). On the duration of civil war. *Journal of Peace Research, 41*(3), 253–273. https://doi.org/10.1177/0022343304043769.

Collins, C. (1976). Colonialism and class struggle in Sudan. *MERIP Reports, 46*, 3–17, 20. https://www.jstor.org/stable/3010898.

Collins, R. (2008). *A history of modern Sudan.* Cambridge University Press.

Collins, T. A., Wink, K. A., Guth, J. L., & Livingston, C. D. (2011). The religious affiliation of representatives and support for funding the Iraq War. *Politics & Religion, 4*(3), 550–568.

Coppedge, M., Gerring, J., Lindberg, S. I., Skaaning, S.-E., & Teorell, J. (2015). V-Dem comparisons and contrasts with other measurement projects. *Varieties of Democracy (V-Dem) Project.* https://www.v-dem.net/media/filer_public/e7/a6/e7a638e3-358c-4b96-9197-e1496775d280/comparisons_and_contrasts_v5.pdf.

Cramer, B. D., & Kaufman, R. R. (2011). Views of economic inequality in Latin America. *Comparative Political Studies, 44*(4), 1206–1237. https://doi.org/10.1177/001041401 0392171.

Cunningham, D. E., & Lemke, D. (2014). Beyond civil war: A quantitative examination of causes of violence within countries. *Civil Wars, 16*(3), 328–345. https://doi.org/10.1080/13698249.2014.976356.

Cunningham, K. G. (2013). Understanding strategic choice: The determinants of civil war and nonviolent campaign in self-determination disputes. *Journal of Peace Research, 50*(3), 291–304. https://doi.org/10.1177/0022343313475467.

308 REFERENCES

Cunningham, K. G., Bakke, K. M., & Seymour, L. J. M. (2012). Shirts today, skins tomorrow: Dual contests and the effects of fragmentation in self-determination disputes. *Journal of Conflict Resolution, 56*(1), 67–93. https://doi.org/10.1177/002200271142969.

Dahl, R. A. (1971). *Polyarchy: Participation and opposition.* Yale University Press.

Davies, J. C. (1962). Toward a theory of revolution. *American Sociological Review, 27,* 5–19. https://www.jstor.org/stable/2089714.

Dawson, L. L. (2010). The study of new religious movements and the radicalization of home-grown terrorists: Opening a dialogue. *Terrorism and Political Violence, 22*(1), 1–21. https://doi.org/10.1080/09546550903409163.

Deitch, M. (2022). Is religion a barrier to peace? Religious influence on violent intrastate conflict termination. *Terrorism and Political Violence, 34*(7), 1454–1470. https://doi.org/10.1080/09546553.2020.1792446.

De Juan, A., & Hasenclever, A. (2015). Framing political violence: Success and failure of religious mobilization in the Philippines. *Civil Wars, 17*(2), 201–221. https://doi.org/10.1080/13698249.2015.1070454.

Della Porta, D., & Diani, M. (2006). *Social movements: An introduction* (2nd ed.). Blackwell Publishing.

Demerath, N. J., III. (2001). *Crossing the Gods: World religions and worldly politics.* Rutgers University Press.

Deutsch, Karl W. (1963). The limits of common sense. In Nelson Polsby (Ed.), *Politics and social life* (pp. 51–57). Boston: Houghton Mifflin.

Dinstein, Y. (1991). Freedom of religion and the protection of religious minorities. *Israel Yearbook on Human Rights, 20,* 155–179. https://doi.org/10.1163/9789004423046_008.

Donnelly, J. (2007). *International human rights.* Westview Press.

Dunn, K. C. (2010). The Lord's Resistance Army and African international relations. *African Security, 3*(1), 46–63. https://doi.org/10.1080/19362201003608797.

Durham, Jr., W. C. (1996). Perspectives on religious liberty: A comparative framework. In J. D. van der Vyver & J. Witte, Jr. (Eds.), *Religious human rights in global perspective: Legal perspectives* (pp. 1–44). Martinus Njhoff.

Edmonds, E. B. (2012). *Rastafari: A very short introduction.* Oxford University Press.

El-Baatahani, A. (2001). Sudan: multiparty elections & the predicament of northern hegemony in Sudan. In M. Cowen & L. Laakso (Eds.), *Multi-party elections in Africa* (pp. 251–277). James Currey.

Ellingsen, T. (2000). Colorful community or ethnic witches' brew? Multiethnicity and domestic conflict during and after the cold war. *Journal of Conflict Resolution, 44*(2), 228–249. https://doi.org/10.1177/0022002700044002004.

Ellingsen, T. (2005). Toward a revival of religion and religious clashes. *Terrorism and Political Violence, 17*(3), 305–332. https://doi.org/10.1080/09546550590929192.

Fair, C. C., & Patel, P. (2019). Explaining why some Muslims support Islamist political violence. *Political Science Quarterly, 314*(2), 245–276. https://doi.org/10.1002/polq.12897.

Fair, C. C., & Shepard, B. (2006). Who supports terrorism: Evidence from fourteen Muslim countries. *Studies in Conflict and Terrorism, 29*(1), 51–74. https://doi.org/10.1080/10576100500351318.

Farr, T. F. (2008). Diplomacy in an age of faith: Religious freedom and national security. *Foreign Affairs, 87*(2).

Fearon, J. D. (2003). Ethnic and cultural diversity by country. *Journal of Economic Growth, 8*(2), 195–222. https://www.foreignaffairs.com/united-states/diplomacy-age-faith.

REFERENCES 309

Fearon, J. D., & Laitin, D. D. (1996). Explaining interethnic cooperation. *American Political Science Review, 90*(4), 715–735. https://www.jstor.org/stable/40215943.

Fearon, J. D., & Laitin, D. D. (1997). A cross-sectional study of large-scale ethnic violence in the postwar period. Unpublished paper, Department of Political Science, University of Chicago, September 30.

Fearon, J. D., & Laitin, D. D. (2003). Ethnicity, insurgency, and civil war. *American Political Science Review, 97*(1), 75–90.

Feierabend, I., & Feierabend, R. (1966). Aggressive behaviors within politics, 1948–1962: A cross-national study. *Journal of Conflict Revolution, 10*(3), 249–271. https://doi.org/10.1177/002200276601000301.

Feierabend, I., & Feierabend, R. (1973). Systemic conditions of political aggression: An application of frustration–aggression theory. In I. Feierabend & R. Fierabend (Eds.), *Anger, violence and politics*. Prentice-Hall.

Feierabend, I., Feierabend, R., & Nesvold, B. A. (1969). Social change and political violence: Cross-national patterns. In H. D. Grahm & T. R. Gurr (Eds.), *Violence in America: Historical and comparative perspectives* (pp. 632–687). National Commission on the Causes and Prevention of Violence.

Feuer, S. J. (2018). *Regulating Islam: Religion and the state I—Contemporary Morocco and Tunisia*. Cambridge University Press.

Filote, A., Potrafke, N., & Ursprung, H. (2016). Suicide attacks and religious cleavages. *Public Choice, 166*(1), 3–28.

Finke, R., & Martin, R. R (2014). Ensuring liberties: Understanding state restrictions on religious freedoms. *Journal for the Scientific Study of Religion, 53*(4), 687–705. https://doi.org/10.1111/jssr.12148.

Finnbogason, D., & Svensson, I. (2018). The missing Jihad: Why have there been no Jihadist civil wars in Southeast Asia? *The Pacific Review, 31*(1), 96–115. https://doi.org/10.1080/09512748.2017.1325391.

Foster, M. D., & Matheson, K. (1999). Perceiving and responding to the personal/group discrimination discrepancy. *Personality and Social Psychology Bulletin, 25*(10), 1319–1329.

Fox, J. (1997). The salience of religious issues in ethnic conflicts: A large-N study. *Nationalism and Ethnic Politics, 3*(3), 1–19. https://doi.org/10.1080/13537119708428508.

Fox, J. (1999a). Do religious institutions support violence or the status quo?" *Studies in Conflict and Terrorism, 22*(2), 119–139. https://doi.org/10.1080/105761099265793.

Fox, J. (1999b). The influence of religious legitimacy on grievance formation by ethnoreligious minorities. *Journal of Peace Research, 36*(3), 289–307. https://doi.org/10.1177/0022343399036003003.

Fox, J. (1999c). Towards a dynamic theory of ethno-religious conflict. *Nations and Nationalism, 5*(4), 431–463.

Fox, J. (2000a). Is Islam more conflict prone than other religions? A cross-sectional study of ethnoreligious conflict. *Nationalism and Ethnic Politics, 6*(2), 1–23. https://doi.org/10.1080/13537110008428593.

Fox, J. (2000b). Religious causes of ethnic discrimination. *International Studies Quarterly, 44*(3), 423–450. https://doi.org/10.1111/0020-8833.00166.

Fox, J. (2000c). The ethnic-religious nexus: The impact of religion on ethnic conflict. *Civil Wars, 3*(3), 1–22. https://doi.org/10.1080/13698240008402444.

310 REFERENCES

Fox, J. (2001a). Civilizational, religious, and national explanations for ethnic rebellion in the post–Cold War Middle East. *Jewish Political Studies Review, 13*(1–2), 177–204. https://www.jstor.org/stable/25834507.

Fox, J. (2001b). Islam and the West: The influence of two civilizations on ethnic conflict. *Journal of Peace Research, 38*(4), 459–472. https://doi.org/10.1177/00223433010380040.

Fox, J. (2001c). Are Middle East conflicts more religious? *Middle East Quarterly, 8*(4), 31–40. https://www.meforum.org/135/are-middle-east-conflicts-more-religious.

Fox, J. (2002a). *Ethnoreligious conflict in the late 20th century: A general theory.* Lexington Books.

Fox, J. (2002b). Ethnic minorities and the clash of civilizations: A quantitative analysis of Huntington's thesis. *British Journal of Political Science, 32*(3), 415–434.

Fox, J. (2002c). In the name of God and nation: The overlapping influence of separatism and religion on ethnic conflict. *Social Identities, 8*(3), 439–455. https://doi.org/10.1080/1350463022000029995.

Fox, J. (2003a). Are ethno-religious minorities more militant than other ethnic minorities? *Alternatives, 28*(1), 91–114. https://journals.sagepub.com/doi/abs/10.1177/030437540302800104?journalCode=alta.

Fox, J. (2003b). Ethnoreligious conflict in the third world: The role of religion as a cause of conflict. *Nationalism and Ethnic Politics, 9*(1), 101–125. https://doi.org/10.1080/13537110412331301375.

Fox, J. (2003c). Do Muslims engage in more domestic conflict than other religious groups? *Civil Wars, 6*(1), 27–46. https://doi.org/10.1080/13698240308402524.

Fox, J. (2004). *Religion, civilization and civil war: 1945 through the new millennium.* Lexington Books.

Fox, J. (2008). *A world survey of religion and the state.* Cambridge University Press.

Fox, J. (2015). *Political secularism, religion, and the state: A time series analysis of worldwide data.* Cambridge University Press.

Fox, J. (2016). *The unfree exercise of religion: A World Survey of Religious Discrimination against Religious Minorities.* Cambridge University Press.

Fox, J. (2018). *An introduction to religion and politics: Theory and practice* (2nd ed.). Routledge.

Fox, J. (2019). *The correlates of religion and state.* Routledge.

Fox, J. (2020). *Thou shalt have no other Gods before me: Why governments discriminate against religious minorities.* Cambridge University Press.

Fox, J., & Akbaba, Y. (2015a). Securitization of Islam and religious discrimination: religious minorities in Western democracies, 1990 to 2008. *Comparative European Politics, 13*(2), 175–197.

Fox, J., & Akbaba, Y. (2015b). Restrictions on the religious practices of religious minorities: A global survey. *Political Studies, 63*(5), 1070–1086. https://doi.org/10.1111/1467-9248.12141.

Fox, J., Bader, C., & McClure, J. (2019). Don't get mad: The disconnect between religious discrimination and individual perceptions of government. *Conflict Management & Peace Science, 36*(5), 495–516. https://doi.org/10.1177/0738894217723160.

Fox, J., & Sandler, S. (2004). *Bringing religion into international relations.* Palgrave-Macmillan.

Fox, J., & Topor, L. (2021). *Why do people discriminate against Jews?* Oxford University Press.

REFERENCES   311

Gabbay, S. M. (2018). Socio-political conditions for Christians in Egypt. *European Scientific Journal, 14*(20), 144. https://doi.org/10.19044/esj.2018.v14n20p144.

Gartzke, E., & Gleditsch, K. S. (2006). Identity and conflict: The ties that bind and differences that divide. *European Journal of International Relations, 12*(1), 53–87. https://doi.org/10.1177/13540661060613.

Gearty, C. (2007). Terrorism and human rights. *Government and Opposition, 42*(3), 340–362.

Ghatak, S., & Prins, B. C. (2017). The homegrown threat: State strength, grievance, and domestic terrorism. *International Interactions, 43*(2), 217–247.

Gill, A. (2008). *The political origins of religious liberty.* Cambridge University Press.

Gill, A. (2013). Religious liberty and economic development: Exploring the causal connections. *The Review of Faith & International Affairs, 11*(4), 5–23. https://doi.org/10.1080/15570274.2013.857116.

Gill, R., & Matheson, K. (2006). Responses to discrimination: The role of emotion and expectations for emotional regulation. *Personality and Social Psychology Bulletin, 32*(2), 149–161. https://doi.org/10.1177/01461672052799.

Gleditsch, K. S., & Ruggeri, A. (2010). Political opportunity structures, democracy, and civil war. *Journal of Peace Research, 47*(3), 299–310. https://doi.org/10.1177/002234331 0362293.

Gleditsch, K. S., &, Rivera, M. (2017). The diffusion of nonviolent campaigns. *Journal of Conflict Resolution, 61*(5), 1120–1145. https://doi.org/10.1177/0022002715603101.

Glendon, M. A. (2019). Making the case for religious freedom in secular societies. *Journal of Law and Religion, 33*(3), 329–339. http://doi.org/10.1017/jlr.2019.3.

Gorski, P. S., & Altinordu, A. (2008). After secularization. *Annual Review of Sociology, 24*, 55–85. https://doi.org/10.1146/annurev.soc.34.040507.134740.

Grim, B. J., & Finke, R. (2006). International religion indexes: Government regulation, government favoritism, and social regulation of religion. *Interdisciplinary Journal of Research on Religion, 2*(1), 1–40. https://www.religjournal.com/articles/article_view. php?id=13.

Grim, B. J., & Finke, R. (2007). Religious persecution on cross-national context: Clashing civilizations or regulating religious economies. *American Sociological Review, 72*(4), 633–658. https://doi.org/10.1177/000312240707200407.

Grim, B. J., & Finke, R. (2011). *The price of freedom denied.* Cambridge University Press.

Grzymala-Busse, A. (2015). *Nations under God: How churches use moral authority to influence policy.* Princeton University Press.

Gubler, J. R., & Selway, J. S. (2012). Horizontal inequality, crosscutting cleavages, and civil war. *Journal of Conflict Resolution, 56*(2), 206–232. https://doi.org/10.1177/002200271 1431416.

Gurr, T. R. (1968). A causal model of civil strife: A comparative analysis using new indices. *American Political Science Review, 62*(4), 1104–1124.

Gurr, T. R. (1970). *Why men rebel.* Princeton University Press.

Gurr, T. R. (1988). War, revolution, and the growth of the coercive state. *Comparative Political Studies, 21*(1), 45–65. https://doi.org/10.1177/0010414088021001003.

Gurr, T. R. (1993a). *Minorities at risk.* United States Institute of Peace.

Gurr, T. R. (1993b). Why minorities rebel. *International Political Science Review, 14*(2), 161–201. https://doi.org/10.1177/019251219301400203.

Gurr, T. R. (2000a). *Peoples versus states: Minorities at risk in the new century.* United States Institute of Peace Press.

312 REFERENCES

Gurr, T. R. (2000b). Nonviolence in ethnopolitics: Strategies for the attainment of group rights and autonomy. *PS: Political Science and Politics, 33*(2), 155–160.

Gurses, M. (2015). Islamists and women's rights: Lessons from Turkey. *Journal of the Middle East and Africa, 6*(1), 33–44. https://doi.org/10.1080/21520844.2015.1027124.

Gurses, M., & Öztürk, A. E. (2020). Religion and armed conflict: Evidence from the Kurdish conflict in Turkey. *Journal for the Scientific Study of Religion*, 1–14. https://doi.org/10.1111/jssr.12652.

Gurses, M., & Rost, N. (2017). Religion as a peacemaker? Peace duration after ethnic civil wars. *Politics & Religion, 10*(2), 339–362. https://doi.org/10.1017/S1755048316000742.

Guth, J. L. (2013). Religion and American public attitudes on war and peace. *Asian Journal of Peacebuilding, 1*(2), 227–252.

Harris, F. C. (1994). Something within: Religion as a mobilizer of African-American political activism. *Journal of Politics, 56*(1), 42–68. https://doi.org/10.2307/2132345.

Hassner, R. E. (2003). "To halve and to hold": Conflict over sacred space and the problem of indivisibility. *Security Studies, 12*(4), 1–33. https://doi.org/10.1080/0963641039 0447617.

Hassner, R. E. (2009). *War on sacred grounds*. Cornell University Press.

Hegghammer, T. (2010). The rise of Muslim foreign fighters: Islam and the globalization of Jihad. *International Security, 35*(3), 53–94. https://doi.org/10.1162/ISEC_a_00023.

Hegre, H., & Sambanis, N. (2006). Sensitivity analysis of empirical results on civil war onset. *Journal of Conflict Resolution, 50*(4), 508–535. https://doi.org/10.1177/0022002 7062893.

Henderson, E. A., & Singer, J. D. (2000). Civil war in the post-colonial world, 1946–92. *Journal of Peace research, 37*(3), 275–299. https://doi.org/10.1177/002234330003 7003001.

Henne, P. S. (2012). The ancient fire: Religion and suicide terrorism. *Terrorism and Political Violence, 24*(1), 38–60. https://doi.org/10.1080/09546553.2011.608817.

Henne, P. S. (2018). Does the UN human rights council help or hurt religious repression? *Journal of Church and State, 6*(4), 705–724. https://doi.org/10.1093/jcs/csy005.

Henne, P. S. (2019). Government interference in religious institutions and terrorism. *Religion, State & Society, 47*(1), 67–86. https://doi.org/10.1080/09637494.2018.1533 691.

Henne, P. S., & Klocek, J. (2019). Taming the Gods: How religious conflict shapes state repression. *Journal of Conflict Resolution, 63*(1), 112–138. https://doi.org/10.1177/00220 02717728104.

Henne, P. S., Saiya, N., & Hand, A. W. (2020). Weapons of the strong? Government support for religion and majoritarian terror. *Journal of Conflict Resolution, 64*(10), 1943–1967. https://doi.org/10.1177/0022002720916854.

Hibbard, S. W. (2015). Religious politics and the rise of illiberal religion. In L. M. Herrington, A. McKay, & J. Haynes (Eds.), *Nations under God: The geopolitics of faith in the twenty-first century* (pp. 103–111). Relations Publishing.

Hodžić, E., & Mraović, B. (2015). Political representation of minorities in Bosnia and Herzegovina: How reserved seats affect minority representatives' influence on decision-making and perceived substantive representation. *Ethnopolitics, 14*(4), 418–434. https://doi.org/10.1080/17449057.2015.1032004.

Hoffman, B. (2004). The changing face of al Qaeda and the global war on terrorism. *Studies in Conflict & Terrorism, 27*(6), 549–560. https://doi.org/10.1080/1057610049 0519813.

REFERENCES 313

Hoffmann, L., Basedau, M., Gobien, S., & Prediger, S. (2020). Universal love or one true religion? Experimental evidence of the ambivalent effect of religious ideas on altruism and discrimination. *American Journal of Political Science, 64*(3), 603–620. https://doi.org/10.1111/ajps.12479.

Hoffman, M. T., & Jamal, A. (2014). Religion in the Arab Spring: Between two competing narratives. *Journal of Politics, 76*(3), 593–606. https://doi.org/10.1017/S002238161 4000152.

Hoffman, M. T., & Nugent, E. R. (2017). Communal religious practice and support for armed parties: Evidence for Lebanon. *Journal of Conflict Resolution. 61*(4), 869–902. https://doi.org/10.1177/0022002715590880.

Holzer, H. J., & Neumark, D. (2006). Affirmative action: What do we know? *Journal of Policy Analysis and Management, 25*(2), 463–490. https://doi.org/10.1002/pam.20181.

Horowitz, D. L. (1985). *Ethnic groups in conflict*. University of California Press.

Houle, C. (2018, *25*(8), 1500–1518. https://doi.org/10.1080/13510347.2018.1487405.

Huber, C., & Basedau, M. (2018). When do religious minorities' grievances lead to peaceful or violent protest? Evidence from Canada's Jewish and Muslim communities. *GIGA Working Paper, 313.*

Hug, S. (2003). Selection bias in comparative research: The case of incomplete datasets. *Political Analysis, 11*(3), 255–274.

Hug, S. (2013). The use and misuse of the minorities at risk project. *Annual Review of Political Science, 16*, 191–208. https://doi.org/10.1146/annurev-polisci-060512-142 956.

Hultman, L. (2012). Attacks on civilians in civil war: Targeting the Achilles Heel of democratic governments. *International Interactions, 38*(2), 164–181. https://doi.org/10.1080/03050629.2012.657602.

Hultman, L. (2017). Battle losses and rebel violence: Raising the costs for fighting. *Terrorism and Political Violence, 19*(2), 205–222. https://doi.org/10.1080/0954655070 1246866.

Huntington, S. P. (1993). The clash of civilizations? *Foreign Affairs, 72*(3), 22–49.

Huntington, S. P. (1996). *The clash of civilizations and the remaking of the world order*. Simon and Schuster.

Iannaccone, L. R. (1995). Voodoo economics? Reviewing the rational choice approach to religion. *Journal for the Scientific Study of Religion, 34*(1), 76–89. https://www.jstor.org/stable/1386524?origin=crossref.

Inboden, W. (2008). *Religion and American foreign policy, 1945–1960: The soul of containment*. Cambridge University Press.

Isaacs, M. (2016). Sacred violence or strategic faith? Disentangling the relationship between religion and violence in armed conflict. *Journal of Peace Research, 53*(2), 211–225. https://doi.org/10.1177/0022343315626771.

Isaacs, M. (2017). "Faith in Contention": Explaining the salience of religion in ethnic conflict. *Comparative Political Studies, 50*(2), 200–231. https://doi.org/10.1177/001041401 6655534.

Ishiyama, J. (2000). Institutions and ethnopolitical conflict in post-communist states. *Nationalism and Ethnic Politics, 6*(3), 51–67. https://doi.org/10.1080/1353711000 8428603.

Ispahani, F. (2013). Cleansing Pakistan of minorities. *Current Trends in Islamist Ideology, 31*. https://www.hudson.org/human-rights/cleansing-pakistan-of-minorities.

314 REFERENCES

Ives, B. (2019). Religious institutionalism: A domestic explanation for external support of rebel groups. *International Interactions, 45*(4), 693–719. https://doi.org/10.1080/03050 629.2019.1621309.

Jazayeri, K. B. (2016). Identity-based political inequality and protest: The dynamic relationships between political power and protest in the Middle East and North Africa. *Conflict Management and Peace Science, 33*(4), 400–422. https://doi.org/10.1177/ 0738894215570426.

Jenkins, J. C., & Schock, K. (2003). Political process, international dependence, and mass political conflict: A global analysis of protest and rebellion, 1973–1978. *International Journal of Sociology, 33*(4), 41–63. https://doi.org/10.1080/15579336.2003.11770275.

Jenkins, P. (2007). Religion, repression and rebellion. *Review of Faith and International Affairs, 5*(1), 3–11. https://doi.org/10.1080/15570274.2007.9523272.

Jenne, E. K., Saideman, S. M., & Lowe, W. (2007). Separatism as bargaining posture: The role of leverage in minority radicalization. *Journal of Peace Research, 44*(5), 539–558. https://doi.org/10.1177/0022343307080853.

Johnston, Jr., D. M. (2011). *Religion, terror, and error: U.S. foreign policy and the challenge of spiritual engagement.* Praeger.

Jok, J. M. (2015). Sudan: Race, religion, and violence. Simon and Schuster.

Joustra, R. (2018). *The religious problem with religious freedom: Why foreign policy needs political theology.* Routledge.

Juergensmeyer, M. (2000). *Terror in the mind of God: The global rise of religious violence.* University of California Press.

Kalyvas, S. N. (2006). *The logic of violence in civil war* (1st ed.). Cambridge University Press.

Karakaya, S. (2015). Religion and conflict: Explaining the puzzling case of "Islamic violence." *International Interactions, 41*(3), 509–538. https://doi.org/10.1080/03050 629.2015.1016158.

Karakaya S. (2016). Ethno-political organization in the Middle East: When do they opt for violence? *Politics & Religion, 9*(2), 332–363.

Kasfir, N. (1977). Southern Sudanese politics since the Addis Ababa agreement. *African Affairs, 76*(303), 143–166. https://doi.org/10.1093/oxfordjournals.afraf.a096834.

Kaufmann, C. D. (1996). Possible and impossible solutions to ethnic civil wars. *International Security, 20*(4), 136–175. https://doi.org/10.1162/isec.20.4.136.

Keels, E., & Wiegand, K. (2020). Mutually assured distrust: Ideology and commitment problems in civil wars. *Journal of Conflict Resolution, 64*(10), 2022–2048. https://doi. org/10.1177/0022002720928414.

Kim, D., & Choi, H. J. (2017). Autocracy, religious restriction, and religious civil war. *Politics and Religion, 10*(2), 311–388.

Klein, G. R., & Regan, P. M. (2018). Dynamics of political protests. *International Organization, 72*(2), 485–521.

Knill, C., & Preidel, C. (2015). Institutional opportunity structures and the Catholic church: Explaining variation in the regulation of same-sex partnerships in Ireland and Italy. *Journal of European Public Policy, 22*(3), 374–390.

Koesel, K. J. (2014). *Region and authoritarianism: Cooperation, conflict, and the consequences.* Cambridge University Press.

Koos, C. (2016). Does violence pay? The effect of ethnic rebellion on overcoming political deprivation. *Conflict Management and Peace Science, 33*(1), 3–24. https://doi.org/ 10.1177/0738894214559670.

REFERENCES 315

Koubi, V., & Böhmelt, T. (2014). Grievances, economic wealth, and civil conflict. *Journal of Peace Research*, *51*(1), 19–33. https://doi.org/10.1177/002234331350050.

Kunst, J. R., & Obaidi, M. (2020). Understanding violent extremism in the 21st century: The (re)emerging role of relative deprivation. *Current Opinion in Psychology*, *35*, 55–59.

Kydd A. H., & Walter, B. F. (2006). The strategies of terrorism. *International Security*, *31*(1), 49–80. https://doi.org/10.1162/isec.2006.31.1.49.

Lai, B. (2006). An empirical examination of religion and conflict in the Middle East, 1950–1992. *Foreign Policy Analysis*, *2*(1), 21–36. https://doi.org/10.1111/j.1743-8594.2005.00018.x.

Lichbach, M. I. (1989). An evaluation of "Does economic inequality breed political conflict?" studies. *World Politics*, *41*(4), 431–470.

Lincoln, B. (2003). *Holy terrors: Thinking about religion after September 11*. University of Chicago Press.

Little, D. (1996). Studying "Religious human right": Methodological foundations. In J. D. van der Vyver & J. Witte, Jr. (Eds.), *Religious human rights in global perspective: Legal perspectives* (pp. 45–77). Martinus Njhoff.

Litvak, M. (1998). The Islamization of the Palestinian-Israeli conflict: The case of Hamas. *Middle Eastern Studies*, *34*(1), 148–163. https://doi.org/10.1080/00263209808701214.

Lobban, Richard Andrew, Jr. (2010). *Global security watch: Sudan*. Praeger.

Lu, Y., & Yang, F. (2018). Does state repression suppress the protest participation of religious people? *Sociology of Religion*, *80*(2), 194–221. https://doi.org/10.1093/socrel/sry029.

Mabee, B. (2007). Re-imagining the borders of US security after 9/11: Securitization, risk, and the creation of the Department of Homeland Security. *Globalizations*, *4*(3), 385–397. https://doi.org/10.1080/14747730701532567.

MacCulloch, R., & Pezzini, S. (2007). Money, religion, and revolution. *Economics of Governance*, *8*, 1–16. https://doi.org/10.1007/s10101-006-0014-z.

MacKenzie, A., & Kaunert, C. (2021). Radicalisation, foreign fighters and the Ukraine conflict: A playground for the far-right? *Social Sciences*, *10*(4), 116. https://doi.org/10.3390/socsci10040116.

Maoz, Z., & Henderson, E. A. (2020). *Scriptures, shrines, scapegoats, and world politics: Religious sources of conflict and cooperation in the modern era*. University of Michigan Press.

Marshall, M. G., & Jaggers, K. (2009). *Polity IV project: Political regime characteristics and transitions, 1800–2002*. Center for Systemic Peace and Colorado State University. http://www.systemicpeace.org/polity/polity4.htm.

Marshall, P. A. (Ed). (2008). *Religious freedom in the world*. Rowman & Littlefield.

Martin, J. P. (2005). The three monotheistic world religions and international human rights. *Journal of Social Issues*, *61*(94), 827–845. https://doi.org/10.1111/j.1540-4560.2005.00434.x.

McAdam, D., McCarthy, J. D., & Zald, M. N. (Eds.). (1996). *Comparative perspectives on social movements: Political opportunities, mobilizing structures, and cultural framings*. Cambridge University Press.

McAdam, D., Tarrow, S., & Tilly, C. (2001). *Dynamics of contention*. Cambridge University Press.

McCarthy, J. D., & Zald, M. N. (1977). Resource mobilization and social movements: A partial theory. *American Journal of Sociology*, *82*(6), 1212–1241. https://doi.org/10.1086/226464.

316 REFERENCES

McCauley, J. F. (2019). Identity, internal state conflict, and religion. *Oxford Research Encyclopedia of Politics*. https://doi.org/10.1093/acrefore/9780190228637.013.843.

Mellor, N. (2017). Islamizing the Palestinian–Israeli conflict: The case of the Muslim Brotherhood. *British Journal of Middle Eastern Studies, 44*(4), 513–528. https://doi.org/10.1080/13530194.2017.1360009.

Mishali-Ram, M., & Fox, J. (2022). Is governmental and societal discrimination against Muslim minorities behind foreign fighters in Syria and Iraq? *Journal of Peace Research, 59*(2), 122–135. https://doi.org/10.1177/0022343320982652.

Mohamoud, Y. A., Cuadros, D. F., & Abu-Raddad, L. J. (2013). Characterizing the Copts in Egypt: Demographic, socioeconomic and health indicators. *QScience Connect, 2013*(1). https://doi.org/10.5339/connect.2013.22.

Monshipouri, M. (1998). The West's modern encounter with Islam: From discourse to reality. *Journal of Church and State, 40*(1), 25–56. https://doi.org/10.1093/jcs/40.1.25.

Muchlinski, D. (2014). Grievances and opportunities: Religious violence across political regimes. *Politics & Religion, 7*(4), 684–705. https://doi.org/10.1017/S1755048314000534.

Muchlinski, D. (2019). The politics and effects of religious grievances. In W. R. Thompson (Ed.), *Oxford research encyclopedia of politics* (pp. 1–18). Oxford University Press. https://doi.org/10.1093/acrefore/9780190228637.013.783.

Muller, E. N. (1980). The psychology of political protest and violence. In T. R. Gurr (Ed.), *Handbook of political conflict: Theory and research* (pp. 69–99). Free Press.

Murshed, S. M., & Tadhoeddin, M. Z. (2009). Revisiting the greed and grievance explanations for violent internal conflict. *Journal of International Development, 21*(1), 87–111. https://doi.org/10.1002/jid.1478.

Nilsson, D., & Svensson, I. (2020). Resisting resolution: Islamist Claims and Negotiations in Intrastate Armed Conflicts. *International Negotiation, 25*(3), 389–412. https://doi.org/10.1163/15718069-25131250.

Nilsson, D., & Svensson, I. (2021). The intractability of Islamist Insurgencies: Islamist rebels and the recurrence of civil war. *International Studies Quarterly, 65*(3), 620–632. https://doi.org/10.1093/isq/sqab064.

Obaidi, M., Kunst, J. R., Kteilly, N., Thomsen, L., & Sidanius, J. (2018). Living under threat: Mutual threat perception drives anti-Muslim and anti-Western hostility in the age of terrorism. *European Journal of Social Psychology, 48*(5), 567–584. https://doi.org/10.1002/ejsp.2362.

Olson, M. (1963). Rapid growth as a destabilizing force. *Journal of Economic History, 23*(4), 529–552.

Omelicheva, M. Y., & Ahmed, R. (2018). Religion and politics: Examining the impact of faith on political participation. *Religion, State and Society, 46*(1), 4–25. https://doi.org/10.1080/09637494.2017.1363345.

Osborne, D., & Sibley, C. S. (2013). Through rose colored glasses: System-justifying beliefs dampen the effects of relative deprivation on well being and political mobilization. *Personality and Social Psychology Bulletin, 39*(8), 991–1004.

Østby, G. (2013). Inequality and political violence: A review of the literature. *International Area Studies Review, 16*(2), 206–231. https://doi.org/10.1177/223386591349093.

Pearce, S. (2005). Religious rage: A quantitative analysis of the intensity of religious conflicts. *Terrorism and Political Violence, 17*(3), 333–352. https://doi.org/10.1080/09546550590929237.

Peled, Y., & Peled, H. H. (2019). *The religionization of Israeli society*. Routledge.

REFERENCES 317

Pemstein, D., Marquardt, K. L., Tzelgov, E., Wang, Y.-T., Medzihorsky, J., Krusell, J., Miri, F., & von Römer, J. (2019). *The V-Dem measurement model: Latent variable analysis for cross-national and cross-temporal expert-coded data*. University of Gothenburg: Varieties of Democracy Institute.

Peretz, E., & Fox, J. (2021). Religious discrimination against groups perceived as cults in Europe and the West. *Politics Religion & Ideology, 22*(3–4), 415–435. https://doi.org/10.1080/21567689.2021.1969921.

Pettersson, T. (2020). *UCDP/PRIO Armed Conflict Dataset Codebook v 20.1*. https://ucdp.uu.se/downloads/

Philpott, D. (2019). *Religious freedom in Islam: The fate of a universal human right in the Muslim world today*. Oxford University Press.

Piazza, J. A. (2011). Poverty, minority discrimination, and domestic terrorism. *Journal of Peace Research, 48*(3), 339–353. https://doi.org/10.1177/0022343310397404.

Pierskalla, J. H. (2010). Protest, deterrence, and escalation: The strategic calculus of government repression. *Journal of Conflict Resolution, 54*(1), 117–145. https://doi.org/10.1177/0022002709352462.

Pierskalla, J. H., & Hollenbach, F. M. (2013). Technology and collective action: The effect of cell phone coverage on political violence in Africa. *American Political Science Review, 107*(2), 207–224.

Pokalova, E. (2019). Driving factors behind foreign fighters in Syria and Iraq. *Studies in Conflict & Terrorism, 42*(9), 798–818. https://doi.org/10.1080/1057610X.2018.1427842.

Polo, S. M.T., & Gleditsch, K. S. (2016). Twisting arms and sending messages: Terrorist tactics in civil war. *Journal of Peace Research, 53*(6), 815–829. https://doi.org/10.1177/0022343316667999.

Rahman, F. Z. (2013). The effects of state-established religion on religious freedom for minorities. *Interdisciplinary Journal of Research on Religion, 9*(8), 1–24.

Raineri, L., & Martini, A. (2017). ISIS and Al-Qaeda as strategies and political imaginaries in Africa: A comparison between Boko Haram and Al-Qaeda in the Islamic Maghreb. *Civil Wars, 19*(4), 425–447. https://doi.org/10.1080/13698249.2017.1413226.

Raleigh, C. (2014). Political hierarchies and landscapes of conflict across Africa. *Political Geography, 42*, 92–103. https://doi.org/10.1016/j.polgeo.2014.07.002.

Razack, S. H. (2008). *Casting out: The eviction of Muslims from Western law and politics*. University of Toronto Press.

Regan, P. M. (2000). *Civil wars and foreign powers: Outside intervention in intrastate conflict*. University of Michigan Press.

Regan, P. M., & Norton, D. (2005). Greed, grievance, and mobilization in civil wars. *Journal of Conflict Resolution, 49*(3), 319–336.

Reynal-Querol, M. (2002). Ethnicity, political systems, and civil wars. *Journal of Conflict Resolution, 46*(1), 29–54. https://doi.org/10.1177/0022002702046001003.

Rieffer-Flanagan, B. (2014). Promoting the fundamental human right of religious liberty in US foreign policy. *GSTF Journal of Law and Social Sciences, 4*(1), 45–51.

Roeder, P. G. (2003). Clash of civilizations and escalation of domestic ethnopolitical conflicts. *Comparative Political Studies, 36*(5), 509–540. https://doi.org/10.1177/0010414003036005002.

Rule, J. B. (1988). *Theories of civil violence*. University of California Press.

Rummel, R. J. (1966). Dimensions of conflict behavior within nations, 1946–59. *Journal of Conflict Resolution, 10*(1), 65–73. https://doi.org/10.1177/002200276601000104.

318 REFERENCES

Rummel, R. J. (1997). Is collective violence correlated with social pluralism? *Journal of Peace Research, 34*(2), 163–175. https://doi.org/10.1177/0022343397034002004.

Russett, B. M. (1964). Inequality and instability: The relation of land tenure to politics. *World Politics, 16*(3), 442–454.

Saideman, S. M., & Ayres, R. W. (2000). Determining the cause of irredentism: Logit analyses of minorities at risk data from the 1980s and 1990s. *Journal of Politics, 62*(4), 1126–1144. https://doi.org/10.1111/0022-3816.00049.

Saideman, S. M., Lanoue, D. J., Campenni, M., & Stanton, S. (2002). Democratization, political institutions and ethnic conflict: A pooled time-series analysis, 1985–1998. *Comparative Political Studies, 35*(1), 103–129. https://doi.org/10.1177/00104140020 3500108.

Saiya, N. (2015a). The religious freedom peace. *The International Journal of Human Rights, 19*(3), 369–382. https://doi.org/10.1080/13642987.2015.1032268.

Saiya, N. (2015b). Religion, democracy and terrorism. *Perspectives on Terrorism, 9*(6), 51–59.

Saiya, N. (2017a). Blasphemy and terrorism in the Muslim world. *Terrorism and Political Violence, 29*(6), 1087–1105. https://doi.org/10.1080/09546553.2015.1115759.

Saiya, N. (2019a). Religion, state, and terrorism: A global analysis. *Terrorism and Political Violence, 31*(2), 204–223. https://doi.org/10.1080/09546553.2016.1211525.

Saiya, N. (2017b). Religious freedom, the Arab Spring, and US Middle East policy. *International Politics, 54*(1), 43–53. https://doi.org/10.1057/s41311-017-0021-4.

Saiya, N. (2019b). *Weapons of peace: How religious liberty combats terrorism*. Cambridge University Press.

Saiya, N., & Manchanda, S. (2020). Do burqa bans make us safer? Veil prohibitions and terrorism in Europe. *Journal of European Public Policy, 27*(12), 1781–1800. https://doi.org/10.1080/13501763.2019.1681494.

Saiya, N., & Scime, A. (2015). Explaining religious terrorism: A data-mined analysis. *Conflict Management and Peace Science, 32*(5), 487–512. https://doi.org/10.1177/0738894214559667.

Salehyan, I., Hendrix, C. S., Hamner, J., Case, C., Linebarger, C., Stull, E., & Williams, J. (2012). Social conflict in Africa: A new database. *International Interactions, 38*(4), 503–511. https://doi.org/10.1080/03050629.2012.697426.

Sambanis, N., Germann, M., & Schädel, A. (2018). SDM: A new data set on self-determination movements with an application to the reputational theory of conflict. *Journal of Conflict Resolution, 62*(3), 656–686. https://doi.org/10.1177/002200271 7735364.

Sarkissian, A. (2015). *The varieties of religious repression: Why governments restrict religion*. Oxford University Press.

Satana, N. S., Inman, M., & Birner, J. K. (2013). Religion, government coalitions, and terrorism. *Terrorism & Political Violence, 25*(1), 29–52. https://doi.org/10.1080/09546 553.2013.733250.

Saxton, G. D. (2005). Repression, grievances, mobilization, and rebellion: A new test of Gurr's model of ethnopolitical rebellion. *International Interactions, 31*(1), 87–116. https://doi.org/10.1080/03050620590919452.

Sayles, M. L. (1984). Relative deprivation and collective protest: An impoverished theory. *Sociological Inquiry, 54*(4), 449–465. https://doi.org/10.1111/j.1475-682X.1984.tb00 069.x.

REFERENCES   319

Schatzman, C. (2005). Political challenge in Latin America: Rebellion and collective protest in an era of democratization. *Journal of Peace Research, 42*(3), 291–310. https://doi.org/10.1177/0022343305052013.

Schock, K. (1996). A conjunctural model of political conflict: The impact of political opportunities on the relationship between economic inequality and violent political conflict. *Journal of Conflict Resolution, 40*(1), 98–133. https://doi.org/10.1177/0022002796040001006.

Schock, K. (1999). People power and political opportunities: Social movement mobilization and outcomes in the Philippines and Burma. *Social Problems, 46*(3), 355–375. https://doi.org/10.2307/3097105.

Selway, J. S. (2011). Cross-cuttingness, cleavage structures and civil war onset. *British Journal of Political Science, 41*(1), 111–138.

Shaver, A., Carter, D. B., & Shawa, T. W. (2019). Terrain ruggedness and land cover: Improved data for most research designs. *Conflict Management and Peace Science, 36*(2), 191–218. https://doi.org/10.1177/0738894216659843.

Shaykhutdinov, R., & Bragg, B. (2011). Do grievances matter in ethnic conflict. *Analyses of Social and Public Policy, 11*(1), 141–153.

Shellman, S. M., Levey, B. P., & Young, J. K. (2013). Shifting sands: Explaining and predicting phase shifts by dissident organizations. *Journal of Peace Research, 50*(3), 319–336. https://doi.org/10.1177/0022343312474013.

Siroky, D., Warner, C. M., Filip-Crawford, G., Berlin, A., & Neuberg, S. L. (2020). Grievances and rebellion: Comparing relative deprivation and horizontal inequality. *Conflict Management and Peace Science, 37*(6), 694–715. https://doi.org/10.1177/0738894220906372.

Smith, H. J., Pettigrew, T. F., Pippin, G. M., & Bialosiewicz, S. (2012). Relative deprivation: A theoretical and meta-analytic review. *Personality and Social Psychology Review, 16*(3), 203–232. https://doi.org/10.1177/1088868311430825.

Snyder, J. (2000). *From voting to violence: Democratization and nationalist conflict.* W.W. Norton.

Solt, F. (2008). Economic inequality and democratic political engagement. *American Journal of Political Science, 52*(1), 48–60. https://doi.org/10.1111/j.1540-5907.2007.00298.x.

Sorens, J. (2009). The politics and economics of official ethnic discrimination: A global statistical analysis, 1950–2003. *International Studies Quarterly, 54*(2), 535–560. https://doi.org/10.1111/j.1468-2478.2010.00598.x.

Stewart, F. (2008). *Horizontal inequalities and conflict: Understanding group violence in multiethnic societies.* Palgrave-McMillan.

Straus, S. (2012). Retreating from the brink: Theorizing mass violence and the dynamics of restraint. *Perspectives on Politics, 10*(2), 343–362.

Sullivan, H. (2019). Sticks, stones, and broken bones: Protest violence and the state. *Journal of Conflict Resolution, 63*(3), 700–726. https://doi.org/10.1177/0022002718763932.

Svensson, I. (2007). Fighting with faith: Religion and conflict resolution in civil wars. *Journal of Conflict Resolution, 51*(6), 930–949. https://doi.org/10.1177/0022002707306812.

Svensson, I. (2013). One God, many wars: Religious dimensions of armed conflict in the Middle East and North Africa. *Civil Wars, 15*(4), 411–430. https://doi.org/10.1080/13698249.2013.853409/.

320 REFERENCES

Svensson, I., & Harding, E. (2011). How Holy Wars end: Exploring the termination patterns of conflicts with religious dimensions in Asia. *Terrorism & Political Violence, 23*(2), 133–149. https://doi.org/10.1080/09546553.2010.516210.

Svensson, I., & Nilsson, D. (2018). Disputes over the divine: Introducing the religion and armed conflict (RELAC) data, 1975 to 2015. *Journal of Conflict Resolution, 62*(5), 1127–1148. https://doi.org/10.1177/0022002717737057.

Sweijs, T., Ginn, J., & De Spiegelire, S. (2015). *Barbarism and religion: The resurgence of holy violence.* The Hague Center for Strategic Studies.

Tadros, M., & Habib, A. (2022). Who speaks for Coptic rights in Egypt today? (2013–2021). *Religions, 13*(183), 1–20. https://doi.org/10.3390/rel13020183.

Tamm, H. (2016). The origins of transnational alliances: Rulers, rebels, and political survival in the Congo wars. *International Security, 41*(1), 147–181. https://doi.org/10.1162/ISEC_a_00252.

Tarrow, S. (1989). *Democracy and disorder: Protest and politics in Italy 1965–1975.* Clarendon Press.

Tarrow, S. (1994). *Power in movement: Social movements and contentious politics.* Cambridge University Press.

Thomas, J. L., Reed, W., & Wolford, S. (2016). The rebels' credibility dilemma. *International Organization 70*(3), 477–511.

Tiedmann, P. (2015). Is there a human right to religious freedom? *Human Rights Review, 16*(2), 83–98. https://doi.org/10.1007/s12142-014-0342-2.

Tiesler, N. C. (2007). Islam in Portuguese-speaking areas: Historical accounts, (post) colonial conditions and current debates. *Lusotopie, 14*(1), 89–102.

Tilly, C. (1978). *From mobilization to revolution.* Addison-Wesley.

Tilly, C., & Tarrow, S. (2006). *Contentious politics.* Oxford University Press.

Toft, M. D. (2007). Getting religion? The puzzling case of Islam and civil war. *International Security, 31*(4), 97–131. https://doi.org/10.1162/isec.2007.31.4.97.

Toft, M. D. (2021). Getting religion right in civil wars. *Journal of Conflict Resolution, 65*(9), 1607–1634. https://doi.org/10.1177/0022002721997895.

Tounsel, C. (2021). *Chosen peoples: Christianity and political imagination in South Sudan.* Duke University Press.

Tsutsui, K. (2004). Global civil society and ethnic social movements in the contemporary world. *Sociological Forum, 19*(1), 63–87. https://doi.org/10.1023/B:SOFO.0000019648.21481.91.

Tusicisny, A. (2004). Civilizational conflicts: More frequent, longer, and bloodier? *Journal of Peace Research, 41*(4), 485–498. https://doi.org/10.1177/0022343304044478.

van Stekelenberg, J., & Klandermans, B. (2013). The social psychology of protest. *Current Sociology Review, 61*(5–6), 886–905. https://doi.org/10.1177/0011392113479314.

Vogt, M., & Rüegger, S. (2021). *The ethnic power relations (EPR) core dataset codebook, version 2021.* https://icr.ethz.ch/data/epr/core/EPR_2021_Codebook_EPR.pdf.

Wæver, O. (1995). Securitization and desecuritization. In R. Lipschutz (Ed.), *On security* (pp. 46–87). Columbia University Press.

Wæver, O. (2011). Politics, security, theory. *Security Dialogue, 42*(4–5), 465–480. https://doi.org/10.1177/0967010611418718.

Wakoson, E. N. (1990). Sudan's Addis Ababa peace treaty: Why it failed. *Northeast African Studies, 12*(2/3), 19–53.

REFERENCES 321

Wald, K. D., Silverman, A. L., & Friday, K. S. (2005). Making sense of religion in political life. *Annual Review of Political Science, 8*, 121–143. https://www.jstor.org/stable/43660312.

Walter, B. F. (1997). The critical barrier to civil war settlement. *International Organization, 51*(3), 335–364.

Walter, B. F. (2017). The extremist's advantage in civil wars. *International Security, 42*(2), 7–39. https://doi.org/10.1162/ISEC_a_00292.

White, P. B., Vidovic, D., González, B., Gleditsch, K. S., & Cunningham, D. E. (2015). Nonviolence as a weapon of the resourceful: From claims to tactics in mobilization. *Mobilization: An International Quarterly, 20*(4), 471–491. https://doi.org/10.17813/1086-671X-20-4-471.

Wilson, M. C. (2019). A closer look at the limits of consociationalism. *Comparative Political Studies, 53*(5), 700–733. https://doi.org/10.1177/0010414019858956.

Wimmer, A., Cederman, L.-E., & Min, B. (2009). Ethnic politics and armed conflict: A configurational analysis of a new global dataset. *American Sociological Review, 74*(2), 316–337. https://doi.org/10.1177/000312240907400208.

Wood, R., & Kathman, J. (2014). Too much of a bad thing? Civilian victimization and bargaining in civil war. *British Journal of Political Science, 44*(3), 685–706.

World Bank. *World Development Indicators.* https://databank.worldbank.org/source/world-development-indicators.

Wucherpfennig, J., Metternich, N. W., Cederman, L.-E., & Gleditsch, K. S. (2012). Ethnicity, the state, and the duration of civil war. *World Politics, 64*(1), 79–115.

Yefet, B. (2019). Defending the Egyptian nation: National unity and Muslim attitudes toward the Coptic minority. *Middle Eastern Studies, 55*(4), 638–654. https://doi.org/10.1080/00263206.2019.1573365.

Zellman, A., & Brown, D. (2022). Uneasy lies the crown: External threats to religious leadership and interstate dispute militarization. *Security Studies, 31*(1), 152–182. https://doi.org/10.1080/09636412.2022.2038664.

Zenn, J. (2020). Boko Haram's conquest for the caliphate: How Al Qaeda helped Islamic State acquire territory. *Studies in Conflict & Terrorism, 43*(2), 89–122. https://doi.org/10.1080/1057610X.2018.1442141.

Zick, A., Küpper, B., & Andreas Hövermann, B. *Intolerance, prejudice and discrimination: A European report.* Friedrich-Ebert-Stiftung.

Index

For the benefit of digital users, indexed terms that span two pages (e.g., 52–53) may, on occasion, appear on only one of those pages

9/11, 28, 45–46

Afghanistan, 1, 28
  Buddhas of Bamiyan, 28
Africa, 59, 61, 138, 151, 176–77
African Traditional Religion, 57–58
Ahmadis, 49, 51
Al-Qaeda, 1
Angola, 61
Animism, 34–36, 57–58, 205, 210, 213–14
anti-Semitism, 1–2, 41–42, 45–46, 64
  anti-Semitism, in Greece, 45–46
Arab, 56–57, 205, 214
Arabic, 38, 214
Arab Spring, 209
Armenian Church, 49
Asia, 151
ATR. *See* African Traditional Religion
Australia, 47–48

Baha'i, 31, 32–33, 205–6
Bahrain, 58, 67–68, 208–9
  al-Khalifa royal family, 208–9
Balkans, 1
Belarus, 41
  Unification Church, 41–42
Boko Haram, 1
Buddhist, 27–28, 34–36, 40, 205
Burundi, 60–61

Canada, 47–48, 189–90, 205
Caribbean, 61
Catholic, 14, 27–28, 34–36, 41–42, 51, 59
Caucasus, 1
Central African Republic, 213
  anti-Balaka, 213

China, 1–2, 57–58, 131, 157–58, 205
  Uyghurs, 1–2, 57–58
  Xinjiang, 131
Christian, 1–2, 14, 27–28, 30, 31, 33–34, 37–40, 41–42, 43, 49, 50–51, 57–59, 64, 66, 67–68, 99, 123, 205, 206, 210, 214
  Christian, Evangelical, 30, 33–36, 152
  Christian, Korean, 38
  Christian, non-Orthodox, 34–36, 41
  Christian, Orthodox, 14, 33–36, 41, 61
Christianity, 27–28, 29–30, 33–34, 37–38, 39–40, 49
Clash of Civilizations Theory, 11
Cold War, 1, 152
Communism, 40
Comoros, 141–42
Copts, 38, 43, 205–7
Cote d'Ivoire, 59
Cyprus, 57–58

Da'esh. *See* Islamic State
Democratic People's Republic of Korea (DPRK), 27–28
  Chondokyists, 27–28
  Juche, 27–28
Denmark, 44, 205

East Asia, 1
Egypt, 43, 58–59, 64, 67–68
  Egyptian Revolution of 1919, 214
  el-Sisi, General Abdel Fattah, 206
  Morsi, Mohamed, 206
  Mubarak, Hosni, 206–7
English Language, 38, 214
Enlightenment, Age of, 122
EPR. *See* Ethnic Power Relations dataset
Eritrea, 60–61

324   INDEX

Ethics of the Fathers, The, 4–5, 242–43
Ethnic Power Relations dataset, 14–15, 19–
      20, 54–55, 56, 83, 85, 131, 142, 223
Europe, 143–44
European Union, 15

Falun Gong, 57–58
Farsi, 33–34
Fiji, 58–59
France, 47–48, 58–59, 205, 229–30
      Charlie Hebdo, 229–30

Gambia, the, 141–42
Georgia, 52–53
Georgian Orthodox Church
      (GOC), 52
Germany, 47–48, 58–59, 64
Ghana, 60–61
Global Terrorism Database, 15, 145,
      152–53
Greece, 45–46
      Golden Dawn party, 45–46
      Greece, Communist Party of, 46
      Karatzaferis, Giorgos, 45–46
Greek Orthodox Church, 45–46
      Kollas, Father Eustathios, 45–46
grievance theory, 2–3, 16–17, 22–23, 68, 83,
      118, 123, 126, 129, 130, 156, 163, 243
GTD. *See* Global Terrorism Database
Gurr, Ted R, 8, 9, 13–14, 121, 122, 129,
      130, 131–32, 223

Hare Krishna, 41–42
Hezbollah, 213
Hindu, 34–36, 50–51, 58–59, 60–61, 205
Holocaust denial, 45–46
Huntington, Samuel, 11
Hussein, Saddam, 59

India, 58–59, 157–58
Indonesia, 48, 58–59, 64, 91
      Aceh, 91
Intifada, Palestinian, 211
Iran, 31, 32–34, 156, 213
      Jundullah, 213
Iraq War, 138–39
Ireland, 58
Iron Curtain, 1

Islamic State, 1, 156
Islamist, 137
Islamophobia, 1–2, 64
Israel, 49, 56–57, 67–68, 122, 211
      Jews for Jesus, 49
      Lev L'Achim, Yad L'Achim, 49
      Ra'am Islamist Party, 56–57
ITERATE dataset, 145

Jamaica, 66
Jehovah's Witnesses, 34–36, 53
Jews, 1–2, 4–5, 14, 34–36, 45–46, 47–48,
      49, 61, 64, 66, 122, 189–90, 205
      Jews, Egyptian, 205–6
      Jews, Greek, 45–46
      Jews, Ultra-Orthodox, 49
Jihadist, 138–39
Josephus, 122
Judaism, 29–30, 34–36

Kenya, 60–61
King, Martin Luther Jr., 3

Laos, 31, 39–40
Latin America, 11–12, 58, 158, 239
Lebanon, 58–59, 213
Lord's Resistance Army, 1

Macedonia, 213
      NLA, 213
Mali, 141–42
MAR. *See* Minorities at Risk project
MAROB dataset, 151, 153, 157
Marx, Karl, 93–94
Marxism, 27–28
Mauritania, 141–42
MENA region, 64
Middle East, 1, 11–12, 59, 67–68, 142, 151,
      153, 158, 239
Minorities at Risk Project, 4, 8, 9, 10, 11–12,
      13–15, 16, 30, 54–55, 78–79, 80–82, 85,
      87–88, 121, 122, 124, 125, 129, 130, 131,
      157, 159–60, 164, 223, 224, 225, 237
modernization theory, 8–9
Mormons, 61
Muslim Brotherhood, 206, 215
      Egypt, 206
      Sudan, 215

Muslims, 1–2, 14, 33–36, 37–39, 43, 44, 51–52, 57–59, 60–61, 64, 66, 67–68, 99, 134–35, 137, 138–39, 143–44, 145, 150, 189–90, 205, 210, 229–30
Muslims, Afghan, 28
Muslims, Alawites, 59
Muslims, Canadian, 210, 211
Muslims, Egyptian, 205
Muslims, non, 38–39
Muslims, Shi'a, 14, 59, 64, 99, 195, 208–9, 213
Muslims, Sunni, 14, 27–28, 59, 64, 99, 208–9, 213–14
Myanmar, 1–2, 43, 205
    Rakhine, 1–2

Nazi, 47–48
Netherlands, 58–59
non-West, 1
North Africa, 1, 142
North America, 64
North Korea. *See* Democratic People's Republic of Korea
Norway, 58–59

Obama, Barak, 46

Pakistan, 1–2, 43, 50–52
PolityIV, 99–100
Protestants, 27–28, 34–36, 48
Protocols of the Elders of Zion, 45–46

Qatar, 58

RAS. *See* Religion and State Project
RASM. *See* Religion and State Minorities Project
Rastafaris, 66
RCDC. *See* Religion and Conflict in Developing Countries dataset
RD. *See* relative deprivation theory
Rebel and Religion dataset, 152
relative deprivation theory, 7–8, 9, 73–75, 76, 77–78, 79, 83–84, 86, 89–90, 141–42, 228, 233, 236–37
Religion and Armed Conflict (RELAC) dataset, 152

Religion and Conflict in Developing Countries dataset, 11–12, 13, 26, 30, 98–99, 158–59
Religion and State Project, 13–14, 87, 141–42, 145, 153, 158–59
Religion and State Minorities Project, 13–14, 26, 30, 42–43, 47, 78, 98–99
Religious Minorities at Risk dataset, 4, 5, 10, 13–16, 18–19, 20–21, 22–23, 26, 30, 54–55, 60, 62, 82, 87–88, 98, 124, 131, 156, 158–59, 160, 164–65, 170–71, 172, 190, 206–7, 209, 210, 212–14, 222–163, 223–25, 228
RMAR. *See* Religious Minorities at Risk dataset
Russia, 34–36
    Chechnya, 1–2
    Law on Extremism, 34–36
    Law On Freedom of Conscience and Religious Associations, 34–36
Russian Orthodox Church, 34–36

Saudi Arabia, 27–28, 58
Scientology, 64
Shari'a, 214, 215
Sikhs, 50–51, 205
Soviet Union, 1
Spain, 58, 131
Sri Lanka, 67
Sub-Saharan Africa, 11–12, 59–61, 158, 239
Sudan, 37–38, 214–15
    Criminal Code, 1991, 37–38
    Mahdists, 214
    Prisons and the Treatment of Prisoners Law, 1992, 38–39
Sudan, South, 213–15
Sudan Civil War
    Addis Abba peace agreement, 214–15
    First (1955–1972), 214–15
    Second (1983–2005), 214
    SSLM, 213
Sweden, 58
Syria, 1, 59, 205

Taliban, 28, 156
Tanzania, 60–61
Timor-Leste, 48
Turkey, 57–58, 67–68

326 INDEX

UCDP/PRIO dataset, 15, 141–42, 152, 210
Ukraine, 1, 51–52
United Kingdom, 47–48, 51–52, 58–59, 208–9
United Nations, 15
United States, 30, 47–48, 61, 123
Universal Declaration of Human Rights, 29
US House of Representatives, 138–39
US State Department International Religious Freedom Reports, 15

Varieties of Democracy (V-Dem), 99–100

Wahhabi, 27–28
West, The, 1–2, 143–44, 145
Western Europe, 58, 60–61, 64
Why Men Rebel, 74
World Development Indicators, World Bank, 177
World Trade Center, 45–46
World Values Survey, 78

Yemen, 213
  Houthi, 213